Kong University Press thanks Xu Bing for writing the Press's name in his Square Calligraphy for the covers of its books. For further information, see p. iv.

To David

Remade in Hollywood

The Global Chinese Presence in Transnational Cinemas

Kenneth Chan

香港大學出版社

HONG KONG UNIVERSITY PRESS

Hong Kong University Press
14/F Hing Wai Centre
7 Tin Wan Praya Road
Aberdeen
Hong Kong

Hardback   ISBN 978-962-209-055-2
Paperback ISBN 978-962-209-056-9

British Library Cataloguing-in-Publication Data
A catalogue record for this book is available from the British Library.

Secure On-line Ordering
http://www.hkupress.org

1006972781

Printed and bound by ColorPrint Production Ltd., Hong Kong, China.

Hong Kong University Press is honoured that Xu Bing, whose art
explores the complex themes of language across cultures, has written
the Press's name in his Square Word Calligraphy. This
signals our commitment to cross-cultural thinking and the distinctive
nature of our English-language books published in China.

"At first glance, Square Word Calligraphy appears to be nothing
more unusual than Chinese characters, but in fact it is a new way of
rendering English words in the format of a square so they resemble
Chinese characters. Chinese viewers expect to be able to read Square
Word Calligraphy but cannot. Western viewers, however are surprised
to find they can read it. Delight erupts when meaning is unexpectedly
revealed."

— Britta Erickson, *The Art of Xu Bing*

Contents

Acknowledgments

Writing a book is like making a Chinese-in-Hollywood movie: the process is transnational in its undertaking. The author, like a film director who receives the main credit, is really only one among a multitude of many agents who have contributed to its materialization. It is with this thought that I wish to offer my thanks to many, in the hope that those whom I have unintentionally left out will be most forgiving of my oversight.

My academic mentors at Clemson University and the University of Florida were responsible for stretching my intellectual horizons and pointing me to paths I would not have otherwise taken. Grateful am I to Nora Alter, Wayne Chapman, Kevin Dettmar, Mark A. Reid, Phillip Wegner, and Harold Woodell; Brandon Kershner for his kind and always thoughtful guidance; Malini Schueller for her Asian-American scholarly expertise and continuing friendship; and to Amitava Kumar for kindling my interest in a *critical* Chinese cultural studies.

Many friends, colleagues, and peers have read parts of the book manuscript and offered their helpful comments and suggestions; while others have shared ideas, criticism, resource material, conversations over coffee, and much encouragement during different stages of the writing process and at various conferences. I am indebted to Chris Berry, Robert Cagle, Evans Chan, Shirley Chew, Ray Edmundson, Ivan Heng, Jeroen de Kloet, Julia Kuehn, David Lim, Shirley Geok-lin Lim, Gina Marchetti, Pen-ek Ratanaruang, Greg Robinson, Stephen Teo, Jan Uhde, Rob Wilson, James Wren, and Ray Yeung. I am especially grateful to Song Hwee Lim for his always insightful comments on my work, challenging me to rethink my arguments and theoretical positions. Of course, my former colleagues both at the National University of Singapore (NUS) and Nanyang Technological University (NTU), Singapore, were among the first people I turned to for advice and ideas. For all their support, particularly during my years at NUS, I must acknowledge Chua Beng Huat, Stephen Donatelli, Donald Favareau, Johan Geertsema, Philip Holden, George Landow, Lo Mun Hou, Andrew Leng, Michael Maiwald, Paul Nerney, Ng Yun Sian, Peter Pang, Stephanie Rupp, Barbara Ryan, Chitra Sankaran, K. K. Seet, Albert Teo, Jeff Webb, and Yew Kong Leong. My former colleagues at

NTU whom I also wish to thank for their support, cheer, and edification include Rebecca Ang, Chang Weining, Chua Ling-Yen, Eddie Kuo, Kwok Kian Woon, Mike Lan Shi-chi, Lee Tang Ling, Francis Lim, Quah Sy Ren, Shirley Sun, Troy Tan, Wee Wan-ling, and Lawrence Wong. Of course, special gratitude must go to those in the Division of English and members of its extended family, whom I am so happy and fortunate to call my friends and intellectual partners: Anne Bergen-Aurand, Brian Bergen-Aurand, James Brady, Sofia Carreras, Terence Dawson, Patrick Dooley, Shameem Fareed, Jeremy Fernando, Angela Frattarola, Jovan Goh, Daniel Jernigan, Koh Tai Ann, Lim Lee Ching, Neil Murphy, Suzanne Nelson, Shanmugapriya d/o Paskaran, Brendan Quigley, Suriyanti Salim, Bede Scott, Sim Wai Chew, Suzana Abdul Tayep, Tamara Wagner, Joy Wheeler, and Andrew Yerkes. To both graduate and undergraduate students, particularly those who have taken my "Asians in Hollywood" course, I can only acknowledge how your enthusiastic discussions of ideas relating to the subject have defined and inflected my thinking as I wrote this book. And, of course, special thanks must go to Elizabeth Tan and Charlotte Qi Yan, my graduate assistants, for their tireless efforts; and to my undergraduate student assistant Clara Geoy for sacrificing her summer vacation time to help see me through the very last months of producing the final draft manuscript: you are a lifesaver.

All my colleagues at the University of Northern Colorado, particularly the School of English Language and Literature, have been extremely supportive of my research and teaching endeavors, for which I am very grateful. I wish to thank especially Sarah Allen, Mary Angeline, Kristin Bovaird-Abbo, David Caldwell, Joseph Chaves, Brenda Cozzens, Joel Daehnke, Barb Dickinson, Lahcen Ezzaher, Gregory Heald, Karen Janata, Karen Jennison, Jeri Kraver, John Loftis, Michael Martinez, Michael Mills, Norman Peercy, Tomas Santos, Ben Varner, Sharon Wilson, and Lloyd Worley. Justin Larsen offered indispensable aid in producing the index for this book. To Marcus Embry, Joonuk Huh, April Miller, and Tracey Sedinger: your friendship and assistance have been particularly instrumental in helping me settle so quickly into UNC as my new university home.

Institutional support is imperative in an undertaking such as this book project. The National University of Singapore, Nanyang Technological University, and the University of Northern Colorado have provided generous university research grants in support of my research. NTU's URECA scheme has also provided additional assistance. Library and archival research are made possible with the help of New York University's Bobst Library, libraries at the University of California at Berkeley and the University of California at Los Angeles, the Hong Kong Film Archive (for their amazingly efficient staff, who respond with such alacrity in assisting helpless researchers like me), the National Library Board Singapore, the National University of Singapore's Central Library, Nanyang Technological University's various libraries, and the Michener Library at the University of Northern Colorado. NTU librarian Wong Oi May has been unstinting in her efforts to assist me with procuring books, DVDs, and other research material. I must also offer my gratitude to the Asian Film Archive, Singapore, particularly Karen Chan, Ong Sor Fern, Tan Bee Thiam, Jacqueline Tan, Kenneth Paul Tan, Mike Wiluan, and Ethan Yeo. As much as I hate to admit it, I do enjoy, albeit perversely, our late-night marathon board meetings.

For the tireless efforts of the staff at Hong Kong University Press I am very grateful. I especially thank my publisher Colin Day for seeing me through the entire process. Your kindness and patience must definitely not go unacknowledged. For guidance and assistance through the editing and proof stages, I am grateful to Associate Publisher Michael Duckworth and Managing Editor Dennis Cheung. Very appreciative am I also of the generous comments and suggestions from the three anonymous reviewers of my book proposal and manuscript; excellent criticisms that have helped me re-conceptualize the book's initial structure. Both the University of Texas Press and the journal *Asian Cinema* have also kindly granted me permission to include in my book extensively revised versions of two previously published essays, listed respectively: "The Global Return of the *Wu Xia Pian* (Chinese Sword-Fighting Movie): Ang Lee's *Crouching Tiger, Hidden Dragon*," *Cinema Journal* 43, no. 4 (2004): 3–17; and "Mimicry as Failure: Jackie Chan in Hollywood," *Asian Cinema* 15, no. 2 (2004): 84–97.

To the always glamorous Bala (aka Beyoncé) and the "gals": thanks for reminding me to stay "fabulous" and to believe that there is more to life than academia. Nick and Tina Melczarek, you guys are fierce! Jeffrey Tan, thanks for your generous friendship. To Kim McEntire and Murray Stone for your kindness and support. To my extended family for being very patient and caring during my long stretches of absence from familial involvement: my parents Edward and Lily, my sisters Adeline and Karen, and the rest of the gang: Bernard, Kenneth, Jonathan, Jeremy, Joshua, Daren, and baby Daryl. Virgil Mooneyhan for unconditionally welcoming me into his family. Coco Chanel for his delightful distractions and inquisitive interruptions. And finally, to my partner David Mooneyhan, this book is as much yours as it is mine. Your patient endurance and devotion have carried me through the toughest of times. It is with love that I dedicate it to you.

1

Introduction:
Remaking Chinese Cinemas, Hollywood Style

When Ang Lee's *Crouching Tiger, Hidden Dragon* (2000) leapt onto global screens, many saw it as a cinematic event that heralded the unprecedented arrival of Chinese cinemas in Hollywood. As part of the recent "Asian invasion"[1] of the American multiplex, where mainstream audiences are now eagerly taking to the various Asian cinemas, this Chinese cultural presence dominated the invasion, thanks in part to the migration of numerous stars, directors, and various players from Hong Kong's film industry: a professional diaspora spurred by the 1997 British handover of Hong Kong to mainland China. Since I began my research in 2000 on this then-emerging cinematic phenomenon, a recurring commentary I encounter is that this trend, like all Hollywood trends, is a transient one: the Chinese are only Tinseltown's current cultural flavor of the month, soon to be replaced by the next big thing capable of revitalizing Hollywood (as Chinese cinemas are believed to be currently doing), thus rejuvenating and sustaining the studios' capitalist productivity and hegemony. In engaging this prediction of the waning interest in Chinese kung fu flicks, sword-fighting spectacles, historical epics, supernatural thrillers, romance/family melodramas, and Chinatown crime stories, one cannot help but wonder how long Chinese cinemas can maintain their current pride of place in Hollywood's multiculturalist approach to cultural appropriation and syncretism? What strategies can these cinemas resort to in order to achieve longevity in the business, and at what cost?

I open with this notion of pop cultural "transience" in my study of the Chinese in Hollywood because it provokes a rather visceral response in me, as both a cultural and film critic; a response that I can only describe, with a deep sense of ambivalence and an eagerness to disavow, as "cultural nationalism." Being an ethnic Chinese from Singapore, I find myself reluctantly cheering on the success of Chinese cinemas in Hollywood in a culturally conflicted fashion: mainly because I bemoan, as a student of film, the often cringe-worthy aesthetic shortcomings of these movies, while questioning, as an anti-Orientalist and anti-essentialist cultural critic, the social, political, and cultural implications of these filmic texts. My painting this personal image of critical and cultural ambivalence and anxiety initiates a theoretical mapping of the kind of cultural politics surrounding this cinematic phenomenon. To bring into further relief the emergent critical questions that color this picture, I now rehearse three very recent moments of globalized Hollywood spectacle where cultural anxieties and contradictions intermingle with the celluloid magic and sparkle that the Chinese in Hollywood have engendered so far.

Hollywood Spectacle One: The much anticipated kung fu fantasy match up between Jackie Chan and Jet Li occurs not in a local Hong Kong production, as fans thought it would.[2] Instead, this über-duel takes place in the number one US box-office hit *The Forbidden Kingdom* (2008), a movie helmed by *The Lion King* director Rob Minkoff and distributed by Lionsgate and the Weinstein Company. This faceoff between Jackie Chan and Jet Li is of such epic proportions from a kung fu cinema standpoint that even the stars themselves decided to downplay audience expectations of the touted fight scene.[3] While he publicly dismissed the script as "nonsense," Jackie Chan chose to sign on to the project because "they told . . . [him] Jet [Li] was doing it." He described his fight scene with Li as one that was "so natural" that they shot the scene only after one rehearsal. In fact, they worked so well together that the director had to ask them to slow down the pacing of the fight sequence.[4] In the eyes of their fans, this representation of their collaboration is indeed worthy of a clash of two kung fu titans.[5] Whether or not this media narrative was part of a marketing ploy, the strategy clearly worked: the film raked in an impressive US$20.9 million during its opening weekend in American cinemas;[6] and an equally stunning US$21.4 million in China, despite Hong Kong newspaper *South China Morning Post*'s criticism that the film "hardly offers a progressive understanding of the multifarious aspects of Chinese culture as it rehashes the themes of kung fu classics" and a Hong Kong magazine characterizing its plot as "unbelievably weird."[7]

The culturally incongruous and "weird" plot, of course, did not go unnoticed by the stars. Chan anxiously reminded viewers that the film was "made for Americans. Chinese viewers may not like it"; while Li concurred by noting how "this is an American production, created by an American screenwriter, about an American child's dream of the Journey To the West story. It would be more interesting to approach this film from a different angle."[8] While its narrative relies on the story of the Monkey King in *Journey to the West* (*Xiyou ji*), a Ming dynasty classic believed to have been written by Wu Chengen, *The Forbidden Kingdom* updates it for American audiences by retelling it from the perspective of American kung fu-crazed teenager Jason Tripitikas (Michael Angarano), who is magically transported to the world of ancient China to free the immobilized Monkey King (Jet Li), with the help of drunken master Lu Yan (Jackie Chan), from the magical spell of the evil Jade Warlord. This narrative premise basically retells *The Wizard of Oz* story, with Jason taking on the Dorothy role in his search for a way home. His encounters with the denizens of a fantastical ancient China — like the culturally colorful but alien characters of the Land of Oz — provide the psychic means for Jason to attain a new sense of heroic confidence (and a requisite set of martial arts skills) to confront the bullies and thugs of his urban American reality. Mainstream American audiences' familiarity with the reformulated Oz tale served to cement *The Forbidden Kingdom*'s successful appeal; while the Monkey King mythology, together with Chan and Li's superstardom, brought Chinese audiences to theaters internationally.

The combination of Hollywood's remaking of the *Journey to the West*, the much-awaited Chan-Li matchup, and the film's impressive global box office success marks for me a spectacular confluence of the critical and cultural issues that this book seeks to investigate. Like many of the films I look at in the chapters that follow, *The Forbidden Kingdom* is an excellent example of a transnational cinematic production, with American company Casey Silver Productions and China's Huayi Brothers and the China Film Co-Production Corporation joining forces in this instance. (Huayi is a rising media group based in China known for co-producing *Kung Fu Hustle* with Sony/Columbia Pictures Film Production Asia[9]; and China Film Co-Production Corporation is credited for *Crouching Tiger, Hidden Dragon*.) With these transnational and multinational collaborative production efforts becoming the norm, what cultural, political, and aesthetic effects will one witness in movies involving the Chinese in Hollywood? What forms of cultural hybridity and filmic synergies will such (un)equal partnerships create? While being thoroughly entertained by the film, I found myself most critically intrigued instead by *The Forbidden Kingdom*'s extra-diegetic elements, particularly the opening credit sequence — Jason's movie poster collection of films like *Monkey Goes West* (1966), *One-Armed Swordsman* (1967), *The 36th Chamber of Shaolin* (1978), *Drunken Master* (1978), and *The Bride with White Hair* (1993)[10] come to vivid life. Using an ingenious animated pastiche of classic, painted poster imagery, the film visualizes symbolically the concepts of cultural appropriation, reconfiguration, and synthesis, which constitute the mechanics of remaking Chinese cinemas in Hollywood.

Hollywood Spectacle Two: The scene opens with our intrepid heroine in a drab sampan-woman disguise creeping into an Oriental pirates' den in order to meet its evil lord. Upon being discovered, she and her companions are dragged into a dark lair fit for the nefarious Fu Manchu. On the platform stands a tall bald figure imposingly decked out in apparently Qing dynasty robes,[11] looking battle-worn but regal. He slowly turns around and deliberately pauses for the classic profile shot. Suddenly, audiences encounter the familiar mien of Hong Kong superstar Chow Yun-fat cosmetically remade into the salt-encrusted pirate captain Sao Feng. With thick bushy eyebrows framing his blood-shot eyes, a sparse but long beard reminiscent of *Flash Gordon*'s Ming the Merciless, a menacing knife scar cutting diagonally across his forehead and face, and frighteningly long, sharp fingernails painted black, Sao Feng smiles sinisterly as he masterfully proclaims in Hong Kong-accented English, "Welcome to Singapore!"

Chow Yun-fat remade into pirate captain Sao Feng

This now familiar episode is the opening sequence in the final installment of Disney's summer blockbuster trilogy *Pirates of the Caribbean: At World's End* (2007). As a seafaring adventure where the protagonist, Jack Sparrow (Johnny Depp), crisscrosses the globe to encounter an array of culturally exotic characters, the film, as a Hollywood blockbuster with indubitable global box office potential, similarly travels well by means of its multicultural representation, giving the film the correctness of a glossy Benetton ad. Representing "Asia" in its multicultural lineup is the epitome of Hong Kong masculine cool, Chow Yun-fat, who has been expertly made up to look like an evil Chinese pirate, hiding out in Singapore and lusting after Elizabeth Swann (Keira Knightley). Chow's role of Orientalist stereotype might be small — his character Sao Feng dies midway through the movie after his attempt to sexually assault Elizabeth — but his presence in this film is nonetheless significant in the context of his career in Hollywood: Chow has indeed arrived in America. His joining a requisite star-studded cast of a blockbuster epic also signals the significant place the Chinese now occupy in Hollywood and American cinema.

But what exactly is the nature of this interest in the Chinese? What motivates it? What sorts of cinematic images and representations does it foster? What precedence in American film history feeds it? In other words, what forms of American cultural politics does this interest turn on and engage? The singular instance of Chow Yun-fat's exoticized appearance in *At World's End* also throws up difficult questions of the cultural cost to attain mainstream Hollywood success: what kinds of roles do ethnic Chinese stars and actors have to play to gain this success? How does the Chinese Hollywood presence affect Chinese cinemas globally? What effect does this presence have on Asian American cinema, considering its independent and alternative cinematic history? Does this presence reinforce Orientalist imagery to pander to American audience expectations of the racist depictions of the Chinese that have emerged out of classic Hollywood? Or are there possibilities of subversive resistance and cultural critique even within a transnational capitalist industry that privileges box office earnings over cultural and political concerns?

The advertising machinery of Buena Vista International kicked into high gear before the film's opening here in Singapore. Ubiquitous posters and huge wall panels dotted the island nation with the tagline "Welcome to Singapore! " turning Sao Feng's proclamation into a tourism-board style marketing strategy. Made up of 70% ethnic-Chinese, Singapore audiences not only love their Chinese-language movies, they absolutely adore Chow Yun-fat and his Singaporean wife Jasmine. This is a textbook case of the power of Hollywood's global appeal accomplished through the specific nodes of cultural localism — in this case, Chineseness and Chinese-language cinemas — within the transnational systems of cinematic production, distribution, and consumption. This global/local nexus that characterizes the contemporary Chinese presence in Hollywood constitutes one of the focal points of critical analysis in this book.

Hollywood Spectacle Three: Flushed with success from *Chicago*'s triumph at the 75th Academy Awards, Rob Marshall goes on to bring Arthur Golden's novel *Memoirs of a Geisha* gloriously to life on the big screen in 2005, a movie destined to be a hysterical camp classic in the likes of, dare I say, *All about Eve* (1950) and *Mommie Dearest* (1981). For who can resist the fabulous gay-iconic performance of Gong Li as Hatsumomo, especially as she threatens Zhang Ziyi's Sayuri with "I shall destroy you!" uttered with the dramatic flourish of a drag-queen?

But clearly not everyone was laughing at the absurdly contradictory image of Chinese actresses playing geishas speaking perfect English. Though being touted by *Time* magazine's Richard Corliss as "Hollywood's Asian Romance, "[12] audiences in Japan and China did not buy into this claim. Having three Chinese stars play the main roles, when high-profile Hollywood acting jobs for Japanese are hard to come by, did not go down well with Japanese viewers, [13] despite the ironic fact that these geisha characters reinforce the Madame Butterfly myth and "the image of sweet, gentle Japanese child-women" as evident in Sayuri.[14] Equally, if not more inflamed, were mainland Chinese audiences. Many denounced the political insensitivity of having Chinese actresses in these geisha roles that are set during the time of World War Two, considering Japan's historic rape of Nanjing in 1937–38 and, more recently, Prime Minister Koizumi's controversial visits to the Yasukuni war shrines in Tokyo.[15] China's State Administration of Radio, Film and Television eventually banned the film.[16]

Of course, mainland China's censorship and outright banning of Hollywood films that inappropriately or negatively depict Chinese culture and politics have a long history. For instance, films such as *Shanghai Express* (1932) and *Limehouse Blues* (1934), both featuring the sensual Anna May Wong playing up the Dragon Lady stereotype, incurred the displeasure of Chinese censors way back in the 1930s.[17] What intrigues me here in the case of *Memoirs of a Geisha* is the way nationalism came roaring back with a vengeance over a Hollywood film, despite the fact that China seeks to insert itself into the network of transnational capital. The central question to ask is: under what cultural political circumstances will Hollywood's deployment of global/local cultural strategies work for their film productions involving Chineseness? For a film that boasts a *trans*national appeal through its pan-Asian casting, the irony is that this multinational casting is the source of discontent. It is also crucial to analyze the motivational factors that spur this kind of cultural nationalist response from the Chinese government and Chinese audiences both in the mainland and across the diaspora. This instance of global Hollywood gone wrong exposes precisely the complex and conflicted cultural and political discourses that mire the tense national-transnational interface, especially as one watches Chinese cinemas enter Hollywood and its network, and as Hollywood remakes, reinvents, and reconfigures Chineseness into its own likeness or the likeness of its perceived Other.

Critical Perimeters: East Asia, Hollywood, the World

Beginning with the premise that post-1997 Hollywood saw a new, resurgent interest in the Chinese presence in its cinema, this book focuses its attention on a number of aspects of this phenomenon. One of its primary concerns is the proliferation of Hollywood and Hollywood-inflected films featuring ethnic Chinese stars like Jet Li, Michelle Yeoh, Gong Li, Chow Yun-fat, and Jackie Chan, in works directed by the likes of John Woo, Wayne Wang, Wong Kar-wai, and Zhang Yimou. This ethnic Chinese presence is clearly not "new" in the sense that it does not form a full cultural/national body of film separate from the commercial and art-house cinemas of mainland China, Hong Kong, and Taiwan. Instead, the long histories and traditions of these national cinemas, together with Chinese-American film, contribute to, overlap with, and provide the contexts for this new Chinese presence. Though this presence is clearly derivative, the various streams of Chinese cinematic histories, traditions, and practices conjoin to produce a nascent film aesthetic and sensibility that offer Chineseness as a commodity for Hollywood's transnational system of cinematic production and consumption. This complex system of interconnections and relationships compels me to address the issue not only from the standpoint of Hollywood films, but also to consider the effects this phenomenon has on films coming out of Hong Kong, mainland China, Taiwan, and Chinese America. In any case, in an age of multinational and transnational co-productions and co-financing (as demonstrated by earlier references to Huayi Brothers and the China Film Co-Production Corporation in my discussion of *The Forbidden Kingdom*), it is becoming increasingly difficult to distinguish these cinemas in strictly national terms. Thus, my analyses would even include films made in and released in theaters in Asia but with the potential to enter the US market, either through limited engagements or DVD sales. In taking on this broader range of cinematic works to transcribe critically the Chinese presence in Hollywood, I am registering the globalizing effects of Hollywood's hegemony. I am also particularly interested in how these Chinese cinemas ride the wave of Hollywood appeal, which is part of its contemporary transnationalization. Like most books of this nature, *Remade in Hollywood* has no ambition, nor the ability, to be comprehensive in its coverage of the various cinemas and its individual films. Instead, it is governed by my own mapping of the topical problematic, through the tracing of the significant and predominant themes, ideas, trends, questions, and concerns.

The temporal framework I have chosen for the book is not arbitrary, but is politically pegged to the July 1997 handover of Hong Kong by the British government to the People's Republic of China. Since the 1984 signing of the

Sino-British Joint Declaration, the territory and its people were plagued by anxieties of what a return to mainland Chinese rule might portend. This anxiety was exacerbated by the 1989 Tiananmen Square massacre, which accelerated the mass exodus of the rich and the mobile to the western countries that welcomed them. The new home for Hong Kong film industry players seemed naturally to be Hollywood, attracting Hong Kong stars, directors, and industry players who were in high demand to make the transition.[18] Such capital-induced diasporas, of course, are complex ones in that their trajectories are never unidirectional, but are bidirectional and even multidirectional in their fluid negotiations of the trans-Pacific capitalist networks that help define the Pacific Rim as a "space of cultural production."[19] Major players like John Woo, Jackie Chan, Chow Yun-fat, Michelle Yeoh, and Jet Li display "flexible citizenship" and are "astronauts"[20] who shuttle between Hollywood, Hong Kong, and wherever film production and promotion take them. The impact of this migration to Hollywood was multifold: film cultures of Hollywood, Asian American cinema, and Chinese cinemas were, in varied ways and to varying degrees, transformed. The rising popularity of the Hong Kong newcomers among American audiences also bode well for those mainland Chinese, Taiwanese, and Asian American players who aimed for Hollywood success, leading many to ride the Chinese/Asian wave of American cinematic fascination.

The Politics of Cinematic Citationality and Transculturation

As the earlier anecdotal examples of monkey kings, pirates, and geishas serve to demonstrate, this book's examination of the Chinese in Hollywood relies on the theoretical nuances of the cinematic remake. My interest lies less in a concern for the remake in its traditional form as a material filmic practice, but more in its critical efficacy as a trope for cultural reinvention, reconfiguration, and rewriting. This theoretical spinning-off from its narrower definitional confines helps one rethink the Chinese-Hollywood connection and its discursive problematic.

Everyone is familiar with the Hollywood remake as a filmic form of secondariness: one removed from its "original" text, but exploited for its box office potential. Yet the remake is much more complex and multifarious in its variations and permutations, in that one could remake a film in many ways and for different purposes. An older film can be updated to accommodate contemporary trends, values, and politics,[21] such as *The Stepford Wives* (1975 and 2004). A film is remade to impress different audience demographics, like Amy Heckerling's *Clueless* (1995). Some remakes are faithful frame-by-frame retakes as in Gus Van Sant's *Psycho* (1998), while others spoof or mimic the original like in the *Austin Powers* series and *The Tuxedo* (2002) starring Jackie Chan. The kind of remakes that are of special interest here are, of course, the "cross-cultural"[22] ones, considering how the commercially successful Scorsese remake of Andrew Lau and Alan Mak's *Infernal Affairs* (2002) into *The Departed* (2006) has now spawned fresh Hollywood interest in also remaking the Jackie Chan-produced *Enter the Phoenix* (2004).[23]

Remaking as a filmic form aside, its structure and character further bespeak of the very nature of cinema itself. In order to make this point, I now turn to Derrida and his theory of the mark of communication. In his essay "Signature Event Context," Jacques Derrida disrupts the purity of the sign by examining its iterability and citationality:

> This is the possibility on which I wish to insist: the possibility of extraction and of citational grafting which belongs to the structure of every mark, spoken or written, and which constitutes every mark as writing even before and outside every horizon of semiolinguistic communication; as writing, that is, as a possibility of functioning cut off, at a certain point, from its "original" meaning and from its belonging to a saturable and constraining context. Every sign, linguistic and nonlinguistic, spoken or written (in the usual sense of this opposition), as a small or large unity, can be *cited*, put between quotation marks; thereby it can break with every given context, and engender infinitely new contexts in an absolutely nonsaturable fashion. This does not suppose that the mark is valid outside its context, but on the contrary that there are only contexts without any center of absolute anchoring. This citationality, duplication, or duplicity, this iterability of the mark is not an accident or an anomaly, but is that (normal/abnormal) without which a mark could no longer even have a so-called "normal" functioning. What would a mark be that one could not cite? And whose origin could not be lost on the way?[24]

In *re*citing Derrida's theory, David Wills constructs the same argument for "the cinematic mark" in what he terms as "cinematic citationality":

> What is being commonly and communally referred to here as the remake, the possibility that exists for a film to be repeated in a different form, should rather be read as the necessary structure of iterability that exists for and within every film . . . The slightest mark is being remarked or remade even as it is being uttered or written, to the extent that it cannot make itself as full presence, as intact and coherent entity. It constitutes itself as reconstitutable, at least it must do so in order to function, that is to say, in order to make sense.[25]

In other words, cinema is a medium of unending citations, quotations, allusions, appropriations, adaptations, remaking, reinventions, rewriting, representations, and hybridizations. Built into the visual and auditory technologies of cinema is this demand for citationality. The power of Derrida's theory and Wills's redeployment of it lies in its deconstruction of essentialist notions of cultural ownership and originality, thus rupturing the boundaries between national cinemas. This is not to say that national cinemas do not exist or that the ideological insistence on those boundaries (real or imaginary) does not have material consequences.

Wills's argument has deep implications for the way we think of transnational Chinese cinemas, of which the Chinese presence in Hollywood is now an integral part. What happens when cinematic citationality leaps cross-culturally, which it must if we are to believe Sheldon Lu's argument that Chinese cinema, in all of its history, is transnational in nature on account that Chinese film is "deeply embedded in the economics of transnational capital"[26]? Patricia Aufderheide offers a telling example of the unpredictable and spiraling way cross-cultural cinematic citationality functions. In her discussion of Sammo Hung's *Eastern Condors* (1987), Aufderheide considers how the film "replays the characters, themes, and plot of" a number of Hollywood war movies.[27] But what is most interesting to me is that at the end of the essay, she gestures to the future where "Hong Kong cinema, itself a pastiche product, may now become the inspiration for tomorrow's Hollywood hits,"[28] an ironic turn that is being realized today. Here we see the possibility of Hollywood citing Hong Kong cinema citing Hollywood, and this is only taking into account a single linear causal thread (that has turned somewhat circular). This irony of cinematic narcissism was not lost on John Woo who similarly observed "that Hollywood began to imitate Hong Kong movies in the late 1980s and 1990s because Hong Kong films (to a certain degree) are imitations of Hollywood films, so Hollywood is imitating Hollywood,"[29] a process that David Bordwell calls "the Hongkongification of American cinema."[30] This mode of citation is naturally much more complex than has been portrayed, in that it is based on the accrual of cinematic sedimentation, one layer transforming itself on the basis of the previous, while adding to or shifting the elements according to its needs. The global cinema industry is a giant network of multiple lines of citation, increasing in its manifold turns and returns, connections and reconnections, particularly as cinematic cultural production intensifies through time. Hence, Tan See Kam takes necessary umbrage at Bordwell's linear formulation of a Hollywood–Hong Kong Hollywood "plagiarism"[31] by arguing that both Hollywood and Hong Kong cinemas have "been produced by, and [are] productive of, the interplay between internal and external forces, filmic, cultural or otherwise" and that "film-artisans from different cultures have used the medium differently, and for different purposes."[32]

This depiction of cinema as a transnational capitalist production of postmodern pastiche and hybridity, marked by interpenetrating and crosscutting loops of citationality, is not impervious to the shaping influences of global cultural politics. Derrida draws out parenthetically, in his discussion of the mark's "iterability," the etymological connotations of the term: "*iter* . . . comes from *itara*, *other* in Sanskrit, and everything that follows may be read as the exploitation of the logic which links repetition to alterity."[33] This connection to Otherness proffers us the idea that cinematic citationality does not flatten out cultural power distinctions, but works through them and sometimes reinforces them, a lesson Gayatri Chakravorty Spivak also offers us in her critique of the politics of cultural translation of the postcolonial text:

> In the act of wholesale translation into English there can be a betrayal of the democratic ideal into the law of the strongest. This happens when all the literature of the Third World gets translated into a sort of with-it translatese, so that the literature by a woman in Palestine begins to resemble, in the feel of its prose, something by a man in Taiwan. The rhetoricity of Chinese and Arabic! The cultural politics of high-growth, capitalist Asia-Pacific, and devastated West Asia! Gender difference inscribed and inscribing in these differences![34]

To study effectively this "with-it translatese" generated by the Chinese presence in Hollywood is to undertake an analysis of the cinema-studies version of what Mary Louise Pratt has so fruitfully described as "transculturation," a term ethnographers deploy "to describe how subordinated or marginal groups select and invent from materials transmitted to them by a dominant or metropolitan culture."[35] The cultural spaces of cinematic production, distribution, and consumption become "contact zones," "social spaces where disparate cultures meet, clash, and grapple with each other, often in highly asymmetrical relations of domination and subordination."[36] The uneven cultural, financial, and political power dynamics in these cinematic contact zones engage an overlapping of Hollywood's projection (on behalf of mainstream America) of an ethnic Otherness on the Chinese, and of the latter's "autoethnography" of Chineseness, a mode of self-representation to suit and engage Hollywood's ideological and cultural conditions.[37] It is in these power differentials and uneven levels of cultural/institutional agencies (often to the disadvantage of the Chinese newcomer) that one can distinguish between the cross-cultural citationality, seen in the Chinese-in-Hollywood phenomenon;

and the sort of cinematic citationality theorized in postmodernist/poststructuralist conceptions of cinema in general.

My critical approach to these cinematic representations of Chineseness and related cultural issues, is to take on the globalized Chinese presence in American and transnational Chinese cinemas as a "problematic," a concept theorized by Louis Althusser.[38] Through "'symptomatic' reading[s]"[39] of these films, I treat them as texts fraught with anxieties, tensions, contradictions, and conflicts produced by the uneven power-relational structures of the Chinese-Hollywood contact zones. Questions of race, class, gender, sexuality, and nation disturb the glossy surface of these transnational cinematic productions — for as in a problematic, what is implied or not represented is just as important as what is visible. Slippages reveal a cinematic unconscious that deserves analysis.

As I examine the construction of a celluloid Chineseness in Hollywood and the self-remaking of transnational Chinese cinemas to exploit the Hollywood paradigm for global box office success, I eschew a prescriptive notion of insisting on cultural authenticity. While historical and cultural facticity are not unimportant issues here, I wish instead to circumvent an essentialist mode of cultural interpretation by questioning less the realism and accuracy of these cultural representations and focusing more on the ideological motivations that spur the production of these images in the first place. Chineseness, as it is configured in these various cinemas, becomes a malleable entity, permitting filmmakers to mold and package it into various ideological, cultural, and aesthetic forms. This malleability is important in enabling a smooth translation of Chineseness into a product that appeals not only to a culturally less discriminating mainstream American and international audience, but also to more critical, global Chinese consumers. In light of the struggling film industries in China, Taiwan, and Hong Kong, a movie like *Crouching Tiger, Hidden Dragon* is eagerly consumed by Chinese audiences because it has the imprimatur of a Hollywood packaging. In other words, Chinese filmmakers in Hollywood have the tall order of presenting a believable formulation of Chineseness while at the same time filtering it through the dominant Hollywood paradigm.

Once Upon a Time in China, Taiwan, and Hong Kong: Hollywood's Adventurism in Chinese Cinematic Histories

The next three sections of this chapter are my attempt to briefly and rather reductively (for reasons of space constraints) chart the historical contours of the interpenetrating relationships between Hollywood and the golden triangle of "pan-Chinese cinema" — China, Hong Kong, and Taiwan.[40] Such a topography will reveal three main streams of cinematic traditions and discourses that intertwine to create the present cultural climate: firstly, Hollywood's adventurism within the Chinese cinematic traditions; secondly, the racist structures of classic and contemporary Hollywood stereotypes of the Chinese; and thirdly, the Asian-American cinematic response of survival and intervention. This discussion of the Hollywood-Chinese cinematic connection foregrounds the notion that what we see as a contemporary development in Hollywood's fascination with things Chinese is not devoid of history, nor has it emerged suddenly out of a cultural vacuum. My hope is to locate this book's discussion of the Chinese in Hollywood within these larger historical and cultural contexts of Chinese and American cinemas and, thus, mark its theoretical contiguity and continuity with these histories and discourses. Because of the survey nature of these sections, advanced students of these cinemas may choose instead to proceed to the final segment where I map out the themes of the book's chapters.

The Asia-Pacific rim, as a zone of cinematic cultural production, has seen an American capitalist encroachment in terms of film distribution and consumption and, to a lesser but growing degree, film production, since cinema's inception. Throughout this century-long history, the relationships that have developed between Hollywood and Chinese cinemas have been ambivalent ones, with the latter fighting off Hollywood hegemony at their respective national box-offices on one hand, and developing a complex network of financial, technological, aesthetic, and cultural interconnections on the other. America has had a historic role in introducing cinema as a capitalist enterprise in China. About a year and a half after the Lumière brothers' inaugural Paris screenings of their film shorts, American James Ricalton accomplished this in 1897 when he screened in Shanghai the Thomas Edison films.[41] Working for the Edison company as a photographer, Ricalton also later traveled to British Hong Kong to capture the city in the form of documentary shorts, which were then brought back to the United States.[42] Together, these landmark moments offer the beginnings of cross-cultural cinematic exchanges and influences. Another important pioneering figure in the early Los Angeles-Shanghai-Hong Kong cinema connection was Benjamin Brodsky, who helped set up the Asia Film Company in Shanghai. Arriving in Hong Kong, Brodsky produced a number of shorts, including Li Minwei's *Zhuangzi Tests His Wife* (1913), which he brought back to Los Angeles to be screened.[43] According to Law Kar, "Brodsky came to the Far East to make money out of the film business and may have never been conscious of his pioneering role. He had inspired a group of young Chinese idealists who founded the local film industry."[44] Before World War II and the Communist control of mainland China, Hollywood was already eyeing China as a huge market for its products and sought capitalist control, especially in Shanghai. In fact, the US government saw Hollywood adventurism overseas as a means to bring American culture, values, beliefs, and capitalist ideology to the rest of the world. When asked about China in 1926, Dr. Julius Klein, who led the Department of Commerce's Bureau of Foreign and Domestic Commerce, noted that movies are "invaluable in all markets where there is a high percentage of illiteracy among the people, for from the pictures they see they get their impression of how we live, the clothes we wear, and so forth . . . I can cite you instances of the expansion of trade in the Far East, traceable directly to the effects of the motion picture."[45] The Chinese naturally perceived in nationalist terms Hollywood's presence as a challenge to the nation's nascent film industry. It did not help Hollywood's cause in China when its filmic imagery of the Chinese tended to be predominantly negative in its racial stereotyping.

In his fascinating study of Chinese film censorship and its relationship to anti-imperialist sentiments in the 1920s and 1930s, Zhiwei Xiao examines instances where censorship and nationalism worked hand in hand to resist Hollywood domination of the film market in Shanghai and the rest of China. In 1930, public protests shut down screenings of Harold Lloyd's *Welcome Danger* (1929).[46] Because "the Chinese characters in this film are all presented as stupid, ridiculous, and uncouth," the film was eventually banned in China. [47] Between 1931 and 1938, the National Film Censorship Committee "adopted an unflinching stand toward both offensive foreign films and foreign film studio activities in China."[48] Xiao deduces from the committee's censorship practices the following approach, which remained unstated on an official level: objectionable elements included "China [represented] as a backward country and her people as an uncivilized race; scenes in which the Chinese appeared as villains, as morally corrupt (smoking opium and gambling), or even as servants; and dialogue that ridiculed the Chinese and the Chinese way of life or referred to the Chinese in a less than respectable way."[49] Because China was (and is even more so today) a very important market to Hollywood, major American studios had to compromise in their dealings to secure their slice of the Chinese pie. Columbia Pictures acquiesced to demands for cuts made to Frank Capra's *The Bitter Tea of General Yen* (1933); Samuel Goldwyn had on their production set of Sidney Franklin's *The Good Earth* (1937) a Chinese censorship committee member; Paramount Pictures' dangling of US$15 million to procure Chinese film studios was subverted by nationalist intervention; and a collusion between American and Chinese investors to create in Shanghai an "Oriental Hollywood" was similarly scuttled.[50] On the other hand, Hollywood domination of the Chinese box office was definitely established in this period, right until World War Two. Hollywood films triumphed mostly in Shanghai while the "hinterland cities" were less receptive of them.[51] An important observation to make here is the fact that this strain of nationalist criticism of Hollywood cinema has reemerged in contemporary form, with Hollywood's renewed domination of the Chinese market. Chinese unhappiness with *Pirates of the Caribbean* and *Memoirs of a Geisha* are just two recent examples.

Under the aegis of British capitalist colonialism, the Hong Kong film industry developed a comparatively more collaborative relationship with Hollywood, despite the competition for box-office dollars. Hong Kong cinema can also trace its trans-Pacific connection to the Chinese diaspora, particularly among Chinese immigrants in America's Chinatowns, who constituted a significant audience sector to which Hong Kong films needed to appeal. In fact, the first Cantonese sound film made was Joe Chiu's *Romance of the Songsters*, through the production company Grandview.[52] Law Kar provides a wonderfully intricate account of Grandview, which was established in 1933 in San Francisco by Joe Chiu and Moon Kwan Man-ching, both of whom were China-born, educated in the United States, and had film-related experience in Hollywood.[53] Chiu's *Romance of the Songsters* has the distinction of being "one of the first films to depict the lives of overseas American-Chinese."[54] With financial support coming from San Francisco, Chiu and Kwan later went on to set up Grandview in Hong Kong, which would become one of the four major Hong Kong film companies in the late 1930s. [55] What is significant, in Law's estimation, of Grandview's history is that it demonstrated how early film production culture was very much "an *interflow* of people and resources between two geographical locations."[56]

Because the exciting and complex history of Hong Kong as a Hollywood of the East is beyond the scope of this short historical overview, I refer readers to Stephen Teo's magisterial account of the various film production companies in Hong Kong from the post-World War II period to the 1970s, especially the Motion Picture and General Investment (MP and GI, or Cathay), Shaw Brothers, and Golden Harvest.[57] As the Hong Kong film industry entered the competitive big-studio model, mega studios like Shaw Brothers produced with assembly-line efficiency, films of a variety of popular genres that appealed to mass audiences in Hong Kong and the Chinese diaspora. Run Run Shaw, who headed film production in Hong Kong, knew his target audiences and their specific cultural/political environment of cinematic consumption. He had "different versions of a film for different markets with varying degrees of censorship: three versions were made, the 'hottest' for the US, Europe and Japan, the 'mildest' for Singapore and Malaysia, and the 'moderate' for Hong Kong."[58] While Shaw did attempt to access the mainstream American market, he was only successful catering to the Chinese community and to Asian cinema enthusiasts. Martial arts cinema, of course, had the strongest appeal, particularly to the African American community in the 1970s (see Chapters Five and Six); and it did have a brief phase where mainstream American audiences experienced what David Desser calls a "kung fu craze."[59] Hong Kong cinema not only introduced new filmic genres and visual aesthetics to America, but Hollywood also offered filmic models for Hong Kong to appropriate and reconfigure for its own purposes. Yingjin Zhang correctly assesses that "by the late 1970s Hong Kong cinema had gained the flexibility of crossing national and regional borders and the advantage of assimilating east and west as well as north and south."[60] This mode of cinematic citationality we see intensified in the contemporary Chinese presence in Hollywood.

One cannot talk about martial arts films in the 1970s without referencing Bruce Lee and his impact on Hollywood-Chinese cinema relationships. As Stephen Teo's portrayal of Lee confirms: "No other figure in Hong Kong cinema has done as much to bring East and West together in a common sharing of culture as Bruce Lee in his short lifetime. In him, Hong Kong cinema found its most forceful ambassador; an Asian role model espousing aspects of an Eastern culture who found receptive minds in the West."[61] For the ethnic Chinese, Lee embodied in his films "an abstract kind of cultural nationalism"[62] that challenged Western (and even Japanese) imperialism, thereby transforming Lee into an appealing icon to audiences in Hong Kong, Taiwan,[63] Southeast Asia, and the Chinese communities across America. He even had a strong following among African Americans. His version of a Chinese masculinity subverted and challenged the older American stereotypes of Asian passivity and submissiveness.[64] Besides his "kung fu style and methods," his "sex appeal and magnetic personality," "to the West, Lee is a narcissistic hero who makes Asian culture more accessible."[65]

Bruce Lee's dramatic film career began when he left Hollywood (see my brief discussion of this in Chapter Six in the context of *Kill Bill*) for Hong Kong to take up Golden Harvest's offer to make his films. *The Big Boss* (1971) and *Fist of Fury* (1972) exploded onto global screens to tremendous applause. In fact, *The Big Boss,* released as *Fists of Fury* in the US, reached number one at the American box office on May 1973, with two other kung fu films rounding off the top three, Golden Harvest's *Deep Thrust – the Hand of Death* (1972) and Shaw's *King Boxer* (1972), re-titled as *Five Fingers of Death*.[66]

The Way of the Dragon (1972) followed, with Chuck Norris adding further American appeal to the film, signaling an acknowledgment of Lee's crossover potential to an American market. Warner Brothers jumped into the production fray in its collaboration with Hong Kong producers to make *Enter the Dragon* (1973)[67] with director Robert Clouse at the helm. The studio continued sporadic involvement with Hong Kong studios to collaborate on cross-cultural projects, such as *Cleopatra Jones and the Casino of Gold* (1975 with Shaw) and Clouse's *The Big Brawl* (1980 with Golden Harvest) starring Jackie Chan in his first crossover attempt into the American market. Other American-Hong Kong collaborations also created films like the B-flick *The Legend of the Seven Golden Vampires* (1974; a Hammer-Shaw co-production),[68] *Shatter* (1974; Hammer-Shaw) featuring Ti Lung as one of the leads,[69] and *The Cannonball Run* (1981 with Golden Harvest) with Jackie Chan and Michael Hui as part of an ensemble cast. Finally, another important role that Bruce Lee played was that he helped create the conditions for the rise of Jackie Chan as a transnational superstar,[70] whose films and career I discuss in Chapters Five, Six, and Seven.

From 1978 to the late 1980s, China, Hong Kong, and Taiwan witnessed dramatic political changes that would not only transform the film industries but also set the stage for the new global Chinese presence in Hollywood in the new millennium. Deng Xiaoping's "Open-Door" economic policies in China, the Sino-British Joint Declaration of 1984 for the Hong Kong handover, and the 1987 lifting of martial law in KMT-controlled Taiwan all created the political, economic, and cultural conditions for "new waves"[71] of pan-Chinese cinemas: the Hong Kong New Wave, the Taiwan New Cinema, and the Chinese Fifth Generation Filmmakers. These rich streams of cinematic creativity would flood the world market through the global network of film festivals,[72] parading Chinese cinematic wares not only to film critics and cinephiles, but also to American filmmakers, distributors, and studio executives.

The works of the Fifth Generation directors, filmmakers who graduated from the Beijing Film Academy in 1982, constitute the "New Chinese Cinema."[73] A beneficiary of Deng Xiaoping's economic liberalization policies, the academy reopened its doors in 1978 to its fifth-generation students, "its first post-'cultural revolution' intake."[74] What was crucial about Deng's policies was that their focus on "market forces" created a new capitalist ethos for the new filmmakers to make sense of.[75] Filmmakers like Zhang Junzhao, Chen Kaige, Zhang Yimou, and Tian Zhuangzhuang were soon gaining international critical attention as art-house filmmakers, with Chen and Zhang Yimou later going on to become commercially important directors whose work found receptive audiences in the United States. After his critically significant *Yellow Earth* (1984), Chen Kaige proceeded to bring down the house at Cannes with *Farewell My Concubine* (1993), only to follow up with lesser films like *Temptress Moon* (1996), *The Emperor and the Assassin* (1998), and *The Promise* (2005). Zhang Yimou similarly took the art-house-to-pop-cinema route from films like *Judou* (1990) and *Raise the Red Lantern* (1991), to his more recent *wuxia* flicks. I look specifically at Zhang Yimou's *Hero* (2002) and *House of Flying Daggers* (2004) in Chapter Four, while I situate Chen Kaige's *The Promise* in the context of Chinese supernaturalism in Chapter Seven.

The two portmanteau films that marked the beginnings of the Taiwan New Cinema were *The Sandwich Man* (1983) and *In Our Time* (1982), the latter featuring a segment directed by Edward Yang, while the former had Hou Hsiao-hsien contributing one section.[76] Joining Hou and Yang were other new Taiwanese directors whose cinematic output though smaller than their Hong Kong counterparts, still made their mark at major international film festivals, with Hou's *City of Sadness* (1989) picking up the Golden Lion at the Venice Film Festival, the first Chinese film to win this award.[77] The Taiwan New Cinema, though short-lived, paved the way for global and Hollywood interest in filmmakers like Tsai Mingliang, Chen Kuo-fu (whose 2002 *Double Vision* I examine in Chapter Seven) and, of course, Ang Lee.[78] Trained in New York University's film school, Lee proved his ability to straddle effectively both the cultural East-West divide and the art-house-Hollywood aesthetic sensibilities. Lee's *Crouching Tiger, Hidden Dragon* (2000), I argue in Chapter Four, signaled the global rise of the *wuxia pian*. His growing body of work, including Hollywood class acts like the Academy-Award winning *Brokeback Mountain* (2005), made him an incredibly marketable filmmaker to mainstream American audiences, Chinese audiences around the world, and, of course, Taiwanese audiences, who happily celebrated their native son's triumph in Hollywood.[79]

The Hong Kong New Wave and Second Wave cinemas represented frenetic bursts of creativity, as they jolted Hong Kong cinema into fresh new directions. This cinematic vitality and aesthetic ingenuity are what Hollywood now sees as fresh blood that it can inject into its tired rehashing of action cinema. (Again, the irony here is that some critics believe that it is *the West* that influenced Hong Kong cinema during the post-World War Two period and, therefore, the New Wave does not really exist.[80] The notion of cinematic citationality may provide an alternative theoretical means to rethink notions of cinematic originality.[81]) The New and Second Wave directors now constitute the mainstays of Hong Kong cinema, with many making the move to

Hollywood since 1997. The incredibly prolific Tsui Hark has close to forty films to his directorial credit, including the highly successful Wong Fei-hong series *Once Upon a Time in China*, which catapulted Jet Li into international superstardom and onto the Hollywood stage. Tsui himself made two Hollywood forays, *Double Team* (1997) and *Knock Off* (1998), both of which were Jean-Claude Van Damme vehicles, before deciding to concentrate on Hong Kong productions. Van Damme's fascination with Hong Kong directors continued with *Maximum Risk* (1996), *Replicant* (2001), and *In Hell* (2003), all helmed by Ringo Lam. Leong Po-chih directed Jude Law in *The Wisdom of Crocodiles* (1998) before proceeding to mainly American television and direct-to-video movies. Taking on both horror and action genres, Ronny Yu added his touch to *Bride of Chucky* (1998), *The 51ˢᵗ State* (2001), and *Freddy vs. Jason* (2003), and then turning around to make the excellent *Huo Yuan Jia*, or *Fearless* (2006), starring Jet Li. Of all the directors to make the Hollywood crossover, John Woo is probably the most commercially successful. Beginning with Universal's *Hard Target* (1993), Woo went on to clinch Hollywood mega-blockbuster deals, such as *Broken Arrow* (1996), *Face/Off* (1997), *Mission: Impossible II* (2000), *Windtalkers* (2002), and *Paycheck* (2003). As with Jet Li and Tsui Hark, Woo's classic crime films *A Better Tomorrow* (1986) and *The Killer* (1989) put Chow Yun-fat on the map of transnational Chinese cinemas, making the latter's move into Hollywood a smooth one. Wong Kar-wai, the art-house film-festival darling, joined the group with his critically celebrated Hong Kong works like *Chungking Express* (1994), *Happy Together* (1997), *In the Mood for Love* (2000), and *2046* (2004); and has now taken on two Studio Canal productions, the recently released *My Blueberry Nights* (2007) and the in-pre-production remake of *The Lady from Shanghai* (2010). A number of newer filmmakers have also dipped their feet in the Hollywood pool: Kirk Wong's *The Big Hit* (1998), Peter Chan's *The Love Letter* (1999), and Stanley Tong's *Mr. Magoo* (1997) — Tong was also responsible for *Rumble in the Bronx* (1995), Jackie Chan's breakout hit in the US. It is interesting to note here that while commercial film directors make the direct leap into Hollywood, the art-house directors naturally take the international film festival route before crossing into Hollywood mainstream when the time is right for them to do so.

My brief but strategically emphatic gallop through the rich and multifaceted histories of pan-Chinese cinema brings us now to the post-1997 present where transnational Chinese cinema has transmogrified into this multi-tentacled creature that entwines itself to Hollywood, together spawning varied versions of celluloid Chineseness, which this book confronts as its main critical challenge.

"Yellow Peril" and the Model Minority: Hollywood's Chinese Stereotypes

"A long time ago in a galaxy far, far away . . ." is undoubtedly the most memorable opening line in science fiction cinema history. It serves as the prelude to all six *Star Wars* films, the first of which is *Star Wars* (1977), the film that launched what has been called the "cult blockbuster" phenomenon, [82] with its spectacular marketing and merchandising paraphernalia.[83] The film's cultural impact, hence, cannot be underestimated, considering the way the series creates for its audience a fantasy space of a mythic reality that is not of this world and yet parallels the human experience that *is* of this world. In this sense, the fantastical distancing of "a galaxy far, far away" in no way reduces the very real structuring presence of the cultural politics of race, class, gender, sexuality, and political ideology in America.[84]

When George Lucas proudly unveiled *Star Wars: Episode I – The Phantom Menace* in 1999, Asian Americans decried the ethnic stereotypes of Asians as a throwback to the older Hollywood representations. The Trade Viceroy Nute Gunray, one of the villainous non-human characters, is spotted speaking English with a suspiciously Asian sounding accent that could easily be mistaken as Chinese in its inflections. One could conveniently dismiss such a reading as a form of ethnic over-sensitivity; but Ed Guerrero's analysis of the first *Star Wars* movie convincingly demonstrates how these films can reveal, rather symptomatically, the conditions of race relations in America:

> The film's construction of race relations arises out of tensions and contestations located in the social here and now . . . But the stark realization of the possibility of a "final solution" to earth's color problem is emphasized in *Star Wars*, in that white people, particularly white males, are constructed as the sole and sovereign human norm, contrasted to "Wookies" and an assorted myriad of exotic creatures and humanoids, especially as depicted in the film's memorable bar scene. Enhancing the film's hierarchical subordination of racial types, *Star Wars* utilizes the mechanism of displacement to recruit and transpose into robots and nonhuman Wookies the friendly "colored" sidekicks, the Tontos, Birmingham Browns, and Nigger Jims of the action-adventure thrillers and novels of America's filmic and literary past. And in much the same way that these sidekicks have always provided emotional comfort in all of the dominant cinema's genres, these alien, exotic, noncompetitive, desexualized contrasts to the reigning "norm" of whiteness continue to be understanding nonwhite "buddies" in times of sharply politicized racial discourse.[85]

The point here is not to label the film series as "racist" per se, but to map the political unconscious[86] of racial socialization that permeates much of contemporary Hollywood cinema. Even in 1999, during an era of multicultural awareness, *Star Wars* characters like Jar Jar Binks and the Trade Viceroy Nute Gunray still come off as racial caricatures locked into the ideological forms of the assimilated non-white or the menacing alien respectively.

What I draw from Guerrero's splendid analysis is also the realization that the racial unconscious forms a cinematic continuum. Racial images of the Chinese, for example, move through distinct phases of Hollywood depiction in accordance with the political and social perceptions of the Chinese throughout American history. The Chinese in the reconfigured form of the alien Trade Viceroy assume an economic menace, not unlike the political and public fears that the People's Republic of China, as a rising global economic powerhouse, might threaten American capitalist might and hegemony in the Asia-Pacific region. Important to consider also is Guerrero's observation that racial stereotypes undergo transmutation into cinematic forms to fit the times, though remaining stereotypes nonetheless. These are significant lessons to keep in mind as one considers the cultural politics of Chinese representation in its new presence within contemporary Hollywood and American cinema.

A number of substantial critical works on the subject of Hollywood stereotypes of Asians were produced beginning as early as the 1950s.[87] A central theme that one gathers from all these works is that the creation of Asian stereotypes and their reproduction on the big screen were enabled by the political conditions of the times, specifically America's trans-Pacific political and military adventurism, and the gradually changing attitudes towards Asian immigrants within the US. While these stereotypes sadly constitute a handsome list, I have chosen to highlight only a select few, with strategic attention placed on their specific relevance to the Chinese and a possible connection to the new post-1997 presence.

The power of cinema lies in its ability to involve the vicarious gaze of its audience, a gaze that is often projected onto a constructed figure of Otherness, be it national, ethnic, gendered, sexualized, or cultural. One of the reasons why Laura Mulvey's analysis of cinematic scopophilia in "Visual Pleasure and Narrative Cinema"[88] had such an impact on contemporary cinema studies is that it engenders discussion of cinema as a phantasmic libidinal space for the construction of alterity to ease anxieties, raise fears as and when necessary, and basically reinforce ideological positions. The formulations of a mythic cinematic Chineseness in recognizable stereotypes and racist clichés ameliorate fears of an invading "alien" culture through visual and narrative containment, particularly by means of the classic Hollywood happy ending where white normality is felicitously restored in America.[89]

This particular tendency in American film one can trace back to cinema's beginnings. In an impressive essay investigating films by both the Thomas Edison company and the American Mutoscope and Biograph, produced between 1898 and 1908 with titles like *Dancing Chinamen, Marionettes* (1898), *Chinese Rubbernecks* (1900), and *The Deceived Slumming Party* (1908),[90] Sabine Haenni demonstrates how these early images of malleable Chinese bodies and of New York City's Chinatown as an exotic tourist space allowed white audiences to "pleasurably experience the newly racialized metropolis by simultaneously consolidating a new kind of 'white' hegemony, and by assigning the Chinese to a limited and constrained space."[91] In other words, Chinatown was turned into a living ethnographic museum, where quick jaunts through it provided the viewer with a Ripley's-believe-it-or-not experience, with speed creating a protective distance from actual human contact. Film as a, then, new media technology furnished a further distancing effect for audiences to experience Chinatown without the consequences or the responsibilities of physical contact. Considering that almost a century has passed since the production of these early film clips, Haenni's argument still resonates for contemporary films like *The Corruptor* (1999), which I analyze in Chapter Five in specific relation to the triad presence in New York City's Chinatown.

An integral fact to keep in mind is that cinema rose as a popular American cultural art form during an intense period of anti-Chinese public sentiments: the Chinese Exclusion Act received President Chester Arthur's signature in 1882 despite his opposition to it, because both houses of Congress passed Representative Horace Page's bill in indication of general public support of these anti-Chinese measures.[92] For, in the public imagination throughout the fin de siècle period and the early twentieth century, the figure of the Chinese transmogrified from that of the pigtailed "coolie," the Chinese indentured laborer, to that of the "deviant" and the "yellow peril," according to Robert G. Lee's taxonomic categorization of "the six faces of the Oriental."[93] Gina Marchetti proffers a culturally incisive definition of the yellow peril:

> Rooted in medieval fears of Genghis Khan and Mongolian invasions of Europe, the yellow peril combines racist terror of alien cultures, sexual anxieties, and the belief that the West will be overpowered and enveloped by the irresistible, dark, occult forces of the East. Given that knowledge about Asia and Asians has been limited in Europe and America, much of this formulation necessarily rests on a fantasy that projects Euroamerican desires

and dreads onto the alien other. Thus, as Western nations began to carve up Asia into colonies, their own imperialist expansion was in part rationalized by the notion that a militarily powerful Asia posed a threat to "Christian civilization."[94]

Her description accurately frames the yellow peril as a mode of Orientalism inflected by Euro-American colonialist and imperialist discourses.[95]

One of the most nefarious yellow peril creations is none other than the character of Dr. Fu Manchu. In light of the Orientalist discourses of British colonialism, it comes as no surprise that Fu Manchu sprang out of the British popular literary imagination.[96] Born in 1883 in Birmingham, England, as Arthur Henry Ward, Sax Rohmer penned thirteen novels featuring Fu Manchu. As Eugene Franklin Wong recounts, Rohmer immersed himself in Limehouse, the area of London where the original Chinatown was first located, to gain inspiration for his famous literary creation.[97] Hollywood came a-calling and the rest was cinematic history. From the 1920s to the 1960s, the doings of the evil doctor filled the big screen, and later, television, with major studios like Paramount and Metro-Goldwyn-Mayer jumping on the Chinese bandwagon and cashing in on the yellow peril scare embodied by Fu Manchu. Boris Karloff, famous for his portrayals of Frankenstein's monster in the James Whale movies, took his turn in MGM's *The Mask of Fu Manchu* (1932).[98] The last English-language Fu Manchu films I am aware of had Christopher Lee play the title character: *The Vengeance of Fu Manchu* (1967), *The Blood of Fu Manchu* (1968), and *The Castle of Fu Manchu* (1969). (It is irresistible to point out here that Shaw Brothers helped co-produce *The Vengeance of Fu Manchu*, adding again to its stable of B-movie international collaborations. Once more, profit triumphed over cultural nationalism in the global film industry.)

The *Flash Gordon* films also delivered a science fiction version of the Fu Manchu character in the form of Ming the Merciless. Robert Barshay's description of him demonstrates a clear parallel between the two villains: "Such is the villain in *Flash Gordon* — a trident bearded, slanty eyed, shiny doomed [sic], pointy nailed, arching eyebrowed, exotically garbed Oriental named Ming, who personifies unadulterated evil . . . [Ming] is the product of perhaps the richest and longest tradition of all of Hollywood's ethnic [racial] stereotypes, one which has spawned many grotesque offspring and conceived innumerable variations of deformity."[99] Could one of its most recent offspring be the pirate captain Sao Feng in *Pirates of the Caribbean: At World's End*, whose image bears an uncanny resemblance to that of its wicked predecessors? My point here is not to advocate a superficial form of cinematic comparison as criticism, but rather to reinforce again the imagistic continuities the character of Sao Feng establishes with the various racist, anti-Chinese discourses of the past that had helped to produce its filmic ancestry, something that filmmakers must continually guard against.

Part of the discursive danger that Fu Manchu and Ming the Merciless were meant to pose was their sexual appetite for white female flesh, a desire invoking the fears of miscegenation. Through her expert readings of early Hollywood films such as D. W. Griffith's *Broken Blossoms* (1919), Marchetti demonstrates how these film "narratives use the fantasy of rape and the possibility of lynching to reaffirm the boundaries of a white-defined, patriarchal, Anglo-American culture."[100] The libidinal forces of Fu Manchu and Ming the Merciless were not only disrupted by the last minute heroics of the white savior, but their erotic inclinations seemed also to have emerged out of the shadows of the grotesquely "perverse" sexual aura, with which Hollywood was wont to imbue its "queer" villains. The desexualized Asian male was another common filmic method used by Hollywood to neutralize this threat to white female sexuality. Even today one is hard pressed to come up with clear instances where the Asian male hero actually wins the white female protagonist in the end,[101] as a quick survey of characters played by Jackie Chan, Jet Li, and Chow Yun-fat will confirm: Jackie Chan and Jennifer Love Hewitt remain friends in *The Tuxedo*; Jet Li pairs up with the *African* American Aaliyah in *Romeo Must Die*; and Chow Yun-fat takes leave of Mira Sorvino for China in *The Replacement Killers*.

White male-Asian female romances, on the other hand, abound, with a rich Hollywood tradition for one to study: *Love Is a Many-Splendored Thing* (1955), *China Doll* (1958), and *The World of Suzie Wong* (1960) specifically featured Chinese women in love with white male heroes. Inhabiting this fantasy world of the white heterosexual male gaze is a passively submissive "Lotus Blossom or a domineering Dragon Lady."[102] These stereotypes frequently do not remain static, but morph from one form to another to engage the libidinal contingencies of the male gaze. A good instance would be Suzie Wong's transformation from the Oriental sex kitten image (as a Hong Kong prostitute) in the beginning of the film, into the sacrificial mother and submissive wife in the end.[103] Part of the white heterosexual male fantasy of the submissive Asian female also revolves around the stereotype of the Japanese "butterfly", popularized by Giacomo Puccini's *Madama Butterfly,* a variation on the Lotus Blossom theme, which David Henry Hwang's play *M. Butterfly* and David Cronenberg's 1993 film adaptation have so thoroughly critiqued.

The recent cultural politics of female empowerment have further spurred the reformulation of the Dragon Lady[104] stereotype, though rather ambivalently

I might add, into the kick-ass martial artist. Michelle Yeoh as a Bond girl in *Tomorrow Never Dies* (1997) marked "the reinvention of the Chinese woman warrior" who, according to Marchetti, "does not drift too far from the formulaic presentation of Asian women in Hollywood as passive but erotic 'lotus blossoms' or villainously dangerous, exotic 'dragon ladies.'"[105] Hopes for a new female heroine who not only matches up to the British colonialist relic that is James Bond, but who is also willing to resist his supposedly irresistible sexual allure, are dashed in the film's genre-conventional finale of Bond getting the girl, once again; this despite the fact that there is little or no sexual charge between Bond and Yeoh's character throughout the film. The eroticism of the kung fu fighting dragon lady here really lies in her dominatrix figuration. The powerful expressivity of the woman-warrior battles one envisions, for example, in the Michelle Yeoh-Zhang Ziyi fight scenes in *Crouching Tiger, Hidden Dragon* is troublingly trivialized into erotic "cat-fights."[106] Lucy Liu's campy turn as the undercover whip-wielding dominatrix teacher figure in *Charlie's Angels* (2000) and her spectacular fight scenes with Uma Thurman in *Kill Bill Vol. 1* (2003) further showcase this problematic update of the traditional Dragon Lady stereotype.

The final figure to round off this array of Hollywood's Orientalist exotica is the rotundly avuncular detective Charlie Chan. Again a literary creation, this time by American author Earl Derr Biggers, Charlie Chan appeared in a series of novels before finding his way onto cinema screens in 1926. His popularity with moviegoers was only later cemented with the film *Charlie Chan Carries On* (1931).[107] Eugene Franklin Wong explains why an America paralyzed by the yellow peril was now ready for a non-threatening Chinese lead character:

> Warner Oland . . . starred as the Chinese detective. Although Oland's personality had much to do with the success of Chan, it is likely that the final immigration measures taken by the United States Government, and the subsequent social relief accompanying the end to the Asian immigration problem, gradually provided a psychological incentive and social climate given to the acceptance of an image of a non-villainous Asian.[108]

So welcoming were audiences of Chan's benign Chineseness that his character appeared in over forty films from 1926 to 1981,[109] the last of which had Peter Ustinov inhabiting the role and confronting Angie Dickinson as the Dragon Queen. The fact that all the Fu Manchu and Charlie Chan roles were played by white actors is no coincidence; it simply testifies to the racist climate of Hollywood in its discriminatory practices of hiring and promoting few Asian actors,[110] and also to the notion that an experienced white actor could more effectively play in yellow face these grotesque caricatures with Orientalist aplomb and hyperbole. When the last Charlie Chan film was first propositioned, Asian Americans were up in arms, with one group calling themselves the "Coalition of Asians to Nix, [sic] Charlie Chan" to express "their disapproval of the proposed film, since the two primary Chinese characters were going to be played by white American actors." Jachinson Chan concludes that the filmmaker's decision to proceed with his casting decision "exemplifies the deep rootedness of a white Charlie Chan," reinforcing the notion of white superiority.[111]

Charlie Chan fails as a "positive image" because he "embodies what Frank Chin and Jeffrey Paul Chan have termed 'racist love,' the image of an ethnic minority who unquestioningly accepts his marginal status even as he serves the social order."[112] The Charlie Chan films are, according to Kwai-Cheung Lo, "always placed in the comedy format through which the stereotypical image of the Asian male is displaced, inverted, and intermingled with European-American traits . . . Charlie Chan is depicted as virtuous, mature, rational, and skillful at solving crimes, while his Asian characteristics, such as his speech, dress, and appearance, are still comically maintained."[113] Charlie Chan, thus unpacked, reminds me of Jackie Chan's methods of mimicry, which I deal with in Chapter Six. This correlation coincides precisely with Lo's own analysis of Jackie Chan, whose film *Rush Hour*, he argues, "shamelessly revives" Charlie Chan, this time in the form of "a muscular Hong Kong body."[114] Both Charlie Chan and Jackie Chan build an unfortunate connection as exemplars of Asians as the "model minority"[115] in America.

Asian American Cinema: Survival Tactics and Critical Interventions

The "new" Chinese presence in Hollywood can now be conceptualized as a merging of the various cinematic streams: the cinemas of China, Taiwan, and Hong Kong, bringing robust traditions and vibrant cultures to bear on this presence; the racial typology and racist iconography produced through a century of Hollywood's reliance on Orientalist imagery, which sadly finds its contemporary revival in reconfigured Hollywood forms; and, finally, Asian American cinema, the last stream, a small but politically important one in the resistance of Hollywood's ethnic stereotypes. By using the notion of "merging," I only seek to register the possible discursive dangers of the Hollywood vortex sucking in these various streams and dissolving them into a homogenous nondescript celluloid Chineseness for transnational consumption. Yet, by highlighting below the lessons from the political activist aspects of Asian American cinema, I am in no way prescribing this cinema's politics as the only approach to engage Hollywood's dominance; for this politics was, and is, multifaceted, and its tactics have been strategically revised through time to meet specific historical exigencies.[116] Furthermore, not all Asian American film is activism-based or is energized by a critical Asian American politics — some instances of this cinema incorporate Hollywood's stereotypes of the Chinese in their narrative and character formulations to earn mainstream acceptance (just as the various streams of Chinese cinemas are equally capable of critical responses to Hollywood's domination of global cinema). Instead, my aim here in transcribing an aspect of the cinema's historical problematics is to offer an instance where a specific cinematic culture can present alternative possibilities in resisting politically questionable discourses in mainstream cinema. (Chapter Two also illustrates this point in the context of the Hong Kong handover.)

To begin to understand the evolution of an Asian American cinema that offers critical interventions, one needs to return to the Civil Rights Movement in 1964 as the crucible of Asian American political awareness and subjectivity. Martin Luther King's efforts on behalf of African America transformed the landscape of all race relations in the United States. When racial discrimination was finally declared illegal by the US Congress in 1964, it had a ripple effect as immigration exclusion laws were also deemed discriminatory.[117] Hence, a year later, the Immigration Act of 1965 came into being, which "abolished the national-origins quotas and provided for the annual admission of 170,000 immigrants from the Eastern Hemisphere and 120,000 from the Western Hemisphere."[118] The gates that were closed to Chinese immigrants were now open, permitting family reunions and a flood of new immigrants that would significantly alter the racial character of the country. Asian Americans began to reexamine their sense of identity, their place in America, their cultural connections to their former homelands, and the political possibilities of asserting their place in a nation that had sought to assimilate them and confine them to the ghettos of America's social margins. The Asian American Movement was thus conceived in the late 1960s followed by the formation of the first Asian American studies program at the University of California at Berkeley and San Francisco State University.[119] The radical politics of the Asian American Movement infused academia and the arts.

In explaining how Asian American cinema emerged out of this politics, Darrell Hamamoto observes that "independent film was but one of many expressive forms that artists adopted to oppose the cultural hegemony of the allied corporate and media industries. Along with film, self-consciously *Asian*

American writing, music, theater, fine arts, and criticism began to assert themselves against the institutionalized racism that had marginalized or excluded creative and intellectual work by Yellow people in the United States."[120] Independent cinema was often the means for Asian American filmmakers to make their mark. Much of the work that was produced during the early years was culturally politicized, engaging and challenging the stereotypes of Hollywood while constructing new artistic spaces for an Asian American expressivity and subjectivity. In her now classic essay on independent Asian American films, Renee Tajima proffers "a broad framework for looking at Asian American cinema": It is "a socially committed cinema" that is "created by a people bound by 1) race; 2) interlocking cultural and historical relations; and 3) a common experience of western domination;" and is also "characterized by diversity shaped through 1) national origin; and 2) the constant flux of new immigration flowing from a westernizing East into an easternizing West."[121] In other words, this framework accommodates the heterogeneity and diversity of Asian Americans in order to challenge the homogenizing reductionism of racial stereotypes, and seeks to lock Asian America into the larger projects of radical political interventions and movements to which such a cinema is indebted.

Tajima historicizes Asian American cinema into two periods: the 1960s and 1970s together form one, while the 1980s constitute another. Out of the former period emerged "an urgent, idealistic brand of filmmaking [that] embodied the energy of the Asian American political movement and sought to be a voice for Asian American people." The latter consisted of "a period of institutionalization, pragmatism, and skills attainment, as filmmakers focused their sights on a mass audience."[122] Tajima also credits certain "Asian American media institutions" like Asian CineVision, Third World Newsreel, Visual Communications, and the Asian American Resource Workshop, among others,[123] for providing the various modes of support to enable independent Asian American filmmakers to accomplish their work. Another important organization that promotes and exhibits Asian American cinema is, of course, the Asian American International Film Festival (AAIFF), which has provided "career boosts to directors such as Wayne Wang and Ang Lee, both of whom later achieved crossover success."[124]

Chinese American directors of feature-length films make up only a handful. Two of the best known feature-length Chinese American directors go by the same last name: Peter Wang and Wayne Wang, the latter achieving greater renown than the former. Hailing from Taiwan, Peter Wang made only three films, all in the 1980s: *A Great Wall* (1986), *The Laser Man* (1988), and *First Date* (1989). Wayne Wang, on the other hand, offers one an excellent instance of a filmmaker who displays the enviable "ability to navigate economic necessity and social perception"[125] by shuttling between Hollywood films and art-house fare, not unlike Ang Lee. In her questioning of Tajima's critique of "mainstream or studio productions as being coopted and politically suspect," Sandra Liu argues that Wang's films should be contextualized within "a complex of conflicting discourses and desires and continuously changing tactics in response to shifting material exigencies."[126] Such tactics enable Wang to stay financially afloat with commercial movies like *Slam Dance* (1987), *The Joy Luck Club* (1993), *Anywhere but Here* (1999), *Maid in Manhattan* (2002), *Because of Winn-Dixie* (2005), and *Last Holiday* (2006); while producing politically urgent and aesthetically creative films like *Chan Is Missing* (1982), *Dim Sum: A Little Bit of Heart* (1985), the adaptation of Louis Chu's novel *Eat a Bowl of Tea* (1989), the X-rated *Life is Cheap . . . But Toilet Paper Is Expensive* (1989), *Smoke* (1995), *Blue in the Face* (1995), *Chinese Box* (1997), the bizarrely kinky *The Center of the World* (2001), *A Thousand Years of Good Prayers* (2007), and *The Princess of Nebraska* (2007). In the next chapter, I consider Wayne Wang's *Chinese Box*, a not-unproblematic cinematic capturing of his former homeland Hong Kong as it momentously changed political hands from Britain to the People's Republic of China.

Apart from the two Wangs, the 1990s saw other efforts that ranged from the critically challenging to the forgettable: Shirley Sun, who co-wrote the script to *A Great Wall*, took on directing duties in *Iron and Silk* (1990); another Chinatown film is Tony Chan's *Combination Platter* (1993); V. V. Dachin Hsu made the horror film *Pale Blood* (1990) and the family comedy *My American Vacation* (1999); and actress Joan Chen made her directorial debut, the incredibly disturbing *Xiu Xiu: the Sent-Down Girl* (1998) and *Autumn in New York* (2000), starring Richard Gere and Winona Ryder. It is only with the arrival of the new millennium that one witnesses a promising group of young energetic directors who are coming into their own. While the present fascination with Chinese and Asian cinemas in Hollywood has probably worked in their favor, a wave that they have ridden to their advantage, this group's small but growing cinematic corpus does not shy away from challenging staid conceptions of the Chinese and Asians in general. Alice Wu's debut *Saving Face* (2004) and Quentin Lee's *Drift* (2000) and *Ethan Mao* (2004) assert lesbian and gay subjectivities in the face of Chinese familial disavowal of their material presence. After shining in the MTV-produced *Better Luck Tomorrow* (2002), Justin Lin went to Hollywood with *The Fast and the Furious: Tokyo Drift* (2006). His latest, *Finishing the Game* (2007), is a wonderful film about the movie industry's attempt to find Bruce Lee's replacement immediately after his death. By playing on the same stereotypes through humor, the film unveils in a non-threatening fashion the impact of Hollywood's stereotyping of the Chinese. (The humor in *Harold and Kumar Go to White Castle* (2004) and *Harold and Kumar Escape from Guantanamo Bay* (2008) functions in the same way.) These new Chinese American players seem to have appropriated Wayne Wang's tactic of straddling both commercially viable and politically avant-garde projects, the two of which may not be mutually exclusive.

As a means of winding down this extended introduction, I quote a statement from an actress and dialogue coach who has been in the American film and television business since 1981:

> The facets to Asian stereotypes, reactions to them, what to do about them are complex. Stereotyping seems an American rite of passage. People I know, upon hearing and dealing with the controversy of Asian stereotypes, have decided to use another minority to avoid it completely. This hurts us in many ways too. We're not seen, we don't work and don't serve as reminders that we are a part of the American fabric.[127]

The complex position she and many others find themselves in, which is this cutthroat business of Hollywood, exposes the material realities that the cultural hierarchies and power structures in the industry have created and imposed on minority participants of the game. Is one willing to pay the price for circumventing stereotypes and standing up against the industry's desire to return to the racist imagistic traditions of Chineseness that are being remade for a contemporary global audience? While her statement commands renewed respect for those struggling in the industry, it also reminds us of the immense cultural and political challenges the various participants of Chinese in Hollywood and the new generation of Chinese-American filmmakers and actors need to confront on a daily basis. As new filmic representations and images emerge in the future, these challenges will become an integral part of a larger historical framework within which to conceive an effective cultural politics to critique, resist, and/or engage Hollywood's hegemony.

Mapping the Chapters

The rest of the book's six chapters follow an idiosyncratic thematic progression (on account of my personal research encounters and interests) in order to isolate specific moments within the Chinese-in-Hollywood phenomenon. Chapters Two and Three, as I have noted earlier, belong together in that they offer a composite reading of the diverse responses to the 1997 Hong Kong handover, which provides the historical point of entry for the book. Chapter Two, "Visualizing Hong Kong," examines the handover through the cinematic gazes of Hong Kong diasporic filmmakers Wong Kar-wai, Wayne Wang, and Evans Chan. Their gazes from afar enable them to grapple cathartically with an important historical moment in their homeland, as they continue to make films in and/or for America. The analysis in this chapter also asks the broader questions of cultural and diasporic identity and politics that the Chinese presence in Hollywood must ultimately face up to, a critical challenge that I present through my discussion of the film's deployment of cinematic visuality as a mode of intervention. In counterpoint to the cultural politics in Chapter Two is Chapter Three's discussion of Hollywood's response to the events through films like *Red Corner*, *Kundun*, and *Seven Years in Tibet*. These films' admirable intention of speaking up against the human rights abuses and lack of democracy evident in China is undermined by the representational excess configured through Hollywood's imaginings of China's terrifying cultural Otherness.

While the Chinese cinematic diaspora was mobilized around the 1997 handover, it is the *wuxia pian*'s (Chinese sword-fighting movie's) arrival in Hollywood in the form of *Crouching Tiger, Hidden Dragon* that signaled the new, sustained presence of Chinese cinema in the United States. Chapter Four, "The Global Return of the *Wuxia pian*," focuses on the strategies of cultural translation and accommodation in Ang Lee's *Crouching Tiger, Hidden Dragon* and Zhang Yimou's *Hero* and *House of Flying Daggers*. The desire to garner global audience appeal in all three films created deep cultural anxieties that left significant traces in the filmic texts for my analysis.

With the *wuxia pian* fueling American and global audience's thirst for Chinese action cinema, Hollywood has diversified its offerings through the crime action genre. However, cinematic representations of criminality and vice in America's Chinatowns have inevitably become a part of the genre's visual landscape, thus sustaining the way mainstream America stereotypically views the Chinese as culturally alien and morally perverse. This mode of representation has resurfaced in the form of the Chinese triads and their involvement in protection rackets, human trafficking, the drug trade, and counterfeiting. Chapter Five, "Enter the Triads," looks at Hollywood films *Lethal Weapon 4*, *The Corruptor*, *Rush Hour*, *Rush Hour 2*, and *Romeo Must Die*, and the way they situate the triads in a global/local nexus and, in turn, ethnicize them into criminally monstrous Others within the discourses of American race relations.

Chapters Six and Seven spotlight Hollywood's evolving fetishism of things Chinese. Discussing the emergence of Sino-chic through Hollywood's appropriation of Chinese action cinema, Chapter Six looks first at how Jackie Chan works the global/local conjuncture by increasing the cinematic Americanization of his work, especially through the themes of cultural adaptation, appropriation, and acceptance of Asian migrants in the US, while simultaneously building his cosmopolitan appeal to a wide global audience, all through the processes of "mimicry as failure" in *The Tuxedo, Shanghai Noon*, and *Shanghai Knights*. The chapter then interrogates the modes of cinematic citationality in Quentin Tarantino's *Kill Bill Vol. 1* and *2*, while at the same time professing an uneasy pleasure for the camp aesthetics in these movies. Treading through a study of the exploitation film, the female revenge genre, and various cinematic allusions to the Shaw Brothers archives, I foreground Tarantino's relishing of an ethnic cinematic chic in his reinvention of Chineseness in *Kill Bill*.

Chapter Seven, "Chinese Supernaturalism," centers on the way *Bulletproof Monk, Double Vision, The Myth,* and *The Promise* pursue a kind of mythic autoethnography, where Chinese religious beliefs and superstitions receive an intensified makeover to emphasize the bizarre, the macabre, the mystical, and the inexplicable. While all these films see it as their responsibility to bridge the East-West divide, they also ironically serve to keep the "monstrous" ethnic Other at bay by deploying ethnic supernaturalism as a cordon sanitaire. This double-edged strategy also reifies racial stereotypes and problematic cultural assumptions on issues such as ethnic assimilation in America, scientific rationalism, and cultural nationalism.

Finally, the book arrives not at a conclusion but a "coda," a musical term I use strategically to suggest the new themes and directions that future work in this area of cinema studies affords, in what I call the "Global Cinematic Technologies of Ethnic (Un)Representation."

2

Visualizing Hong Kong:
Diasporic Cinematic Gaze on the 1997 Handover

> The tradition of the oppressed teaches us that the "state of emergency" in which we live is not the exception but the rule.
>
> Walter Benjamin
> *"Theses on the Philosophy of History"* [1]

July 1, 1997, the day of the British handover of Hong Kong to the People's Republic of China, a day of historical reckoning, has come and gone. The critical and media discourses that swirled around the event, particularly those that were wary of the mainland Chinese government's intentions towards the new SAR (Special Administrative Region), initially invoked the notion of "crisis" to frame the historicity of the moment. Much of the anxiety over the fate of the Hong Kong people lay in the terrifying and undeniable fact that the Chinese political machinery was willing, in the past, to shed innocent blood to maintain political control. The world watched in horror as Chinese military tanks were rolled out to ruthlessly crush the student-led protests of Tiananmen Square in 1989, a mortifying image that could not but define global perception of China's pursuit of national reunification with Hong Kong, Macau, and Taiwan. In light of China's post-Tiananmen retreat to an embattled hard-line position and its willingness to deploy repressive and violent state strategies in dealing with political resistance, one could not but wonder if and to what extent China would honor the principle of "one country, two systems," set in place by the Sino-British Joint Declaration in September 1984, whereby the Chinese government had agreed to allow Hong Kong to stay "a free port and a separate customs territory" and to "remain unchanged for 50 years"?[2] What would become of democratic politics and human rights activism, which Hong Kong only began to experience briefly (as a form of political tokenism) during the office of Christopher Patten, the last governor of British Hong Kong?[3]

Significantly, these questions, which have been rehashed in endless permutations in global media discourses, have become muted or at least greatly diminished in the post-handover era. The handover transpired with much celebratory fanfare but with no major incidents of political "crisis" worthy of sensationalized media attention. Ultimately, this representation of the peaceful and uneventful transfer of power in Hong Kong and the successful continuity of Hong Kong as an economic powerhouse for China only highlights the priority given to the safeguarding of capital in the logic of Hong Kong's "progress" and "modernity." What is also at stake is that attention would be deflected from Hong Kong's alternative political cultures in the global media's eye.

It is precisely this concept of "progress" in Hong Kong's smooth transition that Walter Benjamin would have critiqued in his metaphoric depiction of the angel of history:

> This is how one pictures the angel of history. His face is turned toward the past. Where we perceive a chain of events, he sees one single catastrophe which keeps piling wreckage upon wreckage and hurls it in front of his feet. The angel would like to stay, awaken the dead, and make whole what has been smashed. But a storm is blowing from Paradise; it has got caught in his wings with such violence that the angel can no longer close them. This storm irresistibly propels him into the future to which his back is turned, while the pile of debris before him grows skyward. This storm is what we call progress.[4]

Benjamin was writing at a time when fascism was on the rise in Europe. He challenges his readers then to understand that for the oppressed, "the 'state of emergency' in which we live is not the exception but the rule." The key is "to bring about a *real* state of emergency" in the fight against fascism.[5] In adapting Benjamin's ideas to the Hong Kong context, I am not advocating crude political spectacles as the best option for politicizing a visuality of Hong Kong SAR, a position that would be insensitive and politically irresponsible to the Hong Kong people. Rather, Benjamin's sophisticated notion of history as a reclamation of what constitutes a "state of emergency," a rewriting of that history as a mode of political intervention, allows me to problematize the writing of Hong Kong's place in a modernist[6] narrative of "progress" depicting China's entry into the global capitalist economy.

What excites about Benjamin's strategic writing of states of emergency is the possibility of (re)defining the notion of political crisis though historical writing, and for the purposes of this chapter, the "writing" of cinematic texts in visualizing handover Hong Kong as a mode of intervention. In her book on the Fifth Generation Chinese filmmakers, *Primitive Passions*, Rey Chow argues that contemporary Chinese cinema is "a kind of postmodern *self*-writing or *auto*ethnography . . . a form of *intercultural* translation in the postcolonial age."[7] While Chow is right in warning us of cinematic visuality's "epistemological coercion,"[8] particularly in the exotic self-writing of the Chinese cinema she examines, I want to analyze instead how certain diasporic cinematic texts on Hong Kong's handover deploy the productive theoretical energies of visuality to negotiate the issues of (trans)national, cultural, and political identities. Not only can this visuality serve an ontological function of reflective analysis within its self-writing possibilities, it can also politically interrogate and critique; more significantly, it can negotiate alternative possibilities and potentialities in visual discourses. In his quest to expose the ideology of bourgeois illusionist cinema, Soviet Montage filmmaker and theorist Dziga Vertov, best known for the silent-era classic *The Man with a Movie Camera* (*Chelovek s kinoapparatom*; 1929), unveils precisely this critical and constructive power of cinema through his theory of the "kino-eye, " where, according to Annette Michelson, "epistemological inquiry and the project of a revolutionary cinema converge in that world of truth seen by the cinematic eye."[9] Vertov systematically defines the "kino-eye" as follows: "Kino-eye = kino-seeing (I see through the camera) + kino-writing (I write on film with the camera) + kino-organization (I edit)." In using "every possible kind of shooting technique: acceleration, microscopy, reverse action, animation, camera movement" and "every possible means in montage, comparing and linking all points of the universe in any temporal order, breaking, where necessary, all the laws and conventions of film construction, " "kino-eye is the documentary cinematic decoding of both the visible world and that which is invisible to the naked eye."[10] What is most important here is not only the fact that the cinematic eye is capable of recording images of the world, but that it also can be deployed to analyze, interrogate, and, in the process, visually *negotiate* its (re)writing of events. "To edit," in Vertov's view, is "to wrest, through the camera, whatever is most typical, most useful, from life; to organize the film pieces wrested from life into a meaningful rhythmic visual order, a meaningful visual phrase, an essence of 'I see.'"[11] Hence, the process of kino-organization finally leads one to what he calls "*kinopravda*" or "film-truth."[12] While Vertov's formulation of this film theory was obviously meant to serve the revolutionary aims of a specific era in Soviet history, my contemporary channeling of its interrogatory and constructive potentiality seeks to theorize "visuality" in this chapter as encompassing modes of cinematic representation, techniques, and discourses that make evident in the filmic text the very mechanisms of visual structuring as a form of political aesthetics.

What does it mean then to negotiate cinematically the meaning of a national/historical moment of "crisis," such as the Hong Kong handover, through this visuality? How can this visuality allow one to deal with the political and cultural consequences that the handover might bring? To begin to answer these questions, I would like to turn to the work of three directors whose recent films focus on or surround the Hong Kong handover: Wong Kar-wai's *Happy Together* (1997), Wayne Wang's *Chinese Box* (1997), and Evans Chan's *The Map of Sex and Love* (2001). One could make the rather strenuous argument that most Hong Kong or Hong Kong-related films of the period are really about the question of Hong Kong's political and cultural identity, whether the films specifically focus on or reference the handover, or if they only function as national allegories of the event. Hence, my strategic choice of these three films is premised on two main nodes of connection. Firstly, all three films are Hong Kong diasporic[13] in varied ways with particular connections to the United States, the first two being directed by filmmakers who are now active participants of the contemporary Chinese presence in Hollywood. As a Hong Kong auteur director, Wong Kar-wai has gained a tremendous following particularly in the independent and art-film circuits globally, and has recently widened his appeal to certain sectors of US mainstream audiences with his latest film *My Blueberry Nights* (2007) starring Jude Law and jazz chanteuse Norah Jones. Wong's *Happy Together* offers a take on a Hong Kong identity at the point just prior to the handover but from the other side of the world: Argentina. Wayne Wang, who is Hong Kong-born and has already made his mark with commercial Hollywood fare, chose to tackle the handover directly in his film *Chinese Box*. Wang is a classic instance of how an independent filmmaker can successfully straddle both spheres of commercial success — with movies like *Anywhere But Here* (1999), *Maid in Manhattan* (2002), and *Last Holiday* (2006) — and artistic respectability — *Smoke* (1995), *Blue in the Face* (1995), and *The Center of the World* (2001). His earlier work, such as *Chan is Missing* (1982), *Dim Sum: A Little Bit of Heart* (1985), *Eat a Bowl of Tea* (1989), and *The Joy Luck Club* (1993), has gained canonical status in Asian American film studies.[14] And finally, there is independent filmmaker Evans Chan, whose residence in New York City has not deterred him from making most of his politically incisive films in and about Hong Kong, one of which is *The Map of Sex and Love*.

The second node of connection is that all three films, though narrative in convention, rely on the power of cinematic visuality to decipher 1997 for themselves and to rewrite a Hong Kong that enables them to negotiate from afar (in this case the United States) the shifting notions of home, culture, and identities, as British colonial Hong Kong became the new Hong Kong SAR.

For me to address this question as a way of kick-starting filmic analysis in this book is strategic: I seek to foreground visuality's interventional potential in these films against the backdrop of my generally critical assessment of the remade Chinese presence in Hollywood, as is evident in the following chapters. Though *Happy Together* and *Chinese Box* are considered commercial works, they offer challenging perspectives from an artistic, intellectual, and political standpoint; while *The Map of Sex and Love* disrupts mainstream cinematic production ideals and aesthetics to present subversive visual alternatives to the discussion of Hong Kong's political future. Of course, I am not here suggesting that Hollywood films are *in toto* "bad" while Hong Kong and diasporic Hong Kong films are politically "good"; as the rest of my book demonstrates, Hollywood-produced cinema can also offer cultural political interventions even through its textual ambiguities and anxieties (just as much of Hong Kong cinematic culture is ideologically co-opted by capital and can often be aesthetically and politically compromised). Rather, my reading of these films serves as a critical challenge by highlighting the potential for politically progressive work that can emerge out of a Hollywood-controlled climate of multicultural commodification and commercialism, where contemporary Chinese cinemas are now being remade in America's film industry and then consumed across the globe. Finally, this chapter is meant to be read in close conjunction with Chapter Three, where I discuss Hollywood's approach to the handover. The composite image that this parallel reading produces would then be a more complete picture of the various responses that this historic event has spawned within the Hollywood-Hong Kong transnational cinematic network.

Absence/Presence: Wong Kar-wai's Happy Together

Happy Together, as it is chronologically sandwiched between Wong Kar-wai's funky *Chungking Express* (1994) and the nostalgic *In the Mood for Love* (2000),[15] constitutes an important part of the visualization of Hong Kong as it moves through 1997. *Chungking Express* presents a frenzied urban vision of postmodernist (or modernist) alienation in late-capitalist, multiculturalist Hong Kong, as the latter propels towards its historical fate in 1997; *In the Mood for Love*, on the other hand, slows down the visual pace of history in order to reminisce upon a Hong Kong of yore, where women in *cheongsam* elegance pine for love that can never be, a kind of nostalgia and retrospection that seemed apt when the film was made and released a number of years after the handover.[16] As these two films enfold 1997, the gap in-between is ironically but significantly filled by *Happy Together*, a film that is very much about Hong Kong by *not* being about Hong Kong. This absence/presence critical dynamic is representative of what Ackbar Abbas terms "the cultural self-invention of the Hong Kong subject in a cultural space that" he calls "a space of disappearance."[17] Hence, the film's ironic denial of a focal visuality of Hong Kong is a means of asserting the cultural and political insistence of the place despite its being subsumed within the transactional discourse and politics of the Sino-British agreement.

To begin to talk about "absence" in the context of a visual framework is obviously not to invoke a material void but to talk about *something*, or more precisely to talk about something *else*. In the case of *Happy Together*, Buenos Aires is that something else that substitutes for Hong Kong. Here I tread very carefully on the notion of political allegory, a point that Jeremy Tambling has so efficiently and effectively addressed in his recent book on the film. In rejecting Fredric Jameson's assumptions about allegory, "derived from the Marxism of Lukács," that posits the possibility of unveiling "a determinate narrative . . . concealed as an allegory,"[18] Tambling turns to the theories of Paul de Man, Walter Benjamin, and Gayatri Chakravorty Spivak to produce a poststructuralist conception of allegory that works wonderfully for *Happy Together*: "Benjamin's approach to allegory — which is much closer to deconstruction — means that there is not a single buried narrative to be retrieved, only fragments and interrupted moments."[19] Tambling arrives at a number of significant conclusions on the implications of approaching the film allegorically, a few of which I would like to highlight and reflect upon. Tambling marks the obvious pitfall of national or political allegorical interpretations by noting that *Happy Together* "disrupts our desire to see the characters as representative of Hong Kong or Taiwan, or the events as symbolic of public events."[20] Allegorical modes of reading tend to fall apart when pushed to their very limit. *Happy Together*, because of its context, tempts you into allegorizing but then pulls the rug underneath such interpretive moves. This is even so for a more obviously political film about Hong Kong like Wayne Wang's *Chinese Box*, a point I return to later in the chapter.

By thus rejecting an extended allegorical reading of the Jamesonian mold and embracing instead Benjamin's conception of fragmented moments, Tambling has to grapple with what defines these moments. He illustrates with what I have earlier called the absence/presence critical dynamic by disavowing any possible dialectic between the two opposites:

> The absence of Hong Kong from the screen, never seen save upside-down in Lai's fantasy, echoes the absence of a referent. There is nothing to be said

about Hong Kong. This is a Hong Kong film, but Hong Kong is not to be spoken about any more than Buenos Aires is. Neither city is an allegory for the other. Nor does either city define the other by being thought of as opposites.[21]

Though I do not quarrel with Tambling's poststructuralist perspective in questioning the allegorical readings of the film, I am discomforted by the gentle slip into "the impossibility of reading,"[22] and the gradual unhinging of the filmic text from its political context. (In his defense, I am not saying that Tambling accomplishes this in any sustained fashion throughout his remarkable book.) I would instead like to take one critical step back by suggesting that while he is right in noting how risky it would be to read Buenos Aires as the allegorical signifier of Hong Kong, its presence in the film can be critically productive when read in counterpoint to Hong Kong's absence from the perspective of visual play and, hence, visuality as cinematic rewriting and negotiation.

Wong Kar-wai made the aesthetic and political decision to turn the cinematic eye away from Hong Kong at a very historic moment. But this "turning away" does not signify disinterest or disillusionment, but simply heightens the need for a "turning back," an ironic point that Wong himself comments on: "One of the reasons I chose Argentina was that it is on the other side of the world, and I thought by going there, I would be able to stay away from 1997. But then, as you must understand, once you consciously try to stay away from something or to forget something, you will never succeed. That something is bound to be hanging in the air, haunting you."[23] This anxiety not only permeates the narrative of *Happy Together* but is also anticipated in the trajectory of the film's cinematic gaze. Lai Yiu-fai (Tony Leung Chiu Wai) and Ho Po-wing (Leslie Cheung) are quarrelling lovers[24] who have made their way to Buenos Aires to "start over again." Their stormy relationship is one imbued with a deep sense of national identity and its impending crisis. Lai punishes Ho for his promiscuity by keeping his passport from him, leaving Ho stranded in Argentina. Lai finally visits the Iguazu Falls, the geographical locus of the couple's idealized relationship, but only does so alone. He then heads to Taipei to attempt to meet his new friend Chang (Chang Chen). Though Lai does not find him, the film ends with Lai on the Taipei MRT train system, looking out onto the tracks in the hopes of revisiting his relationship with Chang in the future. Lai and Ho's attempts to start over in another land is premised on the assumption that when their problems are resolved, they will eventually return home to Hong Kong. This anticipation of home is not only revealed in their sense of transience as tourists in Argentina, but also in the few casual references to Hong Kong: Lai's voice-over reflections on how he does not "want to start over [with Ho] but [to] return to Hong Kong," his musings about Hong Kong being on the other side of the globe, or his calling home to his estranged father, who has rejected him on the grounds of Lai's absconding with the boss's money. These instances of tourist or exilic flight on the characters' part create in the narrative a "turning back" effect that propels them towards Hong Kong.

The anxious turn of the narrative back to Hong Kong as its originating point informs the trajectory of the cinematic gaze. The film opens with the Hong Kong passports of Lai and Ho being stamped "with the opening credits . . . colored in the red and white of the Hong Kong flag," imprinting the question of nation and nationality.[25] As the cinematic gaze moves from Buenos Aires to Iguazu Fall and then to Taipei, it anticipates Hong Kong as its telos but Wong prevents Hong Kong from entering the film's diegesis and, hence, the visual expanse of the camera's eye. This is where the absence/presence dynamic appears, where what is not seen can be equally or even more emotive than what is seen. Hong Kong is then articulated through the notion of *différence*, in Jacques Derrida's conceptual play on the term,[26] where Hong Kong is not only visually *differ*ent from Buenos Aires (or any other randomly chosen city for all practical purposes) but is also *defer*red indefinitely in the temporal and visual framework of the movie, until the non-diegetic arrival of 1997, which Wong marks as a temporal plot point in Lai's voiceover at the end: "It's afternoon when I wake up in Taipei. On 20 February 1997, I'm back on this side of the world. I feel like waking up from a long sleep." Because the final shot in the film is the scene that Lai espies from the window of Taipei's MRT,[27] the film's temporal trajectory is truncated and, hence, the visuality of Hong Kong 1997 is textually prevented, creating a circular deferral. This visual deferral, therefore, offers the viewer a Sisyphean experience of anticipating a traumatic event in each viewing of *Happy Together*.

I cannot end this segment of the chapter without returning briefly to the only scene of Hong Kong featured in the film: an upside-down sequence capturing "Causeway Bay, Kwun Tong, and East Kowloon."[28] This sequence functions as a visual representation of what Lai only muses in a state of insomnia, after working the night shift at the abattoir, a vocational arrangement that permits him to get "back on Hong Kong time": "Again I can't sleep. Watching TV, I realized Hong Kong is on the opposite side of Argentina. How does Hong Kong look upside down?" The spatial reversal inherent in the geographical positioning of Hong Kong and Argentina in reference to each other mines precisely their extreme physical opposition on the globe in order to plot an ideal of exilic return: if my life in Hong Kong is troubled, maybe going to the very furthest point of the globe from it will allow me enough distance to reevaluate and sort out my problems. This is where the notion of Ho's "starting over" comes in. Song Hwee Lim makes the sound argument that these inverted images of Hong Kong "do not evoke a sense of nostalgia and longing for home; rather, they serve to disorientate and defamiliarize Hong Kong and even, by their inversion, subvert (as it is, from below) Hong Kong to the point of no return. From Argentina, the images of Hong Kong conjured up by [Lai Yiu-] Fai are images of discomfort."[29] In combining the logic of exilic distancing and defamiliarization, one still arrives at an ambivalent notion of visual return, an anxiously negotiated turning back to Hong Kong, but a return nonetheless. This logic, therefore, reinforces the narrative and visual insistence of Hong Kong in this film, as I have discussed earlier.

Finally, the visual impact of an upside-down Hong Kong conjures the notion of the *camera obscura*, where the upside-down image is the right one because the camera lens reverses every image it produces as light passes through it. The human eye is actually a *camera obscura* in that the retina receives light from an image that is upside down, which the brain then reverses in order for one to perceive the image as right-side up. Marx and Engels's frequently cited metaphoric use of the *camera obscura* in *The German Ideology* may be productive here. They argue that the Young Hegelians' suggestion that mere consciousness of ideology's workings being sufficient to change the material existence of humanity is problematic: "If in all ideology men and their circumstances appear upside-down as in a *camera obscura*, this phenomenon arises just as much from their historical life-process as the inversion of objects on the retina does from their physical life-process."[30] Their point, hence, is that one needs to transform directly the material existence of humanity, which would then further effect ideological change. My rather reductive reading of the Marx and Engel metaphor here is to imbue the upside-down image of Hong Kong in *Happy Together* not only with ideological resonance, but also to suggest that the material being and political existence of the Hong Kong people are foregrounded through this mode of visuality. In other words, the only image of Hong Kong in this film, despite, or rather because of, its inversion, does not detract from but rather accentuates Hong Kong's ideological and material presence.

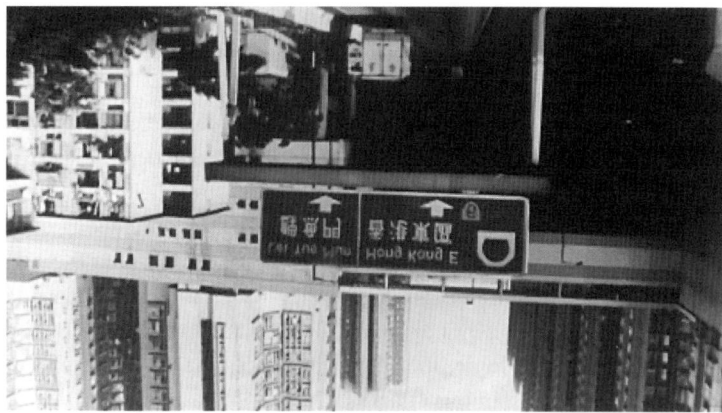

Hong Kong upside down

Visuality and the "Real": Wayne Wang on the Crisis of the Handover

Unlike *Happy Together*'s turn on a visual absence, Wayne Wang's *Chinese Box* is a more visually concrete attempt at coming to terms with the 1997 handover. As most of his earlier works deal with life in America, *Chinese Box* marks a filmic return for Wang to the place of his cultural and national origin, a return that enables him to grapple with the conflicting emotions produced by Hong Kong's (post)coloniality and by Wang's own diasporic displacements. As a result of leaving Hong Kong at the age of eighteen for the US, Wang has developed ambivalent feelings towards his former homeland: "I love it because it's my home, it's Chinese, the food is great . . . But I also hate it because there's no history, nothing is kept, the air is bad. There's a certain aggressiveness about it that wears you down." One can account for this "love-hate relationship"[31] Wang has with Hong Kong by tracing the tensions and contradictions within the hybrid cultural space occupied by the Hong Kong people. It is a hybridity inscribed by the cultural legacy of British colonialism, American cultural imperialism, and a Chinese upbringing, producing a cultural schizophrenia that, as Wang tells bell hooks in an interview, characterizes his childhood:

> I guess it was growing up in Hong Kong, being Chinese, living under a British colony, watching Rock Hudson and Doris Day movies, listening to *The Eagles* . . . I've always been, in a sense, on the border, because my parents were always very Chinese. At the same time they wanted me to be more

American, more, you know, "Western" . . . So I have really been sort of schizophrenic and torn as far back as I can remember.[32]

Migrating to the US only further intensified the complexity of this border mentality:

When I go back to Hong Kong . . . people say that I'm not Chinese; they say I'm American. I'm not Chinese like the people in Hong Kong or China. I was born and raised in Hong Kong, but I'm also completely bastardized by the English culture and the American culture. When I look at things I will look at them from both perspectives. It's unfair to say I'm not Chinese, because I am Chinese; I'm just not pure. But what does that mean today anymore, you know?[33]

The arrival of July 1997, of course, lent Wang's struggle with the demands of Chinese cultural purity greater intensity and significance. The political crisis of the homeland transformed into a crisis of cultural contestation. Hence, while the historicity of the Hong Kong handover provided an exciting, dramatic, and opportune canvas for a film about his homeland, it also permitted him a space to negotiate his ambivalent feelings towards the place and basically to make peace with it — to offer "the movie [as] a love letter to Hong Kong."[34] I want to suggest again that visuality plays a critical role in these negotiations, assisting him in confronting the contradictions of his own cultural identity. But what turns problematic is the way this visuality slips in and out of an oddly exoticizing gaze, creating the ambiguous lines of affiliation and identification with colonialism and neo-imperialism. In order to analyze this gaze and its implications, I would like to visit briefly the movie's plot as political allegory and what it foregrounds and displaces. This analysis provides the context to question cinematic visuality as a mode of the colonialist gaze, and the way Wang uses it to visualize his version of Hong Kong.

John Spencer (Jeremy Irons) is a British journalist who has spent the past fifteen years covering the financial news of Hong Kong. He falls in love with Vivian (Gong Li), a former dance hostess whose "contacts" have helped her boyfriend Chang (Michael Hui) establish himself as a rich and influential player in the business community. Vivian remains faithful to Chang despite the fact that he is unwilling to bear the social stigma and the economic consequences of marrying what traditional Chinese society would consider a tainted woman. While John is unhappy with Vivian's choice, his own world is further disrupted not only by the handover of Hong Kong but also by a personal crisis: he has contracted a form of leukemia which gives him only a few months to live. Choosing to hide his illness from everyone, he embarks on a quest to know the "real" Hong Kong by videotaping the crowded streets and its denizens. This search leads him to discover how Vivian had earlier sacrificed herself for Chang, thus forcing John to confront them both. When Vivian finally decides to leave Chang and reunite with John, it is only then that she hears of John's illness. After spending the final days of the British rule of Hong Kong together with Vivian, John lies down by a pier and dies on July 1, 1997.

Unlike the textual structuring of *Happy Together*, the homology between the political narrative in *Chinese Box* and the cross-cultural love story more strongly insists on the legitimacy of allegorical readings, an instance of which could go something like this: John represents the dying British presence in Hong Kong; Vivian is the culturally "tainted" Hong Kong that China must now make her own but also deal with in terms of the seeds of democracy that have been supposedly planted by the British; and Chang is, of course, China, the traditional patriarch. I think the point here is not to ascertain whether Wang intended the political allegory, but what the critical risks are of such a reading and its attendant effect on the question of visuality?

The first question that comes to mind is: what does it mean to narrate the Hong Kong crisis as a love story? Though the love relationship offers the kind of gendered hierarchy that emblematizes the power relations evident in Hong Kong's coloniality and postcoloniality — the submergence of Hong Kong's political and cultural presence in the British-Chinese transaction — and reflects the ambivalent feelings of the Hong Kong people towards their British rulers, the love story ultimately masks the exploitative agenda of British colonialism. To say that the colonizer does all he does out of love for the native is not unlike using the rhetoric of the white man's burden to justify imperialism. Furthermore, the depiction of Hong Kong as a woman who prostitutes herself reinforces the idea that Hong Kong (according to the Chinese) has not kept itself culturally pure. At the same time, this metaphor supports the idea held by many that Hong Kong people are overly materialistic and politically pragmatic, and lack the moral fiber to stand up for their own political rights. As one critic notes of the love story's resolution, "by dying, 'Britain' forces 'Hong Kong' to wake up from its long reliance on imaginary British support . . . [W]hat was good of the old Empire, despite having drawn its last breath (i.e., John), is enough to send the reborn Hong Kong off in a brave new direction free of its ancestral moorings and illusory obligations."[35] In attributing her courage to John, Vivian, in the final voice-over of the movie, meditates on how she, "like the city . . . [has] to start over again."[36] To suggest that Hong Kong must now learn to stand on its own without Britain's support is obviously problematic, as it implies that Hong Kong must assume the blame for its political immaturity, despite the fact that Hong Kong did not *choose* its colonial status in the first place. If the raison d'être for Britain's colonial presence and final "death" is to encourage in Hong Kong independent political thinking through democracy, where then is democracy during Britain's more than 150 years hold on the territories? In other words, Britain conveniently waited till the approach of 1997 to promote (as tokenism) democratic thinking so as to valorize the rhetoric of democracy, when to do so any earlier would have obviously contradicted the very ideology and presence of Empire. Is Britain's "dying" in the end, therefore, a way of cementing the legacy of democracy in a colonialist nostalgic glow, which ultimately promotes the "benefits" of imperialist rule and relieves Britain of any further responsibility in moving Hong Kong along in its democratic growth or in offering the Hong Kong people the alternative of British citizenship? What then is this "brave new direction" that Hong Kong is portrayed as taking when it can never be free from the "ancestral moorings and illusory obligations" while under Chinese rule? Nor can it be free to pursue this "virtual democracy," as Rey Chow calls it, which has been "hastily planted and left behind . . . like a land mine," producing "a political situation that was guaranteed to be a permanent source of irreconcilable conflict among the supposedly decolonized natives."[37]

Wang has himself questioned the legitimacy of political readings of his film and even denies the film's allegorical connections to the handover: "Some people have misread this as symbolism about the handover . . . We did shoot a lot of real things that were happening during the handover, but this is a complicated love story. It's about the heart of the place."[38] Although his disavowal of the allegorical possibilities feels like a hermeneutical setup, it is nonetheless fascinating the way he conceptualizes the film as a treatise on "the heart of the place." (Of course, one wonders how the political reality of place can be extracted from its "heart" or its identity.) Wang has suggested that "the movie is about the city of Hong Kong more than about a character and a story."[39] Stephen Holden of the *New York Times* also believes "the film is essentially a poetic meditation on the meaning of Hong Kong. The characters' ambiguous personal histories are metaphors for the city, which in turn becomes a metaphor for the elusiveness of historical truth itself."[40] *Chinese Box*, therefore, becomes for Wang an ontological/epistemic excavation of Hong Kong through, what I would argue, the techniques of cinematic visuality.

The study of the cinematic gaze and its structuring of the subject/object relation are of great theoretical importance to the critique of cinematic Orientalist discourses.[41] The issue is one of power relations, where the cinematographer, in controlling the roving eye of the camera, also controls the framing of the object. Hence, film as an ethnography of the "East"[42] allows the filmmaker to stage the object of study in Orientalizing poses, all in the attempt to know more about it. Cinematic visuality, hence, "become[s] the law of knowledge and the universal form of epistemological coercion."[43] However, Rey Chow warns us against the danger of situating this problematic solely in terms of an East-West schema where only the "West" retains the power of gazing upon the "East." She instead argues that the "East" is as capable of self-Orientalism through cinematic autoethnography[44] when "'the East,' too, is a spectator who is equally caught up in the dialectic of seeing."[45] The kind of self-Orientalizing primitivism that Chow pinpoints appears especially in Chinese films that are particularly popular in the United States and in Europe, which suggests that many of these filmmakers may be catering to an Orientalizing gaze.[46]

In the case of *Chinese Box*, whose gaze and what kind of gaze has Wang adopted in order to understand Hong Kong, to know the meaning of the city of his birth? Is the film complicit in perpetuating the colonialist mode of visual penetration? To answer these questions, one should first turn to Wang's use of, what I call, a *double* gaze, where John Spencer's videotaping of the "real" Hong Kong, at certain moments, overlaps and telescopes into Wang's own framing of the movie, the two gazes becoming one. What then is John's vision of Hong Kong, and does it represent Wang's own quest to know Hong Kong in order that he might eventually come to understand himself?

The motivation for John's sudden desire to capture Hong Kong on video springs from a personal crisis. His spiritual and philosophical poverty, after years of writing about the material aspects of the city as a financial reporter, dawns upon him when he is faced with his own mortality. He then turns to Hong Kong in the belief that by understanding the city and its inhabitants, he can arrive at a better understanding of himself and his own existence. Together with Jim (Reuben Blades), his photographer friend, John scours the dirtiest and sleaziest parts of the Hong Kong streets in the hope that by capturing the darker aspects of the city he can also capture its essence.[47] As John puts it, "So much of Hong Kong exists beneath the surface." What he creates is a video montage in intense colors — images spliced in a jump-cut MTV style with Wayne Wang inserting a pulsating Canto-pop soundtrack as an extra-diegetic element, allowing John's video frame to merge with Wang's cinematic frame — disparate but often disturbing glimpses of the city's seamier underbelly, for instance prostitutes peddling their trade, workers in sweatshops, gamblers at the mahjong table shouting vulgarities, the abusive training of a scrawny fighting dog (with which John seems to especially identify), and butchers at work slaughtering various animals. Correlating this last video element of animal slaughter to another scene Wang includes within *his* film's framework, is a special close-up of a freshly cut-up fish whose heart is seen beating its last; an image that Vivian witnesses in person as she walks through the crowded market streets at the end of the film. This image of the fish in the throes of death is of particular significance as a signifier for Britain's, and John's, own dying moments in Hong Kong.

John's videotaping exercise is essentially an Orientalist mode of staging the Other as a route to self-definition. As Edward Said argued almost three decades ago, the Orient is not only discursively constructed so as to justify colonialist domination of it; it is also formulated to help "define Europe (or the West) as its contrasting image, idea, personality, experience."[48] John chooses the dark, sensual side of Hong Kong, just as Joseph Conrad chooses the primeval in the Congo to stage Kurtz's journey into the heart of darkness. The epistemic violence here involves not only a colonialist visual penetration but also the fixing (or more interestingly, fixating) on film, of a stereotypical image of Hong Kong in all its negativity, a visuality that unfortunately hides the lines of imperialist and capitalist exploitation at which these images only hint. Hong Kong, therefore, has been reduced to a tool to help one European man attain moral redemption.[49]

John's videotaping quest also leads him to Jean (Maggie Cheung), a quirky individual with an unusual scar on her face who spends her time peddling strange wares such as bottled "colonial" air of Hong Kong. Jean becomes for John the elusive signifier, an embodiment of Hong Kong that escapes his ability to comprehend it. In his fixation of wanting to get "her story," John insists on interviewing her, which she finally agrees upon only if she gets to frame her own interview (without questions from John) and to wield the video camera herself (a moment of agency?). She then proceeds to recount her life story on tape, a sordid, titillating tale of sexual abuse and castration, a tale that she knows her male audience would want to hear (a moment of strategic, erotic self-Orientalism?). But she leaves out the crux of the interview: "What about the scar and how I got it," she asks in a stoic yet teasing fashion. "This is what I have to say about it. Nothing." The visual epistemic penetration of the camera interview ends in coitus interruptus, an anti-climax emblematized by Jim's question to John, "Did you fuck her?" John's desire to know about Jean is frustrated on a number of levels: she not only fails to reveal the source of the scar, but she is obviously telling a fabricated story of herself, of which John is painfully aware. Furthermore, when confronted with a newspaper clipping of her suicide attempt, Jean finally reveals how she was jilted by her British boyfriend and how she attempted suicide. John then arranges a meeting between Jean and her ex-boyfriend William, which ends with the man walking out on her again and a sobbing Jean rushing out of the stationary bus she and John are in, leaving John with the cryptic and ambiguous "That wasn't William." Jean, therefore, remains as enigmatic as ever to John, for her parting words basically throw into question again the veracity of her story.

Another point about the agency of visuality that needs to be made is how Wang (to his credit) allows the power of visuality to reverse itself momentarily as a way of destabilizing the possibility of ever knowing Hong Kong completely through the cinematic gaze. This reversal ultimately reflects his own realization of the hybrid cultural space that Hong Kong occupies and that defies culturalist definitions. It also undermines his own attempt at self-knowledge through a search for the "real" Hong Kong. He accomplishes this by allowing the reins of visual power to pass from John to Jean as she videotapes herself in close-ups. As Gilles Deleuze explains, the facial close-up is an "affection-image" that invites the viewer to ask questions: "What are you thinking about? Or, what is bothering you, what is the matter, what do you sense or feel?"[50] What we get in Jean instead is an impassive countenance that problematizes reading. To further complicate matters is the way she wields the camera in a fashion that impressionistically ruptures the visual framing: the face is rotated one-hundred-and-eighty degrees, the image is often tilted at odd angles, and one gets half-faced shots of Jean. This rupturing of the frame and the destabilizing of images, hence, resist the violence of cinematic visuality's staging of its object as a mode of domination through seeing and knowing.

The camera also returns to haunt John in two scenes. The first is where Jim projects the image of Jean onto John as he leans against the wall. Jean's projected face neatly overlaps John's, forming a single entity. The second is when John finally lies down at the pier to die: the video camera rests on his heaving chest and produces an image of him closing his eyes and slowly slipping away. These two instances provide symbolic moments that demonstrate how the goals of both John and Wang's visual/cinematic quests ultimately lie in the inward search for a resolution to the moral emptiness (John's) and the cultural contradictions (Wang's) that plague their respective souls. But more importantly, the shifting reversals of subject/object positioning produced by the visual technology of the camera present the images of Jean/ Hong Kong as slippery ones that defy and resist epistemic violation and definition.

To conclude my analysis and critique of the film, I must again credit Wang for his willingness to question the interrogatory power of film by allowing Hong Kong to continually slip from his grasp despite his attempts at immobilizing it within the cinematic frame. By conceptualizing it as a "Chinese box," which "[l]ike one of those Russian dolls . . . [that] can open layer after layer, but you still never know what's going to be inside,"[51] Wang may have incidentally succeeded in expressing the liminality that the Hong Kong people and culture have been relegated to in the scheme of Sino-British relations. On the other hand, Wang's staging of Hong Kong in his technique of visuality requires critique. If John's visual quest aligns with Wang's, is Wang then guilty of deploying an Orientalizing visuality to negotiate his own cultural difficulties? Maggie Cheung, who plays Jean in the movie, offers a rather ironic extra-textual gloss (especially in light of Jean's radical place within the film) on Wang's vision of Hong Kong: "Wang's point of view of Hong Kong kind of stayed in the 70's, or whenever he left . . . I can't say it's not accurate, but for a local Hong Kong person, it's not really the life."[52] Though Cheung is referring to Wang's inappropriate use of a particular setting for the film, her point can be applied in a general sense to his vision of the place as a form of cultural atavism or nostalgia. Wang's Hong Kong, therefore, is a staged or constructed imaginary homeland, to borrow Rushdie's terminology,[53] that arises from his own remembrance and (mis)understanding of it. According to his vision, it is a city that cannot be pinned down culturally, symbolizing Wang's own struggle to come to terms with Hong Kong and its contradictions. It also signifies a desire to resolve these cultural difficulties by a nostalgic yearning for the Hong Kong of his youth, a Hong Kong located in its colonial past. Unfortunately, this colonialist nostalgia can also reinforce the stereotypes of Hong Kong's cultural "absence" and "inscrutability," and to shift attention away from the reality of the cultural and political presence of the Hong Kong people, which British imperialism and Chinese culturalism want the world to reject and forget. As John sadly muses, "I used to write about Hong Kong's future as if it had a definite direction and predictable outcome. But everything about this city is always changing; maybe I wasn't meant to figure you out." The figure of Hong Kong as the pragmatic shape-shifter, which can adapt itself to any political condition, is a logic that eliminates the political and cultural voice of the Hong Kong people, rendering it as inconsequential and dispensable — in other words, "Don't worry about them as they return to Chinese rule; they will survive through change and adaptation."

Visual Interventions: Evans Chan's The Map of Sex and Love

To conclude this chapter's study of visuality in Hong Kong diasporic cinema, I wish to hold up the exciting work of Evans Chan as an instance of the numerous aesthetic possibilities to engage the politics of a post-1997 Hong Kong.[54] Chan's growing oeuvre is eclectically innovative. His works shuttle between New York, Hong Kong, and China, developing a radical activism and cultural politics that foster a kind of trans-Pacific political consciousness.[55] Highly intellectual in his endeavors, Chan asserts a profuse interventional energy in his films that Marchetti considers to be reminiscent of Godard's work, a kind of "counter-cinema."[56] Chan's first feature *To Liv(e)* (1992) grows out of the horror of Tiananmen, where a Hong Kong woman writes letters to actress Liv Ullmann in order to come to terms with the massacre's cultural and political impact. His second film *Crossings* (1994) grapples with the state of Chinese migrancy in New York City. *Journey to Beijing* (1998), his first documentary, tackles the four-month philanthropic walk from Hong Kong to Beijing. Although this film is the first to emerge out of the 1997 handover period, I will look instead at a later narrative film, *The Map of Sex and Love* (2001), which presents the kind of visual intervention with which this chapter is specifically concerned, and which responds to a post-handover political landscape.

The Map of Sex and Love charts the relationship between three characters. Wei Ming (Bernardo Chow), who lives in New York City with his gay Jewish-American partner, returns to Hong Kong for a visit and decides to make a news documentary about the arrival of Disneyland in the SAR. He begins a sexual relationship with Larry (Victor Ma), a dancer, and a friendship with Mimi (Cherie Ho), who happens to fall in love with the two men. All three of them struggle with the demons in their lives: Wei Ming's affair with Larry begins to help him redefine his relationship with his American partner in postcolonialist terms, while he himself is plagued by the ethical conflicts raised by his family's questionable acquisition of wealth in Macau, which may have links to Hitler's holocaust. Larry confronts a guilty conscience stemming from the belief that he has caused the crippling of his homophobic high school teacher; while Mimi experiences a "sense of futility" in her life after she travels to Belgrade and witnesses firsthand the effects of war on human life in the city and, at the same time, receives news that a publisher has rejected her work. She then turns to making her deceased mother's pomelo fish stew, a complex recipe that requires extended periods of time and effort to prepare, in order to reconnect with a quotidian material reality as a means of maintaining her sanity. In finding a connection in their struggles, these characters embark on a journey together to define their personal and political places in post-handover Hong Kong.

Like Wang's *Chinese Box*, the narrative's premise allows Chan to foreground visuality in *The Map of Sex and Love*. Both films feature its central protagonist videotaping Hong Kong, albeit for slightly different reasons. While

John's video quest has ontological motivations founded on Orientalist assumptions, Wei Ming's documentary undertaking unveils a radical political questioning of the direction of China-ruled Hong Kong after the handover. My earlier analysis of Wang's double gaze finds similar application here in that Wei Ming also wields a video camera in order to capture aspects of Hong Kong, and Chan's vision of the place is channeled through Wei Ming's video adventures. The fact that Chan also uses the digital video format for this feature strengthens the homology.

While both films use the video camera diegetically by hiding behind a pseudo-documentary mode to capture the realism of everyday Hong Kong, *The Map of Sex and Love* unabashedly constructs and stages for the camera political narratives and performances that create a visual intervention akin to Vertov's and Benjamin's. I see Chan's visual constructions and staging as a form of Benjamin's writing of a "state of emergency," where the ideologically commonsensical national narrative of Hong Kong's place in global capitalism is challenged. The first of two instances which I analyze is the Mickey Mouse sequence. While Disney movies are already a cinematic mainstay in Hong Kong, the corporate giant Disney makes its physical presence in the form of Disneyland Hong Kong. Covering 310 acres of Lantau Island along Penny's Bay, the new Disneyland opened in September 2005.[57] By using this actual event to premise the opening fictional sequence, the film's critique registers sharply and urgently in a real historical sense. Wei Ming's decision to film a news documentary of the new Disneyland turns into a visual essay on the contradiction of Hong Kong's "postcoloniality." Riding Hong Kong's subway train system, the MTR, upon his arrival, Wei Ming begins videotaping Hong Kong's housing landscape and then talks into the camera as he does so:

> Some people call this the Post-colonial Age. So here's Hong Kong — post-colonial, but self-governed with China. People moving here from China are dubbed "new immigrants." But the most popular, beloved immigrant of the future will definitely be him. [*Shot of someone dressed as Mickey Mouse seated at the other end of the train.*] Hi Mickey? [*Wei Ming starts to address "Mickey Mouse"*] How are you going to guarantee democracy and the rule of law? [*Another shot of Mickey this time blindfolded and holding a weighing scale that symbolizes the law.*] How are you going to renew our love for Hong Kong?

Wei Ming even inserts himself into the second shot of Mickey blindfolded and carrying a weighing scale. Here, he wields the video camera and films himself talking to Mickey. Unlike Wang's and John's "documentary" mode of recording the "real" Hong Kong in *Chinese Box*, Chan, through Wei Ming,

"Mickey Mouse" on Hong Kong's MTR

plays up the performative quality of visuality. The meeting of Mickey Mouse on the MTR cannot but be a tongue-in-cheek mise-en-scène depicting symbolically the arrival of the beloved rodent icon to Hong Kong. By shifting seamlessly from a documentarian cinema verité to an overtly constructed moment of narrative fantasy, Chan interrogates China's embracing of the "democratic" logic of free-market capitalism whose "freedom" privileges transnational corporations like Disney while, at the same time, controls the number of "new immigrants" from China entering Hong Kong SAR.[58] Therefore, when Wei Ming asks Mickey how he is "going to guarantee democracy and the rule of law," he is posing a rhetorical question in a visual setup that writes the contradictions of Hong Kong's place in China's scheme of economic restructuring. Finally, the sight of a less than authentic-looking Mickey in this scene (particularly in contrast to the newsreel images that Wei Ming later views on his desktop computer, where the "real" Mickey and Minnie are seen frolicking behind Hong Kong officials signing agreements) suggests that when Disney brings to the Hong Kong people a consumerist pleasure, it also unfortunately crowds out and distracts them from the more important and pressing questions of democratic politics and cultural identity in the post-handover era.

The second moment of visual intervention is in a sequence where Wei Ming accompanies Larry to Tai O Village to celebrate the latter's birthday.

Inspired by the fishing culture of the village, Wei Ming attempts, through rather crude cardboard drawings, to visually animate the story of Lu Ting, a rebel who was half-fish and half-human. Speaking again into the camera, Wei Ming videotapes himself telling the story while using the sketches as a storyboard:

> I met this dancer a little over a week. Here we are in Tai O Village for his birthday. Hong Kong is luring Disney to this island with $25 billion. There's already a mermaid myth here. Tai O fishermen's mythical ancestor is Lu Ting – a part-fish-part-human rebel. There are times when Larry reminds me of Lu Ting. Because of his passionate nature? Is passion only part-human? During the 11th century, fanned by some millennial, utopian ardor, these fish (er)men rose up against their repressive Chinese rulers. Unfortunately, the Chinese army cracked down on the island, resulting in a bloody massacre.

Wei Ming's drawing of the massacre of the fish-men

Wei Ming's telling of the Lu Ting massacre visually rewrites the mermaid myth as a counterpoint to Disney's frequent appropriation of cultural narratives for its animated extravaganzas: *The Little Mermaid* (1989), *Aladdin* (1992), *Pocahontas* (1995), *The Hunchback of Notre Dame* (1996), *Hercules* (1997) and *Mulan* (1998), among many others, come quickly to mind. While Disney neutralizes the cultural politics of many of these texts to create Americanized yet globally marketable products, Wei Ming's crude drawings demonstrate the contemporary significance of these mythic stories by highlighting the violence enacted upon minority politics and positions, as symbolized by the fish-men rebels led by Lu Ting. While the drawings may be unsophisticated sketches depicting the cruel massacre, they evoke a visceral terror in their allusion to the Chinese government's violent suppression of the student protestors at Tiananmen Square and, hence, draw out a frightening dystopian political vision of Hong Kong. But beyond this obvious political analogy, the simplicity of Wei Ming's sketches and the rather uncomplicated visual technology involved also mobilize a radical visual critique from the ground, in contrast to the complex machinery of corporate and institutional relationships of complicity and, at times, contradiction, involving mainland China, Disney, and transnational capital. This visual moment unpicks further the narrative of capitalist modernity that the Hong Kong success story offers for China's entrenchment in a global capitalist economy.

Conclusion: Visualizing the "Fragmented Commonplace"

In an essay that engages the alternative arts of Hong Kong, including Evans Chan's 1991 movie *To Liv(e)*, Hector Rodriguez conceptualizes the use of various narrative textualities "to produce the kind of collage effect that distinguishes the culture of the fragmented commonplace."[59] This "culture of the fragmented commonplace" incorporates "specific references to well-known Hong Kong streets and landmarks, historical events and situations, vanished architecture, old popular songs, local slang or myths or folktales, disposable everyday objects, and other concrete elements that produce a strong sense of place." In creating "an assemblage of fragments . . . and impression of intense heterogeneity,"[60] these works open up fissures in the official national discourses regarding Hong Kong and its place in China's modernity. Rodriguez's theory is helpful in bringing together the three filmic texts in this chapter: Wong Kar-wai's centrifugal turn on a Hong Kong exilic existence moves the visual from absence to presence through the personal longing to return, while marked by the threat of an uncertain national future. Wayne Wang's visual excavation of ontology in the material context of national and cultural specificities, though may unveil Orientalist tendencies, still succeeds in its failure to pin down Hong Kong categorically, hence allowing the latter's heterogeneity to slip from a coercive visual gaze. And finally, Evans Chan's visual take on a post-handover landscape attempts radical interventions from the position and viewpoint of the fragmented commonplace, challenging the hegemonic discourses of capitalist success and progress while suggesting the viability and hope of alternative voices and politics. These heterogeneous alternatives may then allow one to form what Wei Ming at the end of *The Map of Sex and Love* calls, "absurd connections," in order to make sense of and to re-envision a brave new Hong Kong.

3
Facing the Red Dragon:
Hollywood's 1997 Response to the Hong Kong Handover

As a complement to my earlier examination of Hong Kong diasporic filmmakers' deployment of cinematic visuality as a mode of cultural political intervention, this chapter turns its focus onto Hollywood's response to the Hong Kong handover, by looking particularly at three films released in 1997: Jon Avnet's *Red Corner*, Jean-Jacques Annaud's *Seven Years in Tibet*, and Martin Scorsese's *Kundun*. While these films are clearly part of Hollywood's continuing fascination with Chinese/Tibetan politics, culture, and spirituality — Bernardo Bertolucci's *The Last Emperor* (1987) and *Little Buddha* (1993) come quickly to mind — they also represent a strategically timed reaction to the return of Hong Kong to the People's Republic of China. Though these films do not directly depict the handover per se, they do address its political implications through their portraiture of Chinese ideological and military aggression and its disregard for human rights, a not-too-subtle index of what the West conjures as the terrifying political fate awaiting Hong Kong.[1] In other words, Hollywood's construction of the filmic imagery and political discourses in these films, to a certain extent, demonizes the People's Republic of China.

In her significant essay on this matter, "King Kong in Hong Kong: Watching the 'Handover' from the U.S.A.," Rey Chow correctly, though maybe too categorically, characterizes these three films as constituting "a spate of China-bashing films" that "form part of the U.S. media's concerted effort to attack China in the name of human rights." These films are American pop culture's contributions to a mediatized political discourse Chow calls the "King Kong syndrome":

[B]y posing as defenders of democracy and liberty, the U.S. media portrays Chinese events as crises that require not only vigilance but also intervention. Typically, such portrayals are dramatized — staged in palpably demonizing terms so that audiences in the West are obliged to identify with an invisible but adamant moralistic perspective in which the United States is seen as superior. In discussing the U.S. media's treatment of the 1989 Tiananmen Massacre, I have compared it with the film *King Kong* and used the term "King Kong syndrome" to refer to this structure of cross-cultural, cross-racial representation aimed at producing "China" as a spectacular primitive monster whose despotism necessitates the salvation of its people by outsiders. It is important to remember that although many countries lack "democracy" and "liberty," it is China that, simply because it is not the United States' ideological ally, regularly bears the brunt of this process of palpable demonization . . . For many in the United States, China is, first and foremost, that "other country" where violence erupts.[2]

Chow's attempt to delineate the impact and limits of this discourse allows her to situate the Hong Kong handover within the context of British colonialism and US imperialism (and their complicity), thus problematizing the conflation of colonialism, capitalism, and Cold War anti-communist rhetoric with democracy and human rights.

While this mode of postcolonial critique is a necessary one and is indeed very useful in enabling my analyses of the three Hollywood films, I am also conscious of how Chow's complex and necessarily nuanced arguments can be appropriated by and incorporated, frequently in a reductive fashion, into cultural nationalist agendas; while Chow's cultural self-criticism is selectively ignored. (As I often warn my students in Singapore, it is too easy, all too easy, when discussing issues of colonialism and imperialism, to bash the West or blame former "colonial masters," so as to produce one-note nationalist critiques of western hypocrisy and disingenuousness that completely ignore, for instance, the complicit roles played by the nationalist and capitalist elite in their perpetuation of the very modes of oppression for which they condemn western imperialism and colonialism in the first place.[3]) What concerns me here is the way a unidirectional questioning of the films' "China-bashing" in these appropriated discourses has the potential of reifying an East-versus-West polemic, thus aligning itself with the unreflective and virulent Chinese cultural nationalism one sees being proliferated today.

The past three decades saw the People's Republic of China undergo a rather successful capitalist makeover since the economic reforms of Deng Xiaoping took effect in 1978. While still nominally communist in its ideological positioning, China has now transformed itself into an economic giant, a "red" dragon so to speak (if I could perversely redeploy Chow's King Kong monster metaphor here) that demands global attention. While in the past, western capitalist nations thought it wiser to acknowledge the PRC's legitimate status in the world community of nations because of its nuclear and military might (as the ousting of Taiwan from the United Nations in 1971 exemplifies), today many see the PRC as a rich and vast capitalist market to tap into. As capital defines international relations, it is becoming harder and harder for one to say no to China,[4] particularly in terms of deploying standard modes of geopolitical leverage to move China toward democratic rule and respect for human rights.

This difficulty is further compounded by a parallel rise in Chinese nationalism not only within the mainland but also throughout the diaspora. While I have nothing against nationalism and patriotism, these discourses of nation and culture become highly problematic when deployed in an essentialist fashion to police behavior and speech and to enforce conformity to a dominant political logic. Any criticism of China, Chinese cultural practice, or Chinese politics immediately consigns one to the status of a cultural traitor. This virulent nationalism has the profound danger of eclipsing attention on China's history of human rights abuses, such as in the cases of Tiananmen and Tibet, thereby drowning out voices of dissent. One saw an instance of this nationalism in the recent global protests against the Olympic torch as it made its way through various countries before arriving in Beijing for the start of the 2008 summer Olympic Games. While it is interesting to reflect on the efficacy of such protests, the emergence of numerous pro-Chinese protestors, and the way certain governments around the world sought to criticize and/or quash pro-Tibet voices,[5] I would like instead to focus on a single Chinese student at Duke University in order to illustrate the violently coercive nature of this us-versus-them cultural rhetoric.

Hailing from the city of Qingdao, Miss Grace Wang approached the issue rather differently. She attempted to bring the pro-Tibet and the pro-Chinese groups at Duke University together so that they could talk to each other. Instead, as she tells her story in the *Washington Post*, "I was caught in the middle and vilified and threatened by the Chinese . . . The Chinese protesters thought that, being Chinese, I should be on their side." She soon found her photo posted online with the accusation that she was a "traitor to . . . [her] country." Telephone and email threats ensued, with one even warning her that "[i]f you return to China, your dead corpse will be chopped into 10,000 pieces. " Vandals attacked her parents' home in China with excrement, and even her high school denounced her by having her diploma withdrawn.[6] Although I might seem to be positioning Grace Wang as an emotive poster girl for the pro-Tibet cause (while the pro-China camp has theirs in the figure of paraplegic athlete Jin Jing[7]), I see in Wang more of a reconciliatory figure whose presence resists and disrupts the emotional rhetoric of victimized China against a bullying West. In fact, Wang has made known her position against the Tibetan desire for a separate state. But that she was caught in the crossfire while advocating peaceful negotiations between the two camps and was subsequently demonized as a traitor, illustrates precisely the irrational and incendiary nationalist fervor I see rising in a post-9/11 age. It is a feverishly essentialist logic that demands ethnic Chinese to take sides — taking sides as a national, cultural, and/or religious imperative, as also witnessed in George W. Bush's "you are either with us or against us"[8]; or as in Islamic fundamentalism's terrifying insistence on waging jihad against the West as a sign of faithful religious practice and devotion to Allah. Grace Wang's stand in "not taking sides" is becoming a frighteningly minority and marginalized position in a world consumed by xenophobia, chauvinism, and violence.[9]

My approach to these films, hence, comes in the form of not taking sides, though not in a politically neutral kind of way (which I consider irresponsible), but in a simultaneous critique and affirmation of both positions, a kind of *anxious shuttling* between extreme poles, so to speak, in order to enact a more complex reading that disturbs the films' simplistic politics while positing their potential critical efficacy. My central argument in the analyses of these films is to demonstrate how the noble intentions of some in Hollywood, in upholding their ideals of democracy and human rights and championing the political underdog, lead them to employ various filmic strategies that unfortunately rely on Orientalist representations, cultural stereotypes, and monstrous caricatures of the Chinese or China. These representations miss the mark in terms of audience reach, thereby losing their effectiveness in their otherwise well-intended goals of promoting political and social change. The political enthusiasm of those in Hollywood who have a special interest in Chinese politics — one thinks of Richard Gere and Sharon Stone[10], for example — produces a certain excess in both public discourse and filmic imagery that ultimately alienates more than it mediates.

Red Corner: Representations of Excess

Jon Avnet's courtroom thriller *Red Corner*, starring renowned Tibet supporter Richard Gere, falls into the category of the Hollywood genre where an American tourist/adventurer finds himself in an exotic land, while embarking on a journey that psychologically transforms him, resulting in a deeper sense of self-awareness. More often than not, this transformation leads to a momentary questioning of American beliefs, practices, and institutions, thus displacing the character's insular naïveté with a newly acquired worldliness.

But this cultural sensitivity seldom if ever ends in the subversion or critique of fundamental American ideals, values that are instead reaffirmed at the end of the journey as ideologically true and culturally transcendent. Classic and contemporary instances of this genre include *Sayonara* (1957), *The World of Suzie Wong* (1960), *The Beach* (2000), *Lost in Translation* (2003), *The Last Samurai* (2003), and *The Darjeeling Limited* (2007).

Richard Gere plays the pragmatic Jack Moore, who is sent by an American telecommunications company to negotiate "the first Chinese-American satellite joint venture" with his Chinese counterpart Minister Lin Shou (James Hong) and his western-minded son Lin Dan (Byron Mann). What Moore does not realize is that he has stepped into a trap laid by Lin Dan. After being seduced by Hong Ling (Jessey Meng), the daughter of a high-ranking Chinese general, Moore wakes to find her dead and is thus hauled away by the Chinese police on the charge of murder. With Moore removed from the scene, Lin Dan proceeds to seal a deal with Moore's German competitor Hoffco Telekom. The odds are now clearly stacked against Moore winning the case, especially with the austere Chinese legal system dead set against him (as an American) and with a court-appointed defense attorney, Shen Yuelin (Bai Ling), who does not believe that he is innocent. But, as one would expect from a Hollywood narrative of American heroism, Moore soon gains the trust of Shen and a friendship, with the usual erotic undercurrent, develops between the two. When an assassination attempt on his life gives him the opportunity to seek asylum and safety within the compounds of the American embassy, Moore selflessly chooses instead to surrender to the Chinese authorities so that Shen will not be persecuted for having staked her reputation to obtain his earlier release from prison. The dramatic final court scene has Moore and Shen joining forces to fight the system. After they expose Lin Dan's role in the murder of Hong Ling, General Hong shoots his daughter's killer in the ensuing chaos within the courtroom, hence freeing Moore from the clutches of the politically implicated Chinese judiciary.

What I find most remarkable is the way the film uses three scenes set in Beijing's Purple Bamboo Park[11] to rhetorically structure and present its political message. The scenes occur in the opening credit sequence, in the crisis or turning point within the middle of the film's narrative, and in a brief touching moment between Moore and Shen as part of the post-trial denouement. Of course, these scenes of bamboo leaves swaying in the wind surrounding a beautiful lake offer both relief and contrast to the inevitable atmospheric tension produced by the film's difficult subject matter. But I would also argue that these scenes create an imagistic rhetoric that is unfortunately founded on Orientalist assumptions about Chinese cultural traditions and philosophy, though masked as a newfound cultural sensitivity implicit in the logic of US multiculturalism. This rhetorical setup provides the scenic plot points in the film to mark significant shifts in character development and ideological awakening.

Opening the film, as part of the credit sequence, is a scene of childhood remembrance, where Shen Yuelin reminisces about her grandmother and the time they spent in the Purple Bamboo Park: "When I was a child, I would come to this park and play. My grandmother told me why the bamboo is here. She said, 'It is waiting for the wind to touch it. It is filled with emotions.'" The fact that the film does not provide an immediate context for this opening voiceover (something that the audience will only discover later in the film) adds to the Oriental mystique of its fortune-cookie style philosophy. Even more crucial is that this inscrutable utterance allows the film to construct an atavistic concept of *traditional* Chinese cultural purity, as located in its semiotic resonance with the bamboo and nature imagery; which provides a sharp contrast to the Chinese modernity that one later sees, where corrupt government apparatchiks entangle themselves in greedy capitalist schemes, and where skimpily dressed Chinese women seductively cavort with white men in clubs to the beat of the Village People's "YMCA."

This contrast deepens with the introduction of Jack Moore immediately following the Purple Bamboo Park opening sequence. Moore arrives in Tiananmen Square in a limousine. As the tinted windows roll down, he espies Chinese boys playing soccer, soldiers marching in lock step, and an ominous surveillance camera panning in his direction and focusing directly on him. The shot here is both symptomatic of the panopticism[12] that permeates an authoritarian state, and symbolic of the political and legal plight in which Moore will soon find himself embroiled. But clearly Moore's pragmatist and capitalist bravado do not deter him: he meets with Chinese government officials and convinces them that their "concerns about . . . [his] programming package" being "pornographic, violent, and superstitious" are misplaced, even citing Mao Zedong's political adage, "Use the West for Chinese purposes," to perversely make the following argument: "If our programming teaches your people that America is imperfect, often violent and prurient, wouldn't that discourage the pursuit of Western values?" The following sequence of "Western decadence" in Chinese urban modernity has Moore visit a dance club, attend a fashion show (which opens with a Chinese operatic display, signaling the "problematic" cultural dilution as the West encroaches on China), and end up in bed with the sexy model Hong Ling whom he meets at the show. The crude morality tale here is all too obvious, as one movie critic from *USA Today* rather facetiously put it: "Beware of one-nighters with comely nightclub performers whose governments are weary of encroaching Western values."[13] One could possibly rewrite this warning to read as "Beware of one-nighters with comely nightclub performers whose governments are manipulating Western capitalist modernity and values to reassert their authoritarian power and rule at the expense of personal freedoms and rights. " While it is laudable for the film's critique to hint at Western capitalism's complicity in furthering China's authoritarianism and human rights abuses, it unfortunately relies on an Orientalist and traditionalist notion of pure Chinese culture as the alternative and panacea for these ills, as my readings of the later scenes of Purple Bamboo Park will demonstrate.

But before doing so, I believe it is significant to comment briefly on the depictions of abuse that Jack Moore suffers at the hands of the Chinese authorities, as a kind of cinematic spectacle and excess for the film to make its political point. Moore's predicament is a result of the political intrigue that Lin Dan's corruption has created. When he is dragged to prison upon the discovery of Hong Ling's murder, Moore is stripped naked and hosed down by the prison guards. He is subjected to interrogation techniques that involve physical and psychological torture: he is punched, slapped, and zapped with an electric prod; he is made to view a video of Chinese prisoners being shot and bayoneted to death, in order to impress on him the idea of "Leniency for those who confess. Severity for those who resist," a notion that even an initially skeptical Shen Yuelin believes, a judicial philosophy that is utterly antithetical to America's belief in innocence until proven guilty. Finally, the scatological horror of a prison guard washing Moore's dinner plate in the toilet before serving him food marks for me the extremity of the film's visual caricature of abuse. I am not here suggesting that this form of abuse does not occur in China. Rather, the visual excess in the film I liken to a politician propagandist drumming up of patriotic fervor or a Christian fundamentalist preacher's hyperbolic invocation of fire and brimstone to terrify his audience into belief. This spectacle of cinematic excess only generates a backlash against the film's good intentions, particularly in a *fictional* film coming out of Hollywood and starring an actor whose stand on China and Tibet is well known.

The crisis in *Red Corner*'s plot development occurs in the calm surroundings of the Purple Bamboo Park. But in order to build up to this narrative crescendo, the film turns its attention to the tense relationship between Jack Moore and Shen Yuelin, its détente, and the eventual development of trust and friendship between the two protagonists. It is useful at this juncture to comment on the gendered structure of this relationship. By making the defense attorney a woman in the figure of the alluring Bai Ling, director Avnet and screenwriter Robert King tap into a robust Hollywood tradition of the white hero and his Asian sexual counterpart. In her discussions of the Hong Kong setting in *Love Is a Many-Splendored Thing* (1955) and *The World of Suzie Wong* (1960), Gina Marchetti registers the cultural/national implications in the gender dynamics of this relationship:

> Hong Kong provides a place where all sorts of social and ideological oppositions can be played out in fiction — East-West, Communist-capitalist, white-nonwhite, rich-poor, colonizer-colonized, European-American, Asian-American, progressive-conservative. Within the context of the Hollywood love story, moreover, all these oppositions can be addressed using the cinematic vocabulary of that fundamental opposition between male and female. By using romance to examine these ideological sore points, Hollywood can make any boundaries between nations and races appear as natural as the differences between men and women. Relationships between nations or races can be seen as the male-female romance writ large, with its patronizing sentimentality and inherent inequality left intact.[14]

Had the filmmakers made the Shen character a man, the heterosexual erotic connection would not only have been lost, but the Orientalist practice of conceptualizing Asia in a feminized guise would also have been disabled. Gone, hence, will be the "Asian mystique"[15] of an exotic, gentle, and traditional China. (It is no coincidence that the role of Chairman Xu, the judge presiding over the trial, is played by the talented Asian American actress Tsai Chin, whose no-nonsense demeanor exudes dragon-lady ferocity, thus reinforcing a stereotype that is also a part of the Asian mystique allure. But her gender also permits the film to suggest her puppet-like position in a politically compromised judiciary where her male political masters are pulling the strings from behind.) While one does find in Shen's characterization a strong feminist streak, especially in her insinuation to Moore that it "must be extremely difficult, to rely on a stranger, a woman, a foreign woman, in such serious matters" as his defense in this trial, the feminist potential collapses under the weight of the film's formulation of a good, traditional Chinese culture, as witnessed in Shen's progressive transformation into the image of a gentle Chinese woman who is eventually in touch with her political/cultural self at the end of the film.

The initial shift in Shen's attitude towards Moore is when she obtains his temporary daytime release from prison by staking her own reputation, in order that they might be able to work on the case. The action moves into the domestic sphere of Shen's house where Moore is introduced to a personal space, thus enabling him to reach out to her on a non-professional basis. The cultural divide is breached through the universality of music as Moore's piano playing encourages reciprocity through Shen's playing of the piba, a Chinese-string instrument. She "softens" in his eyes as Moore notes that she has "beautiful hands," an erotic point of contact. They exchange marital information: Shen proclaims how she has "not found a man who's not threatened by a woman's intelligence," an idea that Moore finds incredible considering that there are "half a billion men in this country," drawing assent from Shen. This moment not only evokes the potential of a sexual relationship between them, but is also suggestive of how men from the West are more secure about their masculinity and more politically open-minded in their understanding of feminism to take on strong and intelligent women like Shen.

But Shen does not succumb to his charms so easily, as she puts him in his place in a wonderful scene where Moore becomes flustered over the way public telephone records are deleted by political operatives, a matter that is crucial to his winning the case:

> *Moore*: General Hong?
> *Shen*: It is not General Hong.
> *Moore*: Why not? He's got influence with the P.S.B., with prisons, with everybody.
> *Shen*: He only wants his daughter's killer punished. General Hong is not corrupt.
> *Moore*: He's old guard. He's losing control.
> *Shen*: You do not understand.
> *Moore*: No, you do not understand! This is a satellite communications deal! For better or for worse, the effect of the McAndrews' deal would have been to open a totally closed system!
> *Shen*: Who are you to criticize?
> *Moore*: Once opened there's no going back.
> *Shen*: You come from a country where the infant mortality rate is higher than ours . . .
> *Moore*: The reason you know that is we don't delete the records.
> *Shen*: . . . where people are punished for their color of their skin.
> *Moore*: Have you ever been there?
> *Shen*: Of course, you find it easy to assume that a Chinese father would kill his daughter to stop your precious business deal!
> *Moore*: No, I do not find that easy to assume.
> *Shen*: How many people are killed each week in your peaceful country? How many, Mr. Moore?
> *Moore*: [*humbled*] Too many.

The verbal sparring between the characters is less about giving the Chinese a voice (though it is a welcomed byproduct) than to allow the film to articulate its position on the manner of American intervention on human rights issues. It is a position in consonant with America's political left's argument that the United States needs to address its own human rights record (as in the recent case of the detention camps in Guantanamo Bay, for instance[16]) so as to deflect criticism of hypocrisy and, hence, to give its global leadership on the issue greater legitimacy. This is an argument that I believe the film is successful in conveying, despite Shen's and the Chinese's instrumentality.

The thaw between Moore and Shen is complete when Moore, in realizing that Shen has put her life and career on the line for him, heroically leaves the safety of the American embassy's compound to surrender himself to his Chinese captors. Though I admire the idealism in the character's selflessness, one cannot help but wonder if it is only in the fairy-tale world of Hollywood that Moore's white-savior complex is activated to rescue his Chinese damsel in distress. Shen is so taken by this selfless act that it catalyzes a profound change in her worldview:

> *Moore*: Why did you risk your life for me if you didn't believe me?
> *Shen*: I always assumed the worst about you. I have never questioned. I have always accepted things. It is the same as when I was a child.
> *Moore*: Why?
> *Shen*: I was blind. I was mute.
> *Moore*: When you were a child . . . It was during the Cultural Revolution, wasn't it?
> *Shen*: Yes.
> *Moore*: What is it?
> *Shen*: I went to school until they closed down, and everything went mad. I do not know if you could understand this, Jack Moore.
> *Moore*: Try me.
> *Shen*: I . . . I watched . . . I watched my father be humiliated, and I said nothing. I watched my father be spat on. I did nothing. I even watched my classmates pour black ink over his head, one after another and after another. What did I do? I hid my head in shame while he was dragged away. I never questioned. I was blind. I'm very sorry that I did not believe your innocence. But now I do. I do.

While Moore's selflessness marks a change in his attitude towards people around him — he has been running away from facing up to the personal trauma of losing his wife and daughter in an automobile accident — his personal transformation functions as the catalyst for Shen's personal and *political* conversion. Shen is made to see that she was once a political child for naively believing all that she is told. It takes an American to bring her into political adulthood, where she develops a deep sense of personal integrity and freedom, the belief that her voice is as, if not more, important than the political collective. The Shen-Moore relationship thus turns into a metaphor for the global role that the United States plays in teaching recalcitrant nations to mend their abusive ways. This critical juncture finds Shen alone in the Purple Bamboo Park reflecting and musing over her changed heart, finding the resolve to fight the system in order to save Moore from an almost certain death.

After this second scene involving the Purple Bamboo Park, the narrative propels towards the final court scene where Moore and Shen unite against the corrupt system. The happy ending, where Moore is finally released without charges, is marred by the perpetuation of a political and legal system that covers over its flaws while continuing to subject many to its heavy-handedness: Chairman Xu announces at a press conference that "the Court would particularly like to thank all levels of party and government leadership involved in this case for their diligence and professionalism. The justice accorded will be swift, as it will be fair and impartial." The film does not let the United States government off either, in its critique of the latter's complicity in viewing Moore's case as "a full-scale incident," a diplomatic fiasco, "an international dick-measuring contest" — the inability to say no to a capital-rich China. Moore puts it best when he tells the US embassy official upon his release to "go to hell."

The impact of this powerful criticism falters somewhat when the Purple Bamboo Park makes a re-appearance in the third and final scene. This time Shen and Moore meet at the park to reflect on what has happened, but without really talking about it. Clouded in the philosophical mysticism that is Orientalist China, Shen's words echo those of the opening voiceover: "When I was a child, I would come to this park and play. Do you know why the bamboo is here? It is waiting for the wind to touch it. It is filled with emotions. Listen to the sounds and you can feel them." Here, in contrast to the power suit she wore when making her first appearance on screen, Shen is now dressed in traditional Chinese clothing that can be worn by both genders (a possible neutering effect that diminishes the erotic charge between her and Moore so as to make parting possible). This concatenation of Chinese cultural traditionalism and personal political integrity and freedom imbues the latter with a veneer of cultural respectability defined here by Orientalist assumptions.

To end my discussion of *Red Corner*, I would like to foreground what I call the film's "rhetoric of authenticity" as part of its political argument. The insert to the film's DVD release takes particular pains to accentuate the realism the filmmakers and actors try to attain. Such realism is crucial for the film to make its political argument against China's human rights record believable and convincing. Not only have the production team spent a week in Beijing

Bai Ling in culturally "appropriate" Chinese dress in the final Purple
Bamboo Park scene

engaging in "'guerilla' shooting (without the knowledge or permission of the
Chinese government!) to capture the first-ever 35mm motion picture footage
of the city to appear in a Hollywood film," the video used in Moore's
interrogation scene also features "actual execution footage . . . smuggled out
of China!" Richard Gere himself contends that he is "working on Chinese and
Tibetan causes all the time and if there were any falsehoods or
misrepresentations, it would be dangerous for all the people that . . . [he]
work[s] for and with."[17] Despite the fact that I do not disagree with Gere and·
the filmmaker's position on China, it is necessary to note that this intense desire
for authenticity has ironically generated the cinematic excess I have discussed
earlier. The desire to project onto screen "authentic" representations of the
very worst of human rights abuses produces instead a compressed text of
fantastical proportions, often ascribed to the mythmaking that is Hollywood.

Slavoj Žižek, in his deliberations on the subject/object dialectic, has
observed how our desire to know the Other, or "the secret of the Other,"
produces a "reflexivity." The subject's "external position *vis-à-vis* the Other
(the fact that he experiences himself as excluded from the secret of the Other)
is internal to the Other itself . . . [T]he very feature which seems to exclude
the subject from the Other . . . is already a 'reflexive determination' of the
Other; precisely as excluded from the Other, we are already part of its game."[18]
This dialectic exposes the contradictory relationship between the Hollywood
subject and its Chinese Other, and vice versa. A film like *Red Corner* projects
its "desire" for a Chinese Other that conforms to its notions of China's
disregard of human rights, but in excess. This is less a question of truth than
it is the way desire and representation intermingle in filmic and political

discourses. (Or course, I do not dispute the truth of China's authoritarianism and its human rights record, which I, in fact, condemn.) In the same way, China played into Hollywood's "desire," much to its own political detriment, by confirming the representation of its Otherness when it chose to censure Chinese actress Bai Ling for appearing in the film.[19] This reflexive dialectic only compounds the East-versus-West polemic that we now see so evident in the current Chinese nationalism that is reacting to the pro-Tibet protests of the 2008 Olympic Games.

Hollywood for Tibet: Historicity in Contention

My discussion of *Red Corner*'s rhetoric of authenticity is really a discussion of the urgency of historicity, history as Truth, in the film's critique of corruption, political intrigue, authoritarian rule, and human rights abuses in China. It is through this idea of historicity that I would like to move on to Hollywood's 1997 releases that deal with the Tibet question: Jean-Jacques Annaud's *Seven Years in Tibet* and Martin Scorsese's *Kundun*. But instead of offering the usual close analyses of the two filmic texts in the way I have approached *Red Corner*, I here take a slightly different tack by offering instead reflections on the concerns of historicity as they affect the issue of Tibet and, specifically, Hollywood's engagement with it.

America's infatuation with Tibet has very much been filtered through Hollywood and, hence, is often based on celluloid constructions of what is considered the Tibet question. In the course of his research on "the West's long-standing fascination with Tibet," Orville Schell, in a literate piece about his visit to the set of the Brad Pitt-vehicle *Seven Years in Tibet*, observes how he "encountered hardly anyone who didn't have something to say on the subject. National infatuation had risen to such a level that almost a dozen feature and documentary films were in various stages of production. Everywhere one turned there were strange cultural collisions happening. Stars, producers, agents, and directors were discovering the spiritual message of Lord Buddha."[20] Everyone, from the usual suspects like Richard Gere, Sharon Stone, and Steven Seagal, to Mia Farrow, Steven Spielberg, Goldie Hawn, Annie Lennox, Harrison Ford, George Clooney, and even will.i.am of the Black Eyed Peas, has weighed in on the matter,[21] as recently as the pro-Tibet protests and boycott of the Beijing Olympics in 2008.[22] But why does Tibet garner the kind of political attention that it does? What role has Tibet played, and still plays, in the Hollywood imaginary and in its inevitable influence on political discourses in the United States and in the West?

Hollywood's political fetishism engenders a "virtual Tibet"[23] that embodies an Oriental Other that Western democracies can champion against a progressively modernizing and contradictorily capitalist China — a China that will not conform to the ideological ideals of capitalist-democratic conflations in the West. This is a Tibet, remade by Hollywood, to eschew what Schell, in his unwitting channeling of Edward Said, has described as "commonplace and at-hand for something that is outré and remote and thus all the more vulnerable to becoming the receptor site for our own [meaning 'American'] yearnings and projections."[24] It remains the "Shangri-La in the Western imagination" as first seen in Frank Capra's 1937 filmic adaptation of James Hilton's *Lost Horizon*, a Shangri-La that in its prelapsarian state of cultural purity, epitomized by its geographical insularity and in the rarefied air that Tibet breathes as it occupies the tabletop of the world, permits the West to recapture what is lost in "the fallen state of grace of our own neoindustrial world and lives."[25]

Out of this Asiatic Eden also emerges a form of Buddhism that is increasingly embraced by some in the West. Disenchanted by Christianity's failings in its epochal clash of civilizations with Islam, an ideological battle that has enabled an event as apocalyptic as 9/11 to occur on American soil, many in the Hollywood set have embraced Tibetan Buddhism and its conceptions of non-violence as a viable religious and political alternative. This spirituality has become intertwined with Hollywood's fantastical creations, not only as evident in historically-based films like *Kundun* and *Seven Years in Tibet*, but also in superhero stories such as *Bulletproof Monk* (2003), which I discuss in the context of a Chinese supernaturalism in Chapter Seven. China's annexation of Tibet, its suppression of Tibetan resistance, and the gradual sinicization of political Tibet through the Chinese government's resettlement policies, are now viewed in both *religious* and political terms, just as the incredibly charismatic Dalai Lama is welcomed as a figure of both *religious* and political significance. The image of Mao Zedong belittling the Dalai Lama with the former's communist dictum "Religion is poison," as powerfully presented in *Kundun*, is ultimately read as both religious and ideological oppression.

Finally, my brief attempt thus far to ascertain America's fascination with Tibet must rest on the political ideals of democracy, freedom of speech and the press, the right to self-determination, and the sanctity of human rights; ideals that are quintessentially associated with the United States of America. Tibet, like Hong Kong, Taiwan, and the minority regions of China such as Xinjiang, for instance, typifies the plight of the (political) underdog that Americans would be inclined to defend. America, as a cultural and ideological space, narrates the eventual triumph of the underdog, as Hollywood films about the American dream, particularly the Hollywood sports movie genre, evince. The timing of Hollywood's theatrical release of *Seven Years in Tibet* and *Kundun* appears strategically aimed at the post-1997 handover visit of Chinese leader Jiang Zemin to the United States.[26] The Tiananmen massacre, the Hong Kong handover, and the Tibet question together constitute a string of concerns Hollywood activists would raise against China. The issue of Tibetan independence has an unresolved presence that allows these films to become the political conduit through which the question of Hong Kong's fate under Chinese rule is conveniently channeled in a post-1997 era. In other words, to talk about Tibet is also to talk about the rights of political and cultural minorities in a China that is ideologically and historically hell-bent on achieving glorious reunification.

As in the case of authenticity in *Red Corner*, the notion of historicity in contention becomes central to the rhetorical thrust of the two Tibet films. *Seven Years in Tibet* is based on the true-life experiences of Austrian mountaineer Heinrich Harrer and his friendship with the current Dalai Lama during the time of Nazi Germany's World War Two aggression.[27] *Kundun* is a brainchild of screenwriter and Tibet supporter Melissa Mathison, who was then married to another Tibet advocate, Harrison Ford. Martin Scorsese's directorial presence was fascinatingly low key, in that the film represents a style which one critic describes as "similar to the tradition of narrationless ethnographic filmmaking which includes Frederick Wiseman's documentaries and, more recently, Ulrike Ottinger's monumental documentary on Mongolia, *Taiga* (1993)." The film is also compared to Tian Zhuangzhuang's *Horse Thief* (1986), a film to which Scorsese himself has "accorded high praise."[28] The point is that both films take pride in laboring under the notion that the historical depiction of this particular moment of trauma in Tibetan history is, to the best of their knowledge, as accurate as the art of cinematic consumerism permits. But this question of accurate history in filmic representation is not just a textual one. The importance of history here also underscores the importance of historical legitimacy in the arguments marshaled by both Chinese and Tibetan supporters. Pro-independence Tibetans foreground the history of Tibet's autonomy prior to China's annexation of the territory. The Chinese government, on the other hand, invokes their version of the historical events to insist on Tibet's inclusion in China's geographical and political sovereignty. So complex are the arguments deployed on both sides, that historians of Tibet have made an institution out of the prolific academic analyses produced on the subject, by studying the complexities and complications of the different histories invoked.[29] While complex historicity has enabled historians to maintain the objectivity to which history as a social science aspires, it also unfortunately permits some to disengage from criticizing the Chinese claim to Tibet by alluding to these historical "complexities."

My gesture of a challenge is ultimately grounded on the notion that historicity is contentious, as contemporary theories on historical revisionism (both positive and negative), metahistory,[30] and minority histories have taught us. For history is never just History with a capital "H." What I hope to achieve here is to lay out bits of Tibet's history in order to tease out a specific strand that highlights Tibet's encounter with Euro-American powers. This strand of history can then serve as the framework with which one could approach the two Tibet films in a way that puts into perspective the multiple complicities on the Tibet question.

To begin to understand the nature of Tibet's entanglements with Britain and the United States and how these relationships, in part, contributed to the current political deadlock between Tibet and China, one needs to return to the time of the Yuan dynasty when China was under Mongol rule. When the great Kublai Khan brought China under Mongol domination in 1279AD, Tibet entered the circuit of Kublai's empire; the Tibetan ruler was greatly respected as the khan's spiritual mentor, developing a "priest-patron" relationship with him. But this entry of Tibet into the Mongolian imperial domain has led "[c]ontemporary Chinese scholars and officials [to] consider this the period when Tibet first became part of China," while Tibetans argue, "that they, like China, were subjugated by the Mongols and incorporated into a Mongol empire centered in China."[31] Even into the Qing dynasty, China's Manchu rulers betrayed a lack of interest in Tibet's place within Chinese rule, apart from using Tibet as a means of leverage against the Mongols. Tibet simply became a "protectorate" of the Qing dynasty.[32]

China's disinterest dramatically changed in the nineteenth century when Britain began its imperialist intrusions into Tibetan territory. Through various British missions and later military "diplomacy," British imperial designs on controlling trade in the area grew. When the thirteenth Dalai Lama refused to entertain British encroachments, the viceroy of India, Lord Curzon, sent Indian troops to capture Lhasa, Tibet's capital, in 1904, making them "the first Western troops ever to conquer Tibet."[33] Like in the case of the Opium Wars and the loss of Hong Kong, this British colonial conquest was another sign of European powers carving out spheres of influence at the expense of China, "the sick man of Asia," thus fueling indignation on the part of the Qing government. This is the seed of Chinese nationalist belief in Tibet's place in China's reunification, planted unwittingly by Britain's imperial greed and meddling. As Melvyn Goldstein observes:

The contradiction inherent in Britain's Tibet strategy was that while Great
Britain had to deal directly with the Tibetan government to achieve its ends,
it had to deal with China to legitimize them . . . The resultant 1906 Anglo-
Chinese Convention modified the 1904 accord (without the involvement of
Tibet's government), reaffirming China's legitimate authority over its
dependency Tibet. The key articles in the convention said: "The Government
of Great Britain engages not to annex Tibetan territory or to interfere in the
administration of Tibet. The Government of China also undertakes not to
permit any other foreign state to interfere with the territory or internal
administration of Tibet." And "The Concessions which are mentioned [in
the 1904 convention] are denied to any state other than China." Thus, at a
time when China was unable to exercise real power in Tibet, Britain
unilaterally reaffirmed Tibet's political subordination to China.[34]

The unfortunate consequence of British involvement is the Chinese government
"beginning a program of closer cultural, economic, and political integration
of Tibet with the rest of China,"[35] a program that assumed different forms
right through the chaotic Nationalist period and into China's communist era.

April 12, 1912 saw Yuan Shikai proclaim Xinjiang, Mongolia, and Tibet
part of the new Republic of China, inaugurating what Goldstein calls the "Tibet
Question in its modern incarnation."[36] The rise to power of the Communist
Party in China did not temper this sense of sovereignty over Tibet; Mao
Zedong sanctioned a military assault on Tibet to force the fourteenth Dalai
Lama's hand. Despite Tibet's appeals to the United Nations, the international
community sat by, with Britain and India arguing that it would be unwise to
offend China by considering Tibet a "state."[37] Tibet was forced to sign the
Seventeen-Point Agreement in 1951, of which Point 1 states that "The Tibetan
people shall unite and drive out imperialist forces from Tibet: the Tibet people
shall return to the big family of the Motherland — the People's Republic of
China."[38] Like the British, the United States was guilty of what Goldstein has
labeled as the "bad friend syndrome": "Western powers professing friendship
for Tibet but refusing to support it in its fundamental objective of political
independence while actually bolstering China's claim of real ownership."[39]
In accordance with its Cold War policy of agitating resistance against
communist regimes, America's support of Tibetan resistance "rang hollow"
because the United States was not willing to go the extra mile of supporting
Tibet's claim to independence to the international community, agreeing only
to recognize Tibetan autonomy within Chinese governance.[40] The historic
arrival of President Richard Nixon to China changed little but instead
strengthened China's hand in its claim over Tibet — "beginning in about 1966,
the official U.S. position ceased talking about 'self-determination' for Tibet,

or even of Tibet as an autonomous country as it had in [Secretary of State Christian] Herter's statement in 1960."[41]

My extremely brief and reductive survey of British and American involvement in the Tibet-China spat is *not* to simplistically point an anti-colonial finger at Britain and America, by accusing them of *sole* responsibility and complicity for Tibet's current predicament. (In fact, China is highly responsible for the way it has ruthlessly crushed Tibet's pro-independence movement all in the sanctified name of nationalism.[42]) Rather, my intention is to paint an often-neglected portion of the historical picture so that one can better understand the historical shortcomings of *Kundun* and *Seven Years in Tibet* as Western cultural products. Jean-Jacques Annaud's adaptation of Heinrich Harrer's story not only sees Tibet from the viewpoint of a Nazi-affiliated Austrian mountain climber but also assumes a detached perspective from the context of Euro-American international politics and the roles that China and Tibet have played, as pawns, in a game of international intrigue. Hence, what one sees in *Seven Years in Tibet* is a filmic visualization of China's aggression against a peace-loving Tibetan people, without being privy to the larger historical context defining Chinese motivations against European imperialism. In the same way, *Kundun*'s ethnographic filmmaking aesthetic fosters a tunnel vision in its political mise-en-scène and its diegetic worldview. The insularity of that world is only ruptured by Chinese military and political incursions, with Westerners hardly making a significant presence on-screen or within the film's historical purview — Scorsese's well-intentioned anthropological detachment, therefore, deserves notation as being participatory in this Western "absence." Because both films seek to critique Chinese oppression of Tibet, they need to eschew the overly simplistic depiction of victim-versus-oppressor and provide, particularly, a more complex representation of Western complicity in this matter. This is the only way that Hollywood can avoid being accused of political hypocrisy and can sustain a clearer appreciation of what it seeks to rectify and undo. Films like *Red Corner*, *Seven Years in Tibet*, and *Kundun* can then hopefully transcend the implication that "commodified experience" is necessarily always negative, as Dominick LaCapra challenges us to rethink in his discussion of cinema's reconstructions of trauma in history,[43] trauma that we have sadly witnessed in Tibet.

4

The Global Return of the *Wuxia pian* (Chinese Sword-Fighting Movie)

The *wuxia pian*, or the Chinese sword-fighting movie, occupies a special place in the cultural memory of my childhood. Growing up in the late 1970s and early 1980s in Singapore, I remember with great fondness escaping from the mind-numbing tedium of the British-based education school I attended, and from the blazing heat of the tropical sun to the air-conditioned coolness of the neighborhood cinema. (This was long before multiplexes became fashionable.) Inevitably, a sword-fighting or kung fu flick from Hong Kong would be screening. The exoticism of one-armed swordsmen, fighting Shaolin monks, and woman warriors careening weightlessly across the screen informed my sense and (mis)understanding of Chinese culture, values, and notions of "Chineseness" more radically than any Chinese-language lessons in school could have imparted.[1] The ideological impact of this genre should clearly not be underestimated, as cinematic fantasy is sutured into the cultural and political imaginary of China, particularly for the Chinese in diaspora.[2] Or, as Stephen Teo so correctly diagnoses, "the cinema catered to the psychic needs of the diasporic Chinese to identify, vicariously or nostalgically, with the motherland and its myths — even though many of the overseas Chinese would not have been born in China."[3]

Hence, like many ethnic Chinese moviegoers, I responded to Ang Lee's cinematic epic *Crouching Tiger, Hidden Dragon* (2000)[4] with genuine enthusiasm and anticipation. For many Chinese in the United States and around the world, Lee's film marks an important critical and commercial breakthrough for Asian and Asian American filmmakers who wish to make it in Hollywood. To the delight of these Chinese audiences, *Crouching Tiger, Hidden Dragon* was showered with critical acclaim, enthusiastically received at major international film festivals, and bagged numerous nominations and awards, including the Academy Award in 2001 for best foreign-language film.[5] It introduced the *wuxia pian* and Chinese-language popular cinema to mainstream American audiences, thereby blazing a trail for films like Zhang Yimou's *Hero* (2002) and *House of Flying Daggers* (2004) to follow in its footsteps.

Despite its general success, ambivalence also characterizes the responses ethnic Chinese audiences have had toward Lee's film, an ambivalence that I cannot help but share.[6] On the one hand, a kind of cultural nationalism lured viewers to root for the film to triumph in Hollywood.[7] On the other hand, the film's success evoked suspicions of stereotyping, exoticism, traditionalism, and pandering to a Western gaze, a critique grounded in the methodologies of Edward Said's anti-Orientalism. When *Crouching Tiger, Hidden Dragon* finally made its debut in Singapore after much hype, I conducted an informal survey of audience responses. Though many viewers were initially slow to declare their dislike of the movie (fueled by the ambivalence to which I have been referring), some finally admitted to disappointment. The main reason they gave for why the film did not live up to their expectations of a *wuxia pian* was its lack of "authenticity." Many members of the audience had been brought up, as I was, on a cinematic diet of sword-fighting flicks in the 1970s and 1980s. Hence, they clung nostalgically to some of the genre's conventions which Ang Lee playfully and purposefully chose to reconfigure. Hence, his film was bound to meet with protests from these purists who considered certain traditions of the genre sacrosanct. The charge of inauthenticity is also leveled on cultural grounds. Specifically, the film is accused of inaccurately representing China's history. Clearly, such criticism arises, first, as a result of the political status the film has attained in the popular cultural annals of Asian filmic achievements in Hollywood; unfortunately, the film is then expected to carry the burden and responsibility of cultural representation. Second, the *wuxia pian*, together with certain period movies, is assumed to offer a kind of cinematic cultural gravitas that efficiently embodies history and tradition. In other words, despite the genre's varied permutations and popular appeal, purists expect the genre to retain at its core a traditionalist, nationalist ideology of Chineseness. Such expectations forget how hybridity, appropriation, and reconfiguration — including cross-cultural borrowings and influences — are part and parcel of global cinematic evolution.[8]

The cultural, historical, and theoretical problematics that I have delineated thus far reveal a cultural anxiety about identity and Chineseness in a globalized, postcolonial, and postmodern world order. This anxiety colors both the filmmaker's approach to and audiences' view of the genre, especially in the context of the Hong Kong and Chinese movie industries' attempts to cross over into Hollywood. As political, cultural, economic, and artistic interests crosshatch, the cinematic creatures that emerge inevitably embody tensions and anxieties, sometimes in a fractured, albeit aesthetically beautiful, fashion. *Crouching Tiger, Hidden Dragon, Hero*, and *House of Flying Daggers* are such postmodernist creatures. To consider how these films grapple with the larger issues of cultural identity, the politics of Chineseness, and the immense pressure of American and global audience appeal, this chapter first interrogates the ideological and cinematic implications of Ang Lee's desire to construct an image of "China" in *Crouching Tiger, Hidden Dragon,* before examining the feminist possibilities that the film's narrative and characters suggest. These two approaches reveal that Lee's reconfiguration of the traditional *wuxia pian* into a postmodernist cultural product for a global audience enables him to critique, often in a rather ambiguous and conflicted manner, the vexing centrality of traditional cultural and patriarchal hegemony in China, in spite of the liberating possibilities that diasporic mobility, globalization, and transnationalism supposedly present. In the final section of the chapter, my analysis of Zhang Yimou's *Hero* and *House of Flying Daggers* demonstrates how the Chinese film industry's production of Hollywood-modeled *wuxia* cinematic spectacles similarly result in a politically conflicted cinema that seduces global audiences through its imaginative reworking of the genre by refracting its thematic concerns through the lens of contemporary Chinese cultural and national politics. *Hero*'s box-office triumph in the United States relies on an effective deployment of its nationalist politics, together with a spectacular visuality, to appeal to middle-America in a post-9/11 era of strident patriotism. My readings unveil the deep-rooted anxieties about Chinese culture, identity, and nationalism in these films, especially as they compete for box-office dollars in a transnational film market that is dominated by Hollywood blockbusters.

Re-imagining "China" in Ang Lee's *Crouching Tiger, Hidden Dragon*

As Fredric Jameson's investigations of the postmodern have revealed, postmodernist aesthetics and cultural production are implicated and shaped by the global forces of late-capitalist logic.[9] By extension, one could presumably argue that popular cinema, as a mass-media art form, can be considered postmodern by virtue of its aesthetic configurations, its means of production, and the global reach of its distribution networks. The *wuxia pian* is no exception[10]: *Crouching Tiger, Hidden Dragon* is a postmodern, globalized, contemporary instance of the genre. Headed by a pan-Asian cast with stars from Malaysia (Michelle Yeoh), Hong Kong (Chow Yun-fat and

Cheng Pei Pei), Taiwan (Chang Chen and Lung Sihung), and China (Zhang Ziyi), the movie's production team was truly global in its makeup.[11] Sources of funding for the movie were similarly international in their reach.[12] In Sheldon Lu's estimation, the film "constitutes a clear expression and a major case of *transnational cinema*."[13]

The pan-Asian cast and the film's global appeal complicate and challenge Lee's restructuring of the genre. Lee's career trajectory has taken him from art house to the mainstream. Beginning with his renowned trilogy, *Pushing Hands* (1992), *The Wedding Banquet* (1993), and *Eat Drink Man Woman* (1994), Lee has taken up more mainstream projects, including an adaptation of Jane Austen's *Sense and Sensibility* (1995), *The Ice Storm* (1997), the wonderful but underappreciated *Ride with the Devil* (1999), the intelligent superhero movie *Hulk* (2003), *Brokeback Mountain* (2005), and an adaptation of Eileen Chang's *Lust, Caution* (2007). He understands how audience appeal and box-office draw can not only keep a film production financially afloat but also help attract backers for future projects. To maintain major studio support, Lee appreciates that his films have to be accessible to Euro-American audiences, while maintaining cultural appeal to Chinese (and Asian) audiences, who are generally more familiar with and nostalgic about the conventions and styles of sword-fighting movies. Negotiating these apparently conflicting objectives has led Lee "to tell a story with a global sense" or, as executive producer and screenwriter James Schamus puts it, to make "an eastern movie for western audiences and in some ways a more western movie for eastern audiences."[14] Although Schamus is describing an end product arising out of a complex process of cultural and linguistic translation during the scriptwriting process, his comments are reflective of the politics of global audience appeal. More significantly, the film is emblematic of a hybrid form that embodies the cultural reconfigurations and tensions resulting from its place in a global capitalist economy. What this filmic form further reflects is a cultural anxiety of representation and identity, particularly about what it means to be Chinese in the context of the Asian "invasion" of Hollywood. In making an "eastern movie for western audiences" and a "western movie for eastern audiences," Lee finds himself in the unenviable position of being culturally stuck between a rock and a hard place. On the one hand, cultural essentialists and purists accuse him of making a *wuxia pian* that has diluted the genre's tradition and has propagated an inaccurate representation of China and Chinese culture. On the other, anti-Orientalist critics suggest that Lee was pandering to a Western desire for Oriental exotica and kung fu stereotypes of Asians.

Interviewed for a special "East Meets West" edition of *Newsweek*, Lee addresses the contention that *Crouching Tiger, Hidden Dragon* "is too

Hollywood," consequently betraying his cultural uneasiness. He frames his response by underscoring the film's place in Hollywood's system of production, which he claims limits the film's aesthetic possibilities:

> That was the only way to make this movie. Hollywood financed it, Hollywood was responsible for the esthetics. I use a lot of language that's not spoken in the Ching dynasty. Is that good or bad? Is it Westernization or modernization? . . . In some ways modernization *is* Westernization — that's the fact we hate to admit. Chinese people don't watch Chinese films anymore. They watch Western movies. In Taiwan, "Crouching Tiger" did so well because it was promoted as a big Hollywood movie.[15]

Lee's lack of any delusions about the parameters within which he could work may constitute the first step towards a tactical[16] reexamination of Hollywood's impact on Asian filmmaking and the complex systems of appropriation and exchange that take place between various cinemas. Even more noteworthy is Lee's willingness to admit that cultural syncretism and hybridization are an inevitable part of a globalized film industry. This view implicitly points to the problem with the cultural purist's position. Later in the interview, however, when asked if he could "make a purely Asian mainstream movie," Lee returned to the idea of Chineseness in a way that exposes his uneasiness about embracing the "Westernization" of movie-making:

> With "Crouching Tiger," for example, the subtext is very purely Chinese. But you have to use Freudian or Western techniques to dissect what I think is hidden in a repressed society — the sexual tension, the prohibited feelings. Otherwise you don't get that deep. Some people appreciate it; others don't because it twists the genre. It's not "Chinese." But to be more Chinese you have to be Westernized, in a sense. You've got to use that tool to dig in there and get at it.[17]

Digging into Lee's justification of his use of "Western" methodologies and techniques reveals his rhetorical formulation of them as means to a cultural end. His desire to displace the centrality of Chinese culture unwittingly and ironically serves to reify it instead.

Anti-Orientalist criticism has become a crucial part of film and cultural studies. Hence, any Asian movie that succeeds in Hollywood is inevitably scrutinized, and probably rightly so, for its possible complicity in the perpetuation of Orientalist discourses in the movie industry. Is Ang Lee guilty of such self-Orientalism in making *Crouching Tiger, Hidden Dragon* an "eastern movie for western audiences"? A closer look at the film's visual stylistics and cultural imagery — the panoramic sweeps of exotic landscapes and the fetishism of sexual repression and Oriental sensuality — provides significant evidence to support such a claim.[18] Consider, for instance, the camera's seductive gaze of Zhang Ziyi's face as strands of her black hair, blown by the gentle breeze, softly caress it, all captured in slow motion in the now-famous fight scene between Li Mu Bai (Chow Yun-fat) and Jen Yu (Zhang) on a bamboo treetop canopy. (Hollywood studios have been all too quick to capitalize on Zhang's exotic sensual mien, appearing, for instance, on posters and DVD covers of *Memoirs of a Geisha* with that same sultry, come-hither look worthy of an Asian Marilyn Monroe.) Although one cannot dismiss or sufficiently reiterate the value and importance of criticizing self-Orientalism in light of the ethics of representation, the continued belaboring of such a critique may ultimately deny the genre any possibility of presence given that the *wuxia pian* is by its very nature traditionally "ethnic" and exotic in its appeal; and the fact that the genre has often imbibed, consciously or unconsciously, these self-Orientalizing discourses through its history as a commercial art form. In other words, can one ever make a mainstream *wuxia pian* for a global market without falling into the trap of self-exoticism?

Again, my aim is not to mute anti-Orientalist criticism but to mobilize a different register of inquiry. For if the need to appeal to a Western gaze turns on self-Orientalism (as problematic and questionable as that is), what modes of ethnic "self-writing" does Lee engage in that might in some ways be salvageable as a productive critical enterprise? In the preface to the coffee-table book of the film, Lee theorizes that the making of *Crouching Tiger, Hidden Dragon* was the making of an imaginary China — an act of reimagining "China":

> The film is a kind of dream of China, a China that probably never existed, except in my boyhood fantasies in Taiwan. Of course, my childhood imagination was fired by the martial arts movies I grew up with and by the novels of romance and derring-do I read instead of doing my homework. That these two kinds of dreaming should come together now, in a film I was able to make in China, is a happy irony for me.[19]

In his seminal essay on psychoanalysis and cinema, "The Imaginary Signifier," Christian Metz likens the cinematic screen to "the mirror of childhood" in the Lacanian Imaginary. The audience, in gazing into that screen, enters into a perceptive state of identification like that of the mirror stage but with a difference — the cinematic image "is more involved on the flank of the symbolic, and hence of secondariness, than is the mirror of childhood."[20] This difference is of significance when we consider Lee's theory that the image of China constructed in *Crouching Tiger, Hidden Dragon* is an image drawn from his childhood imagination. This image is a mirror of secondariness in that it is implicated by the Symbolic, by the Law of the Father. But what is critical is the reverse pull of the image that Lee enacts as a mode of intervention. His conceptualization of the film as a dream of a China "that probably never existed" reflects a nostalgia not for a China of yesteryear but a hope for a better China, politically and culturally. Hence, his return to the innocence and idealism of childhood is achieved through the film's suturing of his boyhood daydreams, fantasies, myths, and legends from Chinese literature and his experiences of the *wuxia pian* and its fantastic images. But how can this suturing of elements that are clearly part of the Symbolic, produce a cinematic product that permits critical intervention and resistance? Like the literary mythopoeic nature of Maxine Hong Kingston's *The Woman Warrior*,[21] Lee uses traditional myths and cinematic conventions to create a fantasy space in which to play out alternative political and cultural concerns that ultimately question the very ideological basis of the superstructure — namely, the myths and conventions with which he starts.

A theme that has permeated Lee's Chinese-language films is the perennial cultural desire for individual freedom and rights versus a concern with social and communal responsibility. This problematic binary opposition is still being stereotypically framed as an East-versus-West issue. It is within this binary that Lee inserts filial piety, Chinese patriarchy, and the social and cultural authority of the father figure, as witnessed in his trilogy *Pushing Hands*, *The Wedding Banquet*, and *Eat Drink Man Woman*. Lee has confessed that these issues have a hold on him and on many other Chinese people:

> The essence of morality in the East is "filial piety": loyalty to your parents, to your family. It's where you come from. It's where your heritage comes from. Filial piety has been holding back Chinese society for many years. But now it's facing destruction because East is meeting West . . . So that's the common theme of my first three movies: society, family, the changing world, people not knowing what to do. I also think that the father is an extension of my idea of Chinese culture — which is patriotic society . . . In Asia [*Pushing Hands* is] . . . still their favorite film. They couldn't get over it. It has some emotional core not only of Chinese but also of Eastern society. It's filial piety inside you. It's been taught for thousands of years. It's the basic moral code and you cannot follow it. You feel total guilt because you cannot fulfil it. You become a Westerner and you betray your parents. Something you feel unable to deal with: total guilt.[22]

Lee turns patriarchal moral traditions into a productive guilt, which enables him to explore the clichéd nature of these issues in creative and complex ways.

In *Crouching Tiger, Hidden Dragon, jianghu*, or the ancient martial arts world, constitutes the habitus[23] where the demands of social and communal responsibility are located. To inhabit this world, the *wuxia*, or martial arts hero or heroine, must abide by its honor code of spoken and unspoken rules. (It is in the context of *jianghu* and its mythos that the *wuxia pian* was capable of functioning as a popular ideological tool for cultural indoctrination, particularly during the height of its popularity in the 1960s and 1970s.) The oppressive nature of the disciplinary machine that is *jianghu* disappears into the spectacularity, the romance, and the epic scope of martial arts displays, the heroic duels to the death, and the freewheeling life of the *wuxia*. Smitten by this idealization of the *wuxia* lifestyle, Jen Yu tells Yu Shu Lien (Michelle Yeoh) near the beginning of the film that she envies her freedom and that of Li Mu Bai: "I wish I were like the heroes in the books I read. Like you and Li Mu Bai. I guess I am happy to be marrying. But to be free to live my own life, to choose whom I love . . . That is true happiness."[24] The more worldly-wise Shu Lien then narrates the story of her love for Mu Bai and the honor code that prevents them from consummating their love. She offers the following reason to Jen Yu in an earlier scene: "Fighters have rules too: friendship, trust, integrity . . . Without rules, we wouldn't survive long." In contrast, Jen Yu's disregard for the code buys her the chance to experience unbridled passion with Dark Cloud Lo (Chang Chen) in the Mongolian desert. With Mu Bai's death comes Shu Lien's regret; her final advice to Jen Yu is a message of self-knowledge and integrity: "Promise me one thing, whatever path you take in this life . . . be true to yourself." In explaining the title of the film, Lee captures the essence of this conflict:

> The true meaning of the film lies with the "Hidden Dragon." *Crouching Tiger, Hidden Dragon* is a story about passions, emotions, desires — the dragons hidden inside all of us . . . So as Li Mu Bai and Shu Lien pursue Jen, they are chasing their own dragons. Jen's youth and energy remind them of the romance and freedom that neither of them has experienced. Having chosen a life of duty, Li Mu Bai and Shu Lien had to suppress their passions and desires, and, most of all, their love for each other. It is always close to the surface, but if they gave in to their true feelings, they would be abandoning the code of honor that shaped their lives.[25]

One could easily deconstruct the binary logic of the social responsibility versus personal freedom opposition, but doing so does not nullify the very real material impact this logic has on Chinese societies and communities and, most of all, on individual lives. Lee confronts this logic in his Chinese films by shuttling between its poles as a way of negotiating an illusive middle ground. In *Pushing Hands*, the protagonist, Alex (Bo Z. Wang), finds himself caught between honoring his tai chi-master father (also a signifier for Chinese tradition and culture) by caring for him in his old age, and fulfilling the cultural needs of his Anglo-American wife for personal space. Wai Tung (Winston Chao), the gay son in *The Wedding Banquet*, arrives at an awkward compromise by setting up an unconventional family unit in order to appease his parents' desire for a grandchild. This confused awkwardness persists in *Eat Drink Man Woman*, in which the daughters find themselves perplexed by their father's new romantic adventures as they struggle to calibrate a response that would satisfy society's expectation of filial piety. In *Crouching Tiger, Hidden Dragon*, Jen Yu likewise engages in cultural calibration and shuttling, as evident in her ambivalent actions and responses: she steals the Green Destiny sword, returns it, and then steals it again; her relationship to Shu Lien shifts between that of sworn enemy and that of sworn sister; and her affair with Lo is consecutively marked by intimacy and distance as Jen battles with her own desires and her need for social respectability and acceptance. Clearly, Jen's behavior reflects her contradictory need to resist Chinese patriarchy and to submit to its social discipline at the same time.

It is important also at this point to consider briefly the significance of the ethnic landscape of Lee's China. The linear narrative of *Crouching Tiger, Hidden Dragon* is punctuated by Jen's sumptuous flashbacks of her illicit liaison with the much-feared outlaw Dark Cloud Lo. Just as the desert sequences fracture the main narrative, her passionate affair dislocates the social respectability of mainstream Chinese society of the time. The radical nature of her liaison lies not just in her transgression of socially acceptable sexual practices but also with *whom* she has these relations. As an outlawed bandit who robs from the rich and their caravans that pass through the deserts of Xinjiang, Lo represents the antithesis of Mu Bai and Shu Lien — the latter being distinguished heroes of *jianghu,* and Shu Lien the head of the security agency often hired by the rich to protect themselves and their wealth from criminals like Lo. Even more significantly, Lo belongs to a minority tribe in China, a point that Jen Yu foregrounds when she calls him a "barbarian." (The costume designs and the locations in China, such as the Gobi Desert,[26] possibly suggest Lo's Turkic roots.) Jen's desire for Lo eclipses this racialist gesture when she identifies with Lo's ethnic minority status by wearing the "tribal" clothing provided by Lo, signifying Jen's shift from embracing the respectability of mainstream Qing society to fully obeying the inner promptings of her heart. This imagistic gesture to China's racial minorities, within the film's minor love story subplot, further provides Ang Lee an additional means to rupture Chinese culture's insistent calls to obedience, submission, and conformity.

Woman Warriors Ascend: A Feminist Reading

Teaching *Crouching Tiger, Hidden Dragon* has generated vigorous in-class discussions of the film's feminist potential. What most of my students cite is the obvious centrality of the female characters and the part they play in precipitating the conflict and crises in the narrative. But the issue that is most contentious is determining the political efficacy of the film's modes of representation and narrative construction in its articulation of a feminist agenda. Or, as my students would more bluntly put it, is this or isn't this a feminist film? To answer this question with a yes or no oversimplifies the issue, for the fact that there is even a need for the question suggests a certain ambiguity in the text. This ambiguity attests to Lee's strategic configuration of the feminist elements in the film, hence allowing for multiple and alternative readings. This ambiguity is also a result of the overdetermined systems of film discourse, production, and consumption. It is therefore critical to flesh out the varied political valences that this ambiguity engenders.

The *wuxia pian* and subsequent kung fu spin-offs can be considered masculinist films. Often powered by heroic male characters, these films invest heavily in the ideological entrenchment of Chinese patriarchal power. Apart from the occasional intrusion of woman warriors and helpless damsels in distress, many of these movies center on male-dominated action sequences and the *wuxia* brotherhood via various modes of homosocial bonding.[27] The machismo of the genre's action sequences — the sheer power, speed, and spectacle of violence in the filmic imagery — further accentuates the masculinist inflections, albeit stereotypically. Hence, when Lee foregrounds the women as the driving force of the action and the narrative, *Crouching Tiger, Hidden Dragon* becomes a subversive moment in the gender history of the genre.[28] "The martial arts film is very masculine," reflects Lee, "but in the end our film finds its center in its women characters. It is the women who, in the end, are walking the path of the [Taoist] 'way.'"[29] One wonders, if the centering of the women and their control of the film's action are attempts to write in female agency as feminist empowerment; or can the reinscription of the women in "walking the path of the 'way'" be construed as their recommitment to the patriarchal order and its ideology? Ambiguity also characterizes readings of the action sequences, where almost every fight scene is dominated by women. Again, the question then is, do we read this as filmic female empowerment and agency? Or should we place it within the context of the hierarchy of *jianghu* power, in which the female *wuxia* joins the lower ranks of petty swordsmen, who are ruled by their passions and aspire to become like the (male) master, epitomized by Li Mu Bai — the ultimate swordsman who achieves enlightenment in the form of a transcendental aloofness from the baser human instincts?

The women of *Crouching Tiger, Hidden Dragon* may also account for its popularity at the US box office, especially when the film is seen as another entry in Hollywood's spate of action-flick offerings with strong female protagonists. Lee's film "particularly impresses the American audience since it relates itself to the current Hollywood trend of feminizing kung fu in popular movies like *Charlie's Angels* (2000)," observes Kwai-Cheung Lo. "The feminization of martial arts within the U.S. context may inspire its female viewers . . . but it could also lessen the masculine nationalist dimension of the Hong Kong genre, thereby containing its threat to American masculinity. The fantasy of all-powerful women could therefore be merely a construction of the patriarchal discourse reasserting the male subjectivity."[30] Of course, this male cinematic gaze[31] on domineering Asian women, in the guise of Oriental exotica and erotica, fetishizes and objectifies Asian femininity for the white, heterosexual male's visual pleasure. The figure of the powerful and fierce fighting woman can also become a variation of the dragon lady stereotype.[32]

The three central female characters in *Crouching Tiger, Hidden Dragon* are Shu Lien, Jade Fox, and Jen Yu. Shu Lien, as the good "hero," functions as the mouthpiece of the patriarchal establishment; she articulates the ideology of *jianghu* and seeks to interpellate Jen Yu into that mainstream. Shu Lien's saving grace is her eventual realization that she has to be true to her own heart, a lesson she shares with Jen Yu in the final scenes of the movie. In this sense, Shu Lien is a less interesting character to analyze than her villainous counterparts, Jade Fox and Jen Yu.

Jade Fox is a slightly more conventional villain than Jen, in that she represents the traditional femme fatale turned disgruntled witch, who is seething with resentment against the establishment. However, Jade Fox offers a twist on this character type in that her "villainy" arises not out of pure evil (as it does in many of the genre's archetypes) but out of her marginalization and exploitation within the male-centered *jianghu*. Jade Fox's sexual tryst with Li Mu Bai's master does not end in her receiving the training manual and instruction that she covets but in her killing Mu Bai's master.

Li Mu Bai : Wudan should have gotten rid of you long ago. It's been a long time, Jade Fox! You don't remember me . . . But you should remember my master. You infiltrated Wudan while I was away. You stole our secret manual and poisoned our master! Now it's time for you to pay!

Jade Fox: Your master underestimated us women. Sure, he'd sleep with me, but he would never teach me. He deserved to die by a woman's hand!

Although the film's plotline involving Jade Fox eventually conforms to the genre's narrative conventions (the "good" Li Mu Bai triumphs over his "evil" nemesis, Jade Fox, and avenges the death of his master), her presence disturbs the essentialist moral categories that these conventions depend on and usurps the moral authority of Chinese patriarchal traditions that legitimize the masculinist social structures of *jianghu*. As an extra-textual note, it was a casting coup on Lee's part to have the 1960s doyen of the *wuxia pian,* Cheng Pei Pei, who appeared in King Hu's *Come Drink with Me* (1966) and Chang Cheh's *The Golden Swallow* (1968), play Jade Fox. This decision added a delicious intertextual and intergenerational gloss that accentuates the subversive nature of Jade Fox as a character in the reemergence of the *wuxia pian* in the new millennium.

Jen Yu provides an extension and a reconfiguration of the Jade Fox character type. Although their character trajectories parallel each other up to a certain point, Jen Yu deviates from this pattern by not surrendering to the dark side as Jade Fox does. The battle between Jade Fox and Li Mu Bai for Jen Yu's soul, so to speak, is a morality tale that problematically predicates the gender divide. But in allowing the young Jen Yu to occupy this middle space, where she has to make decisions that will radically transform her life, Lee throws into relief the ways and means of patriarchal interpellation and cooptation.

The subordination and oppression of women in nineteenth-century China is represented by Jen Yu's fantasy and desire for a life of freedom as a *jianghu* swordswoman, a life that circumscribes the constraints of arranged marriages. Even if she has misread the "freedom" that membership into *jianghu* supposedly brings to women, Jen appears to grasp the relationship between gender and power, and its symbolic manifestations — she steals the Green Destiny sword, a phallic symbol of *jianghu* authority, in the belief that it will mysteriously garner the freedom she seeks. The mystification of the phallic power of the sword is further reified when Shu Lien protectively exclaims to Jen Yu, "Don't touch it! That's Li Mu Bai's sword . . . Without the Green Destiny, you are nothing." The two women then enter into a battle to the death for the possession of the sword, in a classic playing out of that Freudian moment.

The idea of possessing the sword/phallus leads Jen Yu into a performance of gender that again plays with the genre's convention of the female swordswoman in drag. While this scenario of the female warrior traversing *jianghu* in male guise is true to form in the *wuxia pian* tradition, Lee offers instead a campy parody of gendered posturing and performativity as a form of subversion. In the teahouse fight scene, a typical aspect of *wuxia pian* mise-en-scène, Jen Yu encounters an ugly mob of roguish swordsmen who constitute a veritable catalog of *wuxia* character types. With names like Iron Eagle Sung, Flying Cougar Li Yun, Shining Phoenix Mountain Gou, these caricatures not only up the camp ante but also exemplify a form of hyper-masculine performativity that typifies the masculinist *wuxia pian*. Not to be outdone by this performance and posturing of masculinity, Jen kicks butt, literally, with the flourish of a whirling dervish, mocking the men's pompous pretentiousness while sending them reeling out of the teahouse. But part of the ingenuity of Jen's spectacular performance as swordswoman is her ability to destabilize the gendered seamlessness by proclaiming at the height of the fight scene, "I am the Invincible Sword Goddess!" This re-gendering appellative, which she bestows on herself in the scene's pivotal moment, is an instance where drag is, as Judith Butler puts it, "subversive to the extent that it reflects on the imitative structure by which hegemonic gender is itself produced."[33]

Zhang Ziyi: "I am the Invincible Sword Goddess!"

The fetishism surrounding Li Mu Bai's Green Destiny sword constitutes the link between its owner and Jen Yu. In desiring the sword, the latter also desires the social and political power that Li Mu Bai holds. The theft of the sword draws the two together into a relationship that shifts uneasily between sexual attraction and tutelage and that mimics Jade Fox's liaison with Mu Bai's master. But sexual attraction and the master-pupil dynamic are not exactly poles apart, in that they intersect, especially on the question of domination and power. Hence, Mu Bai's sexual attraction to Jen Yu gets framed in terms of his desire to take her as a disciple (against Wudan's male-only rule). "She needs direction . . . and training," Mu Bai tells a wary and almost jealous Shu Lien, confirming her suspicions that Jen Yu would "intrigue" him.

Discipleship in the martial arts world involves the total submission of student to master. This is the rite of passage into that world where a distinct stratification of positions of power is obsessively adhered to. The goal of this hierarchy is, in part, to shore up Chinese patriarchal strength. Jen's continued resistance to Mu Bai's efforts to subject her to this disciplining tutelage punctures the moral legitimacy of his claims and reveals the erotic conflicts bubbling beneath Mu Bai's upright veneer. Ang Lee has constructed two intricately artful and stylish scenes to convey these tensions, the first of which is the bamboo treetop fight sequence, a mise-en-scène that alludes to King Hu's *Touch of Zen* (1969).[34] Perched high on top of the trees, Mu Bai and Jen Yu effortlessly float and sway with the wind, conveying, as I have noted earlier, a fluid sensuality. Close-ups of Jen's face reveal her intoxication with the ecstasy of the moment. Mu Bai's cool and masterful countenance expresses his confidence in winning her over, in taking complete control.[35] (The coolness that Chow Yun-fat has perfected in his screen roles works wonderfully here, in that it conveys the condescending attitude which Mu Bai has towards Jen Yu: Mu Bai chooses always to fight Jen with some form of handicap, be it with one hand behind his back, his sword sheathed, or using a stick instead of a sword.) The body positions of the two figures on the treetops are also pregnant with erotic symbolism. Mu Bai at one point bends forward and hovers over Jen, who falls backward into a lying position so that their bodies almost but never quite touch. Sheng-mei Ma's dizzyingly wonderful exegesis of bamboo symbolism in the film correlates for me the sexual charge in this scene: "Bamboo bends and is soft at one moment, then straightens and erects itself the next. The drama of submission unfolds as a power play, the hypnotic eroticism written on Jen's youthful and almost translucent face as it flows across in slow motion."[36] This scene prepares the audience for the final erotic confrontation between Mu Bai and Jen Yu. Having been drugged and dragged into a cave by Jade Fox, Jen awakens to find herself face to face with Mu Bai. Drenched in rainwater, she suggestively pulls back her outer garment to

Zhang Ziyi and Chow Yun-fat's erotic fight sequence

bare her breasts through her wet, hence see-through, blouse. In her drugged state, Jen points the phallic Green Destiny sword at Mu Bai and utters the most erotic line in the movie, "Is it me or the sword you want?" The lowering of psychological inhibitions has enabled Jen Yu to speak more truth in this single question than what Mu Bai would ever have had the courage to face in his unquestioning ideological subscription to *jianghu*'s master-student conventions.

As a final assessment of Jen Yu's effectiveness as a feminist character, one needs to pose a troubling question: how do we account for Jen Yu's apparent cooptation into Chinese patriarchal hegemony when she reflects regret for her actions and hurries off to obtain an antidote to save Li Mu Bai's life? One could conceivably read this as the success of patriarchy disciplining Jen Yu to acknowledge the folly of her ways and to reinsert herself into her rightful place as a woman in Chinese society's hierarchy of power. Li Mu Bai's death may then be read as a "noble" sacrifice to bring Jen Yu back to the fold; for even in death, the patriarch maintains his legitimacy and moral authority. Obversely, one could view the notion of "responsibility" here as just an ideological tool of patriarchal hegemony (which it often can be). Lee may be saying that Jen Yu regrets that she has hurt individuals by her actions but that this regret need not be at the expense of her greater quest for personal freedom. I prefer a more ironic take to the textual play that Lee engages in: the film unsatisfactorily retreats to the genre's conventional "good" triumphing over "evil," where all is (almost) restored in the world of *jianghu*: this imperfectly sutured ending, however, no longer presents the same pleasure when its ideological seamlessness, which has been ripped earlier through Jen Yu's "transgressions," now betrays the contradictions and injustices inherent in *jianghu*'s system of gender oppression and conformity.

It is also important to link our evaluation of Jen Yu to the final "suicide" scene, in which she leaps off the mountain of Wudan. Although this scene lends itself to the conservative interpretation that the suicide depicts the dire consequence of Jen Yu's unruly actions (that is, suicide as punishment), I sense instead that Ang Lee has lifted a page from the American fin-de-siècle novel *The Awakening* by Kate Chopin.[37] Chopin's heroine, Edna, walks into the sea in the final scene of the novel, a gesture that has invariably been construed by literary critics either as a sign of cowardly surrender or as a powerful feminist existential statement denouncing the impossibility of existence in a society where patriarchy assumes complete control. Likewise, in jumping off the mountain despite her reunion with Lo, Jen demonstrates a realization that her relationship with Lo cannot be structured in any way but in accordance with society's (and hence patriarchy's) expectations of gendered practices and norms — Lo wants to "make . . . [his] mark on the world" and to "earn . . . [her] parent's respect." Marriage to Lo, in spite of her love for him, means Jen's giving up the personal freedom that she has been struggling to achieve. My students have tended to resist this rather pessimistic reading, with one of them even ingeniously suggesting that Jen Yu's leap is a catapult to freedom and escape and that she might indeed be alive and well, considering that she has displayed such expertise in the art of *qinggong* (literally "light skill," or the ability to defy gravity, jump over buildings, and leap to and from great heights)[38] — the shots of Jen Yu seemingly floating upwards (as one would see in video sequences of skydivers freefalling) instead of plunging downwards appear to justify this interpretation. Such a view unites this scene with the narrative's fulfillment of Lo's story of hope, whereby God grants a young man his wish when he jumps off a mountain and floats off into eternity unharmed. This interpretation turns on a politics of hope, a possibility that the ambiguity of Lee's filmic imagery permits. Stephen Teo believes this "ambiguous ending . . . plays to the Western sensibility of an art house movie rather than to the Chinese sense of a satisfying action movie finale."[39] True as that might be, contemporary Hollywood cinema has also sufficiently cultivated audience expectations of suicide finales as glorious anti-establishment statements of resistance — the classic freeze frames capturing the eponymous protagonists in *Butch Cassidy and the Sundance Kid* exiting in a bullet-showered blaze of glory, and *Thelma and Louise*'s 1966 Thunderbird convertible flying off the Grand Canyon cliff into temporal suspension, cinematically immortalize the desire for individual freedom against society's oppressive constraints.[40]

The discussion of the ambiguity of the final scene of *Crouching Tiger, Hidden Dragon* brings me full circle to my opening question about the ambiguity of the film's feminist possibilities. I think the semiotic and narrative richness of the film sufficiently foregrounds a feminist critique that complicates this issue on the basis of Chinese culture and the ideological foundation of the *wuxia pian*. In this way, the feminist elements of the movie tie up with Lee's reimagining of China. By depicting the plight of Chinese women, Lee also accentuates and problematizes Chinese patriarchy as a sign of the oppressive nature of Chinese cultural centrism and traditionalism.[41] However, the ambiguities that surface in the filmic text, which may allow Lee to articulate his own complex and often ambivalent sense of obligation and engagement with a return to a paternal figuration of Chinese culture, may ultimately blunt the critiques that I see the film offering. Of course, one must also not dismiss the fact that Lee, as a renowned filmmaker, had to keep as a high priority, his desire to make a film with wide audience appeal. So, in a way, Lee's ambiguous configurations of a feminist politics appeal both to politically conservative and liberal audiences across the East-West divide, depending on how one wishes to read the moments of ambiguity in the film. I am not accusing Lee of "political correctness" (the way conservatives have used the expression) or exonerating him of political accountability. Rather, my purpose here is to reflect on the complex and overdetermined factors and systems that made it possible for this new breed of Chinese sword-fighting films to be successful in a transnational cinematic framework.

Nationalist "Heroics" and the Politics of Ambiguity: Zhang Yimou's Hero and House of Flying Daggers

Crouching Tiger, Hidden Dragon demonstrates how a filmmaker with art-house sensibilities like Ang Lee can take on this popular genre to both critical acclaim and box-office success. Hence, close on the heels of Lee's film come Zhang Yimou's twin *wuxia* epics *Hero* and *House of Flying Daggers*. While acknowledging a certain debt to *Crouching Tiger, Hidden Dragon*'s generation of "unprecedented international interest in Chinese films and in martial arts," Zhang, in an interview with *Time* magazine for a special feature on *Hero*, takes particular pains to distinguish his own attempts on the genre by noting how "everyone's imagination is different" and how "each director has his own goals, his own aesthetic and dramatic aspirations."[42] Zhang's personal background, his cultural and national allegiances, and his career trajectory[43] sufficiently inform this celebrated Fifth Generation Chinese auteur's conceptions of the *wuxia pian*, enough to make *Hero* and *House of Flying Daggers* distinctive though uneven entries in the recent evolution of the genre.

But, not unlike Lee, Zhang's experiments with this popular classic Chinese cinematic form are also fraught with cultural anxieties. Zhang confesses, "I'm a huge fan of martial-arts cinema. I can't get enough of the stuff. I've been that way since I was a kid. I'm completely in agreement with something Lee once said on the subject: 'Every male director's dream is to make a martial-arts flick.' It's been my dream since I was little."[44] As genuine as this fanboy enthusiasm may be, Zhang's embrace of this populist genre is couched in terms of an indulgence in a guilty pleasure. Though this admission betrays his anxiety at helming a major action movie after fifteen years of working on mostly small independent art films,[45] it also signals his desire to gain popular acceptance after years of his films being rejected by the Chinese government and his being accused of pandering only to festival audiences in the West.[46] Zhang belongs to the fifth graduating class of the Beijing Film Academy, which includes luminaries such as Chen Kaige, Zhang Junzhao, and Tian

Zhuangzhuang. As Mary Farquhar nicely puts it, "Their films dare to be different and dare to deconstruct the China they know."[47] The cinematic depictions of Zhang's China in *Judou* (1990) and *Raise the Red Lantern* (1991) so disturbed the Chinese censors and the Chinese government that the films were banned from display in their native country when they were first released.[48] Despite these setbacks, Zhang still hopes to be accepted by his country: "When I'm making a film I'm thinking from the perspective of what's in a Chinese person's mind, what does the audience see, what do they make of it."[49] At the same time, he aspires "to do a film for the whole world": "As a director, I would feel happier if my films can get worldwide appreciation."[50] With *Hero* and *House of Flying Daggers*, Zhang's time in the glare of the mainstream popular spotlight has arrived. With China's then-Prime Minister Jiang Zemin providing logistical support through the People's Liberation Army during the film's production,[51] *Hero* received its grand premiere in December 2002, at Beijing's Great Hall of the People,[52] which is an achievement, considering his reputation as the once rebellious *enfant terrible* of Chinese cinema. Zhang's earlier agreement to make changes to *Happy Times* (2000) under the Chinese Film Bureau's suggestion, his video production efforts for China's bid to host the Olympics, and his Forbidden City staging of Puccini's opera *Turandot* seem to indicate a change of heart, which certainly did not hurt *Hero*'s reception in China.[53] With the blessings of the Chinese government, *Hero* went on to win an Academy Award nomination for best foreign-language film in 2002 and *House of Flying Daggers* for cinematography in 2004. Jenny Kwok Wah Lau correctly identifies "the coming of *Hero*" as "the final institutionalization of a new era in Chinese filmmaking, one that single-mindedly pushes for market success," with slickly produced Hollywood-style films that she calls "Chinese cultured blockbuster [s],"[54] and with Zhang patriotically leading the fore.

Zhang's strivings for global recognition through *Hero* — approval from the Chinese government for its apparent cultural and political message, and acclaim from Western film critics for its spectacular aesthetics — have courted its share of controversy in terms of the political implications of the film's philosophical ruminations on heroism and the Chinese cultural understanding of it, especially in the context of the 1989 Tiananmen massacre, the return of Hong Kong to the PRC, Taiwan's nationalist separatist intents, and the increasing national and cultural chauvinism and xenophobia in a post-September 11 world order.[55] In my analysis of the film that follows, I argue that *Hero* is an anxious and strategically ambiguous text in its attempt at accomplishing multiple levels of audience appeal, a text that unfortunately deconstructs itself ideologically in its overt desire to please. I follow this reading with a short examination of *Hero*'s reception in the United States, and a reflection on why middle America has been so quick in its embrace of the film. A brief discussion of the rather textually light follow-up, *House of Flying Daggers,* forms an interpretive coda, construing the film as Zhang's weak cinematic response to the controversy that *Hero* provoked.

As in my earlier consideration of *Crouching Tiger, Hidden Dragon, Hero* rides on the cultural gravitas of the *wuxia pian* but ratchets it up a notch to a nationalist level. While most films of the genre occupy the mythic habitus of *jianghu,* with the occasional foray into or reference to Chinese history and politics, *Hero* diegetically faces head-on the Chinese individual's relationship and responsibility to national and cultural leadership. In the film's prologue, the audience is ushered into an almost mythic faraway historical past of "two thousand years ago . . . during the Warring States period" where "China was divided into seven kingdoms" fighting "for supremacy while the people suffered." Arising out these warring states is "the King of Qin" who was thought of as "the most ruthless in his effort to conquer the land and unify all under heaven . . . The annals of Chinese history are abound [sic] with tales of the assassins sent to kill the great King. This is one of the legends." This narrative setup of recounting a legend within the greater historical framework of the unification of China helps intensify the cultural and political weight of the film, turning it into a filmic historical rewriting of a pivotal moment in Chinese history for a contemporary audience. The legend of Nameless (Jet Li) attempting to assassinate the King of Qin (Chen Daoming), with help from his *jianghu* friends, occupies the narrative core of this *wuxia pian*. But in breaking off from its narrative specificity of being just *one* of many legends and by taking on allegorical overtones, the legend evolves into an über-cautionary tale of contemporary political and cultural significance. In this light, the characters' assumption of archetypal names instead of realistic ones seems to make sense: Nameless, Broken Sword (Tony Leung Chiu Wai), Flying Snow (Maggie Cheung), Moon (Zhang Ziyi), and Sky (Donnie Yen). A glorious pan shot of the Great Wall of China closes the film, with an accompanying epilogue describing, in classic textbook fashion, how the unification of China produced "the Qin Empire . . . the first dynasty of China" with "Qin Shihuang . . . the First Emperor." This historicism in the prologue and the epilogue strategically functions as bookends to the tale of Nameless, repeatedly impressing on the viewer the national and cultural significance of the values articulated in the film.

The title of the film obviously turns on the concept of heroism in order to make its cultural political message. As an ideological reference point, heroism is not an alien concept in the *wuxia* genre. When characters address themselves as *yingxiong haohan*, they invoke a value system of honor that draws on filial piety, respect for elders and fellow swordsmen, fighting with integrity and for justice, and the belief in righteous vengeance.[56] This *jianghu* heroism holds the pugilistic society in place and defines various human relations and social hierarchies. The masculinist and patriarchal valences of this value system I have touched on earlier; now I wish to focus on heroism as it touches on China as nation and China as cultural center.

Hero begins with the *wuxia pian*'s heroic concept of justice and righteous vengeance and then eclipses it with a cultural nationalist heroism. Nameless is a citizen of the Zhao Kingdom, whose family was killed by Qin soldiers. Out for revenge, he solicits the help of Sky and, later, Broken Sword and Flying Snow, to concoct an assassination plan that will get him within 10 paces of the King of Qin so that he can kill the latter with his special skill "Death within 10 Paces." Flying Snow is eager to assist him, though Broken Sword isn't. In an earlier attempt on the King's life, Flying Snow and Broken Sword had a chance to finish the job, but Broken Sword backed out at the last minute much to Flying Snow's utter dismay and disbelief. In order to convince Nameless to abandon his mission, Broken Sword offers this cryptic explanation:

> When we [Flying Snow and Broken Sword] first met . . . I was living a carefree life. She's the daughter of a Zhao general who died in battle against Qin. She inherited his sword. I knew she would avenge her father. I promised to help her. Calligraphy and swordplay share the same principles. We did calligraphy to inspire our swordplay and to heighten our powers. She knew I'd drifted since childhood, calling no place home. Once we'd killed the King, she said, she would take me to her home. There'd be no more swordsmen, only a man and a woman . . . The essence of calligraphy is from the soul. Swordsmanship is the same. Both aspire to truth and simplicity. Gradually I recognized a greater cause . . . Three years ago we had perfected our skills. Flying Snow insisted on going ahead. Together, we stormed the palace. She asked why I abandoned the mission. I told her the King must not be killed. That is what calligraphy taught me. I didn't kill the King. After that she refused to talk to me. Please abandon your plan . . . Allow me to convey my conviction, in three words. [*Broken Sword writes "All under heaven"*[57] *in the sand.*] These words express my mind. Please consider . . . The people have suffered years of warfare. Only the King of Qin can stop the chaos by uniting all under heaven.

Nameless paraphrases Broken Sword by saying that "one person's suffering is nothing compared to the suffering of many. The rivalry of Zhao and Qin is trivial compared to the greater cause."

As the epilogue notes, "Nameless was executed an assassin but buried a hero." The heroism here is founded on self-sacrifice for the nation and for Chinese culture. For without Nameless being the nameless hero who dies so that the King of Qin can live and go on to be the Yellow Emperor, we would not have, as the film implies, China as a unified nation and Chinese culture as we know it today. Zhang's film distinctly reflects his own cultural patriotism in this fashion (if one were to take this message without considering the film's purported ambiguities that critics have identified). But the notion of self-sacrifice for the greater good in the film's diegesis is only retrospectively possible and effective with a form of historical hindsight. For how is Broken Sword to know that unity is the best thing for China? How could he assume that the King of Qin is the one to accomplish this unity? Why would Nameless be willing to sacrifice his own life in the belief that the King of Qin will honor his request that there be "no more killing" and "peace for all men"? The cultural assumptions of this historicity that Zhang brings to the film in his definition of heroism involve certain risks that I want to address. One of the dangers is that it mythologizes the King of Qin into a kind of cultural a priori of historical determinism and, hence, discursively dissolves the violence and the complexities of political empowerment that inflect historical events, an understanding of which, ironically, the film is supposedly concerned with. In other words, historical and cultural place eclipses historical realities, even as the prologue tells us that "the King of Qin was the most ruthless in his effort to conquer the land and unify all under heaven."

Another risk that *Hero* faces is the fact that the concept of a self-sacrificing heroism can incur criticisms of complicity with Chinese authoritarianism. The heroism that Nameless displays is premised on the idea that the individual must always forego his or her own desires and rights in order to achieve social, cultural, and political unity — in other words, sacrificing the self for the greater good. Firstly, this logic suffers from the stereotypical cultural construction of an inflated sense of an Asian sociality.[58] Secondly, it risks criticism that Zhang has capitulated to the ideological pressures from the Chinese government to make a film that encourages a submissive citizenry even in the face of violent oppression, all in the name of Chinese cultural tradition and authority. Of course, it is too tempting to categorize *Hero* as either pro- or anti-government in a clear-cut fashion, a point I will deliberate later. But suffice to say here, Zhang probably calculated this risk knowing that while such criticism would be inevitable, bearing it outweighs the advantages; that the film's supposed ambiguity could allow the Chinese censors to read it one way while anti-government viewers could see it in another. Zhang, hence, gets to have his political cake and eat it at the same time.

Zhang also defended his film as one of pacifism, transcending the violence of the *wuxia* genre and the political violence of the unification of China: "In my story the goal is the negation of violence. The characters are motivated by their desire to end the war. For real martial-arts masters, true heroes, the heart is far more important than the sword."[59] This is probably *Hero*'s major contribution to the contemporary reconfigurations of the *wuxia pian* in that the shift from "justice" to "peace," as Jenny Kwok Wah Lau points out, "indeed subverts the genre."[60] My criticism of Zhang's approach is not that I disagree with pacifism but that I am critical of the film's conception of how this peace is to be achieved, especially what it implies for those who have to suffer and die for that peace. One of the key moments where this issue is addressed is in the discussion between the King and Nameless on the philosophical underpinnings of the calligraphic writing of the word "sword" (*jian*) that Broken Sword has produced for Nameless:

> *Nameless*: There are nineteen different ways to write it. I asked Broken Sword for a twentieth way. Both calligraphy and swordplay rely on one's strength and spirit. The twentieth style would reveal the essence of his swordsmanship.
> *King*: How odd that one character can be written in nineteen ways. It makes the written language impossible to comprehend. Once I've conquered the six Kingdoms and all the northern tribes, I will eradicate this problem by mandating one style of writing. Wouldn't that be ideal?
> *Nameless*: Your majesty won't stop at the six Kingdoms?
> *King*: The six Kingdoms are nothing! I will lead my army to conquer vast lands and establish a great empire.

Later, when Nameless is at the cusp of deciding whether to kill the King, his majesty has an epiphany after meditating on Broken Sword's scroll:

> *King*: It's just dawned on me! This scroll of Broken Sword's isn't about sword technique but about swordsmanship's ultimate ideal. Swordsmanship's first achievement is the unity of man and sword. Once this unity is attained, even a blade of grass can be a weapon. The second achievement is when the sword exists in one's heart, when absent from one's hand. One can strike an enemy at one hundred paces even with bare hands. Swordsmanship's ultimate achievement is the absence of the sword in both hand and heart. The swordsman is at peace with the world. He vows not to kill and to bring peace to mankind.
> *Nameless*: Your majesty, your visions have convinced me that you are committed to the highest ideal of ultimate swordsmanship. Therefore I cannot kill you.

Nameless' inexplicable trust in the King's philosophical reformation may have been misplaced, but it does highlight that peace, through the philosophical word, can be attained.

What is fascinating is that the calligraphic inscription of "sword" mutates into the semiotic signifier for the merging of word (discourse as peaceful intervention) and sword (war as violent intervention) — Broken Sword's calligraphy and swordsmanship, with calligraphy, or peace, winning over sword, or violence: the Chinese equivalent of the pen being mightier than the sword. Lau describes this genre-subverting moment as "a shift from 'wu' (skill of fighting) to 'wen' (skill of words),"[61] where *wen* triumphs over *wu*. But what I also argue is that Broken Sword's calligraphic depiction of "sword" ironically collapses the distinctions between peace and violence, and deconstructs the correlation between word and peace. In other words, the word (discourse) is as violent as the sword. Examine how the King's utopian desire to bring together the Babel-like polyglot of the various kingdoms and tribes into a unifying tongue has a violent and violating effect, both materially and culturally. Not only does he wish to conquer even more lands, but implicit in his desire to "eradicate this problem by mandating one style of writing" is a violation of both the linguistic and the cultural, a rooting out, as the English-translated word "eradicate" suggests, of a cultural menace. The King of Qin's use of the verb *fei,* meaning "to abolish," or more literally "to disable" in *wugong* (kung fu skill) terminology, connotes precisely the violence inflicted on one's opponent.

Finally, the violence of the word is locked into the violent *logos* of imperial pronouncement and the violence of maintaining power. In his discussion of the paradoxical relation between "constituting power" and "constituted power" in *Homo Sacer*, Giorgio Agamben argues that "if constituting power is, as the violence that posits law, certainly more noble than the violence that preserves it, constituting power still possesses no title that might legitimate something other than law-preserving violence and even maintains an ambiguous and ineradicable relation with constituted power."[62] The sovereign power of the King, in the attempt to call into being his imperial reign, has to see itself outside of that domain, the domain of established law, in order for it to have constitutive or creative power. The constituting call into existence of his empire is a violent one, but he is not held accountable for this violence, being outside of the law and culture (the constituted power), which he has violently constituted in the first place. But the violence of the King's constituting power is, as Agamben suggests, implicated in the violence of maintaining constituted power, the same violence we see when the legions of arrows plow into Nameless in the name of legality. The courtiers of the

King become the voice of the law that impresses upon the King to execute his would-be assassin: "He conspired to assassinate Your Majesty. Show no mercy! This is the law of Qin! To conquer all under Heaven, the law must be enforced. Set an example for the world!" The King, who constituted the law, is hence being supposedly constrained by the law unto violence. This paradoxical trap of sovereign power is also the rhetorical corner that the King chooses to step into when he gives his word to execute Nameless. Agamben's exposé of this paradox is intended to rupture its compulsory rhetoric, something the King could have done by pardoning Nameless in the name of peace and magnanimity. The King's failure to do so clearly is one of a number of ways Zhang's film offers ambiguity to allow for a means of hermeneutical escape from the cultural insistence of obedience to authority.

This notion of ambiguity permits, on one hand, Chinese cultural centrists and the Chinese government to celebrate the film as a paean to self-sacrifice for the good of society and country; while, on the other hand, allowing liberal critics to embrace the film as an ironic critique of blind submission to institutional power, hence further offering a criticism of Chinese authoritarianism. Others offer interpretations that suggest the film's subtle modulations of these binary positions. Chris Berry and Mary Farquhar observe that the male heroes "choose sacrifice for a *principle* that promises an end to the people's suffering."[63] Their argument is plausible on the grounds that the notion of "all under heaven," or "*tianxia*," was historically constituted as what Stephen Teo terms as an "abstract nationalism," which has appeared in the films of Bruce Lee and other Hong Kong works, enabling a form of "cultural nationalism" that was de-linked from the PRC as nation-state.[64] Movie critic Charles Taylor, writing for *Salon.com*, also suggests that "the anti-'Hero' arguments don't take into account that the film ends not in a surge of patriotic feeling but on a pronounced mournful note of contingency and skepticism."[65] This reading is derived from Nameless' death even after he tells the King that there should be "no more killing." One should hold in suspicion the final honor being bestowed on Nameless as a nameless "hero." This is the violence, loss, and sacrifice demanded and yet eventually elided and forgotten, all in the name of Culture and Nation. Shelley Kraicer sums it up nicely by noting that "the director's careful balancing act — presenting films that seem to offer enough to win mainstream (and censor board) approval while maintaining their moral autonomy, richness, and provocative ambiguity vis-à-vis power — is always vulnerable to being (sometimes deliberately, by now automatically) misread by all sides."[66] This balancing act that engages a politics of ambiguity deserves critique: Zhang gets to proffer a filmic message of Chinese patriotism that is in complicity with Chinese authoritarianism's expectations of sacrifice and martyrdom, while maintaining sufficient authorial distance through textual ambiguity[67] in order not to lose the critical support of his advocates in the West, whom he has already won over with his earlier films.

Hero was released by Miramax Pictures in the United States, with the imprimatur of "Quentin Tarantino presents" as a marketing strategy. The film rides the surge of interest in America for the *wuxia pian*, beginning with *Crouching Tiger, Hidden Dragon*. It opened at number one in the box office when released in August 2004, after two years of delays on the part of Miramax.[68] But more than that, *Hero* also comes at a time when American patriotism is at its fever pitch. America has suffered from the trauma of the September 11 attacks and heroism is feted not only in the context of survival and sacrifice in the aftermath of the attacks, but also in terms of George W. Bush's Iraq war policy. Criticism against this policy was then political anathema, silencing even the Democrat side of the congressional aisle, a silence that is now finally being rectified with the intense unpopularity of the war. *Hero* arrived at an opportune moment when national heroism was beginning to be reexamined: What constitutes heroism? Why must heroism be construed in nationalist and patriotic terms? Is one nation's hero another's terrorist? Must heroism follow strictly the conditions of personal sacrifice of life and limb? Can one heroically question the nation's leaders and their policies and still be viewed as heroically patriotic? Directly or indirectly, *Hero* raises these questions and leaves them ambiguously unanswered. As Gary Wu observes, "Zhang Yimou's favorable portrayal of Qin Shihuang was suspected of being a paean to George W. Bush and American 'warmongers.' The central theme of the film, that conquering the world is the best way to stop violence in separate regions of the world, seems eerily resonant of the purported American neoconservative strategy of preemptive strikes."[69] Arguments advocating war for peace or for the need of a more empowered central government can easily be extracted from the film, while references to China's authoritarianism are conveniently contained within the film's "alien" historical context and, hence, dismissed. Audiences of varied political ilk will find something to identify with in Zhang's film, thereby attesting again to its disturbingly timely and politically problematic audience appeal.

To offer an illustration of how and why, as producer Bill Kong delightedly points out, "people in the Midwest, people in the south, not just the metropolitan areas" have gone to see the film,[70] I look at what American media film critics are saying in general and what motivates their evaluation of the film, thus identifying the kind of ideological pull *Hero* seems to assert at a time of high American patriotic fervor and a militarism spearheaded by conservative forces. Critics from the major American newspapers and popular magazines have been generally happy with the film. Responses range from exuberant praise to careful ambivalence, which frequently leans toward the positive, thus leaving those critical of the film's politics to a small minority. Roger Ebert of the *Chicago Sun-Times* reads the film as "a visual poem of extraordinary beauty" where "the sets, costumes and special effects are of astonishing beauty."[71] Mike Clark of *USA Today* lauds its "hypnotic visuals . . . despite [its] shortcomings in storytelling."[72] *New York Times'* Robert Mackey calls it "a spectacular film" from the "unlikely collaboration between two dazzling visual stylists: the Chinese director Zhang Yimou and the Australian cinematographer Christopher Doyle."[73] "Zhang Yimou may have dipped his cinematic pen in 'mere' genre," proclaims *Time* magazine's Richard Corliss, "but in doing so, he has inscribed a masterpiece."[74] Charles Taylor of *Salon.com* combines Mackey's and Corliss's praise by proclaiming the film as "one of the most ravishing spectacles the movies have given us," and arguing that "[t]he real shame of the political quibbling that has taken part in some quarters over 'Hero' is that those arguments have nothing to do with how enjoyable the film is. Above everything, it's a great adventure tale with both scenes of individual combat and battle scenes whose grandeur and geometric formations of troops recall Akira Kurosawa and the Stanley Kubrick of 'Spartacus.'"[75] Writing in *Christianity Today*, Jeffrey Overstreet overstates the film's value by criticizing Academy voters for not giving the film an Oscar. The fact that the film was held back from release in the United States he even attributes to "political bias." While he accurately posits the film's uneasy logic of promoting "the value of unification and peace," he concludes that "American viewers may be unsettled by the conclusion, as there seems to be no room for democracy in *Hero*'s paradigm. In a worldview that reveres the will of a conqueror over the will of a benevolent God, "peace" comes at a cost that will give no one true peace. That is why, in the end, *Hero* remains a conflicted, colorfully turbulent film."[76]

Almost all these critics celebrate *Hero*'s ostentatious visuality, chromatic ingenuity, and technical virtuosity, emphasizing aesthetic form over discursive content. The demand for journalistic "objectivity" may require them to circumvent political comment, and formal filmic analysis and appreciation provide the ideal strategies to achieve this goal. But unfortunately, some also use them to establish the primacy of aesthetic beauty over ideological content, making this the central means of evaluating filmic quality. In not confronting the film's politics, critics risk engaging in a formalist/New Critical approach to textuality, a form of literary criticism that has been debunked for its spurious claim to apolitical aestheticism.[77] Such a position also produces readings of *Hero* that ignore, in contradiction, the very political values of democracy and individual freedom that America supposedly holds dear. It additionally consigns representational China to a traditionalism that antiquates Chinese politics into an imagined infantile or immature modality, a state that America and other Western nations have gone beyond (if one is to buy into this narrative of political progress). What I am suggesting here is that embracing the film's aesthetics (which is not a problem in itself), without taking on its politics, is a way for moderate and even politically left critics (and possibly viewers) in America to enjoy the film at a time when the politics of patriotic loyalty are all the rage, thereby skirting the unpopular criticism of dangerous nationalisms both at home and around the world. And, finally, mainstream acceptance of *Hero* also reflects audience and critical identification with a film that grapples uneasily with the logic of a nationalist unity that advocates military intervention, while simultaneously promoting personal sacrifice and submission, all in the name of achieving a peace that seems perpetually out of reach. The conflicted *Hero* thus helps audiences psychically narrate, in an alternate universe that is ancient China, a desire for peace and restoration in a nation gripped by the fear of terrorism and its disruptive effects on personal security and safety.

Taking into consideration all the controversial responses *Hero* has drummed up, Zhang's immediate follow-up, *House of Flying Daggers,* feels like a troubled attempt, even if it were done unconsciously, to deflect the criticism directed at *Hero*. In radically scaling down the narrative's cultural and historical placement, this second *wuxia pian* removes the burdensome historical weight of the unification of China and strategically situates the plotline in a relatively obscure moment in 859 A.D. during the Tang Dynasty. The film's intimacy, again another unusual take on the genre, rests on the love triangle between only three characters, Mei (Zhang Ziyi) of the House of Flying Daggers, an anti-government "underground alliance," and two government captains Leo (Andy Lau) and Jin (Takeshi Kaneshiro). But this narrative simplicity is deceptive, as audiences are taken for a ride in its labyrinthine twist and turns: Leo turns out to be a Flying Daggers mole planted in the government forces he helps lead. Though he is deeply in love with Mei, he has to suppress his desire for her in order to carry out his missions. Instructed by the leader of the Flying Daggers to lure Leo's colleague Jin to the alliance's hideaway, Mei falls in love with him instead. The climax of the film features a battle scene between Leo and Jin. Leo injures Mei with his flying dagger so as to stop her from running away with Jin who, together with Mei, wishes "to be free . . . like the wind." Mei dies when she pulls out the dagger from her heart in an attempt to stop Leo from killing Jin.

By zeroing in on the intimate and very personal concerns of the three protagonists, *House of Flying Daggers* foregrounds the significance of individual freedom through romantic love. The characters have been burdened with the politics of their time and cannot be free like the wind, as desired by Jin and Mei. As one of the female leaders reminds Leo of his commitment to the House: "We're facing a battle that will decide the fate of the 'Flying Daggers.' The troops are closing in. This is not the time for love." Jin unconsciously echoes this even in his exhortation to Mei to flee with him: "A decisive battle is imminent. You and I are just pawns on a chessboard. Nobody cares if we live or die. Let's go away together and roam the world, as free as the wind." *House of Flying Daggers*, therefore, provides a political counterpoint to *Hero*. While the latter extols the virtues of personal sacrifice for the greater cause, the former pines for freedom and the expression of individuality and desire.[78] Again, the ending of *House of Flying Daggers*, like the ending of *Hero*, presents viewers with interpretive alternatives that are politically troubling. One can see the death of Mei and the suffering it inflicts on Jin and Leo as the impact that an oppressive politics can have on individual freedom. On the other hand, the ludicrously clumsy and unintentionally humorous fight scene at the end (which leaves audiences wishing a quick death for the characters in order for the film to come to a rapid conclusion[79]) almost suggests love's "pettiness" in the context of the more serious political concerns. It reiterates the raison d'être of the Broken Sword-Flying Snow romance in *Hero*'s narrative agenda, which is to accentuate the significance of the larger social, cultural, and political issues at hand. The official sanction of *House of Flying Daggers* as China's entry in competition for the Academy Award for best foreign-language film in 2004 comes as no surprise. The ambiguity of the ending and the supposedly apolitical nature of a *wuxia* romance allow Zhang's global audiences to embrace it as the kind of film that they want to see it to be.

Conclusion

The arrival of the *wuxia pian* in Hollywood and its renewed ascendancy in the global film market promises new configurations of the genre, as Lee's and Zhang's films demonstrate. Its popularity has also encouraged further interest in Chinese cinema as a whole, leading American and global audiences to experience other hybrid *wuxia*-period genres like Stanley Tong's *The Myth* (2005), Chen Kaige's *The Promise* (2005), Feng Xiaogang's *The Banquet* (2006), and Zhang Yimou's latest film *Curse of the Golden Flower* (2006). (This most recent film of Zhang's interestingly finds him returning to the old stomping grounds of *Judou* and *Raise the Red Lantern*, but elevating them into the settings of a Chinese imperial family.) Of course, the pressure is on these films to succeed in the global Chinese film market and to appeal to the finicky American moviegoer brought up on a diet of slick Hollywood-style productions. It is in this an uphill battle that we see the unfortunate compromises made to the production of these postmodern and transnational *wuxia pian*, resulting in the cultural politics of textual ambivalence and ambiguity, where a desire to please all can only risk the ultimate pleasing of none. Still, the box-office successes of *Crouching Tiger, Hidden Dragon*, *Hero*, and *House of Flying Daggers* idealistically command the hope that this revival can and will challenge the makers of future *wuxia* classics to step up to the plate and bring the genre to greater heights.

5

Enter the Triads:
American Cinema's New Racialized Criminal Other

As a genre category, police, detective, and crime films constitute a robust tradition in Hollywood's history.[1] Everyone loves a sordid tale of crime, where an Otherness of illegality (which may often be further associated with a racial, national, ideological, sexual, and/or cultural Otherness within the United States) is briefly entertained, before its eventual safe re-containment through the requisite triumph of the law in the classic Hollywood happy ending.[2] The box-office success of this formula must definitely have had an impact on other national traditions of popular cinema. Witness, for instance, the way audiences have lapped up tales of police intrigue and criminal violence in Hong Kong cinema. In fact, the careers of John Woo, Jackie Chan, Chow Yun-fat, and Andy Lau have been built on this significant genre. Of course, it is unfair to say that Hong Kong simply mimics Hollywood; these Hong Kong police and crime flicks reconfigure the narrative formula in order to allow specificities and idiosyncrasies of culture and filmic tradition to emerge. The Hong Kong versions of this genre, hence, take on a new life of their own.

This difference and edginess (as least through the eyes of American audiences) that Hong Kong cinema contributes to the genre's development in American cinema are particularly evident with the arrival in Hollywood, of Hong Kong's megastars and directors, in the late 1990s. While audiences are rediscovering the stylistic freshness of Hong Kong police and crime films, Hollywood executives are already examining ways of using this freshness to inject a new lease of life to the crime genre in its contemporary form, creating what David Desser has recently christened as "global noir."[3] For instance, John Woo's very stylized aesthetics made popular in his classic films *A Better Tomorrow* (1986), *The Killer* (1989), and *Hard Boiled* (1992) were translated, though with mixed success, into Hollywood films like *Broken Arrow* (1996), *Face/Off* (1997), and *Mission Impossible II* (2000), all directed by Woo himself. *The Replacement Killers* (1998), directed by Antoine Fuqua and executive produced by Woo, is also highly reminiscent from both a narrative and aesthetic standpoint of Woo's *The Killer*, both of which incidentally (or intentionally) feature Chow Yun-fat in the lead roles. Woo's influence on this genre is palpably clear in the way Hollywood continues to look East for more crossover or synergistic possibilities. Johnnie To's *Election* films on triad intrigue generated buzz among foreign-film viewing audiences (*Election* was screened at the Toronto Film Festival; and *Election II*, re-titled *Triad Election*, opened in New York City in 2007), while Andrew Lau and Alan Mak's impressive *Infernal Affairs* (2002) found recent incarnation in Martin Scorsese's *The Departed* (2006), which won a 2007 Academy Award for best picture and garnered Scorsese his long-awaited and much overdue Oscar for best director.

For purposes of historical accuracy, it is significant to note here that the presence of the triads in Hollywood is not new in this Hong Kong crossover. American films made in the 1910s to the 1930s reveal a tradition of constructing Chinatown as a space of criminal terror, with some films deploying triad and tong characters.[4] The Hong Kong entry into Hollywood's production line of police and crime films simply raises again the Chinese ethnic factor in the contemporary redrawing of the genre's configuration of racial Otherness within its narrative structure. A quick and partial survey of the films emerging from 1997 onwards is rather telling: *The Replacement Killers* (1998), *Lethal Weapon 4* (1998), *Rush Hour* (1998), *The Corruptor* (1999), *Romeo Must Die* (2000), *Rush Hour 2* (2001), *Cradle 2 the Grave* (2003), *Rush Hour 3* (2007), and *War* (2007) all involve either Chinese criminal elements or representations of triad and gangland violence. What provokes my readings of these representations of the triads here, as I have mentioned earlier in Chapter One, has less to do with a concern for authenticity than a need to understand the ideological, cultural, and filmic motivations fueling their presence. In other words, one should ask: what is their function in this group of films, and what cultural implications do they produce? Of course, at the same time, one cannot and must not ignore the historical and very real presence of triad and criminal elements in America's Chinatowns, considering the impact they have had on the structuring of cultural and quotidian experience in these ethnic urban spaces. Thus, I seek to trace briefly both the historical place of the triads in Chinese cultural consciousness, and the historical trajectory of Chinese criminality in American cinema, in order to locate these representations as part of a filmic continuum, as a way of accounting for their recent popularity. This historical and contextual framing, on the other hand, will also help foreground a sense of difference and/or development in the modes of representation from their historical precedence, thereby lending a contemporary specificity to the shifting politics of the genre, especially in light of contemporary Asian American cultural politics, and of the recent arrival of the major Hong Kong film industry players in Hollywood.

In examining Hollywood's latest fascination with triad and Chinese gangland criminality, I look first at the fourth installment of the *Lethal Weapon* series and its introduction of Chinese ethnicity into the film's "politically correct" interracial interplay to a mainstream cinematic gaze. Next, I study *The Corruptor*'s attempt to adopt a Chinese cultural sensibility by its addressing the stereotypical notions of Chinese corruptibility through cultural loyalties. Many of the films that feature triad, tong, and other Chinese gangs also often draw connections to African American culture and identity, an issue which the third segment of this chapter addresses. Finally, I close with a very brief reflection on the representations of violence in these films and its critical implications.

The Triad Connection

Louis Koo's chilling portrayal of Jimmy, the rising triad leader in Johnnie To's Hong Kong crime flick *Triad Election* (*Election II*), combines the refined and socially respectable businessman role with that of a vicious and inhumane triad persona. In an incredible Dr. Jekyll-and-Mr. Hyde transformation, where he demonstrates what it means to instill fear among triad members, a usually distinguished and seemingly benign Jimmy interrogates and tortures a disloyal subordinate by smashing him with a hammer and then tearing him up in an utterly gruesome scene of dismemberment. While this iconic cinematic moment indelibly reinforces the triad figure's association with criminal violence and cruelty, it also demonstrates how social/cultural respectability and corrupt criminality can reside, in an apparently contradictory and conflicting fashion, within the same figure. It is this complex and conflicted characterization of the triads that I wish to invoke in order to discuss briefly the problematic one-dimensional stereotyping of triad criminality, while addressing the cultural place that the triads occupy in Chinese national, political, and cultural histories.

In no way can one begin talking about the triads without asserting the undeniable criminal nature of modern triad culture and practices. This is a point I will continually reference throughout this segment of the chapter. But it is equally important to establish that the triads began in the seventeenth century in China as patriotic secret societies whose aims were to oppose the reigning Qing government in order to restore China to Ming rule.[5] In describing the famous Hung Society, Martin Booth observes how it "proclaimed its aims of moral reform, the furtherance of religious belief and practice, the encouragement of Chinese nationalism and coined the famous catchphrase which has echoed down the years of Triad history, *Fan q'ing — fuk ming*: 'Overthrow the Q'ing — restore the Ming.'"[6] These secret societies found political empathy and identification among the Chinese, who viewed the Qing rulers as foreign oppressors. Furthermore, they offered the people material assistance, such as the way the Heaven and Earth Society, the *Tiandi hui*, extended a hand to those who were persecuted and who suffered under the Manchus. The society became a *hui guan*, a self-help association, a cultural practice that has survived to the present, especially within the Chinese diaspora.[7] In other words, cultural links between these societies and the Chinese people were established prior to the emergence of modern China, links that will complicate the relationship between the ethnic Chinese and the now totally criminalized triads.

Triad criminality did not emerge *ex nihilo* after the fall of the Qing dynasty. The *Tiandi hui*, for instance, did dabble in criminal activity but not at the expense of its own members.[8] A look at early triad history reveals that political goals and criminal practices intermingled and intertwined, with the criminal slowly gaining in emphasis through time, especially when the post-Qing era eroded the triad's original patriotic raison d'être. With their deep involvement in the Opium trade and in the Boxer Rebellion,[9] the triads became a force to be reckoned with and major players in Chinese political history could not ignore them. Even Sun Yat-sen and Chiang Kai-shek were important triad members.[10] In a sense, the triads have helped to shape China's history, despite their criminal associations.

The triads also realized that for their operations to succeed they needed to go global. Riding on the coattails of the Chinese diaspora and global capitalism, the triads have their tentacles in both legitimate businesses and criminal enterprises. "Crime pays" is a cliché-reversal that works well for them: narcotics trade, protection rackets, prostitution, pornography, robbery, kidnapping, loan-sharking, gambling, counterfeit-goods trading, smuggling, and illegal immigration are all major contributors to their coffers.[11] The smuggling of illegal immigrants into the United States is an incredible source of revenue, with the yearly global income approximating US$3.5 billion.[12] Many of the Chinese who arrive on American shores find themselves corralled into a criminal underground network.[13] *Lethal Weapon 4* and *The Corruptor* illustrate this phenomenon cinematically. The impact of triad criminality cannot be sufficiently underscored, particularly on the ethnic Chinese communities and on their daily lives. Timothy Mo's novel *Sour Sweet*, for example, offers a literary portrait of precisely the anguish and suffering endured by the Chinese migrant communities in Britain, a depiction that could just as easily be transposed onto an American Chinatown.[14]

Part of the suffering of the Chinese immigrant community lies in the fact that the triads cannibalize their own kind, knowing precisely that these cultural links — or what is called in Chinese, *guanxi* — foster the ease of exploitation. Many among the Chinese are connected or indebted to the tongs, or Chinese "self-help societies," often run by the triads. The tongs offered succor during the difficult times when anti-Chinese racial sentiments translated into anti-Chinese legislation in the US.[15] *The Corruptor* presents audiences with a contemporary example of the ambivalence in which the Chinese community is mired when they struggle to disentangle the criminal aspects of the triads from their cultural and historical connections. The notions of cultural nationalism and indebtedness, hence, make Chow Yun-fat's Nick Chen a more understandable and sympathetic character, despite his "corruptibility." The issue ultimately is that while the Chinese seek to distance themselves from and condemn the violence that the triads have wreaked on American society, they also find themselves frustrated by the cultural holds that these secret societies have on them.

The depiction and characterization of triads in the media, of course, complicate an already complex cultural association between these criminal fraternities and the Chinese communities. Martin Booth accurately diagnoses the emergence of specific cultural stereotypes engendered by this association:

> Every outbreak of tong violence hit the national headlines and pulp magazines. Gory tales of Oriental mayhem captured and coloured the public imagination, reaching a climax in the Fu Manchu stories of Sax Rohmer. They did the Chinese community no good, showing them to be brutal, lawless and corrupt although, the tong fighters aside, the Chinese were the most law-abiding ethnic group in America. Caucasians generally avoided Chinatowns.[16]

Booth is right in drawing a discursive continuity between older representations of Oriental evil (Fu Manchu) and that of triads in contemporary media. Hollywood has rather conveniently resorted to the spectacular nature of triad violence to satiate cinema audiences' appetite for crime action and gore. As a result, in a metonymic fashion, the triads have become synonymous with the Chinese, creating in the latter another racial Other to demonize and to attribute blame for social ills. Therefore, there is a critical need to separate and distinguish the two; unfortunately, this separation could also lead to the possible reification of the good-Chinese-versus-bad-Chinese paradigm that risks the return of the "model minority" cultural politics — Booth's "the Chinese were the most law-abiding ethnic group in America" falls precisely into this particular trap. A critique of this paradigm I will engage next in my analysis of Richard Donner's *Lethal Weapon 4*.

Lethal Weapon 4 and the Politically Correct Interracial Buddy Film

The Reagan-Bush decade predictably saw the muscle-bound figures of Conan the Barbarian, the Terminator, and Rambo storm the big screen. But it was also during this period of conservative masculine posturing on celluloid that we witness, in apparent counterpoint, the arrival of the "racially sensitive" buddy cop film. With the calls for more minority representation on both the big and small screens, black-white interracial pairings seemed to make political and financial sense to Hollywood studios. In calling "the biracial buddy film of the 1980s" an evolution of "the 'white male' buddy film," Ed Guerrero explains how "Hollywood put[s] the black filmic presence in the protective custody, so to speak, of a white lead or co-star and therefore in conformity with white sensibilities and expectations of what blacks, essentially, should be."[17] With the trend beginning with the Richard Pryor and Gene Wilder combination in *Silver Streak* (1976) and *Stir Crazy* (1980), the biracial buddy film exploded onto the scene with Eddie Murphy in films like *48 Hours* (1982), *Trading Places* (1983), and *Beverly Hills Cop II* (1987).[18] Murphy's convict and Nick Nolte's detective characters hit it off as strange but electrifying bedfellows, turning *48 Hours* into a big box-office smash.

On the heels of *48 Hours'* success came the television series *Miami Vice*, which introduced viewers at home to the detectives Sonny Crockett and Rico Tubbs, played by Don Johnson and Philip Michael Thomas respectively. Thomas is of African, Native American, and Irish descent. The fact that the series lasted for five seasons from 1984 to 1989 indicates how it struck a chord with American television audiences. The pairing enabled the possibilities for interracial television drama and humor in the context of an America dealing with racial discrimination and prejudice. It is in the midst of *Miami Vice's* success that the first installment of the *Lethal Weapon* movies emerged. Directed by Richard Donner, the first *Lethal Weapon* was released in 1987, starring Mel Gibson and Danny Glover. Their combination proved to be such a hit that the movie was turned into a franchise: *Lethal Weapon 2* (1989), *Lethal Weapon 3* (1992), and *Lethal Weapon 4* (1998) followed, with Donner at the helm of all the movies. These interracial buddy cop films clearly present

American viewers with the cinematic fantasy of a racially harmonious America that they want to see on screen. This cinematic imaginary has since sustained a string of different genre films featuring interracial buddies from the early 1990's right to the present: *Another 48 Hours* (1990), *White Men Can't Jump* (1992), *Pulp Fiction* (1994), *Men in Black* (1997), *Men in Black II* (2002), and, of course, the filmic remake of *Miami Vice* (2006), featuring Colin Farrell, Jamie Foxx, and the now seemingly ubiquitous Gong Li.

Part of the success of the *Lethal Weapon* film series lies in the chemistry between the lead characters Martin Riggs (Mel Gibson) and Roger Murtaugh (Danny Glover). Their relationship is built on differences of age, class, and race; the films focus on the tensions between the two characters and how, in the midst of battling crime and grappling with personal demons and relationships, they come to find common ground for bonding. While the comedy and action of the films are a major attraction, viewers also become invested in the changing lives of Riggs and Murtaugh: Riggs turns from being a young maniacal "lethal weapon" to become an older and more responsible character, thanks to the experience he has with work partner Murtaugh, and his attachment to his life partner Lorna Cole (Rene Russo) and their newborn child — Cole's character was introduced in the third installment, and she becomes pregnant and gives birth in the fourth. Murtaugh, on the other hand, learns to take more risks in life after being partnered with Riggs, while being forced to embrace a larger extended family — in *Lethal Weapon 4*, he discovers that his daughter is married to Detective Lee Butters (Chris Rock), whom he dislikes, and with whom she is also pregnant with child. In a sense, as characters, Riggs and Murtaugh inversely mirror each other. Their relationship with each other achieves a leveling effect: they attain a kind of commonality of experience and sensibility.

Thus, in the context of black-white race relations, the Riggs-Murtaugh partnership seems to demonstrate a state of progress in racial politics that appeals to mainstream white American audiences. The characters are not one-dimensional figures whose concerns are primarily or solely race and racism; they lead lives that are complex and conflicted, in other words "real" lives, thereby making the question of race an overdetermined one (to borrow the term from Louis Althusser, who borrowed it from Freud[19]). While I agree this reading of race relations in the United States is a significant one, it is equally disturbing that these mainstream Hollywood films, which are supposedly sensitive to the issue of race, in their attempt to reflect the complex social reality of racial lives, consciously or unconsciously risk the elision of *racism* itself in cinematic representation and discourse. This phenomenon is particularly so, for instance, when we see Roger Murtaugh and his family living upper-middle-class lives in contrast to Riggs' working-class background. I am not here suggesting that one returns African American representation to the housing projects or the "hood" for racial "authenticity," but rather I am critical of mainstream Hollywood cinema's tendency to displace the realities of racism with supposedly more "complex" depictions of race relations.[20] It is in this sense that I count the *Lethal Weapon* films to be problematic as "politically correct" interracial buddy cop films. In *Lethal Weapon 4*, the addition of the Chinese into the mix creates another complicating layer to the notion of race relations in this series.

Before I begin examining what the entry of the Chinese and the triads will do to the racial dynamics of the film, it is essential to pinpoint how I am using the phrase "politically correct" in the context of labeling *Lethal Weapon 4* a "politically correct" interracial buddy cop film. I come to the term in a rather troubled fashion because I am *not* using it the way political conservatives are currently using the term. "Political correctness" is invoked to categorize in a derogatory manner any supposed attempt to pander to liberal and/or radical political ideologies or trends. Hence, any expression of sensitivity, genuine or otherwise, to racial, gender, sexual, and class differences, for example, will be ridiculed for its political cowardice in acquiescence to the "oppressive" strategies of liberal "Nazis."[21] What conservative pundits have frequently accomplished in their anti-PC rhetoric is to use it as a means of redefining and celebrating their crude sexist, racist, and homophobic ideologies and practices as modes of political bravery and chutzpah. It is deeply unfortunate that much of this usage of "political correctness" has seeped into mainstream parlance, with many not realizing the ideological implications of its deployment. My brief detour here into the terrain of the culture wars is intended firstly to locate the phrase in its proper discursive context, and then secondly, to unpack the atypical way I am using it, so as to redeploy its reactionary rhetorical strategies as a means of undermining them, all through a critique of race relations in *Lethal Weapon 4*.

To describe the film as "racially sensitive" is to be too generous; therefore, I have chosen instead to risk being politically misunderstood by labeling it "politically correct." The good intentions on the part of the *Lethal Weapon* series to engage questions of race are unmistakable; my goal here is not to question their sincerity. Rather, I am more fascinated by what this "politically correct" approach to race relations in America hides.

As noted earlier, while it offers a more complex view of race relations, the *Lethal Weapon* series unwittingly circumvents the contemporary realities of white racism against African Americans. In *Lethal Weapon 4*, a new racial triangle develops with the entry of the Chinese, complicating the racial dynamics. This triangle of white-black-Chinese relations is enabled by the film's narrative progression from its three predecessors: Martin Riggs comes to the realization that he is getting too old for the rigors of police action when he decides that marriage to Lorna Cole may be the right thing for him, especially with the pending arrival of their baby; Roger Murtaugh *finally* gets to settle down to the idea of retirement and the notion of an extended family. These ideas of domestic peace are quickly shattered when Riggs and Murtaugh accidentally run into a ship full of illegal Chinese immigrants one evening on their night out fishing. Murtaugh's compassion for a group of these stowaways compels him to hide them in his home. However, this move leads to a violent encounter with the triad criminals running the illegal human smuggling racket. Murtaugh's house is torched by them, while Hong (Eddy Ko), Murtaugh's new-found friend, is brutally killed by Wah Sing Ku (Jet Li), the most deadly, and least communicative[22] triad leader. Murtaugh and Riggs thus embark on a hot trail to uncover a triad syndicate of illegal human smuggling, counterfeiting, and international political intrigue.

A number of aspects of the racial triangle deserve close analysis, the first of which is the way the Chinese are being made the new racial Other in the filmic America of the *Lethal Weapon* franchise. Portrayals of interracial buddy couplings on television and cinema in the 1980s have fostered a filmic culture where mainstream audiences are now accustomed to seeing white-black pairings (though one could convincingly argue that these pairings are but only token gestures in the larger scheme of Hollywood's prolific output). This interracial pairing in the *Lethal Weapon* films, hence, is "politically correct," from a politically leftist standpoint, in that it is tokenism that acts as a salve for a white American social conscience. Even more problematically, the "politically correct" relationship between Riggs and Murtaugh, thereby, dissolves any responsibility for the cinematic representational racism that might be directed at the Chinese, because the white responsibility for racism directed at African Americans has already been "addressed" in the film. The Riggs-Murtaugh connection becomes the narrative cover not only for the Orientalist stereotypes that emerge in the film's representations of the Chinese, but also for the incredibly overt stream of "chinky" jokes emanating from Martin Riggs — "flied lice," "enter the drag queen," and "speaky English," as peppered in Riggs' dialogue lines, are all not beneath him. In one scene, he taunts Jet Li's character by simultaneously referencing Bruce Lee and traditional Chinese male attire: "Hey Bruce, nice pajamas." My reading here could be construed as an overly sensitive reaction to racial jokes, particularly when this type of humor is so in character for Martin Riggs, the "lethal weapon" of the LAPD.[23] However, racial humor and its intent are clearly determined by context and tone. In the context of a "politically correct" film that boasts the ability to bring together black and white, the humor seems to reflect a selective racial sensitivity that unfortunately produces a new racial Other in the Chinese, in the form of triad criminals, upon which racist barbs can be aimed with impunity.

It would be incorrect, however, to say that the caricature of the Chinese in this instance is one-dimensionally negative in the figure of the triad criminal. The Othering process also splits the Chinese into an oppositional double: the good Chinese versus the bad Chinese. This doubling is clearly not unique to the cinematic depictions of the Chinese in America, but seems endemic to representations of US ethnic minorities in general. For example, in his discussion of the black gangster film, Mark Reid cautions critics to "transcend the narrative limitations of Manichaean constructions of 'good' and 'bad' blacks and describe the social construction and ideological function of particular types of black gangsters."[24] One cannot but take such good advice to heart even when looking at Manichaean configurations of Chinese characters in *Lethal Weapon 4*.

The good Chinese versus bad Chinese discourse allows the film to lay claim to a supposedly more "complex" representation of the ethnic Chinese, when in actuality it simply deploys two, as opposed to one, stereotype of them. When the Chinese character is good, like illegal immigrant Hong, he is good to a fault: Hong is gentle, soft-spoken, kind, and compassionate, almost passive, one could say. So pliant is his passivity that he is speedily and casually dispatched, by his Manichaean opposite Wah Sing Ku played by Jet Li, as if he were a lowly life form. As the bad Chinese, Jet Li's character, on the other hand, epitomizes the cruelty and ruthlessness one has come to expect of the triad criminal, replaying in contemporary guise the nefarious Fu Manchu caricature. Again, so evil is this character that he is willing to exploit and destroy his own kind: witness particularly the scene where Wah Sing Ku strangles to death the Chinese captain of the ship, after the latter has escaped apprehension despite being chased through Chinatown by Riggs. The extreme typology that the good and bad Chinese characters represent here serves a distinct narrative and ideological function. The bad Chinese's inhumanity and cruelty make him so irredeemable that the racist epithets Riggs hurls at him are not only deemed forgivable but even well-deserved. Audiences are then permitted to cheer on Riggs and Murtaugh as they violently finish him off in the rather bloody final fight sequence. In contrast, the death of the good Chinese, Hong, creates a masculine vacuum that Riggs and Murtaugh, in line with their parental roles within their own families, are now called upon to fill, hence, allowing them to assume a composite American patriarchal savior figure of the Chinese. Riggs' days as a wild young rogue are over, and he can now reassume his rightful role as white patriarch. (The ironic statement that these two Chinese deaths seem to suggest is that "an acceptable Chinese is a dead one.") Of course, together, these Manichaean opposites ultimately have a social disciplining effect: the good Chinese rhetorically reworks the "model minority" logic, while the bad Chinese acts as its foil.

Concluding my analysis of *Lethal Weapon 4* without commenting on the rather significant interracial connection established between Roger Murtaugh and the Chinese character Hong would be to do it critical injustice. This question of the Asian and black connection I will resurrect in detail in the penultimate segment of this chapter; for now, some scattered observations on the ideological place of the Murtaugh-Hong relationship need to be made. Murtaugh's chance encounter with Hong begins in the opening sections of the film, where Riggs and Murtaugh run into the ship that is smuggling Chinese immigrants into Los Angeles. After a vicious gun battle, the duo "rescues" these immigrants and hands them over to the police (and, implicitly, the immigration officers) for processing. These illegal immigrants from China have to suffer six weeks in a hellhole on the ship with little food and only one toilet, till they are sold by snakeheads "like slaves" as a means of paying off the $35,000 passage fee,[25] the audience is told. The white police officer who offers this information betrays a rather nonchalant attitude towards these Chinese immigrants, which in turn greatly disturbs Murtaugh, as the following dialogue exchange between them unveils:

> *Police Officer*: They'll claim asylum and say they're persecuted like everybody else. And we'll send them packing. Cost you and me a goddamn fortune.
> *Murtaugh*: What happened to "bring me your tired, your poor, your wretched masses, yearning to be free," huh?
> *Police Officer*: Now it reads "no vacancies."
> *Murtaugh*: I guess your parents are Native Americans?

Murtaugh's racial minority status enables him to empathize with the Chinese as he sees the parallel between the experiences of these illegal Chinese immigrants and that of the middle passage and slavery in African American history. By alluding to the tragic and violent oppression of Native Americans in US history, his sarcastic quip, in retort to the police officer's aggrandized sense of white racial entitlement, further draws out the relational and collaborative possibilities between American racial minority groups. In breaking the *letter* of the law by illegally taking in Hong and his family, Murtaugh affirms the *spirit* of the law, as he exasperatedly tells an oddly reticent and uninvolved Riggs: "Wait a friggin' minute! The way I see it: these are slave ships out there. And I'm freeing slaves! I'm freeing slaves! Like no one did for my ancestors, ok Riggs? This is my chance to do somethin' and do it right." This is a highly impressive political conjuncture that the film, through Murtaugh, has established. While the history of black slavery is significantly different both materially and ideologically from the kind of slavery we see in the case of the Chinese — the comparison here is not intended to diminish the greater severity and intensity of the former — the point of similarity converges on the exploitation of certain impoverished segments of humanity, through the global processes of capitalist development. While black slavery's genesis and progression lie in the exploitation of African humanity for the eventual rise of the industrial capitalist juggernaut that is the United States, the exploitation of the Chinese immigrant emerges out of a global capitalist demand for cheap human labor, in an age of flexible accumulation.[26] This point by no means exonerates the complicity of the triads in the way they ride these capitalist structures for their own greedy purposes, as Jet Li's Wah Sing Ku tells his father: "America has many laws, but written by men. Money can change everything."[27]

While the circularity of global capitalist exploitation may be far from Murtaugh's mind (and probably even further from the filmmaker's intent), the emotional current flowing from Murtaugh's empathy is an important one, especially when one views this filmic moment retrospectively from a post-September 11 perspective. Whatever Murtaugh's motivations may be, he sees how human and historical connections cannot but inform a personal ethics of social responsibility, a theme that is increasingly resonant for philosophers and critical theorists today. In invoking the notion of the "precarious life," Judith Butler critiques what she calls the "hierarchy of grief"[28] for human life:

> It would be difficult, if not impossible, to understand how humans suffer from oppression without seeing how this primary condition [of human vulnerability] is exploited and exploitable, thwarted and denied. The condition of primary vulnerability, of being given over to the touch of the other, even if there is no other there, and no support for our lives, signifies a primary helplessness and need, one to which any society must attend. Lives are supported and maintained differently, and there are radically different ways in which human physical vulnerability is distributed across the globe. Certain lives will be highly protected, and the abrogation of their claims to sanctity will be sufficient to mobilize the forces of war. Other lives will not find such fast and furious support and will not even qualify as "grievable."[29]

Slaves fall under lives not worth grieving for because they slide easily into the category of the exploitable in the human economy of capitalist utility. When Murtaugh draws up a relationship between black slavery and illegal Chinese immigration, he (un)wittingly develops two critical themes for us: firstly, all life is equally precarious; it deserves to be grieved for, and is, therefore, precious — a principle that goes against the racial hierarchies defining the nationalist politics that advocate anti-immigration in the United States. Illegal immigrants are abused, exploited, and killed daily, but because they occupy the liminal spaces between nations, they are often deemed not worth grieving for within the ideological boundaries of the nation and national identity. Secondly, Murtaugh's attempt "to do somethin' and do it right" evinces a cosmopolitical[30] ethics of responsibility: what one does in a specific point in time and space is not solitary and disconnected; instead, it forms a part of a complex global network of relationships of causes and consequences. This interconnectivity produces an ethics where a consciousness of one's actions and its consequences are greatly heightened.[31]

Admittedly, my interpretation of Murtaugh's desire to assist the Chinese is very much a contemporary and retroactive one. It is not my intention to imbue *Lethal Weapon 4* with a radical cultural politics that it does not possess. For, ultimately, the film's depiction of Murtaugh's sense of kinship to Hong, and its place in the film's narrative, return the audience to a more mainstream and politically less challenging perspective on minority race identities:

Hong: In America, my children have a chance to make a good life.
Murtaugh: We want the best for our children and our grandchildren.
Hong: You believe I'm a grandfather?

Murtaugh bonds with Hong and then gives him his watch as a memento. What is significant about this rather simple and touching scene is the way the bonding through children and grandchildren serves to inscribe and re-inscribe Hong and Murtaugh respectively into the greater logic of the American dream, hence displacing and diminishing the immediacy of their racially specific sufferings and oppressions. The final interpellation of Hong and Murtaugh into the American capitalist ideology of the good life rewards the film's "politically correct" sensibilities with a return to an idealized but naïve notion of a race-free America where minorities can successfully assimilate and disappear into the material comforts of middle-class anonymity.

The Corruptor: Triad Chinatown and Cultural Corruptibility

Directed by James Foley and executive produced by Terence Chang[32] and Oliver Stone, *The Corruptor* offers a tale of tong turf wars and police complicity set within the confines of New York City's Chinatown. I want to begin my analysis of the film by zeroing in on four brief and seemingly insignificant moments of geographical framing. The film opens with a shot of Chinatown streets with the twin towers of the World Trade Center distinctly in the background. Shots of the towers repeat themselves in later sequences, one during a police raid on whorehouses and another during a chase sequence in Chinatown's labyrinthine alleys. The film then closes with a final shot of the lower Manhattan skyline with the World Trade Center and the Statue of Liberty clearly in focus. Anyone who has ever visited New York City's Chinatown prior to September 11, 2001, will remember the visual ubiquity of the twin towers: at almost any point from the streets in and around the Chinatown and Little Italy areas, you could catch a glimpse of the towers looming on the skyline. Hence, it is not a surprise to find that urban crime films set in New York City, and shot prior to 9/11, like *The Corruptor*, would include the towers as part of their stylistic montage sequence to locate their narrative. Revisiting the film and viewing these scenes now cannot but create an eerie but sad sense of absence/presence; a sense of loss for these iconic buildings that are at once so familiar and yet so alien; and a sense of a continued filmic presence enabled by these scenes, which function as a sort of unconscious pop cultural archive. (My nostalgia is testament to New York City's status as a global city; and also, admittedly, to the global mobility afforded by my class position as an academic. I must further attribute this connection to my lifelong infatuation with this city of all cities.)

But indulgent nostalgia aside, this "archive" of four shots of the twin towers provides a significant filmic loop, repeatedly reinserting into the filmic eye images of these imposing architectural structures. Jacques Derrida, in an interview discussing the 9/11 attacks, reflects on the recurring filmic images of the twin towers playing in the media immediately after the planes smashed into them. He characterizes the almost incessant screening of these images as a "loop": "The loop is also meant to refer to the circular and narcissistic spectacularity of this painful elation, of this climax, terrified by the other and terrified to discover that there is something we are elated about seeing here, terrified to find ourselves allaying our terror by our voyeurism."[33] Of course, Derrida is theorizing about a specific traumatic moment in 9/11 and its very particular spectacularity that my discussion of *The Corruptor* is not meant to parallel or even compare with. What I wish to do instead is to appropriate the notion of the filmic loop and the Othering process that the twin towers on film coincidentally avails itself in both instances. The soaring phallic towers were a visual proclamation to the world of the capitalist might of the United States. Nestled in New York City's financial district, with Wall Street just a block or two away, the World Trade Center was the symbol of America's First World economic status. But its awe-inspiring presence also had an Othering effect, especially on the surrounding ethnic enclaves, as a reminder of the racial and class divides. The filmic repetition or "loop" of the twin towers in *The Corruptor*, therefore, works not only to frame spatially the location of Chinatown in lower Manhattan, but also to create a visual and imaginary *cordon sanitaire* that ghettoizes Chinatown, encapsulating the crime and violence within that space. While the close juxtaposition of the towers and Chinatown terrifies mainstream American audiences with the physical closeness of the violent and criminal Other, it also conversely comforts them with the notion that such terror is safely confined within the crime-infested space of that Other and, hence, cannot harm them. The ever-present image of the twin towers serves as concrete reminder of this idea. Hence, it is in this manner that the visual impact of the towers becomes, to use again Derrida's words, a filmic mode of "allaying our terror by our voyeurism."

The twin towers framing New York City's Chinatown

The loop that Derrida is referring to is a filmic repetition of a single moment of apocalyptic trauma that is symptomatic of a perpetual state of terror that we are witnessing in a very real way in the world today. The loop in *The Corruptor* of the World Trade Center/Chinatown juxtaposition is also one of perpetual terror, but one related to the triads, their criminal activities, and the violence that they wreak. The fear of the triads lies not only in the terrifying thought that their mode of terrorism will spill outside of Chinatown and into mainstream America, but that their (Chinese) culture of corruption will infect American society. This fear of moral corruption, thereby, structures the relationship between the film's two main protagonists: Nick Chen (Chow Yun-fat) and Danny Wallace (Mark Wahlberg). Nick Chen is a much-decorated police officer who leads the NYPD's Asian Gang Unit. His success in dealing with the tongs and Asian gangs in Chinatown relies on his connection to the two tong leaders, Benny Wong (Kim Chan) and Henry Lee (Ric Young), who feed him information for his celebrated crime busts. Lee's interests, in turn, are guarded by Chen. Into this scenario of police "corruption" enters Danny Wallace, a young and upcoming cop sent by Internal Affairs to investigate Chen and his tong connections. But Wallace soon develops a mentor-pupil relationship with Chen, while becoming embroiled in a morally questionable relationship with Henry Lee, who has entrapped Wallace by offering to help the latter's father out of his debts to the Italian mafia. Wallace discovers that keeping clean in this community is easier said than done. When Chen uncovers Wallace's real identity and purpose, the two come to a violent confrontation. In attempting to rescue a boat full of illegal Chinese immigrants, Chen takes a bullet for Wallace and dies. Acknowledging that they are now truly partners, and coming to terms with the notion that right and wrong in Chinatown are not so easy to keep straight, Wallace writes a report to Internal Affairs exculpating Chen of any corrupt wrongdoing.

What the film tries to establish is the relationship between corruptibility and the culturally specific lure of *guanxi*, the Chinese concept of relationships. Nick Chen's corruptibility is related to his deep sense of indebtedness to the tongs, specifically Benny Wong, as Chen tells a curious Wallace:

> I was the first Chinese cop in the 15th. I was going to clean up Chinatown. The white cops wouldn't work with me. And the people wouldn't talk to a cop, Chinese or not. Only Benny Wong will talk to me. He took me around, took care of my debts, fed me a few busts, made me look good and I like it. Then he became a godfather. At that time Henry Lee was nothing. One night my father walks into a gambling house and ends up dead. Turns out Lee knew that there was a contract on him. He made it clear. He could have told me. I could have saved him.

Therefore, Chen sees that *guanxi* with Benny Wong and Henry Lee will not only help him further his career in the police force, but also believes that he can do some good for the people of Chinatown through it.

According to Martin Booth, this "particularly Chinese concept of *guanxi* . . . arises from the Confucian ethos of revering one's ancestors and forming family, clan, place or name associations. Wherever Chinese go in the world, they never lose touch with their roots and are always open and welcoming to other Chinese if they share something in common with them. The result of this is the global perpetuation of ancient social structures."[34] Though Booth is trying to establish here the method with which the triads create a hold on the people they exploit, he has also offered a definition of *guanxi* that accurately presents it as having wider social, political, and cultural resonance. For instance, in her analysis of the transnational capitalist forms of Chinese "flexible citizenship," Aihwa Ong argues that global business relationships between the Chinese are often forged through *guanxi*.[35] The point I am making here is that while *guanxi* can lend itself to corrupt practices, it is not always and exclusively the case. The danger then for *The Corruptor* to enmesh *guanxi*, Chinese culture, and triad corruption and criminality within the narrative space of Chinatown is to further reify essentialist stereotypes of Chinese corruption and degeneracy as culturally inherent.

One must, however, give the film credit for trying to resist these stereotypes, despite the fact that it is not entirely successful in doing so. By having Danny Wallace enter the world of Chinatown through his joining the NYPD's Asian Gang Unit, the film acknowledges the ethical and moral dilemmas and complexities involved when cultural relations assert their ideological demands. When Wallace first joins the unit, he comes to it as a white savior figure, one who idealistically believes in performing his duty as a cop "to save the yellow people," as his Asian female colleague rather sardonically puts it to him. (Another colleague exclaims, "I knew it! Yellow fuckin' fever! Junior's here to walk the street and to get his wick licked by a nice diamond-eyed beauty." In this scene where the unit's members confront Wallace on his motivations for wanting to join them, the filmmakers seem to suggest a certain cognizance of the Orientalist discourses that permeate the genre. Reflecting this understanding and sensitivity only makes the film politically superior to *Lethal Weapon 4* and its "politically correct" professions.) Whether Wallace indeed has "yellow fuckin' fever" or is making up his political ideals of helping the Chinese in order to accomplish his goal of infiltrating the unit, one thing is evidently clear: his principled belief in right and wrong are so sterilely held that he is even ambivalent about responding to his father's call for financial help to get the latter out of trouble with the mafia. His strained relations with his father, his growing student-mentor relationship with Chen, and his questionable alliance with Henry Lee all parallel one another and become instrumental in teaching him, because, as Chen sagely frames it, "you don't change Chinatown . . . It changes you."

The "corruption" of Danny Wallace, hence, forms a pivotal moment in the film. In the following dialogue sequence where Henry Lee, with a rather feminized lilt in his voice and with the diabolical seductiveness of Fu Manchu, draws Wallace into his web, one is almost convinced by the persuasiveness of his pragmatic logic:

> *Lee*: I want to help you because I want you to help me.
> *Wallace*: What do you mean help you?
> *Lee*: My business is victimless. I supply services people want and are forbidden to them by politicians. However, you have seen there are those whose business is not victimless, whose tactic is violence. I can help you rid Chinatown of those elements, and help keep your father alive. All I ask is that you look out for my interests in return.
> *Wallace*: I think you are asking for more than that.
> *Lee*: Long after you and I are gone, there will be gambling in Chinatown; there will be men willing to pay a woman for her favors. And the police will always be the last to know. That's a fact. Well, you can chase your tail in the dark and accomplish nothing, or you can really do some good for the people of Chinatown, for your career, and for your father. Think of how many more young women would end up in dumpsters if not for your acceptance of my help. Do we have a deal? Or do you want me to call the Italians and rescind my offer and let them deal with your father? . . . Good.

The camera shifts from Lee to Wallace as the conversation progresses, until finally the audience only sees an extended facial close-up of Wallace and hears Lee's voice as he elegantly dispatches his rhetorical coup de grâce. This sequencing structure symbolizes the shift in power between the two, and Wallace's eventual acquiescence to Lee's "persuasiveness."

Wallace's corruption not only complicates the ethical and legal boundaries of right and wrong for him, but also demolishes his righteous sense of what he believes he is capable of, vis-à-vis his father's vices and failures. The latter even shames Wallace by returning the ten thousand dollars that Chen offers to Wallace, because he believes that Wallace is planning to betray his partner, which to him is an act that is more immoral than any criminal transgression. When Chen sacrifices his life to save him, a remorseful Wallace can only ask for forgiveness, affirm their partnership as fellow police officers, and submit a report exonerating Chen of any suspicion of criminal wrongdoing. In other words, Wallace's relationships with his father and Chen have complicated his ethical choices; and this experience becomes a kind of personal illustration of the impact that the Chinese notion of *guanxi* has on the community and its relationship to triad criminality.

While this reading suggests that *The Corruptor* is arguing for a more nuanced cultural understanding of the Chinese's ambivalence towards the triads, which is a necessary and significant point to make, I am less convinced by the film's critical efficacy. While Wallace's time with the Asian Gang Unit may have helped him build bridges of cultural understanding that span the gulf between white and Chinese America, a gulf symbolized by the last of the four shots of the World Trade Center sitting at the edge of Chinatown, Wallace's gaze is still ultimately that of a tourist. Like Marlow's experiences in Joseph Conrad's *Heart of Darkness*, Chinatown functions as Wallace's Congo. His journey into the heart of a dark, crime-infested Chinatown has given him insight into his own soul, uncovering his own vulnerability and corruptibility. The convenient instrumentality of Chen's life and death, not to mention the deaths of many Chinatown inhabitants (lives which are "unreal" and, hence, not worth mourning for, as Butler has questioned in *Precarious Life*), initiates the psychological unpicking of one (white) man's moral follies, in order that he might be set right again.[36]

Black and Chinese Gangland Turf Wars

Hollywood's representation of American ethnic minorities as lives which are "unreal" and, thereby, dispensable, is a parallel one can draw between popular cinematic depictions of African and Chinese American urban experiences. While this parallel allows for the two ethnic communities to find empathetic identification in their criticism of such representations, it also furthers a black-Chinese cultural connection that began in the 1970s. It is, therefore, not unusual to find that contemporary urban crime films featuring the Chinese, such as the *Rush Hour* films and the Jet Li vehicles *Romeo Must Die* and *Cradle 2 the Grave,* rely on an African American presence to imbue them with an element of urban cool, which allows the studios to market these films to African American audiences. A number of film scholars have mapped this cultural connection,[37] and so I do not wish to traverse the same critical terrain here. But I do want to highlight a number of moments in this cinematic history in order to situate my discussion of the triads within this black-Chinese cultural connection, and then use it to frame my brief analysis of *Rush Hour, Rush Hour 2*, and *Romeo Must Die.*

The image of a shirtless Bruce Lee we see emblazoned on t-shirts and posters exudes an in-your-face, anti-establishment coolness that speaks to many African Americans politically. David Desser describes kung fu film's crossover appeal in terms which explain Bruce Lee's iconic status in the black community:

Outside of the blaxploitation genre it largely replaced, kung fu films offered the only nonwhite heroes, men and women, to audiences alienated by mainstream film and often by mainstream culture. This was the genre of the underdog, the underdog of color, often fighting against colonialist enemies, white culture, or the Japanese. The lone, often unarmed combatant fighting a foe with greater economic clout who represented the status quo provides an obvious but nonetheless real connection between kung fu films and black audiences.[38]

The cultural nationalism in Bruce Lee's films provides for black audiences images of an identifiable, ethnic minority figure who confronts white racism and imperialism, and basically "kicks ass."[39] Lee's popularity paved the way for Jackie Chan to enter the scene. Gina Marchetti examines this continuity between the two dragons[40] by tracing Lee's influence on Chan, Chan's apprenticeship in Lee's films, and Chan's continued deployment of black culture to populate his films.[41] Marchetti's observation of Chan's ability to reconfigure this black-Chinese connectivity for audience consumption is spot on: "the use of 'blackness' as a signifier in each of these [filmic] vehicles enhances their marketability across various audiences, including white, middle-class, suburbanites who can place Chan within the defined parameters of 'multicultural' spectacle found in the Hollywood action genre."[42] Laleen Jayamanne gives Chan's appeal a transnational scope by suggesting that "in these films Chan has made for himself a transnational kinship group by creating filial networks with familiar generic types."[43]

While the black connection that Bruce Lee offers has a stronger political subversive potential, Jackie Chan's appropriation of this connection loses some, though not all, of the political potential of the former. In fact, this connection is reconfigured and repackaged with cinematic capitalist consumption in mind. The political edge in Lee's films comes out of a post-Civil Rights era, marking a significant distinction from the kind of globally palatable cultural politics of Chan's oeuvre, which bears an I-can-be-everything-to-everyone appeal in Chan's character and star persona. This appeal, unfortunately, has the ability to blunt the critical sharpness of its political good intentions, as its politics is often deterritorialized from its material historicity, thus becoming a commodity within the circuits of global cinematic consumption. Of course, one cannot naively identify the capitalist complicity in Chan's work without realizing that the iconography of Bruce Lee is equally vulnerable to this mode of cooptation — Lee's image, like those of Mao Zedong and Che Guevara, has been fashioned into revolutionary chic — but the difference may lie in the way Jackie Chan and Jet Li's films represent a more immediate level of involvement, vis-à-vis the retroactivity in Lee's case.

It is in this context of the "'multicultural' spectacle found in the Hollywood action genre" that I wish to locate the tenuous connections and relationships between blackness, Chineseness, the triads, and the violence and turf wars between African American and Chinese American gangs, as they are represented in Hollywood urban crime cinema involving both races. My use of the word "tenuous" is meant to highlight the essentialist tendency of many to stereotype both the Chinese and African Americans in terms of their associations with gang-related crime and violence — the triads with the Chinese, black crime gangs with the black community, and the horrendous notion of the two coming into conflict with each other in a dystopian vision of racial conflagration. But more particularly, the word points us to the constructed nature of these representations and their cultural political deployment in popular Hollywood cinema. The Jackie Chan-Chris Tucker partnership in the *Rush Hour* films and the Jet Li-Aaliyah collaboration in *Romeo Must Die* are hyperbolic black-Chinese concatenations that idealize not just racial harmony (between two "troublesome" minority groups) but also a racially infused version of the model minority (as if allowing Asian "passivity" to calm the black "beast" in a cross-cultural twist). This interracial pairing forms a hybrid version of the good minority figure, which serves to contain and repulse the onslaught of gangland crime and violence for a white majority audience.

Brett Ratner's *Rush Hour* heralded the incredibly successful on-screen partnership between Jackie Chan and Chris Tucker, playing Hong Kong Chief Inspector Lee and LAPD Detective James Carter respectively.[44] The narrative circumstance which brings the characters Lee and Carter together is one of marginalization by the establishment. Consul Han's daughter is kidnapped by Hong Kong-linked art thieves; and Lee, Han's good friend, comes to their aid. However, he is waylaid by a reluctant Carter, who is sent by the FBI and the LAPD because Carter is seen as a loose canon. Lee and Carter, hence, are coerced into their partnership because they are both seen as hindrances and nuisances to the FBI solving the case. Of course, as in most Hollywood films, the dynamic duo circumvents the system to rescue the kidnapped girl and to find a personal connection that promises filmic sequels in this franchise. While this first film introduces the relationship formula between Carter and Lee, it also sets up a narrative paradigm that ameliorates white social fears of ethnic criminality and unrest. Lee and Carter, as the combined, hybrid, good-model minority, save the day by foiling the designs of ex-British colonialist bad guy Thomas Griffin, also known as Juntao in Hong Kong circles (Tom Wilkinson), another culturally hybrid criminal figure. Lee's good-guy likeability, though combined with a clownish persona, counterbalances Carter's grating character to offer an acceptable ethnic minority "heroic" figure. Their combination works to smooth out racial sensitivities for a white audience, as the scene where Lee's verbal faux pas of greeting black bar patrons with "What's up, my nigga?" exemplifies. Lee, fending off the angry black men, is presented as a figure of cultural innocence who is also capable of putting out racial violence, while putting so-called racial "hyper-sensitivities" in their place.

Rush Hour 2 reverses the geographical placement in the trans-pacific framework of the series' narratives. This time we have Carter traveling to Hong Kong as a tourist, visiting his buddy Lee. Before long, Lee and Carter encounter the triads in the form of Ricky Tan (John Lone)[45] and Hu Li (Zhang Ziyi). Involved in the counterfeiting of greenbacks, Tan and Hu Li draw Lee and Carter into a web of intrigue and deception. The trail left by the triads eventually leads the detectives back to the US, specifically Las Vegas. The transnational mobility of the triad characters — particularly the way they move fluidly in and out of embassies, easily smuggle goods across borders, and seamlessly draw criminal connections between Hong Kong and Las Vegas — captures the revivalist strain of the yellow peril in the cinematic figure of the triad criminal. Of course, Lee and Carter arrive in time to save the day once more. This time Carter obtains insider information from his source on the ground, Kenny (Don Cheadle), the owner of Chinese Soul Food Restaurant. Married to a Chinese woman and well-acquainted with kung fu skills, Kenny, and his love for things Chinese, represents "another great set piece on miscegenation,"[46] precisely because he functions as a metonymy of black-Chinese connectivity, thereby articulating the social and political value of black-Chinese connectivity to the resistance of bad Chinese triads and their criminal encroachment onto white American territory.

Finally, *Romeo Must Die* pushes black-Chinese relations to the brink of dystopian conflict by setting them within the morality tale of Shakespeare's *Romeo and Juliet*. This loose adaptation of the classic play allows director Andrzej Bartkowiak to bring together Jet Li (in his follow-up to *Lethal Weapon 4*) and the late recording star Aaliyah. Li plays Han, who escapes from a Chinese prison, to investigate his brother's death and to prevent his family, the Sings, from clashing with their rivals, the O'Days. Aaliyah is Trish O'Day, the daughter of Isaak O'Day, patriarch of the black mafia family, from whom she wishes to distance herself. The tit-for-tat killings of each other's family members stem ultimately from a turf war: as Sing's second-in-command Kai (Russell Wong) impresses on Han, "The waterfront is only four square miles. Half the businesses belong to us, the other half to them. It's just a matter of time." The turf war between the O'Days and the Sings is a microcosmic depiction of the dire dystopian descent to which the lethal combination of ethnic strife and tribal criminality could lead. Only the transcendent love of Romeo and Juliet, that is Han and Trish, can help prevent this scenario.

I often relish in alternative adaptations of literary classics such as Baz Luhrmann's MTV-style *Romeo + Juliet* (1996) because such quirky approaches fracture the classic text and force audiences to rethink traditional interpretations and their assumptions. In the case of *Romeo Must Die*, I prefer to reverse the interpretive method by suggesting that here the reputation of the classic text and its traditional lesson encourage audiences to map and structure a rather simplistic understanding of ethnic strife and criminal turf wars. The lesson that mainstream audiences are wont to arrive at is that not only should ethnic minorities embrace love as a universal means of peaceful coexistence, but also that blacks and Chinese must seek to abandon their culturally specific tendencies of criminality and violence to make peace a reality. I may seem to be building an interpretive straw man for the sake of toppling it; but one need only draw a parallel with the 1992 riots in Los Angeles to see the very real correlation. Lisa Lowe observes that "though the U.S. media consistently attempted to construct the crisis as a racial conflict between Blacks and Koreans, the looters enraged by the [Rodney] King verdict were not only Blacks but also Chicanos, Latinos, and working-class whites; all violently objected to the denial of brutally racialized economic stratification."[47] Lowe's analysis is instructive in that the US media engaged in a reductive and essentialist reading of the riots, pointing to race as their central cause, hence making invisible the capitalist machinery of economic exploitation and its role in forming a racialized structuring of the various economic classes in America. In a similar way, *Romeo Must Die* lays the blame at the doorsteps of the Chinese and the African American communities, and hence on the categories of race and culture, while eliding any critique of the collusion of economic exploitation and white racism.[48] The fact that Han and Trish survive, in a rather dramatic reversal of Shakespeare's ending, registers a misplaced utopianism that audiences want as an ending to this cinematic dramatization of racial strife and ghettoized crime in minority America.

A Violent End

In my discussion of these triad-related crime films that Hollywood has produced, I have subjected triad violence, directly or implicitly, to the glare of critical analysis and condemnation. Rather than ending here with a reiteration of this critique of triad violence, I choose instead to redirect our gaze onto the physical and cultural violence enacted against the Chinese Other, metonymically through the triads, in the name of national legality and cultural respectability. Triadic cruelty and violence in all these films command a reciprocal and, hence, permissible cruelty and violence on the part of the police and the cultural mainstream to bring these wayward elements into social and cultural conformity. In his renowned essay on the "Critique of Violence," Walter Benjamin zeroes in on the idea that "police violence is emancipated from both conditions" of lawmaking and law preservation. "The assertion that the ends of police violence are always identical or even connected to those of general law is entirely untrue. Rather, the 'law' of the police really marks the point at which the state, whether from impotence or because of the immanent connections within any legal system, can no longer guarantee through the legal system the empirical ends that it desires at any price to attain."[49] That triad violence and police brutality occupy the same space external to institutional legality confers on them both a sense of fantastical terror that deserve equal condemnation and reproach. These films, in projecting one form of violence, expose the Other, thereby deconstructing the comforting fantasy of ethnic containment and assimilation by and through the law for a mainstream cinematic gaze in the reconfigured form of the Hollywood crime film.

6

Hollywood's Sino-Chic:
Kung Fu Parody, Mimicry, and Play in Cross-Cultural Citationality

Kung fu Sino-chic was the hot commodity hitting theaters across America in the summer of 2008 as DreamWorks Animation unleashed the lovably rotund but surprisingly dexterous Po on eager young audiences. Unfortunately, *Kung Fu Panda*, starring the vocal talents of the amazing Jack Black as the main character, offers only a marginally entertaining parody of the kung fu comedy genre[1] popularized by Jackie Chan in the 1970s through classics of Hong Kong cinema such as *Snake in the Eagle's Shadow* (1978) and *Drunken Master* (1978). Of course, *Kung Fu Panda* is clearly not original in its parody (that is if one can talk about parody in terms of originality in the first place) in that it belongs to a growing line of Hollywood films that exaggerate and make fun of martial arts films and kung fu comedies from Hong Kong: *Big Trouble in Little China* (1986), *Beverly Hills Ninja* (1997), *Kung Pow: Enter the Fist* (2002), and the bizarre sports-kung fu hybrid *Balls of Fury* (2007), where kung fu meets table tennis. These films thrive on and are protected by their (sometimes questionably) ironic play on ethnic stereotypes, from which much of the humor is derived.[2] On the other hand, the popularity of these films does signal an increasingly mainstream interest in martial arts cinema in America, beyond the realm of subterranean, fan-boy, cult fascination.[3]

But what is intriguing to me is that Hollywood's parodic attempts may have also influenced in some way the evolution of the genre in Hong Kong. Stephen Chow's *The God of Cookery* (1996), *Shaolin Soccer* (2001), and *Kung Fu Hustle* (2004) not only capitalized on the popularity of kung fu comedies as we know them in Asia, but also permitted an element of self-parody to refashion the genre for a new generation of kung fu cinema fans. In an ingenious reading of how kung fu cinema "betrays a tremendous anxiety over the hitherto not-so-successful negotiation with Western modernity," Siu Leung Li confronts *Shaolin Soccer* "as one of the attempts in commercial cinema to further commodify kung fu beyond the conventional 'kung fu genres,' crossing kung fu over to other genres to produce an often hybrid form in order to make money."[4] Apart from identifying, in *Kung Fu Hustle*, allusions to *The Matrix* film series, Peter Hitchcock also lists visual references, which constitute in Chow's borrowings, a veritable catalog of Hollywood cinematic history, including the work of Quentin Tarantino.[5] One encounters elements of frenetic slapstick comic violence reminiscent of Robert Zemeckis' *Who Framed Roger Rabbit* (1988) and typical of the elastic Jim Carrey as in *The Mask* (1994). The cross-cultural citationality occurring here sees Hollywood and Hong Kong crisscross the Pacific in its cultural and cinematic appropriation and hybridization, allowing filmmakers on both sides to tap, often collaboratively, into the transnational capitalist circuits of global filmic production, distribution, and consumption. Parody, mimicry, and cultural play are part and parcel of this citationality flow. However, the concern one needs to raise in noting this phenomenon is the kind of cultural politics this citationality invokes or implicates, and the attendant risks and consequences its generates. In order to avoid the one-note and unidirectional critique of simply identifying and judging good/bad cinematic representations, I approach the more recent films of Jackie Chan and Quentin Tarantino to map out my own shifting and ambivalent readings of their work as a means of demonstrating how the political dexterity of these texts contributes to their transnational success. As Jackie Chan playfully mimics Western pop culture and Quentin Tarantino irreverently stitches together elements of Chinese (and Asian) cinemas, they jointly compose a picture of chiasmic mirroring that is symptomatic of the complex nature of Hollywood's strategies of remaking.

Mimicry as Failure: Jackie Chan in Hollywood

Watching the career transformations of Jackie Chan is like watching one of his movies with all the action-packed twists and turns, always exciting and never without surprises.[6] Together with millions of his fans around the world, I have derived great pleasure in witnessing his various incarnations: he has transformed himself from the young and rebellious Wong Fei-hong in *Drunken Master* to the globe-trotting Chinese Passepartout in *Around the World in 80 Days* (2004). In becoming a transnational cinematic superstar,[7] Chan realizes that part of his success lies in his ability to morph, sometimes in subtle ways, to keep pace with audiences' changing demands and their shifting demographics, while maintaining the highly appealing star persona that he has cultivated through the years.[8] This formula has not only enabled Chan to remain one of Asia's top action superstars, but has also allowed him to build a substantial fan base in the United States, since the success of the *Rush Hour* franchise. It would seem overly simplistic, however, to characterize Jackie Chan's strategies of transformation *solely* in terms of his place within the capitalist machineries of the Hong Kong film industry and now Hollywood. Though he is undeniably a savvy entertainer and businessman (with box-office success being a significant and key measure of achievement for him[9]) and although he prefers to exclude the overtly political in his films,[10] social and cultural politics still do have a place in his work. They determine certain politicized aspects of his transformations, particularly in relationship to the strategy of audience appeal. Hence, his films invoke issues of cultural, national, and racial identities that resonate with his viewers' concerns, exemplifying what globalization theorists have characterized as the capitalist deployment of the local in the global.[11]

Any brief biographical, filmic, and critical survey of Jackie Chan's life and work will account for us his interest in certain issues of cultural politics, as they appear in his films, which are often marked by a careful balancing act between a "true" political consciousness and a calculated strategy of audience appeal, both of which help structure the transformations of Chan's star persona. Embedded in some of his earlier Hong Kong movies are plot scenarios and characters that hint at the oppressive nature of British colonial rule or espouse various forms of Chinese cultural nationalism. The presence of such subtle anti-colonialist critiques should come as no surprise, considering the fact that the work of Bruce Lee has ideologically impacted Chan's own career choices. While most critics are quick to note that Lee paved the way for Chan's own meteoric rise[12] (Chan's Chinese adopted stage name *Cheng long*, "To become a dragon," takes off from Bruce Lee's *Li Xiaolong*, "Lee, the Little Dragon"), some are careful to reflect that Chan wanted to be his own man (as the idiom *Wangzi chenglong*, meaning "wishing one's son become a dragon," foregrounds every Chinese family's auspicious wish for their male offspring to succeed in life[13]). Lisa Stokes and Michael Hoover are on the mark to call Chan "an anti-Bruce Lee"[14] as he sought "to remake himself."[15] Remake himself he did, not just in terms of a new martial arts style and a new visual aesthetic, but also through an extension and a reformulation of Bruce Lee's Chinese nationalist politics.[16] While such a cultural nationalist agenda allows Chan to embed subtle anti-colonialist critiques in his earlier films, a position that often elicits positive responses from his Hong Kong and Chinese audiences, Chan globalizes this critique by reconfiguring Lee's cultural nationalism into a *trans*national anti-imperialist politics. This shift is also important in that it enables him to insert himself into the contemporary discourses of globalization and diaspora. The narrative of *Who Am I?* (1998), for instance, sees Chan's character traverse the globe in a search for his identity, while connecting him to a postcolonial Africa.

This form of political connection paves the way for a trans-Pacific crossover that in a sense parallels Chan's recent success in relocating his career from Hong Kong to Hollywood. *Rumble in the Bronx* (1996), *Rush Hour* (1998), and *Rush Hour 2* (2001) incorporate the issues of race and racism against minorities in the United States. Here marks what Gina Marchetti terms Jackie Chan's "black connection."[17] With Bruce Lee's cultural nationalism acting as a trailblazer, Chan is able to offer African American audiences movies that they can both enjoy, and politically connect with and appropriate. [18] But Chan updates Lee's racial pride message of the 1970s by turning to the interracial alliances and tensions between African Americans and the growing Asian migrant community in the US. Chan has subtly but successfully retooled his macho-comic star persona into an image of a bumbling, though humane, anti-racist champion of immigrant rights and racial harmony.[19]

I have thus far mapped out briefly the contours of Chan's strategies of transformation in the initial phases of his Hong Kong-to-Hollywood career move. What is especially intriguing to see is how Chan works the local/global conjuncture by balancing the gradual cinematic Americanization of his work, especially via the themes of cultural adaptation, appropriation, and acceptance of Asian migrants in the United States, while simultaneously building what David Bordwell has classed as a "calculated cosmopolitanism"[20] in his appeal to a wide global audience. What one must keep in mind too is that the Hollywood phase of his career is also marked by a limited agency on his part: Chan has directed quite a number of his earlier Hong Kong films, choosing not only to do his own stunts despite the physical dangers involved, but also to have a greater sense of control of the films' direction and, hence, their ensuing cultural politics. Coming to Hollywood, however, has involved a diminishment of that agency, as he now has to negotiate complex studio bureaucracies, especially when it comes to his safety during stunt work; and to grapple with the hierarchy of control involving numerous studio executives, directors, producers, and screenwriters. His superstardom to the rest of the world notwithstanding, Chan is basically new to Tinseltown and needs time to build his cultural capital there. It is with this understanding of his transformed status that I devote this section of the chapter to an examination of Chan's shifting star persona as it appears in three of his recent movies: *The Tuxedo* (2002), *Shanghai Noon* (2000), and *Shanghai Knights* (2003). In reconfiguring his macho-comic image and inserting himself into Hollywood genre-specific settings and character types, Chan performs a humorous mimicry that can be both subversive and self-mocking, a playfulness that permits him to interrogate the limits of his own agency while affirming his commercial relevance within Hollywood's transnational hegemony. Through the processes of a (post)colonial mimicry, these films also hint at an anti-imperialist critique that can serve to connect Chan to his Chinese and non-Western audiences, a critique that unfortunately does not quite push the radical envelope far enough but instead resorts to locating Chan in a political comfort zone that reinforces his universal cosmopolitan appeal, that is, a politically correct Jackie Chan for everyone. It is this contradictory embodiment of potentiality and limitation — both personal and institutional — that allows me to respond ambivalently to both the critical pleasures and political difficulties in his recent work.

To understand Jackie Chan's use of mimicry to reshape his cinematic persona for an engagement with the racism and the neo-imperialism in US culture and history, I want to turn to Homi K. Bhabha's analysis of colonial mimicry as a framework to read Chan's recent films. In "Of Mimicry and Man," Bhabha approaches "colonial mimicry" as a discourse of colonial subjugation and hegemony that springs from a "desire for a reformed, recognizable Other, *as a subject of a difference that is almost the same, but not quite.*" Hence, the success of colonial mimicry relies on its "strategic failure," where "mimicry must continually produce its slippage, its excess, its difference"; and "is therefore stricken by an indeterminacy."[21] It creates what Bhabha labels as a "partial presence" or a "metonymy of presence."[22] This critical definition of mimicry has led Gina Marchetti to make the following application on Jackie Chan's performances:

> He can slip effortlessly between imitations of James Bond, Indiana Jones, and other white masters of global order and Michael Jackson's moon walk or Chris Tucker's version of playing the "dozens." He takes on various roles as masks; however, no authentic self is promised behind the persona . . . [A]lthough Chan may turn ethnic and racial stereotypes on their head and he may mimic the white hero, he does so from a position of uncertainty and questionable power. His deracination frees him in many ways, but limits his legitimacy in other ways. He easily shifts form and position, but, ultimately, accommodates himself to the postmodern condition without much critical footing.[23]

The ambivalence of Chan's critical position is what ultimately undermines the effectiveness of any political critique of imperialism or racism that his films only begin to offer, as my reading of his three movies reveals. Chan mimics the James Bond super-spy figure in *The Tuxedo*, and, in *Shanghai Noon* and *Shanghai Knights*, he inserts himself into the Wild Wild West to be like John Wayne. While it is true that his "deracination," or what one critic calls his "disembedding,"[24] grants him the cinematic license of "flexible citizenship,"[25] Chan's rather successful attempts at inserting himself into the Hollywood machinery, in the case of these films through mimicry and hybridity, cannot but be racialized. This mimicry turns on a "failure" grounded in racial terms: as James Bond or John Wayne, he is "almost the same but not *white.*"[26] Yet ironically, this racial "failure" is the essence of Chan's success in these movies. The comic element, which has been an integral key to successful Jackie Chan movies, rests on the discomfort of the new racialized roles he inhabits and the disjuncture between his star persona and the cultural traditions of these well-worn figures of James Bond and John Wayne.

I find it hard not to be ambivalent about Chan's cinematic mimicry and its political functions and effects. On the one hand, I take to heart Bhabha's argument that colonial mimicry can present moments of critical resistance in its very structure. The "failure" of mimicry produces an ironic questioning by "the *splitting* of colonial discourse,"[27] where the very foundation of the discourse deconstructs itself, revealing its ideological and political investment and its constructedness. The demystification and denaturalization of colonial discourse assumptions reveal that there are alternatives, be they cultural, national, racial, class, gendered, or sexual. By taking on Bond and John Wayne, Chan "splits" the discursive underpinnings of these figures, while gesturing towards absent or hidden alternatives.[28] Furthermore, it heartens one to see the subversive potential in Chan's performativity of these Hollywood figures, the sanctity of which he playfully disrupts in his inept mimicry. On the other hand, scholarly critics are right in pointing out the limitations of the political critiques in his films, especially when Chan's films work towards winning mass audiences and, of late, ensuring him a place in the Hollywood pantheon of stars. Hence, the politicization of his films assumes a muted or moderated quality. One could say that the films offer a politics of mass appeal, a position that accommodates many while offending few. In so doing, Chan blunts the potential of anti-imperialist and anti-racist critiques, as the following readings of his three films demonstrate.

The Tuxedo: Mimicry through Sartorial Insertion

"My name's Tong, James Tong," proclaims Jackie Chan's character to a villain who confronts him in a scene from *The Tuxedo*. Although Chan, in his earlier films, never played a character that directly mimicked James Bond, many of his roles, such as in *Police Story* (1985), *Armour of God* (1987), *Armour of God II* (1991), and *Supercop* (1992; US release 1996) feature his trademark reinvention of the super spy/action hero to incorporate his comedic star appeal. *The Tuxedo* presents Chan with the opportunity to take his fascination with Bond to a new level. Here we see him not only assuming a Bond-inspired character, but also reinventing it to accommodate his own star persona and cinematic image. However, his parodic mimicry of the famous James Bond response to an identity inquiry ("My name's Bond, James Bond") betrays an anxiety of racial difference, identity desire, and national belonging, an anxiety that also symbolizes Chan's ambition to succeed in America. This is, after all, *the* Bond-inflected Jackie Chan movie that is set in the United States and that primarily targets American mainstream audiences who are extremely familiar with the Bond film series and, hence, can be assumed to be more critical of any parody of it.

From *Dr. No* (1962) to the recent *Quantum of Solace* (2008), James Bond is a cinematic figure of British imperialist nostalgia, desire, and fantasy. Bond also has an important place in American popular culture, thereby symbolizing the historical and ideological continuities and connections between the British Empire and US imperialist hegemony. Part of the pleasure of Bond as imperialist fantasy, rests on his being an agent endowed with global mobility and access, unrestrained by national borders and laws as demonstrated in his having a "license to kill." (It is tempting here to extrapolate from these cinematic fantasies the complicit relationship between the forces of globalization and Anglo-American imperialist desires). Against this reading of Bond, I would like to juxtapose *The Tuxedo* as an American immigrant text that at moments subverts, and yet, eventually, re-inscribes this fantasy.

Chan's character James Tong hints (because the movie does not reveal this) of F.O.B., fresh-of-the-boat, Asian migrancy with its attendant stereotypes. Speaking in halting English, Tong works as a New York City taxi driver, while struggling to woo a sophisticated Asian woman he fancies, and to attain the American dream (as his studying of a *Dummy's Guide to Amassing Wealth* attests). What distinguishes him from other immigrant taxi drivers is his manic ability to speed-drive through the crowded and labyrinthine streets of the Big Apple. His notoriety earns him a chance to work as the chauffeur of the British Bond-like agent Clark Devlin (Jason Isaacs), whose suave debonairness Tong admires and to which he aspires. Devlin's secret weapon is a US government-issued tuxedo which enables him to perform remarkable feats. During an assassination attempt on his life, Devlin is temporarily put out of commission, leaving Tong to use the tuxedo to pick up where Devlin left off and to save the world, with the help of agent Delilah

Del Blaine (Jennifer Love Hewitt), from the dastardly evil schemes of Diedrich Banning (Ritchie Coster). The way the narrative sets up Tong to assume Devlin's place and mimic his Bond-like characteristics forces into clear view the stark distinctions between certain forms of immigrant immobility and Bond's access to a transnational mobility. The factors of race, class, and, most of all, political power determine these distinctions. To move Tong from the restricted confines of his taxi (which is made ironic by the notion of speed through his manic driving style) to his newfound world of unlimited access as Devlin's flexible mobility offers, the movie accentuates the widening gulf between the rich and the poor, the powerful and the powerless, and the North and the South, in an era of globalization.

These notions of distinction and difference produce also the humor in Tong's attempt at mimicry. The device which allows Tong to take the place of Devlin is the tuxedo. This sartorial weapon of masculinist fantasy furnishes its wearer with an array of abilities including the superhuman power to climb walls, to fight like Jackie Chan, to be a brilliant sharpshooter, and to dance and sing like James Brown. Hence, the suit becomes an extension of the Bond persona. When Tong inhabits the suit, he symbolically inserts himself into that persona, thereby leading him into uncomfortable but humorous situations. The suit becomes a "metonymy of presence," where Tong may be able to do all that the suit enables him, but still "fails" to live up to the image of Bond — or as he puts it, "Being a Clark Devlin is not easy." This failure of Tong's mimicry of Bond is ultimately a racial failure, "almost the same but not *white.*" The racial demand of Bond is best represented by Del Blaine's injunction for Tong to "stop using the ridiculous accent!" This mimicry as "failure" effectively exposes the racial construction of Bond as an Anglo-American cinematic hero.

Substantiating this critique is Siu Leung Li's suggestion that "the tuxedo itself is an assimilation of the kung fu body. The tuxedo/object moves the body/subject, not the other way around. It is the tuxedo fighting through the human body."[29] To move beyond Li's and my own argument, I want to posit a more fluid dialectic within the tuxedo-body relation, as offered in theories of the cyborg figure.[30] Taking this relation out of the confines of the film's diegetic framework allows Chan to mischievously deploy the Bond tuxedo for its subversive self-parodic quality. The fact that Devlin's/Bond's invincibility can be attributed to the suit brings into question the innate heroism of Bond, making ironic the superficiality of sartorial debonairness that the tuxedo brings — Bond, in many instances of both the book and the movie series, is ultimately a parody of himself[31]; Chan is thus parodying a parody. Tong's uneasy wearing of the tuxedo also results in an inventive playfulness that undermines the political seriousness of Bond as a cinematic figure of Cold War ideology. Furthermore, on a star performative level, the tuxedo becomes a narrative device through which Jackie Chan, the kung fu star, can again demonstrate and authenticate to his audiences his daredevilry, hence making invisible the tuxedo: Chan does not require any special suit to perform the incredible stunts, to fight like a pro, and to sing and dance (no matter how absurd and incongruous a Chinese James Brown might seem).[32] This authentication of Chan's star persona is no different in effect from his inclusion of outtakes in almost all his films. The final point that Chan makes here is once again his fearless inventiveness in taking on a genre that racially and culturally challenges him through its insistent taunting of "mimicry as failure."

But with the film's ending, the tuxedo, or the lack thereof, reasserts Tong's "correct" racial place and reaffirms white superiority in the film's diegetic world, through a message of human potentiality and possibility despite (and even through) differences. When Tong asks how Devlin has acquired the ability "to be so smooth" in his dealings with women, Devlin replies, "The same way as you drive. I have the same instincts as you do." Instead of chalking it up to the tuxedo, Devlin offers an "inspirational" message to Tong to believe in one's self. What is inevitably problematic in this message is the essentialism and determinism of "instincts" that lock James Tong and Clark Devlin in their difference. This difference further creates a hierarchy when Devlin produces a new version of the tuxedo for Tong, which the latter uses in the final fight scene to defeat the villain, who now wears the tuxedo. If clothing symbolism is anything to go by, the new suit does not share the class significance of a tuxedo. Instead, as a regular suit, inferior in material and stylistic convention, though with the same special technological features of the tuxedo original, it is more of a "downgrade," marked by class difference.

Ultimately, the motivations behind Tong's/Chan's mimicry of Devlin/ Bond diminish *The Tuxedo*'s potential as an effective Asian American immigrant text. The motivations work on two levels. Firstly, Tong desires to be smooth and suave like Devlin, especially when it comes to the ladies. Bond's sexism hardly makes for model behavior, nor is it an attitude to emulate. The sexualizing of James Tong as a character is understandably important, not only to Jackie Chan's choice of roles he has made thus far,[33] but also as a contribution to the filmic representation of Asian men as sexual beings. But the movie ends with the bumbling Tong not getting the girl of his dreams despite his misadventures with the tuxedo, thus leaving the stereotype of the socially incompetent and sexually inept Asian male intact.

Secondly, Tong's goal as an immigrant is to become a part of the United States. This is accomplished at the movie's end when he is recruited to be a part of Devlin's team of secret agents. The critique that the mimicry of Bond offers is again muted when Tong is co-opted into the establishment and set in his appropriate place within the racial and political hierarchy. He becomes the model minority figure, the good "chink," by articulating that "it is an honor to help the United States of America." The patriotic discourse here merges with the cultural logic of assimilation. In a sense, such an ending symbolically parallels Chan's desire to please; and, hence, to be accepted and to succeed in Hollywood and in America.

Shanghai Noon and *Shanghai Knights:* The "Eastern Westerns"

Sandwiching *The Tuxedo*, in terms of theatrical release dates, are two movies of a successful series, *Shanghai Noon* and its sequel *Shanghai Knights*. According to Chan in his autobiography, these movies constitute a genre he calls "an Eastern Western,"[34] a formula he had his eye on since declaring Sammo Hung's *Once Upon a Time in China and America* (1997) to be his brainchild.[35] The box-office success of Chan's new films definitely strengthened his Hollywood career beyond the *Rush Hour* movies, and would certainly cement his reputation as the master of comic reinvention of action cinema. Once again, the processes of reinvention in these films involve parody, hybridity, and mimicry.

Shanghai Noon is, according to Chan, "a very smart pun on the John Wayne film *High Noon*,"[36] reflecting Chan's love for Hollywood films and his interest in Western popular culture. What director Tom Dey does with this East-West fusion is to turn it into another American immigrant story, but told on a historically grander and more spectacular level. The year is 1881 and the place is the Forbidden City in China. Princess Pei Pei (Lucy Liu) harbors the American dream, but her attempt at migration transforms into a nightmare when her American tutor assists Chinese traitor Lo Fong (Roger Yuan) in kidnapping her to extort a ransom from the Chinese Imperial Court. Imperial guard Chon Wang (Jackie Chan) is sent to rescue the princess. Upon arriving at Carson City, Nevada, he hooks up with outlaw Roy O'Bannon (Owen Wilson), turns cowboy, and together they save the princess. In a turn of events typical of immigrant narratives, Chon Wang and Princess Pei Pei decide to remain in the United States.

By relying on the filmic tradition of the Western, *Shanghai Noon* invokes the American frontier imaginary, with its literary and cinematic images of land settlement and new beginnings, the colonial immigrant's dream of "Westward ho!" This imaginary, however, is imperialist, as Ella Shohat and Robert Stam argue:

> If the imperial adventure film conveyed the pleasures and benefits of empire, the western told the story of imperial-style adventures on the American frontier . . . The myth of the frontier has its ideological roots in some of the [following] discourses . . . the competitive laws of Social Darwinism, the hierarchy of the races and sexes, the idea of progress. It gave exceptionalist national form to a more widespread historical process — the general thrust of European expansion into Asia, Africa, and the Americas . . . A narrative paradigm is enlisted to serve teleological notions of national progress and manifest destiny.[37]

Chan's fascination with the Western as a genre encourages him to locate himself within this mythology, by pilfering a page from American television Westerns such as *Gunsmoke* (1955–75), *How the West Was Won* (1978–9), and *Bonanza* (1959–73) that also featured Chinese characters or elements. (For instance, *Bonanza*'s Hop Sing, as the Cartwright's manservant, was a regular on the popular TV series.)[38] But Chan's "Eastern Western" engenders a postcolonial critique that the historical specificity of his Chineseness offers. It is here that his work becomes politically interesting, especially in the way he capitalizes on his own postcoloniality to create audience appeal via political identification. Confronting the imperialist and Anglo-American formulation of the "Wild West" is the presence of both Chinese immigrant slave/indentured labor in the construction of the transcontinental railroad, and the Native American communities that Chon Wang encounters. These elements in the movie give an important historical revisionist slant, with the Chinese presence complicating the white bias in the nationalist history of the transcontinental railroad,[39] and the Native Americans disturbing the self-proclaimed right of colonial settlers to the land of America.

Like his ability to work his "black connection," Chan forges political links as and where possible. The film's narrative allows him to connect with Native Americans through Chon Wang's unwitting and serendipitous marriage to a Native Indian girl. The Chinese imperial guards are mistaken for Jews by the white settlers, hence enabling the movie to reference briefly anti-Semitism. And for the Chinese, Chon Wang maintains his cultural allegiance through the notions of filial piety, respect for the Emperor, and a healthy sense of cultural pride, despite his eventual decision to remain in America. I think it is praiseworthy of Chan and director Tom Dey to take on certain issues of political relevance in their otherwise very Hollywood movie. However, it becomes problematic when the movie does not allow these issues to run their critical course, producing instead a postmodernist pastiche that only glosses superficially various political concerns — the movie becomes a politically correct, multiculturalist romp. Its desire to please, like *The Tuxedo*, leads eventually to the neutralizing of any critical edge. A painful instance of this would be the presence of the Chinese villain Lo Fong, who basically exploits his people for his own gain. Though the character does complicate the model minority stereotype, the good Chinese versus bad Chinese framework serves to shunt any direct accusation of white racism and its responsible role in the exploitation of Chinese indentured labor. This partial presence of a critique eventually makes the movie politically palatable to white mainstream American audiences.

I believe one of the main appeals of the movie is the humorous spectacle of a cultural clash: a Chinese imperial guard, in all his "exotic" costuming and accent, is transplanted into the alien (though very familiar to an American mainstream audience) environment of the frontier West. In order to survive and to succeed in his mission, Chon Wang must adapt and transform himself into a cowboy. Like in James Tong's imitation of Bond, Chon Wang also faces the inevitable failure of mimicry on account of his race. However, Chan turns this "failure" into a playful parody that resorts to camp as a way of resisting the figure of the cowboy and his place in a racist imperialist imaginary. "Chon Wang" is a strategically chosen Chinese name that puns on "John Wayne," an onomastic Americanization with which Roy christens his new partner. John Wayne is the imposing figure of classic Westerns, with a mythic image of traditional masculinity and gung-ho heroism; an image that has extended itself into the popular and political discourses of US global might. But the "seriousness" of John Wayne's star persona cannot but give way to its own deconstruction, as Richard Dyer proposes in his examination of gay camp readings of the man: "Gay camp can emphasize what a production number the Wayne image is — the lumbering gait, drawling voice and ever more craggy face are a deliberately constructed and manufactured image of virility. In this way, gay camp can stop us from treating John Wayne as an embodiment of what it 'really' means to be a man."[40] Nathan Lane's hilarious attempt in *The Birdcage* (1996) at using Wayne as the model in his character's performance of what society considers as heterosexual masculinity is a classic instance of this queer subversion. From the standpoint of race, Jackie Chan similarly rides on this reexamination of Wayne by his turning his failure of mimicry into a racial resistance of the white cowboy as the all-American hero of the Western. With Roy O'Bannon's continued insistence that "this is the West not the East," Chon Wang agonizes, though with much humor, over his gradual transformation into a cowboy in terms of speech, action, and dress.

But as funny as it is to see him awkwardly struggle in this spectacle of mimicry, Chon Wang's difficulties also expose the cultural violence involved in the processes of immigrant assimilation, in this case pitched against the racial impossibility of measuring up to the mythic standards of a John Wayne. The ultimate violation, of course, comes when Lo Fong cuts off Chon Wang's queue, a moment of symbolic "racial castration," to borrow David Eng's terminology.[41] Chon Wang, however, reasserts himself by elevating the "Shanghai Kid," a racialized title that Roy gives to him, from the status of *sidekick* to that of heroic *partner*.

The strategy of mimicry unfortunately shifts into hyper-drive in the sequel *Shanghai Knights*. In this movie, Jackie Chan's goal of global audience appeal takes the notion of postmodern pastiche into the incredulous realm of multicultural farce and fantasy. The story of Chon Wang's adventures in the Wild West continues when his sister Chon Lin (Fann Wong) sends news that their father has been killed by the British Lord Nelson Rathbone (Aidan Gillen), who has stolen the imperial seal for the Chinese traitor Wu Chow (Donnie Yen). Both Rathbone and Wu Chow have claims to the thrones of their own countries, and they conspire to help one another become king and emperor respectively. Chon Wang heads to New York City to find Roy O'Bannon, and together they arrive in London, England, to help Chon Wang's sister avenge their father's death, to save Queen Victoria from the villains' assassination attempt, and to protect the Chinese empire from falling into the hands of traitor Wu Chow. What director David Dobkin has achieved with this plotline is to transplant the American Wild West into the British Empire, enabling a double return to the imperial center with Jackie Chan in the midst of it all.

Shanghai Knights could conceivably achieve an anti-imperialist critique of British empire-building and Chinese authoritarianism, extra-textually enriched by Chan's Hong Kong origin. Such opportunities begin to present themselves in the movie with, for instance, the historical references to the Opium War[42] and the Chinese Boxer Rebellion, and Chon Wang's spirited response to Rathbone's audacious proclamation of the hope that "the Chinese people will follow India's example and one day embrace British rule." But these opportune moments are squandered when Chan instead puts mimicry (in the form of the traveling American Western hero) in the service of empire, of both the British and the Chinese. In fighting the villains Rathbone and Chinese traitor Wu Chow, and eventually being knighted by Queen Victoria for his bravery, Chon Wang becomes part of empire and is ideologically co-opted, thus displacing villainy from empire to the empire stealers. Hence, any critique of imperialism is lost in the narrative framework of the good imperialist versus bad imperialist.

Despite its critical flaws, *Shanghai Knights* is a marvel of Chan's inventive remaking of Hollywood. His mimicry of the Hollywood legends produces a work of self-referentiality that can be seen as an allegory of Chan's aspirations to become a Hollywood star and legend. As he notes in his autobiography, "I had long watched American films with envy, wishing I had the budgets and resources they boasted with every frame; I'd danced along with Fred Astaire, hummed to Frank Sinatra and Julie Andrews, laughed at Chaplin and Keaton and Lloyd, the great comics of the silent classics."[43] *Shanghai Knights,* as postmodernist pastiche, allows him to pack them all in, making it a cinephile's dream text. Charlie Chaplin and Sir Arthur Conan Doyle appear as characters, and Chan reenacts the revolving door chase scene with the New York City police, reminiscent of the energy and style of Keaton,[44] Chaplin, and Lloyd. Chan also replays the clock-tower scene from *Project A*, this time with London's Big Ben and with the eye-popping slide down the tower using the Union Jack as a make-shift parachute. Both of these clock-tower stunts mimic Harold Lloyd's 1923 *Safety Last.*[45] And finally, the market fight scene is a stroke of comic action genius, where Chan does Gene Kelly's classic song-and-dance routine in *Singin' in the Rain* while dispatching the London thugs. The movie ends with Roy O'Bannon offering a business proposition to Chon Wang that they enter the movie business together:

> *Roy*: I believe these movies can play to your strengths. There is no sound. We don't have to deal with the language problem. I think the kung fu stuff could be huge. We are dying for a good action picture.
> *Chon Wang*: John Wayne, movie star? Could work!

Chan completes the circle of self-referentiality by making *Shanghai Knights* a vehicle of both his Hollywood success story and the humble beginnings of his own cinematic birth. This takes chutzpah befitting a Hollywood star.

Jackie Chan has come a long way since his earlier failures to break into the US market with box-office flops such as *The Big Brawl* and *The Cannonball Run*. Just prior to his recent success, Chan asserts his sense of self: "If I ever go back to America again . . . I'm not going as Bruce Lee, or Clint Eastwood, or John Wayne. I'll go back as *Jackie Chan*, or I won't go at all."[46] The irony here is that Chan's series of successful movies rely on a cinema of mimicry and reinvention in spite of his anxiety of influence. Hence, the Jackie Chan persona that he alludes to can only emerge partially through a process of configuring Otherness, in reaction to the mainstays of Hollywood tradition. Could this be a reason for the sort of politics we see emerging from his films, a politics that is ambivalent or, at best, half-hearted? Will this politics become braver and edgier with each successful movie? In a recent cultural nationalist attempt to promote Asian cinema over Hollywood cinema, Chan rather unselfconsciously stressed to Indian news reporters, "Why do we need to ape their culture?"[47] His all-too-sincere question, unfortunately, encapsulates the contradictions produced in his attempts to fuse, on one hand, his own mimicry of Hollywood, and on the other, his strong sense of cultural loyalty. This fusion is supposed to transform him magically into the all-appealing international superstar that he desires to be. But then again, just like the mythological character of the Monkey King, in the Chinese literary classic *Journey to the West* (which also happens to be the title Chan uses for the final chapter of his autobiography), Jackie Chan might just have more transformational tricks up his sleeve. We can only hope, wait, and see.

Reinventing Grindhouse: Quentin Tarantino, the Female Revenge Film, and Bite-Size Chinese Cinemas

Moving from one cinephilic film star to another, I now turn to Quentin Tarantino and begin with *Grindhouse,* the double-bill Robert Rodriguez-Quentin Tarantino spectacular, which opened in theaters in the United States in April 2007. This movie event's unabashed titular labeling — itself a marketing strategy[48] — of the Tarantino *Death Proof* as a grindhouse exploitation flick demonstrates how far Tarantino has come in helping shape American cinematic taste by moving B-movie aesthetics into mainstream acceptability. Together with films like *Reservoir Dogs* (1992), *Pulp Fiction* (1994), and *Jackie Brown* (1997), *Kill Bill Vol. 1* and *2* (2003 and 2004) have played a definitive role in initiating and sustaining this phenomenon.

For those who are new to the term, a grindhouse refers to a usually run-down theater, frequently located in a seedy part of town, screening B-grade, low-budget movies that feature gobs of gratuitous sex and violence. Hence, it is a theatrical space that denotes and connotes class differences through its appeal to the lowest denominator. As purported purveyors of bad taste, these theaters offer movies that generally fall into the category of the "exploitation film." In his extensive history of the genre, Eric Schaefer observes that the "classical [American] exploitation film," which "emerged in the early 1920s and existed throughout the 1950s,"[49] exhibited a number of characteristics, only two of which I will mention here. Firstly, "their primary subject was a 'forbidden' topic. The major exploitation topics included sex and sex hygiene, prostitution and vice, drug use, nudity, and any other subject considered at the time to be in bad taste." Secondly, these "films were made cheaply, with extremely low production values, by small independent firms."[50]

Exploitation films took on a "more fluid" classificatory nuance as they emerged out of the 1950s with, for instance, the "blaxploitation" films of the 1970s.[51] Beginning with the seminal *Sweet Sweetback's Baadasssss Song* (1971) by Melvin Van Peebles, Hollywood's major studios rode the ethnic exploitation wave with, for instance, the *Shaft* movies, the Pam Grier[52] starring vehicles *Coffy* (1973) and *Foxy Brown* (1974), and *Cleopatra Jones* (1973) with Tamara Dobson in the lead.[53] In fact, Dobson's follow-up outing in the role, *Cleopatra Jones and the Casino of Gold* (1975), was another semi-successful Hollywood-Hong Kong collaboration that reflects the mutual influences these two mega industries of global cinema had on each other. Jointly produced by Warner Brothers Pictures and Shaw Brothers, this "white-authored sequel . . . sent Cleo to Hong Kong where she destroys a Chinese, female-headed drug ring."[54] What was of special significance to this lesser known B-movie is that it similarly represented the Hong Kong Chinese in a racially exploitative fashion the way it did African Americans; and its Hong Kong connection symptomatically drew Chinese cinema into the American capitalist circuit of the exploitation film. I say "symptomatically" because it is not the first Chinese-language film to enter the market this way; other Hong Kong films, particularly genres like the *wuxia pian* and kung fu films, had already found their way into US grindhouses, often being paired as double-billed features with "blaxploitation" movies.[55]

United States censorship of cinema, as its long history reveals, has contributed to the classification of exploitation films as morally and aesthetically questionable commodities. Their marginality in American pop culture has led film scholars like Jeffrey Sconce to envision the genre as a "paracinema," a cinematic culture "in opposition to Hollywood and the mainstream US culture it represents."[56] Unconvinced by this binary distinction established between exploitation cinema and the Hollywood mainstream, Paul Watson prefers to view exploitation cinema within the larger history of cinema, cinema technology itself being inherently "exploitative." His theory basically throws into relief mainstream Hollywood cinema's complicit relationship to exploitation:

> Exploitation — the embodiment of tastelessness — is now itself, paradoxically, part of dominant taste, and its processes and discourses have become integral even to cinema's most official and mainstream manifestations. This suggests that if the concept of exploitation survives today, it does so neither as a paracinema, a beyond, an outside to cinema, nor as "cultural detritus" or the "cinematic dregs" that [Jeffrey] Sconce describes. Nor is it an intrinsically oppositional discourse, a "bad film" counter-aesthetic capable of filling the void vacated by the historical avant-

gardes. On the contrary, the significance of exploitation cinema now lies precisely in its proximity to the present capital-intensive patterns of film production. That is, if the concept of the exploitation film can be translated into the present at all, it is as a framework for discussing the production and marketing strategies of the most mainstream manifestation of cinema — Hollywood.[57]

Tarantino's oeuvre brings into form Watson's theory by reinventing exploitation aesthetics and re-presenting them as Hollywood blockbusters, a cinematic coming-home, so to speak — exploitation is Hollywood and Hollywood is exploitation. This issue has deep implications as one considers the place of Hong Kong cinema in Hollywood-exploitation films like *Kill Bill Vol. 1* and *2*.

For now I come to the more vexing question of taste and the pleasures that one derives from exploitation films. Taste is political in that one's ideological, philosophical, religious, and/or cultural makeup determine how one approaches the violence, gore, and sex seen in exploitation cinema. For example, Tarantino's films feature what some would consider intentional camp. Camp ruptures the good-bad distinctions in critique of the elitism of cultural stratification, as Susan Sontag delineates in her classic essay: "Camp taste turns its back on the good-bad axis of ordinary aesthetic judgment. Camp doesn't reverse things. It doesn't argue that the good is bad, or the bad is good. What it does is to offer for art (and life) a different — a supplementary — set of standards."[58] Hence, the playfulness of camp in daring to engage that which is taboo and abject is subversive in its politics, in the same way that gay sexuality's conceptions of play and playfulness disturb the boundaries of heterosexual male anxieties of the homoerotic, and that transvestism and transexuality cause "gender trouble,"[59] both often through the excesses of camp. But in acknowledging camp's political usefulness, I am also conscious of its function, as a hermeneutical barrier behind which one conceals modes of exploitation, be they sexual or violent, in the name of aesthetic play and sheer giddy fun. In other words, a politics of ambiguity emerges in the use of camp to indulge visually in politically questionable modes of exploitation and violation, particularly of women, racial minorities, and sexual minorities. (An extremely troubling illustration would be where Bruce Willis's Butch Coolidge rescues Ving Rhames's Marsellus Wallace from the rapists using a samurai sword in *Pulp Fiction*.) This visual pleasure can, for instance, be formally achieved through a sub-genre of the exploitation film, the female revenge movie, of which *Kill Bill*[60] is the ultimate contemporary example.

In order not to be misconstrued as attempting to play the role of moral police, I do admit to enjoying *Kill Bill* greatly. But the pleasures to me are utterly vexing because they are ambiguous, dubious, and ultimately troubling in their contradictions, complicities, and convolutions. One cannot reduce these pleasures to a simplistic Manichaean duality of good and bad, much less tease out the ethical implications of each of these pleasures and their originating motivations, particularly when much of my pleasure is derived from the notions of camp and ironic readings. Yet at the same time, I am unwilling to let Tarantino off easily, by arguing that the critical distancing of camp must not delude one into believing that the politically offensive elements of his films' originating sources are thus neutralized or diluted through his mode of cinematic pastiche and allusion. Furthermore, in terms of Chinese cinematic culture, the line between intertextuality and neocolonial pilfering is a fine one indeed, especially when Tarantino sutures disparate elements from the various cinemas by stripping them out of their original context. I am not here arguing that one must therefore treat these often B-grade Chinese films with an extremist form of reverential respect, nor am I suggesting that Tarantino's allusions do not pay homage to Chinese cinemas and thus help generate American mainstream interest in these filmic traditions: his love for and active promotion of Hong Kong cinema has in many ways helped filmmakers like John Woo and Yuen Woo-ping make their mark in Hollywood. My own anxious shuttling here between criticism and praise of Tarantino is to register the contradictions and conflicts his films' citationality generates, "visual quotation[s]"[61] that have enabled his works to enter the popular cultural mainstream, thereby making Tarantino a hot commodity in the American film business.

I want to start my analysis of *Kill Bill*'s cross-cultural citationality by noting that as the über-female revenge film, it incorporates and synthesizes not one, or two, but multiple revenge film traditions from various national and alternative cinemas. As Tarantino the ultimate film geek puts it, "it's like taking 30 years of my favourite [sic] grind-house movies and genres and sticking them into a press and that's this movie."[62] He references François Truffaut's *The Bride Wore Black* (1968), Burt Kennedy's *Hannie Caulder* (1971), Toshiya Fujita's *Lady Snowblood* (1973), Gary Sherman's *Dead and Buried* (1981),[63] and of course, I might add, Shaw sexploitation B-classics of the1970s. Uma Thurman's character Beatrix Kiddo, more symbolically called The Bride, sums up *Kill Bill*'s revenge motif in the opening sequence of *Vol. 2*:

> Looked dead, didn't I? Well, I wasn't. But it wasn't from lack of trying, I can tell you that. Actually, Bill's last bullet put me in a coma. A coma I was to lie in for four years. When I woke up, I went on what the movie advertisements refer to as: A roaring rampage of revenge. I roared and I

rampaged. And I got bloody satisfaction. I've killed a hell of a lot of people to get to this point. But I have only one more. The last one. The one I'm driving to right now. The only one left. And when I arrive at my destination I am going to kill Bill.

In this signature *in media res* start of *Kill Bill Vol. 2,* Tarantino through The Bride establishes the core ethos of the revenge motif: the female protagonist must emerge out of the fires of suffering and injustice to seek revenge on her victimizers, thus setting up the character's motivation and justification for the bloody carnage she will enact. In systematically killing from bottom to top a hierarchy of her victimizers, she arrives at the top honcho, in this case Bill, the killing of whom she will derive the most "bloody satisfaction," as the emphatic repetition of the "last one" signifies.

While Tarantino's filmic allusions are numerous, I want to focus specifically on the Shaw movies of the 1970s that Tarantino had immersed himself in during the script-writing process — "I had the fortunate fun of being able to watch at least one Shaw Brothers movie a day, if not three, and the reason I was doing it is that I wanted to immerse myself so much in that style of filmmaking so that the things that they did would be second nature to me. "[64] The revenge motif is part and parcel of popular Chinese cinemas, a theme which populates the vast catalog of the Shaw film archives in genres as disparate as horror, melodrama, *wuxia*, kung fu, fantasy, and soft-core erotic cinema. Three films of the 1970s stand out particularly: Chor Yuen's *Intimate Confessions of a Chinese Courtesan* (1972), Ho Meng-hua's *Kiss of Death* (1973), and Kuei Chih-hung's *Spirit of the Raped* (1976).

As a *wuxia*-erotic hybrid, Chor Yuen's *Intimate Confessions of a Chinese Courtesan* is a classic entry in Shaw's stash of "blue" films, the erotic or sexploitation films that titillate through their soft-core porn elements. Among the first mainstream Hong Kong films to bring lesbian sexuality to a viewing public, *Intimate Confessions of a Chinese Courtesan* recounts the experiences of Ai Nu (Lily Ho) — whose name means "love slave" and is also the Chinese title of the film — and how she was kidnapped and forced into prostitution by the lesbian Chun-i (Betty Pei Ti) who owns the Four Seasons Brothel. Ai Nu learns martial arts from Chun-i, who has fallen in love with her. Upon acquiring her skills, Ai Nu proceeds to plot her revenge by methodically killing all the men who have raped her or have forced her to have sex. She then confronts Chun-i in the final fight scene where Chun-i's arms are cut off in what must be an extremely stylized sequence of cinematic violence for audiences of the day. Ai Nu, as narrative conventions dictate, dies in the end when she kisses Chun-i as a final act of pity, and the latter poisons her with a literal kiss of death. Ho Meng-hua's *Kiss of Death* follows the same revenge narrative arc with the voluptuous Chen Ping playing Chu Ling, a young woman who was gang raped, and as a consequence contracts an incurable venereal disease called "Vietnam Rose." She becomes a bar girl, meets its owner (Lo Lieh), and learns kung fu from him. The film exploitatively moves from one scenic set-up to another, where Chu Ling is repetitively exposed to sexual assaults of various kinds, including one where she is molested by the doctor who is supposed to treat her disease. Like Ai Nu in *Intimate Confessions of a Chinese Courtesan*, Chu Ling dies after a violent enactment of revenge against her exploiters. Finally, the figure of the raped bride emerges in the horror-gore fest that is Kuei Chih-hung's *Spirit of the Raped*. A young woman who is engaged to be married is raped and killed after she witnesses her fiancé's death at the hands of thugs. Her spirit returns as a specter in a red Chinese wedding dress to wreak revenge on her victimizers, who die horrible and gruesome deaths befitting their crimes. While the revenge takes on a supernatural form and, hence, differs from the other two Shaw films, what is significant is the figure of the angry bride on a rampage, a figure we find repeated, of course, in *Kill Bill*.

These three films of Shaw cinema from the 1970s demarcate the cinematic parallels and references that *Kill Bill* collectively synthesizes and reinvents. The obvious plot and thematic similarities include the bride figure, rape, assault, martial arts, systematic revenge, and extreme violence. But my interest in this comparative study is less with the detailed pinpointing of similarities than the structures of cinematic pleasure that these revenge narrative arcs offer to audiences. When Bill (David Carradine), in a self-reflective manner, analyzes the libidinal impulse in his attempt to kill The Bride, he is not far off the mark in describing the cinematic pleasure of viewing these female revenge films: "You know, Kiddo, I'd like to believe that you're aware enough even now to know that there's nothing sadistic in my actions. Well, maybe towards those other . . . jokers, but not you. No Kiddo, at this moment, this is me at my most . . . [*cocks pistol*] masochistic." Clearly, the masochism in Bill's murderous criminality is structurally and morally worlds apart from the sadomasochistic pleasure of the heterosexual cinematic gaze in which *Kill Bill* lures its audiences to partake. What I want to draw on instead are the sexual resonances of this gaze and their moralistic emplacement within the female revenge film narrative.

Like its Shaw cinema precedents, *Kill Bill* takes its audience on a wild trip of exploitative indulgence in the guilty cinematic pleasures of sexual fetish and spectacularly gory violence. In order for revenge killings to occur, all these films must open with some form of violation of the female protagonist. The central characters in the three Shaw films emerge out of a prelapsarian state of sexual innocence, from which their subsequent violation strips them of. Though The Bride is in no way innocent — she is one of Bill's assassins and bears his child — Beatrix Kiddo as a bride intentionally foregrounds her desire to retreat away from the violent world of the Deadly Viper Assassination Squad to one of domestic bliss. Bill's attempt at killing The Bride in her white wedding dress as she is absorbed in her new world of church, friends, and a new family, brings her two worlds into confrontation and deadly collision, thereby accentuating the stark differences between them. The bridal dress and Beatrix's fragile pregnant state parallel the supposed girlish frailty and delicate innocence of Ai Nu and Chu Ling. In their rupture lies the sadomasochistic pleasure of the cinematic gaze.

Specific scenes of further sexual violation and exploitation create filmic depictions of sexual fetishes and tendencies, which later contribute to the just nature of the revenge killings. The so-called rape scenes dangerously offer titillation in their sanitization of rape's actual violation, with audiences feeling further moral absolution as they leave the theater knowing that the rapists have received their just deserts and the female protagonist, in her violated and hence "impure" state, is conveniently contained through her death, as in the case of *Intimate Confessions of a Chinese Courtesan* and *Kiss of Death*. *Kill Bill* replicates somewhat this narrative strategy. Like the character Chu Ling in *Kiss of Death* where the actress Chen Ping was provided every means of shedding her clothes in scenes that depict molestation or rape, The Bride suffers, during her four-year coma, possible multiple rapes by the hospital attendant and his lascivious male trucker buddy. Her violent retaliations become acceptable in the context of her exploitation. Similarly, the life stories of O-Ren Ishii's (Lucy Liu) revenge against the pedophilic murderer of her family, and Gogo Yubari's (Chiaki Kuriyama) phallic knife penetration of a leering Japanese businessman fall into the same pattern of the cinematic pleasures of exploitation and retaliation.

The significance of the narrative structure of violation-revenge-justice places what are the extremely problematic pleasures of the cinematic exploitation of sexual violence directed against women within a moralizing framework of justice served through vigilante executions. These films, hence, morph into morality tales that supposedly warn against sexual exploitation and criminality. In other words, the narrative's brief excursion into the taboo terrain of sexual violence and fetishism is redirected back into the moral mainstream, allowing audiences to experience visually the scandalous and questionable while salving their sense of propriety through their final identification with the film's narrative endorsement of a violent justice. The pleasures of sexual "perversity" shift into the pleasures of a post-violation exploitation of violence — The Bride's Hattori Hanzo sword becomes the phallic weapon in this pornography of violence that stabs, amputates, and decapitates.

Finally, the erotic pleasures that heterosexual male audiences derive in seeing girl-on-girl action come in both sexual and violent forms in these films, first in terms of lesbian contact (seen in *Intimate Confessions of a Chinese Courtesan*) as a prelude to heterosexual ménage à trois, and then in terms of the typical "cat-fight." This latter mode of filmic sexist violence panders to the heterosexual male gaze, as is typified in blaxploitation films such as *Coffy*, which Tarantino pays tribute to in *Jackie Brown*. The women-on-women violence is also seen in another Jack Hill film, *Switchblade Sisters* (1975), rereleased on DVD by the now defunct Rolling Thunder imprint also created by Tarantino. The Bride in *Kill Bill* has her share of this violence as she battles the maternal and yet deadly Vernita Green (Vivica A. Fox), the nubile Gogo Yubari in her Japanese school-girl uniform, the kimono-clad O-Ren Ishii, and the one-eyed Elle Driver (Daryl Hannah), whom many will remember in the naughty nurse outfit in *Vol. 1*. Every male heterosexual fetish is catered to here.

I want to return to where I started in this section, that is the question of the vexing pleasures of this film. Tarantino points out that "this whole movie takes place in this special universe" and that "this isn't the real world."[65] The rhetorical turn in his argument is one that correlates with camp, which places "everything in quotation marks,"[66] in its playful ironic distancing. Though I relish this ironic play, I am equally troubled by its apparently clear cut distinction between cinematic fantasy and the real world. The world of *Kill Bill* is an overdetermined one, not only by its appeal to a range of cinematic fantasies and fetishes but also by the very real cultural politics that all these fantasies and fetishes feed into. The film's professed removal from or disavowal of real-world cultural politics through its postmodern aesthetics only deepens the tensions of cinematic pleasure and its complicit relation to various modes of exploitation in a capitalist film economy.

The foregoing analysis of *Kill Bill* has indirectly demonstrated so far that Tarantino's film-buff inclinations have produced a work of cinematic excess, especially in its uncanny ability to cite copiously from the history of Chinese-language cinema. These references appear as commodities of Chinese cinematic culture in bite-size form for easy transcultural and transnational consumption. Tarantino expertly sutures these bits into an almost seamless collage of Chinese chic, where the barriers and boundaries of time, history, and culture are ignored or dismantled in the fabrication of the fantasy cinematic world of fluid cultural interpenetration and interchangeability; a world made possible through the "global/local synergy" of a capitalist "transnational imaginary."[67] For the uninitiated, this frenzy of cultural citation disembodies bits of Chinese-language cinema in order to offer the film a gloss of Oriental stylishness with little or no historical rootedness. This is, of course, the means through which Tarantino's cinema sells itself to the world, a cinema of cultural instantaneity, dazzlingly packaged in the form of exploitation cinema's shock tactics.

My criticism notwithstanding, I am still drawn to the self-congratulatory pleasure of picking out Tarantino's often obscure B-movie references of Hong Kong cinema, where in the remaining pages of this chapter I do not resist. However, to simply produce a veritable catalog of these references remains for me a less fruitful critical enterprise than to examine these points of citation as nodes of cultural abrasion and contortion, as various cinematic and cultural elements rub against each other like tectonic plates, producing some fascinating results. Here one must credit Tarantino for his ingenious play and playfulness that make him the directorial phenomenon that he is. The analysis that follows will coextensively assume the form of scattered notations on the various Chinese cinematic permutations that emerge in *Kill Bill*.

The Shaw Scope Logo: Tarantino obtained permission to use the Shaw Brothers' branding sequence to open *Kill Bill Vol. 1,* which provides for him a touch of cinematic nostalgia: "The Shaw Brothers, the Shaw Scope Logo and then, the Feature Presentation thing which I grew up watching, I always hear that tune before a movie starts. That just lets you know right away where I'm coming from and just sit back and have a good time and know from whence this came."[68] Mainstream American audiences will find Tarantino's nostalgia baffling, but Chinese audiences, especially those from Hong Kong and the Chinese diaspora, deeply empathize. I share completely Tarantino's sentiments, for I was a kid who grew up in the 1970s and early 1980s with a staple diet of Shaw films. Even today I bathe these films in a nostalgic glow that remembers, often erroneously, the pleasures of a good Shaw title, only to find how truly disappointing the film is in subsequent viewings. This nostalgia, in a sense, creates an amnesia of the almost Fordist assembly-line mechanical reproduction of Chinese-language B-flicks emerging rapidly out of Shaw studios to fill its theaters across the Hong Kong and Southeast Asian markets, hence accounting for its low production values and exploitation elements.[69] Tarantino's use of the logo deterritorializes it from its Hong Kong-British colonial capitalist history and embeds it in a postmodern assemblage of cinematic traces. Another fascinating point that one needs to note is that this logo itself represents a form of semiotic borrowing, as it looks almost exactly like the one used by Warner Brothers. This appropriation provides a material and symbolic representation of the citational circularity of the Hollywood-Hong Kong connection: Tarantino borrowing Shaw borrowing Warner Brothers.

The Chinese-Japanese American O-Ren Ishii: One of my favorite scenes in the film is where Lucy Liu's O-Ren Ishii is presiding over a meeting of the Japanese Yakuza heads where she is now the most powerful overlord:

> *Boss Benta*: Boss Tanaka! What is the meaning of this outburst? This is a time for celebration.
>
> *Boss Tanaka*: And what exactly are we celebrating? The perversion of our illustrious council?
>
> *Boss Honda*: Tanaka, have you gone mad? I will not tolerate this! You're disrespecting our sister! Apologize!
>
> *O-Ren Ishii*: Tanaka-san, of what perversion do you speak?
>
> *Boss Tanaka*: My father . . . [*to Benta*] along with yours . . . [*to Ozawah*] and along with yours, started this council. And while you laugh like stupid donkeys, they weep in the afterlife over the perversion committed today.
>
> *Boss Ozawah*: Outrageous! Tanaka, it is you who insults this council! [*Throws rag at him*] Bastard!
>
> *Boss Tanaka*: [*Throws rag back*] Fuck face!
>
> *O-Ren Ishii*: Gentlemen. Tanaka obviously has something on his mind. By all means, allow him to express it.
>
> *Boss Tanaka*: [*Last words*] I speak, of the perversion done to this council . . . which I love . . . more than my own children, by making a Chinese Jap-American half-breed bitch its leader!
>
> [*O-Ren quickly runs across the table and cuts off his head.*]

Lucy Liu's brilliantly campy geisha-like quick shuffle across the long meeting table in her kimono and Japanese slippers is followed by her terrifying beheading of the Yakuza boss. The jump cut of the initial humorous moment to the traumatic scene of decapitation with its fountainhead of blood spewing forth is fascinating in the context of O-Ren Ishii's mixed race heritage as the diegetic point of contention. Her decapitation of Boss Tanaka with her samurai sword not only reverses ironically the racial power relations between the Chinese and the Japanese — one is reminded of how the Japanese were so quick to chop off Chinese heads during World War Two — but it also microcosmically represents a transnational world order where global capitalism has helped engineer cultural mobility and hybridity that displaces and fragments the older systems of racial and nationalist insularity, parochialism, and centrism. What takes their place is not a new understanding of racial sensitivity and cooperation, but a power struggle forged ahead by US global hegemony as violently embodied by the Chinese-Japanese American O-Ren

Ishii. Her decision to address the other stunned Yakuza bosses in Lucy Liu's strongly Americanized English registers the new cultural power order:

> So you all will know the seriousness of my warning, I shall say this in English. As your leader, I encourage you from time to time, and always in a respectful manner, to question my logic. If you're unconvinced that a particular plan of action I've decided is the wisest, tell me so, but allow me to convince you and I promise you right here and now, no subject will ever be taboo. Except, of course, the subject that was just under discussion. *The price you pay for bringing up either my Chinese or American heritage as a negative is . . . I collect your fucking head.* Just like this fucker here. Now, if any of you sons of bitches got anything else to say, now's the fucking time![70]

Mish-Mash of Chinese Kung Fu Cinema: With Yuen Woo-ping — who is now becoming the requisite martial arts guru of Tinseltown after his stint in *The Matrix* trilogy — as the martial arts advisor on the film, Tarantino leaves nothing to chance in ensuring the authenticity of the fight sequences. He references Chinese martial arts in visual pop culture so extensively that *Kill Bill* is a rich goldmine of obscure kung fu cinema allusions — for instance, Neu!'s "Super 16" was originally used in Jimmy Wang Yu's *Master of the Flying Guillotine* (1975)[71]; and Quincy Jones' *Ironside* theme, which cues the murderous looks of The Bride, is also found in Cheng Chang-ho's *King Boxer* (1972) — Tarantino knows this film as *Five Fingers of Death*[72] because it was one of the few Shaw Brothers kung fu films that made it to the American box-office top ten, actually peaking at no. 3 on May 16, 1973, during what David Desser has termed the "kung fu craze" period in the 1970s in the United States.[73] These cinematic curiosities aside, three major references to Chinese kung fu deserve special mention and analysis: David Carradine, Bruce Lee, and Gordon Liu.

David Carradine-Bruce Lee Face-off: *Kill Bill* could conceivably be Tarantino's alternate universe restaging of the David Carradine-Bruce Lee face-off. Anyone familiar with Bruce Lee's short show-business career will know that there was no actual showdown between the two. Flushed with success from playing Kato in *The Green Hornet* (1966–1967) on Twentieth Century Fox's television show, Lee was supposed to star in the new Warner Brothers television drama *Kung Fu* (1972), to be aired on the American television network ABC. Instead, the role of Caine, the Shaolin monk who flees from his assailants to the United States, went to David Carradine. According to the cultural nationalist mythology surrounding his return to Hong Kong, Lee left the United States because "of his disappointment in losing the role of Kwai-chang/Caine . . . and the realisation [sic] that prejudice still ruled in the film capital."[74] There is a playful mythic tracking in Tarantino's use of David Carradine to star as Bill: his long slightly disheveled hair style, his flute playing, and his speech and physical mannerisms all echo a more mature version of Grasshopper, the nickname that Caine's Shaolin master had bestowed on him. With the flute, Tarantino is consciously pointing to another reference, the 1978 film called *The Silent Flute* (or *Circle of Iron*),[75] which also "ironically . . . starred David Carradine in the roles [Bruce] Lee envisioned for himself."[76] Tarantino admits that "if Bruce Lee was [sic] still alive, he'd be in" *Kill Bill*.[77] The next best thing is to have Uma Thurman dress up in the iconic yellow jumpsuit that Lee popularized in *Game of Death* (1978). It does not quite matter that a blond Anglo-American woman steps into the shoes of the Chinese cultural nationalist hero that Bruce Lee had become, because Tarantino is simply updating the intercultural sexploitation flicks from Shaw Brothers, such as Ho Meng-hua's outrageously cheesy *The Mighty Peking Man* (1977) and Pao Hsueh-li's *Deadly Angels* (1977), both starring Russian blonde bombshell Evelyne Kraft. (But unlike her 1970s predecessors, Beatrix Kiddo assumes the mantle of a 1990s Hollywood violent female protagonist, asserting a rather ambiguously feminist agency.[78]) What matters though is that in playing out the Carradine-Lee conflict on the screen for B-movie thrills, Tarantino is, consciously or not, re-inscribing traces of the historical context of the industry's and American society's race-conscious efforts to situate Chineseness and the virile Chinese masculinity that Bruce Lee embodied, into the mediatized spaces of racial containment. One only wonders if the cultural politics of race has indeed changed much in Hollywood since the days of Bruce Lee's flight back to Hong Kong.

Gordon Liu: Kung fu cinema aficionados revere Gordon Liu, who is better known in Hong Kong and the Chinese-cinema viewing world as Liu Chia-hui. Liu starred in a number of important Shaw martial arts classics such as *The 36ᵗʰ Chamber of Shaolin* (1978), *Clan of the White Lotus* (1980), and *Return to the 36ᵗʰ Chamber* (1980). Tarantino made maximum use of Liu in having him play Johnny Mo with the Kato-looking mask in *Vol. 1* and the cruel Pai Mei in *Vol. 2*. I wish to locate the film's "Chapter Eight: The Cruel Tutelage of Pai Mei" as part of Tarantino's mythic construction of the legend of The Bride. In the campfire scene, Bill recounts for Beatrix's benefit a "Once upon a time in China" story of Pai Mei's incredible skills and his utter cruelty, before sending her off to be tutored by this White Lotus Clan master. (Interestingly, Liu appeared in *Clan of the White Lotus* where he battled Lo Lieh's similarly white-haired villain.) Pai Mei subjects Beatrix to the usual sexist, patriarchal putdowns before starting her training. Beatrix, in undergoing the standard kung fu discipleship one sees in almost every other Chinese martial arts film, emerges as Pai Mei's best pupil, hence leading him to teach her his dreaded and deadly Five-Point-Palm Exploding-Heart Technique, which she uses to finish off Bill in the end. For the average Chinese audience, this Pai Mei sequence is so familiar, and yet so alien at the same time. A process of defamiliarization[79] has occurred where the genre's once familiar convention of cruel tutelage is now made new or strange again when stripped off its generic, temporal, and cultural context. Pai Mei's attire, hairstyle, mannerisms, and speech have undergone temporal dislocation in their emplacement within the narrative context of the modern-day setting in *Kill Bill*. Even the Technicolor quality of the scene, its cinematography (especially in the zoom-in[80] close-ups of Pai Mei), and the standard kung fu training "sequence where the characters [in black silhouette] were doing martial arts in front of a [red-colored] background"[81] seem out of joint from the rest of the film in terms of cinematic technique. The B-movie aesthetic quality of Hong Kong flicks becomes more evident in the film's postmodern pastiche, lending a heightened quality of kitsch to its Chinese cinematic chic. For American audiences, Pai Mei's cultural idiosyncrasies will probably be lost in translation to many, as one film scholar even misconstrues the character as "an almost parodic dandy,"[82] attesting again to the cultural consequences of Tarantino's technique. Finally, to be fair to Tarantino, his casting of Liu not only pays homage to a kung fu cinema icon but Liu's star turn in *Kill Bill* also possibly helped kick start a potential Hollywood film career: he was supposed to star in *Heroes of Shaolin*.[83]

Uma Thurman and Gordon Liu in a stylized fight-training sequence

Kill Bill displays the cinematic chutzpah of Quentin Tarantino, represented by the kind of unrestrained license he takes in appropriating and suturing a wide range of Chinese and other national cinematic elements into a postmodern product for global consumption. His reinvention and remaking of Chinese cinema, if you can call it that, may be excessive, exploitative, and exaggerated; but it is also indicative of what Hollywood transnational cinema can accomplish through its processes of cultural repackaging and commodification, albeit in the most heightened of ways. While I ambivalently look forward to more, I fear, in contradiction to this pleasure, what the cannibalization of Chinese cinema may eventually lead to.

7

Chinese Supernaturalism:
Mythic Ethnography and the Mystical Other

Remaking Asian horror is presently big business in Hollywood. Hideo Nakata's *Ringu* (1998) first crawled onto American cinema screens as Gore Verbinski's *The Ring* (2002), terrifying audiences enough to bring them back for more, thus conjuring a host of other similar haunting remakes: *The Grudge* (2004), *The Ring 2* (2005), *Dark Water* (2005), *The Grudge 2* (2006), and *The Eye* (2008). Jaded horror fans seek a different and unusual kind of thrill to jolt them out of Hollywood's tired and predictable formulae of vampires, zombies, and exorcisms. What these new Asian horror remakes bring to the fear of the supernatural unknown is the xenophobic dread of the inscrutable ethnic "alien" Other.[1] This figurative correlation has been well established by film scholar Robin Wood, who argued more than two decades ago, that the horror film allows for monstrous representations "of the figure of the Other," which includes various marginalized groups such as ethnic minorities.[2] Cultural estrangement undoubtedly scares the living daylights out of white American suburbia.

Of course, Asian supernaturalism, mysticism, religion, and the occult unfortunately occupy a troubled place in the history of Asians in America. The fin de siècle period that saw anti-Chinese legislation also witnessed the emergence of the "yellow peril," which white America perceived as "a threat to nation, race, and family,"[3] particularly the Christian family. Gina Marchetti draws out this connection between the yellow peril and the "pagan" religions and mysticism of Asia, which serves as the Manichaean Other to Christian civilization: "Rooted in medieval fears of Genghis Khan and Mongolian invasions of Europe, the yellow peril combines racist terror of alien cultures, sexual anxieties, and the belief that the West will be overpowered and enveloped by the irresistible, dark, *occult* forces of the East."[4] Early Hollywood films like D.W. Griffith's *Broken Blossoms* (1919) constructed images of an Oriental religious Other, which would soon become contiguous with other representations of inscrutable alterity.[5] These cinematic images formed a part of a larger discourse that painted Chinatown as a den of sin, degradation, and evil, epitomized by Sax Rohmer's Fu Manchu of classic Hollywood. Asia hence became the repository of spiritual corruption and Faustian seduction.

Unfair it would be to leave this discussion of Orientalist conceptions of Asia at its historical worst; for multiculturalist politics in recent decades have helped modulate, for mainstream Anglo-Americans, stereotypes of Asian religiosity and superstition by elevating them into the realms of spiritual transcendence and enlightenment, all this in spite of (or probably because of) their perceived primitivism. The newly acquired spiritual and cultural sensitivity, as embodied in stars like Richard Gere, Steven Seagal, and Brad Pitt, has become yoked to a Hollywood activism critical of mainland Chinese politics, a critique that is both deserving in its identification of human rights abuses, and yet problematic in its neo-imperialist capitalist agenda.[6] (I dealt with this issue in greater detail in Chapter Three.) But what is fascinating to me here, for the purposes of this chapter, is that spirituality and the supernatural continue to engage the earthbound politics of international relations and intercultural conflict. In the context of Hollywood's latest symbiotic relations with, and incorporation of, transnational Chinese cinemas, the supernatural would become the point of transcultural contact and intercultural contestation.

Coterminous with the Asian horror fad is a recent spate of films dealing with Chinese elements of the supernatural, the occult, and the mystical. Beginning with the Disney-fication of the *Mulan* (1998) story, Hollywood, East Asian, and Hollywood-East Asian co-productions have generated a cinematic cornucopia on the subject: Taiwanese director Chen Kuo-fu's *Double Vision* (2002); *The Touch* (2002) directed by Peter Pau and starring Michelle Yeoh[7]; *Bulletproof Monk* (2003) starring Chow Yun-fat and produced by Terence Chang and John Woo; the Stanley Tong-directed Jackie Chan vehicle *The Myth* (2005); and Chen Kaige's dismal attempt at the *shenguai wuxia* genre,[8] *The Promise* (2005). The phenomenon common to all these films is what I call a "Chinese supernaturalism," a term that refers to the frenzied cinematic representations of religious, mystical, superstitious, spiritual, and/or supernatural elements in Chinese culture, which dizzyingly spiral within the vortex of transnational audience appeal as filtered through or inflected by the Hollywood system.

The fantastical and grotesque imagery that populate these films come at us with such a frenzied speed, which Bhaskar Sarkar, in his reading of Hong Kong martial arts films, has identified as having "a distinctly absurd or hysterical quality about them." These films "become allegories of their context: anxieties over the new economic realities, the effects on social and cultural life, and the emerging political alignments are played out onscreen with hysterical abandonment."[9] Though Sarkar's point concerns Hong Kong's pre-1997 political realities, it rings true for these films of Chinese supernaturalism, particularly as commodities of transnational capital. Not only do these films have to meet the demands of Chinese audiences around the world, but they also have to find various means to meet the production standards of Hollywood while connecting with non-Chinese American and global viewers. Supernaturalism as cinematic trope becomes "the uncanny site of a contact zone crowded and haunted by various forces."[10] As part of the process of "transculturation," "where subordinated or marginal groups select and invent from materials transmitted to them by a dominant or metropolitan culture,"[11] Chinese supernaturalism appropriates, hybridizes, and reconfigures Chinese history, myth, fantasy, and popular culture, especially Chinese cinematic genre traditions, to achieve a transcultural, or "universal" resonance, so as to attain global marketability. But these contact zones are also zones of anxiety, slippage, and fragmentation, unveiling the uneasy suturing of the local to the global. The narrative deployment of the supernatural as it transgresses and transcends both temporality and spatiality become the filmic means of erecting the fantasy of transcultural connectivity and universal meaning.

In order for Chinese supernaturalism to spin its magic of temporal transcendence, it needs first to traverse back and forth *in* time. The notion of the supernatural works through and ruptures, what Rey Chow has called, "primitivism" in contemporary Chinese cinema. Primitivism deploys "modes of signification" that shuttle between "'culture' and 'nature.'" The cultural rhetoric of "primitivism" rests on the following premise: "if Chinese culture is 'primitive' in the pejorative sense of being 'backward' (being stuck in an earlier stage of 'culture' and thus closer to 'nature') when compared to the West, it is also 'primitive' in the meliorative sense of being an ancient culture (it was there first, before many Western nations)." The double cultural turn here allows for Chinese culture to assert both its victimized status, while foregrounding its cultural superiority in terms of its antiquity.[12] Chinese supernaturalism, therefore, rides on this notion of antiquity and takes it to a superlative level: it does not only argue for an ancient beginning, but it goes beyond that beginning to a time before time, to a time transcendent of time. The supernatural forms a kind of third term in the triangulation of culture-nature-supernatural. The supernatural produces the illusion or the fantasy of a transcultural or trans-human space that enables the possibilities of human identity, existence, mediation, and connection. So, the themes of immortality, morality, predestination, and free will are important concepts that are repeatedly invoked in these films, ideas and themes that everyone can appreciate. Many of these films, for instance, seek to use the supernatural as a means of bridging or negotiating between East and West. In other words, while the supernatural affirms its superiority or precedence through antecedence, its "trans" status, it remains rooted in human and cultural signification and is invoked for human and cultural purposes. To approach this issue from another angle, like the nature and culture divide, the supernatural is as cultural as nature is cultural. It is only defined by culture to be transcultural. Its transculturalism or "universality" is, therefore, a fantasy through which these films offer global audience appeal.

The rest of this chapter examines four films from this perspective: *Bulletproof Monk*'s turn to fictitious Tibetan myths of immortality; *Double Vision*'s cultic forms of Taoist beliefs; and *The Myth*'s reworking of reincarnation and the semi-mythic story of the first Chinese emperor's obsession with the pill of immortality. I conclude the chapter with a brief meta-textual analysis of the histrionics surrounding *The Promise* and its failure to be the film that it so anxiously aspires to be.

Translating the Mythic in *Bulletproof Monk*

"The Bulletproof Monk is a mythical hero in a modern world. He is here to teach people to believe in themselves against overwhelming adversity. Once again, a person must fight to discover the right thing to do and fight even harder to get it done," writes John Woo, in the foreword to the comic book original upon which the 2003 movie is based.[13] As the co-producer of Paul Hunter's film, Woo lends his imprimatur because he believes in the story's universal ethic of doing the right thing. It is this "universal" appeal that ultimately sells the film to an American audience. How it accomplishes this "universality" is the focus of my analysis.

Bulletproof Monk really had the luxury of a guaranteed comic-book fan base to tap into, but the timing of its production and release clearly also took advantage of Hollywood's new fascination with Chinese action cinema, including the casting of the ever cool Chow Yun-fat in the lead role for superstar power. In addition, its plot configurations of having the character Monk (Chow) hand over the guardianship of an ancient Tibetan scroll, which apparently offers its bearer both invincibility and a form of immortality, to Kar (Seann William Scott) and Jade (Jaime King), young Anglo-American characters, articulates a multiculturalist sensitivity that is appealing to the general American audience. In this sense, *Bulletproof Monk* should really be read as the superhero version of the Asian-American immigrant success story. The narrative structuring of ethnic incorporation (as assimilation) and eventual invisibility is what makes this immigrant success story comforting to the Anglo-American mainstream and, hence, "universal" in its telling.

In order to achieve this ethnic invisibility, the film needs to initiate the process of cultural translation by taking the mythic and the supernatural that are in Tibet and relaying them into an American context. The opening exposition sequences not only construct historical and cultural distancing — in the spiritualized spaces of Tibet, against the backdrop of the crude material violence that is Nazi Germany — but they also prepare audiences for their later relocation to a nondescript, major American urban center,[14] which functions as modernity's stand-in. The time is 1943 and Monk's master has guarded the Scroll for a long six decades. According to the fulfillment of the Prophecies, he has finally identified Monk as his successor:

> When you first came to me, you were the most undisciplined youth I'd ever laid eyes on, yet you proved yourself worthy to be the Next Guardian. You have fulfilled the Three Noble Prophecies. You defeated an army of enemies while a flock of cranes circled above. And then you battled for love in the Palace of Jade. And finally, you freed brothers you never knew with the family you never had. Now you must make the final sacrifice — give up your name.

Monk is thus expected, within the film's diegetic and audience-reception framework, to bring the Scroll and the Prophecies into present-day America.

In viewing *Bulletproof Monk* as supernatural fantasy, one is expected to suspend questions and disbelief — what is this Scroll about? Why must it be protected when it can grant powers of healing and regeneration to its bearer? Is one protecting the truth that is in the Scroll or the power that it brings? Because these questions are not to be asked, the point of the film shifts from that of the Scroll to that of the notion of prophecy as an enabler of human involvement and agency. A prophecy projects into the future before disabling itself upon its fulfillment. What then matters is the person who has been prophesied about and what that person brings to humanity. This emphasis is important in that Tibetan spirituality and supernaturalism are only instrumental, a means to an end, to the shift of human agency from Monk to the characters Kar and Jade. The writers of the film could have constructed any Asian mythic story to fill the place of this one, and it would not have mattered. What truly matters is that the morality tale of finding the right thing to do and doing it is being culturally translated via the instrumentality of the myth, and brought into the realm of the American everyday through the agency of Anglo-American versions of the bulletproof hero.

Cultural translation, of course, is both apt metaphor and linguistic reality that *Bulletproof Monk*'s narrative invokes, reiterating my earlier discussion of its connection to the concept of remaking as it involves the Chinese in Hollywood.[15] The idea of cultural translation, hence, resonates on both textual and contextual levels, at times even intertwining diegetically. For instance, as the atypical American immigrant, Monk waxes philosophical in stereotypical "fortune cookie" speak when he tries to "put it in language . . . [Kar] will understand," such as "Why do hot-dogs come in packages of ten while hot-dog buns come in packages of just eight?" Like the invention of the fortune cookie, this Americanized pseudo-Confucian wisdom of the quotidian panders to the comforting misconceptions of the Chinese. Another episode of translational misadventures is found in the scene where Monk secretly espies Kar brandishing his martial-arts skills alone in a cinema hall. Living in this battered old theater called the Golden Palace where classic Chinese kung fu films are being screened, Kar has acquired his skills through mimicking the pugilistic moves of these actors who come from a time and place far removed from his own. This moment of the film's clever self-referentiality mimics its own moves of cultural translation in the reconfiguration of Chineseness through Hollywood — the film is itself a translation of other Chinese kung fu movies. Kar's kung fu skills may be based on cinematic fantasy, but it does not really matter, because it achieves a level of reality all on its own. In other words, the mode of cultural translation works through a poststructuralist circularity where Chineseness moves from signifier to signifier. Hollywood's conception of Chineseness similarly translates one cinematic form of cultural fantasy to another, ultimately serving only its own transnational capitalist goals of increasing US and global box-office takings.

The ultimate case of cultural translation resides in the Three Noble Prophecies, which Monk (mis)reads in the most humorous of ways. He takes great exegetical liberty in construing the "flock of cranes" to mean the mechanical cranes — machinery as signifier of American capital — that hang over Kar as he almost single-handedly (with the surreptitious aid of Jade) battles Funktastic's gangster crew. The mystical battle "for love in the Palace of Jade" is reread as a love story between Kar and Jade, who flirtatiously tussle with each other in Jade's Russian mafia father's mansion. And, their freeing the "brothers you never knew with the family you never had" reflects the immigrant context of Monk and the "family" of American-based Tibetan monks, to whom Jade and Kar find themselves connected. What is remarkably entertaining is the creative interpretive work that the cultural translation of the Prophecies calls for to suit America's needs. The interpretive results become "modernized" in very American terms of emphasis: its technologism (capitalist machinery), its narration (the love story), and its social context (multicultural America).

One of Monk's philosophies in his approach to Kar is that "everyman's life concerns every other man, especially if he is on the noble path to true enlightenment," a philosophy permitting Monk to believe that Kar could possibly be the "Next Guardian." As he tells his fellow American Tibetan monk, "the Prophecies must apply to everyone, or they mean nothing." This transcultural rhetoric of universal applicability of the Prophecies is the film's narrative means of bestowing on Kar and Jade this guardianship, turning its universality into Anglo-American specificity. The film ends with an American replication of the earlier Tibetan ceremony, this time with Monk laying hands on Kar and transferring the text of the Scroll into both Kar and Jade. In a final marriage-like ceremony, the now wrinkled Monk, with a quiet ministerial dignity, confirms Jade and Kar as the new Guardians of the Scroll: "You both fulfilled the Prophecies. Not two lives that are incomplete. One complete life. " After he whispers in their ears the two halves of the final verse of the Scroll, he offers the following benediction: "Now you're inseparable, the unity of opposites." The harmony of yin and yang is transmogrified into an Anglo-American heterosexual union.

The wrinkling of Chow Yun-fat's Monk

Kar and Jade represent the incorporation of Tibetan/Chinese culture for their own and society's betterment. In other words, ethnic differences must and should serve the greater national good. Ethnic specificity embodied by Monk as the Asian-American immigrant must then be translated into the culturally assimilated forms embodied by Kar and Jade's whiteness, which bleaches ethnic peculiarities into safely homogenized forms of the multiculturalism[16] and cosmopolitanism that the new bulletproof heroes now share, a refigured version of what Frantz Fanon rather ingeniously and catachrestically calls "lactification."[17] With his ethnic usefulness expended, Monk's final goodbye wave as he visually disappears, like magic, into a sea of people, signals his assimilation into mainstream invisibility, thus preserving intact the white body politic.

Double Vision: Supernaturalism as the Love That Unites

Taiwanese director Chen Kuo-fu's *Double Vision* belongs to a new breed of Asian films that target markets within and beyond Asia. The film is produced by Columbia Pictures Film Production Asia, part of the Columbia TriStar Motion Picture group, Sony Pictures Entertainment — the production giant responsible for Zhang Yimou's *The Road Home* (1999), Ang Lee's *Crouching Tiger, Hidden Dragon* (2000), Tsui Hark's *Time and Tide* (2000), Corey Yuen's *So Close* (2002), He Ping's *Warriors of Heaven and Earth* (2003), and Stephen Chow's *Kung Fu Hustle* (2004). What is interesting about this film is that it does not only have a pan-Asian cast including Tony Leung Ka Fai and Rene Liu, but it also features David Morse, who lends a cross-cultural, Hollywood element to its appeal. Though the film did not make it into general theatrical release in the US, Morse's presence provides the American draw for its DVD release and signals the film's Hollywood branding that has become an important element in ensuring the box-office success of Chinese films internationally.

Tony Leung stars as a Taiwanese cop, Huang Huo-tu, who is not only plagued by the social alienation and trauma of exposing corruption within the Taiwanese police force, but also battles a crippling sense of helplessness as he relives in his mind the moment where his daughter Mei Mei (Huang Wei-han) was held hostage by a relative who was criminally involved in the corruption he helped identify. Though she survived the ordeal, Mei Mei has withdrawn into complete silence — she refuses to utter a word. These events have led to a straining of the relationship between Huo-tu and his wife Ching-fang (Rene Liu). Meanwhile, the police force is faced with a series of murders, one more baffling than the other. The first victim is the chairman of a chemical company, who has been accused of dumping toxic waste. He drowns in the summer heat of his office. What is more baffling is that crime-scene investigators discover ice in his lungs. The second victim is a senator's mistress, who is burnt to death in her apartment, with no apparent signs of fire in the aftermath. The priest of a church is the third victim discovered to have been disemboweled while reading in bed one night. He is, however, no ordinary priest, in that he has played a significant role in facilitating Taiwan's purchase of weapons from the United States. In order to allay public fears of the supernatural nature of these killings, the Taipei police invites FBI serial murder specialist Kevin Richter (David Morse) to help with the case. Together, Richter and Huo-tu follow the evidence trail to an immortality-seeking Taoist cult, led by a young girl with double pupils. The girl and her followers have already claimed a fourth victim, who has had his heart ripped out. According to the cult's mythology, each of the killings must replicate one of the five representations of Taoist hell. Just when the case is believed to have been solved and the perpetrators caught, Richter becomes the fifth and final victim. Huo-tu discovers him dead the morning Richter is scheduled to leave for the United States; he has apparently ripped out his own tongue in his sleep. This ritual killing parallels the fifth and final hell in the mythology. Richter's death sends Huo-tu into a tailspin, leading him to the final confrontation scene with the girl with the double pupils. After killing the girl, he enters into an apparently fatal coma. The film ends with the possibility of his miraculous recovery when his daughter Mei Mei breaks her silence by calling out to her father.

Double Vision falls into the genre category of the contemporary serial killer film, such as *Se7en* (1995) and *The Silence of the Lambs* (1991); but it distinguishes itself with its Asian religious slant. The director uses this context to frame the predictable East-versus-West cultural conflict, a theme that appeals to audiences' stereotypical understanding of East-West cultural differences. The arrival of FBI investigator Kevin Richter intentionally throws into relief these apparent cultural differences: Richter is accosted by Taipei reporters asking him how he is going to investigate the case if he cannot speak Chinese. Richter's American take-charge attitude does not go down well with Huo-tu's colleagues, leading Huo-tu to advise him to "be more respectful and not talk so much." More importantly, the film offers a critique of how this perception of East-West cultural differences can be deployed and manipulated by the powers-that-be for various political purposes. Richter has been requested by the Taipei police to assist in the investigation in order to give the impression that its privileging of scientific methods in forensic work represents progress, as the police chief's press statement indicates:

> After an initial investigation, we have discovered that the deaths of Father Lorenzo, the Chairman of Tai Feng, and Chiu Miao-fang are all possibly

related. These are serial murders. Because this case has generated many rumors causing anxiety among our society, our police force wishes to solve this case *logically*. Through the American Institute in Taiwan, the FBI has agreed to send an agent specializing in serial murder to Taiwan to assist in solving this case. We hope he can use a *scientific* method to move us forward.
18

The East is thus linked to religious superstition and mysticism, while the West is credited with rationalism, positivism, and hence, progress. Instead of deconstructing this binary opposition, the film's critique becomes a cultural nationalist one that reifies the logic it seeks to question in the first place. Take the following conversation between Huo-tu and Richter, for instance:

Huo-tu: You just don't understand. You can't see all the evil in your country.
Richter: We see it. And we managed to lock it up once in a while.
Huo-tu: That's impossible.
Richter: Look. But I rely on science, not talismans, not good luck charms.
Huo-tu: Your so-called scientific methods are only useful when dealing with mortals like ourselves. There are beings that cannot be controlled by our laws.
Richter: What are you saying? Are you saying that the killer is an evil spirit? Or some kind of . . . or something from another world?
Huo-tu: What's wrong with you, Mr. Richter? All your years in the FBI, you have never encountered with [sic] a demon before?

The cultural nationalist logic is married here to the supernatural, as the very nature of the genre creates the narrative conditions for this logic to be an acceptable one. When Richter becomes the fifth and last victim despite their having scientifically "solved" the case, this cultural nationalist logic is brought to filmic narrative conclusion. Richter has to die and be sacrificed because, like the other victims who were morally corrupt, his crime or sin is one of unbelief — during a television interview immediately after he has helped crack the case, Richter offers this statement that is retrospectively ironic: "It could be a lot easier for us if there were ghosts and evil spirits. Unfortunately, man is worse than any figment of our imagination." Because of the way the narrative sets up Richter's fall, the film could be read as anti-West in its cultural rhetoric; but I want to suggest that the scenario offers two possible interpretations, thereby lending to a wider audience appeal. The notion that a cocky American "had it coming," so to speak, for being culturally arrogant has a kind of appeal to certain sectors of the global audience; yet, the film could also be seen in the light of a multicultural correctness, a sensitivity to other religious and spiritual beliefs, a kind of cultural self-flagellation, making it equally marketable in the United States.

Richter's death almost seems to give the film license to launch completely into the supernatural. Huo-tu, in losing consciousness, soon finds himself in the hospital room of the girl with the double pupil. She flees, he gives chase, and they arrive at the temple where the girl's followers had an earlier violent encounter with the police. This cat-and-mouse sequence becomes a surrealistic mind-blowing moment for Huo-tu as he enters into a life-and-death tussle with the girl. Time and space are ruptured, as Huo-tu moves through various temporal frames and spatial dimensions represented by quick jump cuts and slow-motion sequences.[19] Cinema, with its various visual techniques, offers here a depiction of a different kind of temporality, a temporality of the supernatural. One could almost call this a "messianic time," which Giorgio Agamben characterizes as an "operational time." It is "not a supplementary time that could be added from outside to chronological time. It is, rather, a time within time — not ulterior, but interior — which measures only my disconnection with it, the impossibility of coinciding with my representation of time — but for the same reason, it also opens up the possibility of grasping and accomplishing it." It is "the time which is left to us,"[20] the time of the present moment,[21] the time for salvation.

Huo-tu's battle with the girl with the double pupils is not just a physical one, it is also a spiritual and psychologically personal one: he is battling his own demons. Part of the prophecy that the film narrative constructs is one that involves immortality: it is believed that the person who achieves immortality has to go through an extremely grave illness. In finally slipping out from this supernatural temporality, Huo-tu slips back into a coma. The final scene in the film has the paramedics carting him out of the temple building,[22] with his wife and child rushing to his side. It is in this moment of mourning that Mei Mei emerges from her long silence and calls out to her dad. Suddenly, tears start to flow from Huo-tu's eyes, signifying that he will probably survive this ordeal. More importantly, it also establishes Huo-tu's role in the prophecy in that he has survived a grave illness and is immortalized. This notion of immortality, as the final postscript of the film suggests, is different in that it involves not eternal life but eternal love. The postscript basically reads in Chinese: *youai buse*, or "where there is love, there is no death." As much as this is a cringe-worthy moment, it is also a fascinating one in seeing how the film at the end reconfigures the supernatural into the universal — the universal appeal of love, cementing the global appeal of the film. In a scene prior to his death, Richter offers Huo-tu the following advice: "Now I may be a foreigner, but there are some things that are universal. What you're doing to your family and yourself I have seen it before. Now you gave me some advice when I first got here; I'm going to return the favor." In a way that he has never intended, Richter brings Huo-tu and his family back together through his death, thereby erasing the cultural distance between them in his role within the film's supernaturalism. East and West are eventually bridged through the supernaturalism that is love.

Crossing Time and Space: Supernaturalism as Cultural Nationalism in *The Myth*

Stanley Tong's *The Myth* reaches out to a specifically core Asian audience, while extending its target outwards, globally. Produced by Jackie Chan's Hong Kong-based JCE Entertainment, the film has been screened almost everywhere but in the United States. It is one of Jackie Chan's more recent Hong Kong movies since his joining Hollywood's A-list of box-office superstars who can command their own — Jackie Chan is an exemplary instance of Aihwa Ong's notion of Chinese "flexible citizenship," with his one leg in Hong Kong and another in Hollywood, straddling the best of both worlds. This flexible or mobile locality is interesting in light of Chan's recent comments on his Asian productions. He argues that his made-in-Asia films allow him to be more experimental, and he seeks to protect "his market value in the U.S. by limiting the Stateside release of his Hong Kong movies that are made on a lower budget than U.S. productions."[23] In realizing his own commodification within the Hollywood star system, Chan exhibits a shrewd entrepreneurial business sense in his strategy of keeping separate the two working spheres, which he knows will never be perfectly insulated from each other in a global cinematic industry dominated by Hollywood. His "experimental" efforts in Hong Kong seldom fail because he has a robust global fan base established way before Hollywood came a-calling, a fan base that will ultimately help him constitute an even larger one for his Hollywood films. His cinematic innovations will also eventually feed into the Hollywood system when the American viewing public tires of the formulaic flicks churned out en masse by studio drones. Jackie Chan will be there again to offer fresh blockbuster ideas, thereby sustaining his longevity in the system. In working with the elements of a fantastical history — China's first emperor's search for immortality[24] — *The Myth*'s Chinese supernaturalism accomplishes two things. Firstly, it presents a strong cultural appeal to Chinese and Chinese diasporic audiences. This appeal parallels the Shanghai cinemas of the 1920s where there "was the return of 'Chineseness' with a vengeance — a kind of legendary, magical 'Chineseness' that spun out of control," according to Yingjin Zhang.[25] (Studios like Tianyi and Mingxing churned out *wuxia pian* and *shenguai pian*.[26]) Secondly, *The*

Myth's intricate intercultural narrative structure and its beautiful pan-Asian cast maintain a broad appeal to global audiences, while never quite fully closing its doors to America, particularly through foreign DVD sales. My inclusion of this non-US film in this chapter is to reiterate again the trans-Pacific cross-cultural flows that enable the production of a film like *The Myth*, particularly in the way Hollywood influences and inflects Chan's work, as much as Chan contributes to Hollywood's remaking. Hence, it is of no coincidence that the film was released during a time when Chinese supernaturalism was asserting a strong presence in Hollywood cinema.

The truly global nature of the film's casting is also reflected in its narrative's geographical scope. Much like his earlier films where the globetrotting Chan crisscrosses various national borders — *Who Am I?* (1998), *The Accidental Spy* (2001), and *Around the World in 80 Days* (2004) — *The Myth* moves Chan's modern-day character, Jack, from Hong Kong to India and finally to China, while allowing his Qin-dynasty character, General Meng Yi, to fall in love with a Korean princess. To facilitate this mode of time traveling and cross-cultural mobility, the film deploys Chinese supernaturalism to cut through temporal and spatial barriers so as to create a narrative of transculturalism where the localism of Chan's Hong Kong/Chinese cultural rootedness is comfortably embedded in, while working through, the film's globalism — the cinematic equivalent of the local in the global for the sake of transnational capital. The key ingredient is Jackie Chan's star persona, which shuttles between the film's twin narratives and between his two characters.

Based on the belief in reincarnation, *The Myth*'s two narratives, set in two different time periods separated by almost two millennia, meet in Dr. Jack Chan (Jackie Chan), Hong Kong archeologist extraordinaire, whose intrepid findings and gutsy attitude have won him the distinction of foiling the Dead Sea Scrolls forgery. But Jack is haunted by dreams of another life in another time: as General Meng Yi during Qin Shihuang's reign. Meng Yi has been tasked by the Emperor to escort and protect Korean Princess Ok-soo (Kim Hee-seon) who is to become Concubine Li of Qin. Because the entourage has been intercepted and scattered by Ok-soo's disgruntled Korean general lover, Meng Yi and Ok-soo find themselves making their way back on their own to Xianyang, the Qin capital. Of course, the two fall in love when unhindered by their social and political roles and constraints, but it is a love that is not to be as their historical destinies dictate. The ailing emperor sends Meng Yi on a dangerous mission to retrieve the Immortality Pill, but the latter is ambushed by court intrigue and betrayal, and is consequently killed in the battlefield. But before Meng Yi leaves on his fateful mission, Ok-soo tells him that she will wait for his return, literally. Forced to be the royal taster, Ok-soo consumes the Immortality Pill and lives into the twenty-first century in the emperor's hidden mausoleum. In the present, Jack is lured by his greedy friend William (Tony Leung Ka Fai) on a trip in search of an anti-gravity stone from outer space, an adventure of the likes of Indiana Jones, that takes them from Dasai, India, to Xi'an, China, where the famed terracotta warriors[27] were found. They discover a cave leading into the Qin Emperor's mausoleum, which uses the anti-gravity stone to levitate an entire imperial palace tomb. Jack and Ok-soo finally meet, with the latter discovering that Jack is only Meng Yi reincarnated and is not Meng Yi himself. She decides to remain in the mausoleum, waiting for her lover to return, despite the fact that William's greed has led him to dislodge the anti-gravity gem from its place, thereby sending a cataclysmic chain reaction that destroys and buries the mausoleum forever.

In order to unravel the intertwining mechanisms of the two narratives, one needs to understand the function of Jackie Chan's star persona, which is an amalgamation of Chan's personality, his philosophies, his background, and the public image he wishes to cultivate. This persona permeates the screen roles that Chan adopts, which in turn contribute new elements and characteristics that help evolve this persona. One of the central representations of himself that Chan keenly maintains is his good-guy image, revolving around a principle of moral integrity. An aspect of this integrity centers on his sense of belonging to Chinese culture. Chan displays a strong sense of cultural patriotism, which one finds liberally peppered in his films, particularly ones that are made in Hollywood.[28] But he is ever so cautious to couch his cultural loyalties in terms of a global multiculturalist sensibility: the notion that all cultures in the world should be respected; ergo, one should similarly respect Chinese culture. In taking on the role of the archeologist adventurer Jack, Chan foregoes the mimicry of Harrison Ford's Indiana Jones to elevate the character type to a higher moral plane. (This is an instance where Chan's made-in-Asia films give him the liberty to abandon the mimicry-as-failure strategy I have analyzed in Chapter Six, although the film does gesture in cinematic tribute to *Indiana Jones and the Temple of Doom* (1984) and its Indian mob attack scenes.) Indiana Jones' Eurocentric and colonialist attitude toward the indigenous peoples he encounters and the cultural artifacts he presumably "unearths" is rewritten in Chan into the laudable terms of respect for cultural ownership, as the dialogue between him, William, and the business woman Maggie unveil:

> *Maggie*: Our foundation financed this project. Anything found should belong to the foundation. How can you donate the sword [of Meng Yi] to the museum [in Xi'an]?

Jack: The sword's a Grade One national relic. It belongs to *all of humanity*. It's only right we return it to the *world* via the museum. Anyway, what's key to the [anti-gravity] project are the meteorites. These two artifacts have nothing to do with them.

William: Before my experiments draw a conclusion, anything may prove to be a critical link. How can you prejudge it by saying otherwise? My experiments will benefit all mankind. Artifacts are old, dead things. They have no life, no future! What science is concerned with is precisely the future!

Jack: Fine, if that's what you say, then why are these 2000 year-old artifacts so important to you?

William: I risked my life for that sword!

Jack: No, I did. (*William looks shamed.*)

William: Ok! In that case, when I find the meteorites, you'll still give them away?

Jack: Yes. As long as it's someone else's artifacts, I'll return them. No one can plunder relics from someone else's country and put them in their own museums. They call it "safe-keeping," but it's theft. It's despicable behavior.
29

Even though Jack's criticism is directed at the foundation's capitalist greed, the final barb provides an equal sting for museums in the West for plundering developing countries of their ancient historical treasures and artifacts in the name of preservation and education. The fact that the villains are Chinese helps blunt this critique enough for him to get his message across without coming off as being patriotically offensive to non-Chinese viewers.

Jack's position on this issue finally leads him to stand guard on behalf of the Qin Emperor's mausoleum and, hence, Chinese history, from being raided by the evil Professor Ku (Zhou Sun). Jack proclaims to the tomb raiders, "No one can take anything from here. This is a part of history. It should stay buried forever!" Clearly, this admonition is not really meant to convince these raiders to abandon their goal, but it really serves instead to register for the audience Jack's own motivation. His cultural patriotism, both literally and metaphorically, turns him into a Qin imperial soldier, like the terracotta warriors *in situ* who are "troops in an eternal vigil" (as Professor Ku puts it) over the mausoleum of Qin Shihuang, the first emperor of China. In this sense, Jack's cultural nationalism flows through time to connect with General Meng Yi's unquestioned loyalty to the Qin Emperor, a fusion that Jackie Chan's star persona cinematically enables. Meng Yi likens himself to "a blade, destined to fight for His Majesty, and die for . . . [his] country." In simpatico, the Master of Dasai Martial Arts informs Jack that he "can become one with . . . [his] sword! It must be a bond from lifetimes ago."

The beauty of Chan's glocalism (the local in the global) in this film lies in his ability to be both stirringly patriotic of his Chineseness, hence reaching out to his ethnic Chinese fans, while, at the same time, so politically acceptable in his consideration for the world at large through his respect for national histories and cultures; his cultural patriotism can be easily adopted and transplanted into any part of the world. Jackie Chan's persona, therefore, wields the dizzying magic of Chinese supernaturalism to flit across space and time, into global movie screens to touch the hearts of audiences the world over.

The Promise: Travesty, Parody, and Camp

The critics panned it and its US release found the film cut shorter and reedited.[30] There is much to dislike about Chen Kaige's *The Promise*; as a contemporary instance of the *shenguai wuxia pian*, the fantasy flick contorts into a hysterical text of over-ambition and bombast. Through its Chinese supernaturalism, *The Promise* aspires to engage audiences with the loftier philosophical concerns of destiny, fate, free choice, and human agency. But its aesthetic excess and imagistic hyperbole, like Icarus' fateful flight, causes the film to crash and burn.[31] By trying too hard to secure cultural and philosophical gravitas on too flimsy a narrative premise, the film becomes "a new-millennium *wuxia pian* that risks all its marbles on nonsensical style and none on storytelling."[32]

The Promise appeared to be a promising enterprise from its inception. The time for a hybrid version of the *wuxia pian* was ripe, considering the immense success of Ang Lee and Zhang Yimou's recent works. The film sent out all the right signals: it had a gorgeous pan-Asian cast, which included Korean star Jang Dong Gun, Japanese Hiroyuki Sanada, Hong Kong starlet Cecilia Cheung, and upcoming Hong Kong film idol Nicholas Tse; Peter Pau helmed its spectacular cinematography; the China Film Group and other investors pumped in US$35 million, making it "the most expensive film ever made in China"[33]; and the film was nominated for best foreign-language film at the Golden Globes. But *The Promise* never quite attained its potential because it suffers from hysteria, "a play of excess,"[34] in its anxiety to be *the* transnational Chinese cinematic blockbuster. Like many Hollywood blockbusters today, good storytelling and effective filmmaking are frequently eclipsed by the spectacles of star power, lavish set design, impressive special effects, and an imperative epic scale, all of which a good film do not necessarily make. Chen, the Fifth Generation director of the impressive *Yellow Earth* (1984), seems to have forgotten what he knew best in his early years of filmmaking. Ironically, aspiring to match Hollywood's expectations of slick production values only resulted in a film of cinematic excess, which is what basically killed the film for *Variety* critic Robert Koehler: "Though the building blocks of a fine epic fantasy are in place, stuttered pacing and transition hiccups in the pic's midsection produce a pattern of characters literally running all over the place for last-minute rescues that soon become comical. Even in fantasy, an internal logic must apply . . . The generous servings of poorly realized CG effects, from the bull stampede on, imprint 'The Promise' with a cartoonish quality that undercuts the tale's emotional textures."[35] Chinese supernaturalism here unfortunately becomes the film's own metaphor for its impossibility, in defying the very logic of good filmmaking. So mortified was one Chinese filmgoer and blogger that he proceeded to make a spoof called "The Blood Case of the *Mantou*,"[36] which generated intense internet buzz when it was released into cyberspace. It turned into "one of the most downloaded video clips on the Chinese Net." Such unwarranted negative publicity only incurred director Chen's displeasure when he threatened suit against Hu Ge, the author of the video spoof, for intellectual property infringements. The whole affair later exploded online into a debate about free speech in China.[37]

Despite all the negative hoopla it has generated, I perversely derive pleasure from *The Promise* as glorious camp. From Nicholas Tse's effete performance, to the outrageous costumes and set-pieces, to the B-movie CG effects of Cecilia Cheung being flown like a human kite, the film is the embodiment of "psychedelia extremis."[38] My pleasure in these moments modulates the supposed seriousness of Chinese supernaturalism into the frivolity of its absurdist commodification — in fact, the *wuxia pian* and the *shenguai wuxia pian* have a great tradition as campy B-movie classics, especially the Shaw Brothers films like *Intimate Confessions of a Chinese Courtesan* (1972), *Na Cha the Great* (1974), *The Web of Death* (1976), and *Buddha's Palm* (1982). This enjoyment of the film's "naïve" camp in no way seeks to reclaim or salvage Chen's film critically. *The Promise* never intended to be campy, which is why it makes reading it as camp so entertaining. Rather, I see my camp approach as symptomatic of the film's overreaching, its oblivion to the irony of its circumstances as an impossible text of Hollywood-fashioned transnational Chinese cinema. It is in this sense that one needs to understand Hu Ge's spoof, not only as an indicator of *The Promise*'s failings but also as a signifier of its global presence, be it positive or negative.[39] It is critical too for *The Promise* to view itself as a spoof of itself.[40] In fact, all the films I have analyzed in this chapter tread this fine line between philosophical and cultural weightiness, and pure pop cultural campy fun, particularly as they remake the tradition of what are generally Chinese-Hong Kong B-movies. Camp is, after all, part of the nature of the Chinese supernatural and fantasy genre. The upshot is how contemporary filmmakers react to the genre's inherent ironies and to audiences' ironic responses will determine their future success, both critically and in the global film market.

Coda:
Global Cinematic Technologies of Ethnic (Un)Representation

Remember Hollywood's not America.

Ferras[1]

In place of a conclusion, I have chosen a "coda," the brief tail end of a musical piece that does not just reiterate themes but also introduces new ones with the purpose of envisioning, or more appropriately in my case, speculating, the future of the Chinese in Hollywood and, thus, penciling in possible lines of future critical inquiry. Like most academics, I do detest going out on a limb to connect the invisible dots that extend into an uncertain future[2] — as the maker of popular cinematic taste, Hollywood is highly volatile in its accommodation and restructuring of filmic trends; who could have predicted two decades ago that there would be such a surge of interest in Chinese cinema in Hollywood today? Despite the risk, I see my speculations as having retrospective self-reflectivity to help me reopen critical spaces that I, or anyone else, could enter into in the future.

This unlikely ending with a coda is also accompanied by another (equally out-of-place) musical reference in the epigraph: a line from a contemporary pop song "Hollywood's Not America." In it, the pop artist Ferras sings of how the search for riches and fame in Hollywood is ultimately "a hollow little game." He reaffirms this message in the chorus, telling the one he is singing to, to "Put your blue jeans / Back on girl / Go home / Remember Hollywood's Not America." Setting aside the ironic fact that Ferras's song was promotionally played twice on 2008's *American Idol* in Hollywood, I want to highlight how the song works out a discourse of American cultural authenticity by appealing to the heartland sartorial simplicity of "put[ting] your blue jeans back on," in contradistinction to the artificiality and constructed gloss of Hollywood's consumerist culture — the song appeals to mainstream America's conviction that Hollywood is not definitive American culture, ameliorating the frightening fact that much of the rest of the world sees the United States through Hollywood lenses, thanks to Hollywood's global cultural hegemony. Bridging this instance of pop music exegesis to the Chinese in Hollywood provides me the opportunity to then point to the inherent contradictions of this Hollywood/American-heartland cultural dichotomy when applied to America's reception of ethnic representations in Hollywood/transnational Chinese cinema. If one were to adopt momentarily, a priori, the framework of this binary opposition, it behooves mainstream American consumers to realize how ironically contradictory it is to accept its logic, while still consuming Hollywood-ized Chineseness *as* Chineseness, with its Orientalist and stereotypical elements, reconfigured and transformed for contemporary audience consumption, remaining more or less intact. These forms of celluloid Chineseness confirm in the minds of mainstream American audiences imageries of the Chinese perpetuated throughout Hollywood's history, which many are already familiar with; and they inculcate in a new generation of audiences freshly reformulated stereotypes that will require much critical work to dislodge. Conversely, if one were to reject this Hollywood/American-heartland distinction (which, to a certain degree, one must), the borders between these cultural positions necessarily blur, allowing for a more nuanced depiction of how Hollywood inevitably influences "real" culture in general, and thus helps define it. It is therefore imperative that we engage, instead of dismiss, the discursive impact of Hollywood commodification on cultural identity in the United States and across the globe, and enter into conversation with the cultural discourses produced on Hollywood screens, beyond a default critique of popular cinema's failings in cultural "authenticity." This approach will, hence, help circumvent the cultural nationalist's inchoate warbling of (an appropriated) "Hollywood Chineseness is *not* Chineseness." While the advocacy of politically incisive interventions in alternative film cultures is necessary and important (a point I have made in Chapter Two), we cannot ignore and reject the cultural (dis)pleasures of encountering filmic Chineseness in Hollywood and Hollywood-inflected transnational Chinese cinemas. These filmic representations and discourses of Chineseness deserve to be politically negotiated, in the same way that Antonio Gramsci negotiates the mechanisms of political hegemony.[3] It is an effort to which I hope this book has contributed, in its own small way, through the unpacking of the crisscrossing and fluid processes of cinematic remaking, citationality, hybridity, appropriation, and transculturation; processes that will continue to characterize the cinematic productivity of the Hollywood-Asia-Pacific film network for years to come.

Looking at films in various stages of production in 2008 and beyond, one can ascertain established trends that my book has already begun to identify. While kung fu and *wuxia* are big and will probably remain so for a while, various permutations of the martial arts genre are given hybrid twists, incorporating historical, mythological, and supernatural elements. This atavistic turn to a mythic or mystical past as part of the cinematic ethnography in Hollywood fictions seems unabated. The deployment of Chinese supernaturalism in *The Forbidden Kingdom*, for instance, extends my discussion of the topic in Chapter Seven into the area of literary adaptations of Chinese classics,[4] which are and will become a significant cultural resource for film producers to tap into.[5] The success of these martial arts/historical drama hybrids has also led to transnational Chinese cinemas' repackaging of the *wuxia pian* into grittier battle epics, such as Daniel Lee's *Three Kingdoms: Resurrection of the Dragon* (2008), Ching Siu-tung's *An Empress and the Warriors* (2008), Peter Chan's remake of the Chang Cheh classic *Blood Brothers* (1973) into *The Warlords* (2007), and John Woo's much-anticipated *Red Cliff* (2008).[6]

Chinese elements also sprinkle forthcoming Hollywood flicks, infusing "ethnic flavor"[7] and creating multicultural spectacles as already seen in *The Pirates of the Caribbean: At World's End*. Martial arts persist as the ethnicizing ingredient, the multicultural flavor *du jour*, so to speak: the third instalment of *The Mummy* series now has Brendan Fraser's Rick O'Connell encounter the mummy of the first emperor of China played by Jet Li. Rumor on the internet has it that Chow Yun-fat is supposedly negotiating with Disney to play Snow White's kung fu instructor in a live-action version of the animated classic.[8] (Whatever the truth may be, it is certain that Chow will appear in a fantasy-action film called *Dragonball* (2009) and has signed on for Johnny To's *The Red Circle*.) Even film projects that usually do not require Chineseness to make an appearance do so to up the ante through ethnic appeal: Gong Li's presence in *Miami Vice* (2006) and *Hannibal Rising* (2007) created enough of a buzz to clinch for her, according to rumors, another role in Paramount's *Ripley's Believe It or Not,* which is currently in pre-production. Zhang Ziyi appears opposite Dennis Quaid in *The Horsemen* (2009), even as her acting fees have now multiplied to US$5 million, ten times what she was receiving when she appeared in *Jasmine Flower* (2004).[9] Liu Ye, known for his role in Stanley Kwan's *Lan Yu* (2001), appears as a graduate student whose loss of the Nobel Prize provokes a violent reaction. *Dark Matter* (2007), helmed by first-time director Chen Shi-zheng, is an American independent film based on a real incident; it tackles the belief that a growing population of Chinese immigrants in the United States may be viewed as a threat to mainstream American positional security in terms of education and jobs. While

I want to read these films as healthy signs that ethnic Chinese actors (or rather a few key stars) are getting acting roles and are appearing in films because of their growing appeal as accomplished artists, it may still be too soon to ascertain if this trend will turn out to be mere ethnic tokenism in the multicultural parading of racial minorities, among which the Chinese are currently flavor of the month.

The issue of Chinese ethnic representation in Hollywood engenders another series of crucial questions that deserve separate venues of research investigation: what kinds of tactics or strategies can Chinese filmmakers, actors, and industry players deploy to deal with Hollywood's reversion to the older ethnic stereotypes but in newly reconfigured forms for global distribution? (A recent example would be Lucy Liu's decision to star in a TV series based on Charlie Chan, where she plays Charlie, the granddaughter of the detective. Liu's point in doing so is "to turn . . . [the stereotype] on its head" by having "a woman play Charlie and to be seen in modern daylight with an Asian person being cast" in the role.[10]) How will the Chinese presence in Hollywood affect the Chinese film industries in Hong Kong, Taiwan, and China, both in terms of industry survival and film aesthetics? In a related way, how do Hollywood-Asian coproductions change the dynamics of the industries and the future work of filmmakers who choose *not* to take the Hollywood route? What possibilities are in store for Chinese and Asian American independent cinema to function within the circuits of transnational cinematic networks, in order to reach a wider audience base, without compromising their political critical edge? What seems certain, though, is that a multi-audience sector approach to filmmaking will become a sustainable trend, as coproduction units from various parts of the Asia-Pacific rim (including Hollywood) bring together stars from various Asian countries to imbue their films with multinational crossover potential, hence allowing them to succeed in one country's box office when they fail in another, assuring a net global profit. It will also be fascinating to see how Hollywood will respond to what Chua Beng Huat has theorized as the emergence of an "East Asia Popular Culture," a term that "designate[s] the development, production, exchange, flow and consumption of popular cultural products between the People's Republic of China (PRC), Japan, South Korea, Taiwan, Hong Kong and Singapore,"[11] of which Katsuyuki Motohiro's *Shaolin Girl* (2008), executive produced by Stephen Chow, may be a recent cinematic instance.

My discussions on ethnic representation thus far assume that ethnicity as a mark of difference on screen is of central concern. While actors do not have the luxury of circumventing the visual presence of their Chineseness (and which they should not have to), directors and other industry professionals working behind the scenes do.[12] Directors John Woo, Wong Kar-wai, Peter Chan, Ang Lee, Wayne Wang, and Stanley Tong have worked or are working on "non-Chinese" projects as a means of demonstrating their adaptability and avoiding being pigeon-holed into the category of directors who solely produce "foreign," "ethnic," or "minority" films. It is not my intention here to criticize these filmmakers or to question their motivations, for some of them have contributed truly engaging films through the Hollywood system, including Ang Lee's *The Ice Storm* (1997) and *Brokeback Mountain* (2005) and John Woo's *Windtalkers* (2002). Instead, my goal is to unpack the discursive dynamics of this trend in order to point to future opportunities for critical re-examination. This is a trend that will become inevitable should (or when) American audiences lose their fascination with the exotic appeal that Chinese cinemas presently hold. Though I am not troubled specifically by ethnic Chinese filmmakers making films with Anglo-American actors and Anglo-American settings, it is disturbing when this move is validated as a mark of "universal" success, as if whiteness on screen is erased of its ethnic specificity and made invisible,[13] enabling it to be a stand-in for global humanity. Their overtly "Chinese" films are then viewed as the more culturally "authentic" but artistically underdeveloped part of their oeuvre, while their entry into Hollywood's Anglo-American cinematic tradition proper transforms into a mark of artistic maturation. In a similar fashion, African-American directors suffered the same dilemma even before Asian directors entered the Hollywood scene. Filmmakers like Spike Lee, the Hughes brothers, Carl Franklin, and Bill Duke worked on films with strong African-American emphases earlier in their careers and then later took on projects that had what Hollywood considers to be mainstream American appeal. Much of this logic resembles a throwback to the racial rhetoric inherent in the politics of assimilation, where ethnic minorities in America are asked to revoke their racial identities by embracing an American one that is marked by an unspoken generic racial whiteness. Part of the problem is also that American audiences (and global audiences through Hollywood's enculturation) are frequently unwilling to accept Asian actors in primary film roles without the need to racialize their presence, a symptom of the long political road ahead for Asian and Asian American activists to challenge the American public's perception of Asians in America as the "perpetual foreigner."[14]

What also fascinates me in this filmic "lactification" is the global Chinese response to it. Allow me to illustrate with an example: though *Brokeback Mountain* predictably received the ban from mainland Chinese censors, the *China Daily* discussed the "Chinese aesthetics" of the film,[15] as an understandable means of claiming and retaining Lee within the realms of

Chinese cultural productivity. In her reading of Lee's film, Rey Chow locates its "sentimental fabulations" as a demonstration of how "contemporary Chinese directors have so noticeably contributed to and transformed the production of global cinematic culture since the 1980s."[16] For the lack of a better description of these hermeneutical maneuvers, I shall label them as cultural allegorical readings. These readings are made possible by the consciousness of the director's ethnicity as the wellspring of the film's discursive content and/or structuring. While Chinese (hence, Asian) ethnicity is visually erased, it has not disappeared completely but has become subsumed into the cinematic text, forcing many Chinese and Chinese American audiences to wrestle with these technologies of (un)representation in order to re-read ethnicity back into the text. Of course, such interpretive moves welcome further debate on how Chinese audiences around the world read and consume these films. What I wish to highlight particularly as a means of closing this book is the notion that *Brokeback Mountain*'s ability to elicit different responses and readings, allowing, for example, American audiences to be either enraptured or scandalized by the story of gay cowboys (depending on their political position on gay sexuality) while permitting global Chinese audiences to frame the film according to their understanding of Chinese cultural specificities, testifies to the effective deployment of Chineseness, both on and off the screen, to accomplish Hollywood's transnational audience appeal. The way Chineseness is continually reshaped by and through the Hollywood paradigm into that which critics call transnational Chinese cinemas commands our attention and deserves our ever watchfulness.

Notes

1 Introduction: Remaking Chinese Cinemas, Hollywood Style

1. Richard Corliss, "Asian Invasion," *Time*, 14 August 1995, <http://www.time.com/time/magazine/article/0,9171,983301-1,00.html>, accessed 27 May 2008. See also Minh-Ha T. Pham, "The Asian Invasion (of Multiculturalism) in Hollywood," *Journal of Popular Film and Television* 32, no. 3 (Fall 2004): 121–131. Pham argues that the very notion of an "Asian invasion itself is an American construct" and that multiculturalism through "the increased presence of Asian and Asian American actors and filmmakers" helps reinforce "Hollywood's image as a racially inclusive, equal opportunity, global industry" (122).

2. When the film opened in Singapore, fans were delighted that the on-screen pairing of Chan and Li had finally happened, though they wished it had occurred much earlier in their careers. One fan notes that he had "been waiting for this dream fight for years," while another believed that "they should have fought in the early 1990s, before they went to the United States." Bernard Koh and Douglas Tseng, "Who Packs a Bigger Punch?" *The Sunday Times*, 27 April 2008, Lifestyle section, 2.

3. "Jackie and Jet's Movie 'Isn't Great,'" *The Straits Times*, 20 September 2007, Life section, 12.

4. "Jackie and Jet: Friends, Not Foes," *The Straits Times*, 19 April 2008, Life section, 12.

5. Li describes his sparring session with Chan as a meeting of "Olympic champions. " "Jackie and Jet: Friends, Not Foes."

6. "Forbidden Kingdom is No. 1 in US," *The Straits Times*, 22 April 2008, Life section, 18.

7. Min Lee, "Kung Fu Film 'The Forbidden Kingdom' a Hit in China," *Yahoo! News*, 8 May 2008, <http://news.yahoo.com/s/ap/20080508/ap_en_mo/film_forbidden_kingdom>, accessed 15 May 2008.

8. "Jackie and Jet's Movie 'Isn't Great.'"

9. Jonathan Landreth, "China's Huayi Bros. Thinking Big," *The Hollywood Reporter*, 24 May 2005, <http://www.hollywoodreporter.com/hr/search/article_display.jsp?vnu_content_id=1000930260>, accessed 18 May 2008.

10. My production of this list of films is based on a quick and probably inaccurate identification as a result of only two theatrical viewings. But the pleasure of this identification of filmic allusions is also the pleasure of positing the cinematic traditions that the character Jason has immersed himself in, traditions that ultimately inform his cultural fantasies (of being a kung fu warrior) as well as ours.

11. The Chinese censors cut, according to *Variety*, a scene where pirate Sao Feng recites a poem by Li Bai, a poet from the Tang dynasty. Chinese audiences questioned the film's negative racial depiction as an "image of the Chinese in the eyes of Hollywood producers." "China Censors 'Cut' Pirates Film," *BBC News*, 12 June 2007, <http://news.bbc.co.uk/2/hi/entertainment/6744245.stm>, accessed 15 June 2007.

12. Richard Corliss, "Hollywood's Asian Romance," *Time*, 14 November 2005, <http://www.time.com/time/asia/covers/501051121/story.html>, accessed 15 June 2007.

13. "Geisha Film Reveals 'Hidden Culture,'" *BBC News*, 1 January 2006, <http://news.bbc.co.uk/1/hi/entertainment/4503454.stm>, accessed 15 June 2007.

14. Sheridan Prasso, *The Asian Mystique: Dragon Ladies, Geisha Girls, and Our Fantasies of the Exotic Orient* (New York: Public Affairs, 2005), 87. Prasso argues that this image of the Japanese child-woman is part of a series of images that depict the submissive Asian woman stereotype, all of which contribute to what she calls the allure of "the Asian Mystique." This allure is so prevalent and naturalized in screen discourses that my students are always stunned, when I teach this film, by how easy it is to miss the pedophilic implications of the relationship between the young Chiyo (Sayuri's birth name) and the Chairman (Ken Watanabe).

15. Clifford Coonan, "'Memoirs of a Geisha' Banned by Beijing in Row over Chinese Stars," *The Independent*, 2 February 2006, <http://www.independent.co.uk/arts/film/news/article342661.ece>, accessed 15 June 2007. One person even went online to say that "Zhang and Gong have brought shame to the Chinese." Andreas Lorenz, "China's 'Geisha' Complex," *Spiegel Online*, 7 February 2006, <http://www.spiegel.de/international/0,1518,399593,00.html>, accessed 15 June 2007.

16. Coonan, "'Memoirs of a Geisha' Banned."

17. Prasso, *The Asian Mystique*, 79–80. Offering a more conflicted and, hence, more complex interpretation of Wong is: Yiman Wang, "The Art of Screen Passing: Anna May Wong's Yellow Yellowface Performance in the Art Deco Era," *Camera Obscura* 60, vol. 20, no. 3 (2005): 159–91.

18. For a discussion of films in this period (1989–1997), see Gina Marchetti, *From Tian'anmen to Times Square: Transnational China and the Chinese Diaspora on Global Screens, 1989–1997* (Philadelphia: Temple University Press, 2006).

19. Rob Wilson and Arif Dirlik, eds., *Asia/Pacific as Space of Cultural Production* (Durham: Duke University Press, 1995).

20. Aihwa Ong, *Flexible Citizenship: The Cultural Logics of Transnationality* (Durham: Duke University Press, 1999), 127.

21. Andrew Horton and Stuart Y. McDougal, introduction to *Play It Again, Sam: Retakes on Remakes,* eds. Andrew Horton and Stuart Y. McDougal (Berkeley: University of California Press, 1998), 2.

22. Ibid., 4.

23. Lee Sze Yong, "Enter the New Dragon," *The Straits Times,* 31 May 2007, Life section, 20.

24. Jacques Derrida, *Margins of Philosophy*, trans. Alan Bass (Chicago: University of Chicago Press, 1982), 320–21.

25. David Wills, "The French Remark: *Breathless* and Cinematic Citationality," in *Play It Again, Sam: Retakes on Remakes,* eds. Andrew Horton and Stuart Y. McDougal (Berkeley: University of California Press, 1998), 148.

26. Sheldon Hsiao-peng Lu, "Historical Introduction: Chinese Cinemas (1896–1996) and Transnational Film Studies," in *Transnational Chinese Cinemas: Identity, Nationhood, Gender*, ed. Sheldon Hsiao-peng Lu (Honolulu: University of Hawai'i Press, 1997), 3.

27. Patricia Aufderheide, "Made in Hong Kong: Translation and Transmutation," in *Play It Again, Sam: Retakes on Remakes,* eds. Andrew Horton and Stuart Y. McDougal (Berkeley: University of California Press, 1998), 193.

28. Ibid., 198.

29. Quoted in Lisa Odham Stokes and Michael Hoover, *City on Fire: Hong Kong Cinema* (London: Verso, 1999), 309.

30. David Bordwell, *Planet Hong Kong: Popular Cinema and the Art of Entertainment* (Cambridge: Harvard University Press, 2000), 19.

31. Ibid., 19.

32. Tan See Kam, "From *South Pacific* to *Shanghai Blues*: No Film Is an Island," in *Hong Kong Film, Hollywood and the New Global Cinema: No Film Is an Island,* eds. Gina Marchetti and Tan See Kam (London: Routledge, 2007), 15–6.

33. Derrida, *Margins of Philosophy*, 315.

34. Gayatri Chakravorty Spivak, *Outside in the Teaching Machine* (New York: Routledge, 1993), 182.

35. Mary Louise Pratt, *Imperial Eyes: Travel Writing and Transculturation* (London: Routledge, 1992), 6.

36. Ibid., 4.

37. Ibid., 7. Pratt deploys "autoethnography" as a reference "to instances in which colonized subjects undertake to represent themselves in ways that *engage with* the colonizer's own terms." See also Chow's use of this concept in her reading of primitivism in the works of China's Fifth Generation filmmakers. Rey Chow, *Primitive Passions: Visuality, Sexuality, Ethnography, and Contemporary Chinese Cinema* (New York: Columbia University Press, 1995), 38.

38. "It is the field of the problematic that defines and structures the invisible as the defined excluded, *excluded* from the field of visibility and *defined* as excluded by the existence and peculiar structure of the field of the problematic; as what forbids and represses the reflection of the field on its object." Louis Althusser, "From *Capital* to Marx's Philosophy," in *Reading Capital,* by Louis Althusser and Étienne Balibar, trans. Ben Brewster (London: Verso, 1997), 25–6.

39. Ibid., 28.

40. Jenny Kwok Wah Lau, "*Farewell My Concubine*: History, Melodrama, and Ideology in Contemporary Pan-Chinese Cinema," *Film Quarterly* 49, no. 1 (Fall 1995): 16–27.

41. Yingjin Zhang, *Chinese National Cinema* (New York: Routledge, 2004), 14.

42. Law Kar, "The American Connection in Early Hong Kong Cinema," in *The Cinema of Hong Kong: History, Arts, Identity,* eds. Poshek Fu and David Desser (Cambridge: Cambridge University Press, 2000), 45.

43. Ibid., 45–6.

44. Ibid., 46.

45. Quoted in John Trumpbour, *Selling Hollywood to the World: U.S. and European Struggles for Mastery of the Global Film Industry, 1920–1950* (Cambridge: Cambridge University Press, 2002), 64.

46. Zhiwei Xiao, "Anti-Imperialism and Film Censorship during the Nanjing Decade, 1927–1937," in *Transnational Chinese Cinemas: Identity, Nationhood, Gender,* ed. Sheldon Hsiao-peng Lu (Honolulu: University of Hawai'i Press, 1997), 38–9.

47. Ibid., 38, 40.

48. Ibid., 41.

49. Ibid., 42.

50. Ibid., 42–5.

51. Zhang, *Chinese National Cinema,* 71–2.

52. Ibid., 152. See also Paul Fonoroff, *Silver Light: A Pictorial History of Hong Kong Cinema, 1920–1970* (Hong Kong: Joint Publishing, 1997), xiv–v.

53. Law, "The American Connection," 50–9.

54. Ibid., 52.

55. Ibid., 52, 57.

56. Ibid., 59.

57. Stephen Teo, *Hong Kong Cinema: The Extra Dimensions* (London: BFI, 1997), 3–109. For a short but effective description of the rise and decline of Shaw Brothers film production, see Stephanie Chung Po-yin, "The Industrial Evolution of a Fraternal Enterprise: The Shaw Brothers and the Shaw Organisation," in *The Shaw Screen: A Preliminary Study,* ed. Wong Ain-ling (Hong Kong: Hong Kong Film Archive, 2003), 1–17.

58. Chung, "The Industrial Evolution," 9.

59. David Desser, "The Kung Fu Craze: Hong Kong Cinema's First American Reception," in *The Cinema of Hong Kong: History, Arts, Identity,* eds. Poshek Fu and David Desser (Cambridge: Cambridge University Press, 2000), 19.

60. Zhang, *Chinese National Cinema,* 187.

61. Teo, *Hong Kong Cinema,* 110.

62. Ibid., 111.

63. Zhang discusses how Taiwanese audiences read Lee's image in a slightly more ambivalent way than Hong Kong audiences did. Zhang, *Chinese National Cinema,* 144.

64. Teo, *Hong Kong Cinema,* 114.

65. Ibid., 113. See also Tony Rayns, "Bruce Lee: Narcissism and Nationalism," in *A Study of the Hong Kong Martial Arts Film* (Hong Kong: The Urban Council, 1980), 110–12; Meaghan Morris, "Learning from Bruce Lee: Pedagogy and Political Correctness in Martial Arts Cinema," in *Keyframes: Popular Cinema and Cultural Studies,* eds. Matthew Tinkcom and Amy Villarejo (London: Routledge, 2001), 171–86.

66. Desser, "The Kung Fu Craze," 20. *Deep Thrust – the Hand of Death* is the US title for *Lady Whirlwind* (1972).

67. Teo, *Hong Kong Cinema,* 117.

68. Desser, "The Kung Fu Craze," 26.

69. Bey Logan, *Hong Kong Action Cinema* (Woodstock, NY: The Overlook Press, 1995), 18.

70. Gina Marchetti, "Jackie Chan and the Black Connection," in *Keyframes: Popular Cinema and Cultural Studies,* eds. Matthew Tinkcom and Amy Villarejo (London: Routledge, 2001), 137–58.

71. Zhang, *Chinese National Cinema,* 225.

72. For an intriguing read on the agendas of various film festivals around the world, see Kenneth Turan, *Sundance to Sarajevo: Film Festivals and the World They Made* (Berkeley: University of California Press, 2002).

73. Tony Rayns, "Breakthroughs and Setbacks: The Origins of the New Chinese Cinema," in *Perspectives on Chinese Cinema,* ed. Chris Berry (London: BFI, 1991), 104.

74. Ibid., 106.

75. Chris Berry, "Market Forces: China's 'Fifth Generation' Faces the Bottom Line," in *Perspectives on Chinese Cinema,* ed. Chris Berry (London: BFI, 1991), 114–25.

76. Chris Berry and Feii Lu, introduction to *Island on the Edge: Taiwan New Cinema and After,* eds. Chris Berry and Feii Lu (Hong Kong: Hong Kong University Press, 2005), 5–6.

77. Zhang, *Chinese National Cinema,* 246.

78. Berry and Lu, introduction to *Island,* 6–7.

79. With even President Chen Shui-bian celebrating the filmmaker's win, the Taiwanese proclaimed Lee a "hero." "The One That Got Away," *The Straits Times,* 8 March 2006, Life section, 6.

80. This argument was raised by Roger Garcia, whom Law Kar references in his essay. Law Kar, "An Overview of Hong Kong's New Wave Cinema," in *At Full Speed: Hong Kong Cinema in a Borderless World,* ed. Esther C. M. Yau (Minneapolis: University of Minnesota Press, 2001), 46. See also in the same collection of essays Hector Rodriguez, "The Emergence of the Hong Kong New Wave," 53–69.

81. In what he calls "cross-pollination" between Hong Kong and Hollywood, Logan provides a short but useful list which includes *City on Fire* (1987)/*Reservoir Dogs* (1992), *Top Gun* (1986)/*Proud and Confidence* (1989), and *Hard-Boiled* (1992)/*Joshua Tree* (1993). Logan, *Hong Kong Action Cinema,* 132.

82. Thomas Schatz, "The New Hollywood," in *Movie Blockbusters,* ed. Julian Stringer (London: Routledge, 2003), 31.

83. Matt Hills, "*Star Wars* in Fandom, Film Theory, and the Museum: The Cultural Status of the Cult Blockbuster," in *Movie Blockbusters,* ed. Julian Stringer (London: Routledge, 2003), 178–89.

84. Ed Guerrero, *Framing Blackness: The African American Image in Film* (Philadelphia: Temple University Press, 1993), 117.

85. Ibid., 117–8.

86. Fredric Jameson, *The Political Unconscious: Narrative as a Socially Symbolic Act* (Ithaca: Cornell University Press, 1981).
87. Dorothy B. Jones, *The Portrayal of China and India on the American Screen, 1896–1955* (Cambridge: Center for International Studies, Massachusetts Institute of Technology, 1955); Eugene Franklin Wong, *On Visual Media Racism: Asians in the American Motion Pictures* (New York: Arno Press, 1978.); Gina Marchetti, *Romance and the "Yellow Peril": Race, Sex, and Discursive Strategies in Hollywood Fiction* (Berkeley: University of California Press, 1993); Robert G. Lee, *Orientals: Asian Americans in Popular Culture* (Philadelphia: Temple University Press, 1999). For quick overviews on the topic and interviews with directors, see Roger Garcia, ed., *Out of the Shadows: Asians in American Cinema* (Milano: Olivares, 2001). On ethnic images in American cinema, see Lester D. Friedman, ed., *Unspeakable Images: Ethnicity and the American Cinema* (Urbana: University of Illinois Press, 1991). Of significance though not concerning cinema directly is Christina Klein, *Cold War Orientalism: Asia in the Middlebrow Imagination, 1945–1961* (Berkeley: University of California Press, 2003).
88. Laura Mulvey, "Visual Pleasure and Narrative Cinema," in *Feminism and Film,* ed. E. Ann Kaplan (Oxford: Oxford University Press, 2000), 34–47.
89. Lisa Lowe makes this argument about the Asian immigrant in America by calling her, in a happy coincidence, "a 'screen' . . . on which the nation projects a series of condensed, complicated anxieties regarding external and internal threats to the mutable coherence of the national body . . . Stereotypes that construct Asians as the threatening 'yellow peril,' or alternatively, that pose Asians as the domesticated 'model minority,' are each equally indices of these national anxieties." Lisa Lowe, *Immigrant Acts: On Asian American Cultural Politics* (Durham: Duke University Press, 1996), 18–9.
90. Sabine Haenni, "Filming 'Chinatown': Fake Visions, Bodily Transformations," in *Screening Asian Americans,* ed. Peter X. Feng (New Brunswick: Rutgers University Press, 2002), 21–3.
91. Ibid., 25.
92. Iris Chang, *The Chinese in America: A Narrative History* (New York: Penguin, 2003), 131–2.
93. Lee, *Orientals,* 8–10.
94. Marchetti, *Romance,* 2.
95. Edward W. Said, *Orientalism* (New York: Vintage, 1978).
96. Lee, *Orientals,* 114.
97. Eugene Franklin Wong, "The Early Years: Asians in the American Films Prior to World War II," in *Screening Asian Americans,* ed. Peter X. Feng (New Brunswick: Rutgers University Press, 2002), 56–8. Excerpted from Wong, *On Visual Media Racism,* 88–119.
98. Wong, "The Early Years," 58.
99. Quoted in Ibid., 59. Robert Barshay, "Ethnic Stereotypes in Flash Gordon," *Journal of Popular Film* 3, no. 1 (Winter 1974): 24–6. The last incarnation of Ming was played by Max Von Sydow in Universal Pictures' *Flash Gordon* (1980).

100. Marchetti, *Romance,* 10.

101. An audacious turn of the sexual tables is Ho Meng-hua's *The Mighty Peking Man* (1977), where Danny Lee's character ends up with the blonde female Tarzan (Evelyne Kraft). Quentin Tarantino is so taken by this Shaw flick that he has released it under his Rolling Thunder imprint in the US.

102. Peter X. Feng, introduction to *Screening Asian Americans,* ed. Peter X. Feng (New Brunswick: Rutgers University Press, 2002), 9.

103. Feng confronts the pleasures of watching *The World of Suzie Wong* and its complex implications, thus complicating the more directly critical readings of the film as racist and Orientalist. Peter X. Feng, "Recuperating Suzie Wong: A Fan's Nancy Kwan-dary," in *Countervisions: Asian American Film Criticism,* eds. Darrell Y. Hamamoto and Sandra Liu (Philadelphia: Temple University Press, 2000), 40–56.

104. For a detailed study of Anna May Wong playing up this stereotype in films like *Daughter of the Dragon* (1931) and *Shanghai Express* (1932), see Cynthia W. Liu, "When Dragon Ladies Die, Do They Come Back as Butterflies?: Re-Imagining Anna May Wong," in *Countervisions: Asian American Film Criticism,* eds. Darrell Y. Hamamoto and Sandra Liu (Philadelphia: Temple University Press, 2000), 23–39.

105. Marchetti, *From Tian'anmen to Times Square,* 20.

106. Lo offers another explanation of the woman warrior's sexual appeal: "There is always a reason for male filmmakers to imagine or sexualise women as warriors or as the copies of masculine heroes . . . Masculinity is effective only as reflected and contrasted with a similar but antagonistic sexed other . . . Sexual antagonism engages a self-propelling process in which men imagine masculine women as an imminent threat and to enhance their own virility and power they seek to contain and control the perceived threat." Kwai-Cheung Lo, "Copies of Copies in Hollywood and Hong Kong Cinemas: Rethinking the Woman-Warrior Figures," in *Hong Kong Film, Hollywood and the New Global Cinema: No Film Is an Island,* eds. Gina Marchetti and Tan See Kam (London: Routledge, 2007), 129. For a reading of earlier martial arts woman warriors such as Angela Mao in *Enter the Dragon,* where her suicide in the face of sexual violation functions as the film narrative's appeal to Western audiences' expectation of female vulnerability, see Yvonne Tasker, *Spectacular Bodies: Gender, Genre and the Action Cinema* (London: Routledge, 1993), 24.

107. Wong, "The Early Years," 59–60.

108. Ibid., 60.

109. Ibid., 60.

110. See Jeff Adachi's excellent documentary *The Slanted Screen* (2006).

111. Jachinson Chan, *Chinese American Masculinities: From Fu Manchu to Bruce Lee* (New York: Routledge, 2001), 58.

112. Feng, introduction to *Screening Asian Americans,* 5. Frank Chin and Jeffrey Paul Chan, "Racist Love," in *Seeing Through Shuck,* ed. Richard Kostelanetz (New York: Ballantine, 1972), 65–79.

113. Kwai-Cheung Lo, *Chinese Face/Off: The Transnational Popular Culture of Hong Kong* (Urbana: University of Illinois Press, 2005), 140.
114. Ibid., 141.
115. For an excellent engagement with the contemporary nuances and implications of the "model minority" myth, see Frank H. Wu, *Yellow: Race in America Beyond Black and White* (New York: Basic Books, 2002), 39–77.
116. Lo correctly argues that John Woo's films "being placed as part of Asian American culture should be understood within the international frame of global capitalism." Lo, *Chinese Face/Off,* 161.
117. Ronald Takaki, *Strangers from a Different Shore: A History of Asian Americans* (New York: Penguin, 1989), 418.
118. Ibid., 419.
119. William Wei, *The Asian American Movement* (Philadelphia: Temple University Press, 1993). See especially Chapter 5, "Activists and the Development of Asian American Studies," which chronicles the links between early Asian American political activism and the subsequent formation of Asian American studies programs within the politically charged climate of these two universities.
120. Darrell Y. Hamamoto, "Introduction: On Asian American Film and Criticism," in *Countervisions: Asian American Film Criticism,* eds. Darrell Y. Hamamoto and Sandra Liu (Philadelphia: Temple University Press, 2000), 1.
121. Renee Tajima, "Moving the Image: Asian American Independent Filmmaking 1970–1990," in *Moving the Image: Independent Asian Pacific American Media Arts,* ed. Russell Leong (Los Angeles: UCLA Asian American Studies Center, and Visual Communications, Southern California Asian American Studies Central, 1991), 12.
122. Ibid., 14.
123. Ibid., 16.
124. Hamamoto, "Introduction," 3. Jun Xing, *Asian America through the Lens: History, Representations, and Identity* (Walnut Creek, CA: AltaMira Press, 1998), 177–78.
125. Sandra Liu, "Negotiating the Meaning of Access: Wayne Wang's Contingent Film Practice," in *Countervisions: Asian American Film Criticism,* eds. Darrell Y. Hamamoto and Sandra Liu (Philadelphia: Temple University Press, 2000), 95.
126. Ibid., 90–1.
127. This viewpoint comes from Karen Huie. Quoted in Lisa Odham Stokes and Michael Hoover, *City on Fire: Hong Kong Cinema* (London: Verso, 1999), 316.

2 Visualizing Hong Kong: Diasporic Cinematic Gaze on the 1997 Handover

1. Walter Benjamin, *Illuminations*, ed. Hannah Arendt, trans. Harry Zohn (New York: Schocken Books, 1968), 257.
2. Hong Kong Government, *A Draft Agreement between the Government of the*

United Kingdom of Great Britain and Northern Ireland and the Government of
the People's Republic of China on the Future of Hong Kong, 1984, 11–13; quoted
in Steve Tsang, *A Modern History of Hong Kong* (Hong Kong: Hong Kong
University Press, 2004), 226.

3. Jeremy Tambling, "The History Man: The Last Governor of Hong Kong," *Public
Culture* 9 (1997): 355–75. While Tambling's essay reads the paradoxical role
that Patten plays, one could also turn to Rey Chow, "King Kong in Hong Kong:
Watching the 'Handover' from the U.S.A.," *Social Text* 55, vol. 16, no. 2 (Summer
1998): 93–108, for a reflection on the belated tokenism of introducing democracy
to Hong Kong and the political consequences on the Hong Kong people after the
handover. I am also particularly indebted to Chow's essay for inspiring the notion
of negotiating homelands in "crisis" from afar.

4. Benjamin, *Illuminations*, 257–8.

5. Ibid., 257. Emphasis mine.

6. For a complex understanding of what constitutes modernity, or more accurately
"modernities," in Asia, "that defy both the prescriptions of the globalists/universalists
and the descriptions of the localists/indigenists," see Jenny Kwok Wah Lau,
introduction to *Multiple Modernities: Cinemas and Popular Media in Transcultural
East Asia*, ed. Jenny Kwok Wah Lau (Philadelphia: Temple University Press,
2003), 3.

7. Rey Chow, *Primitive Passions: Visuality, Sexuality, Ethnography, and Contemporary
Chinese Cinema* (New York: Columbia University Press, 1995), xi.

8. Ibid., 10.

9. Annette Michelson, introduction to *Kino-Eye: The Writings of Dziga Vertov*, by
Dziga Vertov, trans. Kevin O'Brien (Berkeley: University of California Press,
1984), xix.

10. Vertov, *Kino-Eye*, 87–8.

11. Ibid., 88.

12. Ibid., 41.

13. The fact that Benjamin's angel of history is a figure in *flight* and in its en*vision*ing
of the historical "wreckage" cannot but be a felicitous coincidence here, particularly
when we consider the processes of a distancing effect in the diasporic eye's
visualizing of homeland from afar.

14. Wang's recent offerings mark a conscious return to Asian American cultural issues:
A Thousand Years of Good Prayers (2007) and *The Princess of Nebraska* (2007).
The latter film opened the 21st Singapore International Film Festival in 2008.

15. While I am aware that Wong also released *Ashes of Time* (1994) and *Fallen
Angels* (1995), I have chosen *Chungking Express* as the point of demarcation
because of the latter's place in the popular reception of Wong's body of work.
Critical work on Wong's cinema has grown significantly: Wimal Dissanayake,
Ashes of Time (Hong Kong: Hong Kong University Press, 2003); Jean-Marc Lalanne
et al., eds., *Wong Kar-wai* (Paris: Dis Voir, 1997); Stephen Teo, *Wong Kar-wai:
Auteur of Time* (London: BFI, 2005); Peter Brunette, *Wong Kar-wai* (Urbana:
University of Illinois Press, 2005).

16. A discussion of nostalgia in *Happy Together* is available in Rey Chow, "Nostalgia of the New Wave: Structure in Wong Kar-wai's *Happy Together*," in *Keyframes: Popular Cinema and Cultural Studies*, eds. Matthew Tinkcom and Amy Villarejo (London: Routledge, 2001), 228–41. A revised version of this essay made its way into Chow's latest book: Rey Chow, *Sentimental Fabulations, Contemporary Chinese Films: Attachment in the Age of Global Visibility* (New York: Columbia University Press, 2007).

17. Ackbar Abbas, *Hong Kong: Culture and the Politics of Disappearance* (Minneapolis: University of Minnesota Press, 1997), 1. See especially Abbas's chapter on Wong Kar-wai, where he reads *Days of Being Wild*, *Chungking Express*, and *Ashes of Time*.

18. Jeremy Tambling, *Wong Kar-wai's* Happy Together (Hong Kong: Hong Kong University Press, 2003), 15. On Jameson's reading of "Third World" texts as "national allegories," see Fredric Jameson, "Third-World Literature in the Era of Multinational Capitalism," *Social Text* 15 (Autumn 1986): 65–88.

19. Tambling, *Wong Kar-wai's* Happy Together, 15.

20. Ibid., 18.

21. Ibid., 18–19.

22. Ibid., 19.

23. Jimmy Ngai and Wong Kar-wai, "A Dialogue with Wong Kar-wai," in Jean-Marc Lalanne et al., *Wong Kar-wai*, 112.

24. The question of gay sexuality in this film, and later in Evans Chan's *The Map of Sex and Love*, brings on a different set of complex hermeneutics that would extend this chapter beyond its intended length. Hence, the issue really deserves an essay of its own.

25. Lisa Odham Stokes and Michael Hoover, *City on Fire: Hong Kong Cinema* (London: Verso, 1999), 268–69.

26. Jacques Derrida, *Margins of Philosophy*, trans. Alan Bass (Chicago: University of Chicago Press, 1982), 3–27. For his theory on play involving presence and absence, see Jacques Derrida, "Structure, Sign, and Play in the Discourse of the Human Sciences," in *Writing and Difference*, trans. Alan Bass (London: Routledge, 1978), 351–70.

27. The political significance of ending the film in Taipei does not go unnoticed by Tambling, who observes that Taipei is "a city whose relationship to its powerful neighbour, mainland China, is as embattled as Argentina's relationship to the USA." Tambling, *Wong Kar-wai's* Happy Together, 63. Equally effective is Song Hwee Lim's contention that "*Happy Together* deliberately designates [Lai Yiu-] Fai's final destination not as Hong Kong but instead as Taiwan, where a militant independence movement rejects Taiwan's reunification with China." Song Hwee Lim, *Celluloid Comrades: Representations of Male Homosexuality in Contemporary Chinese Cinemas* (Honolulu: University of Hawai'i Press, 2006), 102.

28. Tambling, *Wong Kar-wai's* Happy Together, 58.

29. Lim, *Celluloid Comrades*, 122.

30. Karl Marx and Frederick Engels, *The German Ideology*, ed. C. J. Arthur (New York: International Publishers, 1947), 47.

31. Quoted in Scarlet Cheng, "The Homecoming," *Far Eastern Economic Review*, 15 May 1997, 67.

32. bell hooks, *Reel to Real: Race, Sex, and Class at the Movies* (New York: Routledge, 1996), 126–27.

33. Quoted in Kristin Hohenadel, "A Human Face for Hong Kong's Identity Crisis, " *New York Times*, 19 April 1998, 38.

34. James Sterngold, "Wang's World in a Love Story," *New York Times*, 9 January 1998, B7.

35. Wena Poon, Review of *Chinese Box* by Wayne Wang, *Film Quarterly* 52, no. 1 (1998): 34.

36. Intriguingly, this final voiceover appears in the original US videotape release and in the Asian VCD version, but is missing in the Lionsgate Signature Series DVD version released in the US in 2003.

37. Chow, "King Kong in Hong Kong," 100.

38. Quoted in Sterngold, "Wang's World in a Love Story," B7.

39. Quoted in Hohenadel, "A Human Face for Hong Kong's Identity Crisis," 38.

40. Stephen Holden, "A Meditation on the Meaning of Hong Kong," *New York Times*, 17 April 1998, B18.

41. Rey Chow critiques the colonialist mode of cinematic visuality in Bernardo Bertolucci's *The Last Emperor* in Rey Chow, *Woman and Chinese Modernity: The Politics of Reading between West and East* (Minneapolis: University of Minnesota Press, 1991), 3–33. The self-Orientalizing mechanism of visual autoethnography in contemporary Chinese cinema Chow explores next in *Primitive Passions*.

42. My use of the terms "East" and "West" in the context of discussing Orientalism is obviously not to essentialize but to problematize these categories.

43. Chow, *Primitive Passions*, 10.

44. This is a term that Chow borrows from Mary Louis Pratt, *Imperial Eyes: Travel Writing and Transculturation* (New York: Routledge, 1992).

45. Chow, *Primitive Passions*, 12–13.

46. Ibid., 38.

47. Scarlet Cheng observes that this film offers Wang a means of "showing some of the dark side of Hong Kong life." Cheng, "The Homecoming," 68. Wang uses fascinating footage from or possibly inspired by the home videos he took of his Hong Kong visits. His 1997 documentary *Home Movies* is available as a special feature on the Lionsgate Signature Series edition. *Chinese Box*, dir. Wayne Wang, 99 min., Lionsgate Entertainment, 2003, DVD.

48. Edward W. Said, *Orientalism* (New York: Vintage, 1978), 1–2.

49. In discussing the role of Africa in Conrad's *Heart of Darkness*, Achebe asks, "Can nobody see the preposterous and perverse arrogance in thus reducing Africa to the role of props for the break-up of one petty European mind?" Chinua Achebe, "An Image of Africa: Racism in Conrad's *Heart of Darkness*," in *Hopes and Impediments: Selected Essays 1965–1987*, by Chinua Achebe (London: Heinemann, 1988), 12.

50. Gilles Deleuze, *Cinema 1: The Movement-Image*, trans. Hugh Tomlinson and Barbara Habberjam (Minneapolis: University of Minnesota Press, 1986), 88.

51. Quoted in Seth Faison, "Hong Kong Plays the Role of a Drama-Filled City," *New York Times*, 1 July 1997, C9, C12.

52. Quoted in Hohenadel, "A Human Face for Hong Kong's Identity Crisis," 38.

53. Salman Rushdie, *Imaginary Homelands: Essays and Criticism 1981–1991* (London: Granta Books, 1991).

54. Evans Chan is part of what Stephen Teo calls the "Second Wave" of Hong Kong filmmakers (vis-à-vis the "New Wave"). Stephen Teo, *Hong Kong Cinema: The Extra Dimensions* (London: BFI, 1997), 184–203.

55. Paul Gilroy's conception of the "Black Atlantic" comes to mind. Paul Gilroy, *The Black Atlantic: Modernity and Double Consciousness* (Cambridge: Harvard University Press, 1993). Read Evans Chan's own reflections on this diasporic sensibility in an interview by Marchetti: Gina Marchetti, *From Tian'anmen to Times Square: Transnational China and the Chinese Diaspora on Global Screens, 1989–1997* (Philadelphia: Temple University Press, 2006), 183–8.

56. Marchetti, *From Tian'anmen to Times Square*, 160. She derives the term from Peter Wollen, *Readings and Writings: Semiotic Counter-Strategies* (London: Verso, 1982). Wollen has a chapter entitled "Godard and Counter Cinema: *Vent d'est.*"

57. For the latest updates and details of this mega-tourist attraction, go to <http://park.hongkongdisneyland.com/hkdl/en_US/home/home?name=HomePage>, accessed 27 May 2008.

58. "Hong Kong Set for Chinese Influx," *BBC News*, 28 April 1999, <news.bbc.co.uk/1/hi/world/asia-pacific/330923.stm>, accessed 16 June 2007.

59. Hector Rodriguez, "The Fragmented Commonplace: Alternative Arts and Cosmopolitanism in Hong Kong," in Lau, *Multiple Modernities*, 133.

60. Ibid., 128.

3 Facing the Red Dragon: Hollywood's 1997 Response to the Hong Kong Handover

1. China's cinematic response can be found in Xie Jin's *The Opium War* (1997). The film is "a RMB100 million production that grossed RMB72 million in China and NT$3 million in Taipei . . . the first PRC feature to premiere . . . [in Hong Kong] on a split-revenue basis." Yingjin Zhang, *Chinese National Cinema* (New York: Routledge, 2004), 286. What this moderate success at the box office indicates is that Chinese nationalism is a strong sentiment when it comes to understanding the place of Hong Kong in the reunification of China. But in a nuanced reading to counteract often naïve and uninformed Western perspectives on the Opium War, Marchetti recommends that Xie Jin's film "should not be so simply dismissed. " Gina Marchetti, *From Tian'anmen to Times Square: Transnational China and the Chinese Diaspora on Global Screens, 1989–1997* (Philadelphia: Temple University Press, 2006), 41.

2. Rey Chow, "King Kong in Hong Kong: Watching the 'Handover' from the U.S.A.," *Social Text* 55, vol. 16, no. 2 (Summer 1998): 94.

3. Of course, it is essential to consider audience needs strategically when engaging these critiques. I find myself encouraging *Singaporean* students, on one hand, to temper their anti-colonial criticism with a healthy dose of self-reflection, while suggesting to students in my *American* classroom the need to understand and even adopt postcolonial and anti-Orientalist perspectives, on the other.

4. Ien Ang, *On Not Speaking Chinese: Living Between Asia and the West* (London: Routledge, 2001). I am here indebted to Ang for asking the question, "Can One Say No to Chineseness?" the title of a chapter in her book where she argues for a dismantling of Chinese centrism located in discussions of diaspora. Her embrace of hybridity as a theoretical concept, in consideration of her *peranakan* identity, is significant (37–51). My redeployment of her question in a geopolitical context is to further suggest that this cultural centrism deepens with China's rise as an economic superpower.

5. Singapore's alignment with the Chinese cause, for instance, finds its form in a series of articles and essays in Singapore's main newspaper *The Straits Times*: Tom Plate, "When Hollywood Hijacks the Plot," *The Straits Times*, 14 April 2008, 20; Hong Xiaoyong, "China Did Well by Tibet," *The Straits Times*, 23 April 2008, 20; and Goh Sui Noi, "Slap in the Face for Chinese," *The Straits Times*, 24 April 2008, 22. It is of no coincidence that Singapore is not exactly known for its human rights record either, and the fact that it has just won the role of hosting the 2010 Youth Olympics.

6. "Chinese Student in US Dubbed 'Traitor,' Threatened with Violence," *The Straits Times*, 23 April 2008, 8.

7. "'Wheelchair Angel' Feted for Fending Off Protesters," *The Straits Times*, 12 April 2008, 8. The Chinese fencer has been dubbed "angel in a wheelchair." Jin Jing's determination to protect the Olympic flame—or as she puts it, "I'd rather die than let go of the torch," a resolve that she believes "[a]ny *Chinese* or Olympics-loving torch-bearer would" have (emphasis mine)—has led one online supporter to conceptualize her as a national symbol of China's victimized status: "Those separatists should feel ashamed. They always talk about human rights, but they attacked a weak and disabled girl."

8. "You Are Either With Us or Against Us," *CNN.com*, 6 November 2001, <http://archives.cnn.com/2001/US/11/06/gen.attack.on.terror/>, accessed 31 May 2008.

9. See how Judith Butler's deconstruction of George Bush's imperative to take sides unveils the coercive binarism of East versus West: "The voicing of critical perspectives against the war [in Iraq] has become difficult to do, not only because mainstream media enterprises will not publish them (most of them appear in the progressive or alternative print media or on the internet), but because to voice them is to risk hystericization and censorship. In a strong sense, the binarism that Bush proposes in which only two positions are possible . . . makes it untenable to hold a position in which one opposes both and queries the terms in which the opposition is framed. Moreover, it is the same binarism that returns us to an

anachronistic division between 'East' and 'West' and which, in its sloshy metonymy, returns us to the invidious distraction between civilization (our own) and barbarism (now coded as 'Islam' itself)." Judith Butler, *Precarious Life: The Powers of Mourning and Violence* (London: Verso, 2004), 2.

10. Sharon Stone's unfortunate gaffe in talking about China's earthquake as "karma" for the Chinese government's suppression of Tibet's pro-independence movements is not only reprehensible but also irresponsible. Stone subsequently apologized to the Chinese people, only to later modulate that apology into one of support for Tibet. It is this kind of spectacular excess that tars with the same brush the good work of other Hollywood celebrity activists on behalf of the Tibetan people. "Stone Says Quake Was 'Karma,'" *The Straits Times*, 27 May 2008, Life section, 14; "Stone Sorry for 'Karma' Comment," *The Straits Times*, 30 May 2008, Life section, 10; and "Apology: Stone and Dior Differ," *The Straits Times*, 2 June 2008, Life section, 12.

11. The park is a tourist attraction with a significant history. See <http://www.china.org.cn/english/features/beijing/31002.htm>, accessed 2 June 2008.

12. Michel Foucault, *Discipline and Punish: The Birth of the Prison*, trans. Alan Sheridan (New York: Vintage Books, 1977).

13. Mike Clark, "Bai Ling Adds Dimension to 'Red Corner' Thrills," *USA Today*, 31 October 1997, Life section, 1D.

14. Gina Marchetti, *Romance and the "Yellow Peril": Race, Sex, and Discursive Strategies in Hollywood Fiction* (Berkeley: University of California Press, 1993), 110.

15. Sheridan Prasso, *The Asian Mystique: Dragon Ladies, Geisha Girls, and Our Fantasies of the Exotic Orient* (New York: Public Affairs, 2005).

16. See Mat Whitecross and Michael Winterbottom's searing *The Road to Guantanamo* (2006). A humorous but no less critical take is *Harold and Kumar Escape from Guantanamo Bay* (2008).

17. The insert is part of the US DVD version: *Red Corner*, dir. Jon Avnet, 122 min., MGM Home Entertainment, 1998, DVD.

18. Slavoj Žižek, *The Sublime Object of Ideology* (London: Verso, 1989), 66.

19. Yahlin Chang, "Can You Go Home Again?" *Newsweek*, 10 November 1997, 78. Despite all the threats from the Chinese government, Bai Ling admirably defends her work by arguing that *Red Corner* "is not an anti-China movie."

20. Orville Schell, "Virtual Tibet," *Harper's Magazine*, April 1998, 39.

21. Guy Dinmore, "Hollywood Filmstar Urges Congress to Act Over Tibet," *Financial Times*, 14 March 2007, Asia edition, 3; "Celebrities Mark Tibetan Uprising," *BBC News*, 10 March 1999, <http://news.bbc.co.uk/2/hi/entertainment/294210.stm>, accessed 5 June 2008.

22. Stars, such as Richard Gere, Mia Farrow, and Steven Spielberg, and world leaders, including Hillary Clinton, British Prime Minister Gordon Brown, and German Chancellor Angela Merkel, supported boycotting the Games to varying degrees. George Clooney and will.i.am believed in moderation and participation as a means of challenging China to change its position on Tibet and Darfur. "Politically Minded Stars Split on Skipping Beijing Olympics," *CNN.com*, 8 May 2008, <http://

edition.cnn.com/2008/US/05/07/olympic.boycott/index.html?eref=edition>, accessed 5 June 2008.

23. Schell, "Virtual Tibet."
24. Ibid., 39–40.
25. Ibid., 40. James Hilton, *Lost Horizon: A Novel* (New York: HarperCollins, 1960).
26. Chow, "King Kong in Hong Kong," 94.
27. The film is based on Harrer's book: Heinrich Harrer, *Seven Years in Tibet* (New York: Tarcher/Putnam, 1981.)
28. Marc Abramson, "Mountains, Monks, and Mandalas: *Kundun* and *Seven Years in Tibet*," *Cineaste* 23, no. 3 (April 1998): 8–12. I am citing from an online version at <http://ccbs.ntu.edu.tw/FULLTEXT/JR-EPT/abramson.htm>, accessed 6 June 2008.
29. The study of these histories is truly beyond the ken of this book. So, in true dilettantish fashion, I have turned randomly to books whose approaches I found either distinctive or user friendly. For an account that features an interview with the Dalai Lama, see John F. Avedon, *In Exile from the Land of Snows: The Definitive Account of the Dalai Lama and Tibet Since the Chinese Conquest* (New York: HarperCollins, 1997). For a "balanced" native-informant historical study, see Tsering Shakya, *The Dragon in the Land of Snows: A History of Modern Tibet Since 1947* (New York: Columbia University Press, 1999). I have relied on and cite exclusively from the following concise historical précis: Melvyn C. Goldstein, *The Snow Lion and the Dragon: China, Tibet, and the Dalai Lama* (Berkeley: University of California Press, 1997).
30. Hayden White, *Metahistory: The Historical Imagination in Nineteenth Century Europe* (Baltimore, MD: Johns Hopkins University Press, 1975).
31. Goldstein, *The Snow Lion and the Dragon*, 4.
32. Ibid., 14.
33. Ibid., 23.
34. Ibid., 25–6.
35. Ibid., 26.
36. Ibid., 31.
37. Ibid., 44–6.
38. Ibid., 47.
39. Ibid., 34.
40. Ibid., 49.
41. Ibid., 58.
42. The Chinese government has chosen to conceal this ruthlessness from its citizens, even as recently as in the 2008 Tibet protests. Censorship is an old technique of preventing a nation's young from learning the difficult truths that state authorities are afraid they might stumble upon. This is also a means of sustaining an unquestioning nationalism in a new generation of citizenry. "China Blocks YouTube over Tibet Protests," *MSNBC.Com*, 16 March 2008, <http://www.msnbc.msn.com/id/23657906/>, accessed 7 June 2008.
43. Dominick LaCapra, *History in Transit: Experience, Identity, Critical Theory* (Ithaca: Cornell University Press, 2004), 46.

4   The Global Return of the *Wuxia pian* (Chinese Sword-Fighting Movie)

1. For an informative study of the history of the *wuxia pian* and the major Hong Kong directors (such as King Hu, Chang Cheh, Liu Chia-liang, Chor Yuen, and Tsui Hark) and their impact on the genre, see Chapters 6 and 7 of Stephen Teo, *Hong Kong Cinema: The Extra Dimensions* (London: BFI, 1997). David Bordwell, *Planet Hong Kong: Popular Cinema and the Art of Entertainment* (Cambridge: Harvard University Press, 2000) foregrounds the global significance of Hong Kong action and martial arts cinema and its formalist aesthetics. See also Chang Cheh, *Chang Cheh: A Memoir*, trans. Teri Chan and Agnes Lam (Hong Kong: Hong Kong Film Archive, 2004); and Kwok Ching-ling and Grace Ng, eds., *Director Chor Yuen* (Hong Kong: Hong Kong Film Archive, 2006).

2. Esther C. M. Yau points out that Hong Kong films provide "light doses of 'Chinese-ness'" as "a panacea for . . . homesick overseas Asian audiences." Esther C. M. Yau, "Introduction: Hong Kong Cinema in a Borderless World," in *At Full Speed: Hong Kong Cinema in a Borderless World,* ed. Esther C. M. Yau (Minneapolis: University of Minnesota Press, 2001), 2. The People's Republic of China, Taiwan, Hong Kong, Malaysia, Singapore, and various parts of the Chinese diaspora constitute an interconnected and interdependent circuit of production, marketing, distribution, and consumption of Chinese-language cinemas, of which Hong Kong movies form a major component.

3. Stephen Teo, *"Wuxia Redux: Crouching Tiger, Hidden Dragon* as a Model of Late Transnational Production," in *Hong Kong Connections: Transnational Imagination in Action Cinema,* eds. Meaghan Morris, Siu Leung Li, and Stephen Chan Ching-kiu (Durham: Duke University Press, 2005), 194.

4. Much of the Ang Lee segment of this chapter was originally published as "The Global Return of the *Wu Xia Pian* (Chinese Sword-Fighting Movie): Ang Lee's *Crouching Tiger, Hidden Dragon,"* *Cinema Journal* 43, no. 4 (Summer 2004): 3–17. See in the same issue Christina Klein, *"Crouching Tiger, Hidden Dragon*: A Diasporic Reading," 18–42; and the film's screenwriter and executive producer James Schamus's response to the two essays: "Aesthetic Identities: A Response to Kenneth Chan and Christina Klein," 43–52. The fact that the journal devoted a major portion of the issue to a single film is testament to its significance.

5. If awards can serve as reliable indicators of a film's success, *Crouching Tiger, Hidden Dragon* is not only an American success story but also a truly global one. It picked up awards for best director and best film at the Twentieth Hong Kong Film Awards; best picture at the Taiwanese Golden Horse Awards; best director and best foreign-language film at the Golden Globes; Academy Awards for foreign-language film, cinematography, art direction, and original score and was nominated for best picture and best director.

6. According to Teo, *"Crouching Tiger*'s reception in Asia was not uniform. In some territories where Chinese preponderate the box-office takings can only be said to be lacklustre compared with its performance in the West." Teo, *"Wuxia* Redux," 200.

7. In her excellent analysis of *Crouching Tiger, Hidden Dragon*'s cultural translatability, Felicia Chan argues that it was "marketed as a Matrix-type film, . . . an art film, a woman's film, as well as a combination of all these" in the United States, while "the film's Oscar triumph saw a revived interest in many parts of East Asia, which basked in a collective cultural pride." Felicia Chan, "*Crouching Tiger, Hidden Dragon*: Cultural Migrancy and Translatability," in *Chinese Films in Focus: 25 New Takes,* ed., Chris Berry (London: BFI, 2003), 57–8. For more on the film's cultural translatability and its reinvention of the *wuxia pian,* see Ken-fang Lee, "Far Away, So Close: Cultural Translation in Ang Lee's *Crouching Tiger, Hidden Dragon*," *Inter-Asia Cultural Studies* 4, no. 2 (2003): 281–95.

8. In his discussion of how he battles these extreme viewpoints on the *wuxia* genre, James Schamus cautions Stephen Teo, in an interview, "to beware of the trap of genre-based criticism that defines genres in such a way that boundaries seem as if they have an existence, but in fact these are ever mutating. The national discourses that underwrite a lot of the work, or at least accompany a lot of the work in terms of its reception, can also be a bit of a black hole too, in the sense that you're dealing on the one hand with cultural formations that work over periods (when you're dealing with China, over thousands and thousands of years) and at the same time you're dealing with national formations that are in themselves actually quite recent and ephemeral. So that even the idea of an 'Eastern point of view' on the *wuxia* genre — to the extent to which it's a nationalist point of view or pertains to a kind of national discourse — could itself be called already a Western point of view; or a point of view that mixes East and West in a dialogue that's quite modern." Stephen Teo, "'We Kicked Jackie Chan's Ass!' An Interview with James Schamus," *Senses of Cinema,* March-April 2001, <http://www.sensesofcinema.com/contents/01/13/schamus.html>, accessed 11 June 2008.

9. Fredric Jameson, *Postmodernism, or, the Cultural Logic of Late Capitalism* (Durham: Duke University Press, 1991).

10. Evans Chan argues that Hollywood has only recently begun to understand and value the impact of Hong Kong action movies on postmodernist cinema aesthetics. However, he laments that the Hong Kong film industry might be in its death throes as it is now being "cannibalized by Hollywood." Evans Chan, "Postmodernism and Hong Kong Cinema," in *Postmodernism and China,* eds. Arif Dirlik and Xudong Zhang (Durham: Duke University Press, 2000), 303. Could *Crouching Tiger, Hidden Dragon* and the resurgence of the *wuxia pian* mark a turnaround for the industry, whereby a kind of trans-Pacific cross-pollination might reinvigorate it through collaborative action?

11. Biographies of the production team and a list of the complete credits for the film are available in Linda Sunshine, ed., *Crouching Tiger, Hidden Dragon: A Portrait of the Ang Lee Film* (New York: Newmarket Press, 2000). This book also includes the complete screenplay in English and essays by Lee, Schamus, David Bordwell, and film critic Richard Corliss.

12. See James Schamus's account of the complex negotiations over financial backing for the film in "The Guardian/NFT Interview: Ang Lee and James Schamus,"

Guardian Unlimited, 7 November 2000, <http://film.guardian.co.uk/interview/interviewpages/0,6737,394676,00.html#early>, accessed 23 May 2007.

13. Sheldon H. Lu, "Crouching Tiger, Hidden Dragon, Bouncing Angels: Hollywood, Taiwan, Hong Kong, and Transnational Cinema," in *Chinese-Language Film: Historiography, Poetics, Politics*, eds., Sheldon H. Lu and Emilie Yueh-yu Yeh (Honolulu: University of Hawai'i Press, 2005), 222.

14. "The Guardian/NFT Interview."

15. Nisid Hajari, "Erasing the Boundaries," *Newsweek*, special ed., Issues Asia, July-September 2001, 79.

16. I have in mind Michel de Certeau's notion of "tactics" here. Michel de Certeau, *The Practice of Everyday Life*, trans. Steven Rendall (Berkeley: University of California Press, 1984), xvii–xx.

17. Hajari, "Erasing the Boundaries," 79.

18. Attending to the exotic in Lee's first three movies is: Sheng-mei Ma, *Immigrant Subjectivities in Asian American and Asian Diaspora Literatures* (Albany: State University of New York Press, 1998), 144–58.

19. Sunshine, *Crouching Tiger, Hidden Dragon*, 7.

20. Christian Metz, "The Imaginary Signifier," in *Narrative, Apparatus, Ideology: A Film Theory Reader*, ed. Philip Rosen (New York: Columbia University Press, 1986), 253. Although Metz's theoretical concern is the spectator-screen relationship, the tropes of the mirror and the imaginary as they play out on identity are useful in thinking about a filmmaker's construction of his work.

21. Maxine Hong Kingston, *The Woman Warrior: Memoirs of a Girlhood Among Ghosts* (New York: Vintage International, 1976). It is clearly not coincidental that in the chapter "White Tigers," Kingston claims that the merging of her mother's "talk-stories" and her own experiences with the *wuxia pian* led to her fantasies of being the legendary swordswoman Fa Mu Lan.

22. "Ang Lee: *Pushing Hands*," in *My First Movie: Twenty Celebrated Directors Talk about Their First Film*, ed. Stephen Lowenstein (New York: Pantheon, 2000), 372–73. For varied interpretations on this issue in Lee's films, see Wei Ming Dariotis and Eileen Fung, "Breaking the Soy Sauce Jar: Diaspora and Displacement in the Films of Ang Lee," in *Transnational Chinese Cinemas: Identity, Nationhood, Gender*, ed. Sheldon Hsiao-peng Lu (Honolulu: University of Hawai'i Press, 1997), 187–220; and Mark Chiang, "Coming Out into the Global System: Postmodern Patriarchies and Transnational Sexualities in *The Wedding Banquet*," in *Screening Asian Americans*, ed. Peter X. Feng (New Brunswick: Rutgers University Press, 2002), 273–92.

23. Pierre Bourdieu, *The Logic of Practice*, trans. Richard Nice (Stanford: Stanford University Press, 1990), 52–65.

24. All English translations of the dialogue from the film are from Sunshine, *Crouching Tiger, Hidden Dragon*.

25. Sunshine, *Crouching Tiger, Hidden Dragon*, 76.

26. According to Schamus, "The film was shot in almost every corner of China, including the Gobi Desert and the Taklamakan Plateau, north of Tibet, near the Kyrgyzstan border." Ibid., 46.

27. For a discussion of male homosocial desire along a spectrum that includes homosexual desire at one end, see Eve Kosofsky Sedgwick, *Between Men: English Literature and Male Homosocial Desire* (New York: Columbia University Press, 1985), 1–20. I am not suggesting here that the homoerotic is absent from the *wuxia pian*; the films of Chang Cheh and Liu Chia-liang exemplify, for instance, the subtext of homoerotic tensions in the relationships and in the machismo displays of the male characters. See Teo, *Hong Kong Cinema*, 102–7; and Michael Lam, "The Mysterious Gayness in Chang Cheh's Unhappy World," trans. Sam Ho, in *The Shaw Screen: A Preliminary Study,* ed. Wong Ain-ling (Hong Kong: Hong Kong Film Archive, 2003), 175–87.

28. Whether one attributes this choice to the source material for the screenplay (Wang Du Lu's novel) or to Chow Yun-fat's lack of martial arts experience, Lee decided to shift the action sequences away from Chow Yun-fat's character. "The Guardian/ NFT Interview." Hence, one can still credit Lee and James Schamus for wanting to pursue a project that deviated from the genre's gender conventions.

29. Sunshine, *Crouching Tiger, Hidden Dragon*, 7.

30. Kwai-Cheung Lo, *Chinese Face/Off: The Transnational Popular Culture of Hong Kong* (Urbana: University of Illinois Press, 2005), 185. See also Sheldon Lu's take on this issue. Lu, "Crouching Tiger," 228–30.

31. Laura Mulvey, "Visual Pleasure and Narrative Cinema," in *Feminism and Film,* ed. E. Ann Kaplan (Oxford: Oxford University Press, 2000), 34–47.

32. In presenting an example of merging kung fu action with the dragon lady persona, Prasso surveys Lucy Liu's film career as she moves from playing "the sadistic dominatrix hooker in Mel Gibson's 1999 movie *Payback*" to her "role of icy Princess Pei Pei" in *Shanghai Noon*, and finally to the "kick-ass" Alex Munday in the two *Charlie's Angels* movies. Liu's response to why she accepted roles that further "the Dragon Lady/Vixen stereotypes" was a truthfully simple "I don't have many options now." Sheridan Prasso, *The Asian Mystique: Dragon Ladies, Geisha Girls, and Our Fantasies of the Exotic Orient* (New York: Public Affairs, 2005), 73–4.

33. Judith Butler, *Bodies That Matter: On the Discursive Limits of "Sex"* (New York: Routledge, 1993), 125. While this cross-dressing mise-en-scène has a Chinese cinematic and literary cultural specificity to its lineage, my application of Butler's idea here emphasizes the very contemporary feminist politics that marks *Crouching Tiger, Hidden Dragon* as the product of East-West pop cultural and intellectual intermingling, as both Schamus and Lee have described their film. Feminist literary critic Elaine Showalter notes how the film "speaks with luminous directness to the aspirations of *contemporary* women." Elaine Showalter, "Sex Goddess," *The American Prospect*, 21 May 2001, 38. Emphasis mine.

34. Teo, "'We Kicked Jackie Chan's Ass!'"

35. Berry and Farquhar read this treetop scene and the teahouse scene in the stylistic terms of Chinese opera. Chris Berry and Mary Farquhar, *China on Screen: Cinema and Nation* (Hong Kong: Hong Kong University Press, 2006), 71.

36. Sheng-mei Ma, "Kung Fu Films in Diaspora: Death of the Bamboo Hero," in

Masculinities and Hong Kong Cinema, eds. Laikwan Pang and Day Wong (Hong Kong: Hong Kong University Press, 2005), 114.

37. Kate Chopin, *The Awakening* (New York: Norton, 1994).

38. Engaging in a rather creative discussion of *qinggong* (and its masculinist valences), see Hsiao-hung Chang, "The Unbearable Lightness of Globalization: On the Transnational Flight of *Wuxia* Film," in *Cinema Taiwan: Politics, Popularity and State of the Arts*, ed. Darrell William Davis and Ru-shou Robert Chen (London: Routledge, 2007), 95–107.

39. Teo, "*Wuxia* Redux," 202.

40. Rather coincidentally, Fran Martin also alludes to Ridley Scott's film in her study of the final sequence where Jen jumps off the mountain. Martin argues that "a significant effect of the film's projection of a simulacral, postmodern, and transnational version of 'Pan-Chineseness' is precisely to fantasize the contemporaneity of third-wave pop-feminism into the heart of a re-imagined 'Chinese tradition.'" Fran Martin, "The China Simulacrum: Genre, Feminism, and Pan-Chinese Cultural Politics in *Crouching Tiger, Hidden Dragon*," in *Island on the Edge: Taiwan New Cinema and After*, eds. Chris Berry and Feii Lu (Hong Kong: Hong Kong University Press, 2005), 158–9. Also arriving at the same allusion are Yeh and Davis, who further read this scene as "an affirmative national allegory" for "Taiwan separatists." Emilie Yueh-yu Yeh and Darrell William Davis, *Taiwan Film Directors: A Treasure Island* (New York: Columbia University Press, 2005), 193.

41. I realize that Lee's use of Chinese patriarchy as a metonymic stand-in for Chinese culture and the oppressive force field it asserts can diminish the specific feminist critique of Chinese patriarchy. Yet cultural and feminist critiques can form a kind of political alliance to take on the same structure that enacts their respective modes of oppression.

42. Stephen Short and Susan Jakes, "This Film Was My Boyhood Dream," *TIMEasia.com*, <http://www.time.com/time/asia/features/hero/int_zhang_yimou.html>, accessed 17 May 2007.

43. Paul Clark, *Reinventing China: A Generation and Its Films* (Hong Kong: The Chinese University Press, 2005), 164–86.

44. Short and Jakes, "This Film Was My Boyhood Dream."

45. Tonglin Lu would probably categorize this as part of the "Zhang Yimou Model" where Chinese filmmakers find initial success in the international film festival scene before turning into profitable commercial filmmakers both in China and around the world. Tonglin Lu, *Confronting Modernity in the Cinemas of Taiwan and Mainland China* (Cambridge: Cambridge University Press, 2002), 157–8.

46. Frances Gateward, ed., *Zhang Yimou Interviews* (Jackson: University Press of Mississippi, 2001). In this excellent collection of interviews, Zhang has been asked on numerous occasions how he would react when being accused of depicting Chinese society and politics in an unfavorable light in order to garner Western critical praise and to pander to Western notions of Chinese authoritarianism. His response has consistently been an increasingly unconvincing appeal to ignorance: he has little comprehension of Western audiences and their cinematic taste. See

particularly the following interviews: Mayfair Mei-Hui Yang, "Of Gender, State, Censorship, and Overseas Capital: An Interview with Chinese Director Zhang Yimou," in Gateward, 41–2. First published in *Public Culture* 5, no. 2 (Summer 1993): 297–313; Renee Schoof, "Zhang Yimou: Only Possible Work Environment Is China," in Gateward, 71. First published on 5 November 1995, The Associated Press; and Kwok-Kan Tam, "Cinema and Zhang Yimou," in Gateward, 114.

47. Mary Farquhar, "Zhang Yimou," *Senses of Cinema*, May 2002, <http://www.sensesofcinema.com/contents/directors/02/zhang.html>, accessed 17 May 2007.

48. The ban was lifted in 1992. Clark, *Reinventing China,* 178.

49. Schoof, "Zhang Yimou," 71.

50. Tam, "Cinema and Zhang Yimou," 114.

51. Jenny Kwok Wah Lau, "*Hero*: China's Response to Hollywood Globalization," *Jump Cut: A Review of Contemporary Media*, no. 49 (Spring 2007), <http://www.ejumpcut.org/trialsite/Lau-Hero/text.html>, accessed 22 May 2007.

52. Susan Jakes, "Playing Safe," *Time*, 15 December 2002, <http://www.time.com/time/magazine/article/0,9171,501021223-400042,00.html>, accessed 17 May 2007.

53. Ibid.

54. Lau, "*Hero.*"

55. In comparing the film with Leni Riefenstahl's *Triumph of the Will*, J. Hoberman of the *Village Voice* cannot but see that "Hero's vast imperial sets and symmetrical tumult, its decorative dialectical montage and sanctimonious traditionalism, its glorification of ruthless leadership and self-sacrifice on the altar of national greatness, not to mention the sense that this might somehow stoke the engine of political regeneration, are all redolent of fascinatin' fascism." J. Hoberman, "Man with No Name Tells a Story of Heroics, Color Coordination," *Village Voice*, 17 August 2004, <http://www.villagevoice.com/film/0434,hoberman2,56140,20.html>, accessed 21 May 2007. This comparison to Riefenstahl is similarly made in Evans Chan, "Zhang Yimou's *Hero*: The Temptations of Fascism," *Film International* 2, no. 8 (March 2004): 14–23.

56. Jet Li makes the following observation about contemporary action films: "Films now are all about killing one's opponent as fast as possible. In the old days, guys had more respect for each other. There was a dignity about the way they fought." Stephen Short and Susan Jakes, "Violence Doesn't Solve Anything," *TIMEasia.com*, <http://www.time.com/time/asia/features/hero/int_jet_li.html>, accessed 17 May 2007. Li's latest *wuda pian* (kung fu film) *Fearless* (2006) returns specifically to this traditional notion of honor.

57. Broken Sword actually writes *two* Chinese words, *tianxia*, which is literally translated as "beneath the sky" or "all under heaven," the latter of which more effectively articulates the extent of the emperor's sovereignty.

58. "The older generation will like it but I'm not sure about the youngsters. The government will definitely like it. It's a film that says country comes first, then city, then family," notes Jet Li. Short and Jakes, "Violence Doesn't Solve Anything."

59. Stephen Short and Susan Jakes, "Making of a Hero," *TIMEasia.com*, <http://www.time.com/time/asia/features/hero/story2.html>, accessed 17 May 2007.

60. Lau, *"Hero."*

61. Ibid.

62. Giorgio Agamben, *Homo Sacer: Sovereign Power and Bare Life,* trans. Daniel Heller-Roazen (Stanford: Stanford University Press, 1998), 40.

63. Berry and Farquhar, *China on Screen,* 163. Emphasis mine.

64. Teo, *Hong Kong Cinema,* 111–2.

65. Charles Taylor, "Hero," *Salon.com*, 27 August 2004, <http://dir.salon.com/story/ent/movies/review/2004/08/27/hero/index_np.html>, accessed 17 May 2007. See also Robert Y. Eng, "Is Hero a Paean to Authoritarianism?" *AsiaMedia*, 7 September 2004, <http://www.asiamedia.ucla.edu/article.asp?parentid=14371>, accessed 22 May 2007. In arguing that *Hero* is critical of authoritarianism, Eng compares Zhang's film to Chen Kaige's *The Emperor and the Assassin* (1999) and Zhou Xiaowen's *The Emperor's Shadow* (1996).

66. Shelley Kraicer, "Absence as Spectacle: Zhang Yimou's *Hero*," <http://www.chinesecinemas.org/hero.html>, accessed 22 May 2007. Originally published in *Cinema Scope* 5, no. 1 (Spring 2003): 9.

67. Literary critics of British colonial literature, for example, have frequently made this argument in order to politically rehabilitate canonical figures like Joseph Conrad, E. M. Forster, and George Orwell from their complicit roles within the structures of British imperialism.

68. Craig S. Smith, "'Hero' Soars, and Its Director Thanks 'Crouching Tiger,'" *New York Times*, 2 September 2004, E1.

69. Gary G. Xu, *Sinascape: Contemporary Chinese Cinema* (Lanham, MD: Rowman and Littlefield, 2007), 27.

70. Ien Cheng, "Hero's Success Sweeps the US," *Financial Times*, 13 September 2004, Arts and Style section, 12.

71. Roger Ebert, "Hero," *rogerebert.com*, 27 August 2004, <http://rogerebert.suntimes.com/apps/pbcs.dll/article?AID=/20040826/REVIEWS/408260304/1023>, accessed 12 June 2008.

72. Mike Clark, "'Hero': Easy on the Eyes But a Little Too Plodding," *USA Today*, 26 August 2004, <http://www.usatoday.com/life/movies/reviews/2004-08-26-hero_x.htm>, accessed 12 June 2008.

73. Robert Mackey, "Cracking the Color Code of 'Hero'," *New York Times*, 15 August 2004, <http://www.nytimes.com/2004/08/15/movies/15MACK.html?ex=1250308800&en=314c0d1ef8845f23&ei=5088&partner=rssnyt>, accessed 17 May 2007.

74. Richard Corliss, "In the Mood for Swordplay," *Time*, 15 December 2002, <http://www.time.com/time/magazine/article/0,9171,501021223-400044,00.html>, accessed 17 May 2007.

75. Taylor, "Hero."

76. Jeffrey Overstreet, "Hero," *Christianity Today*, 20 August 2004, <http://www.christianitytoday.com/movies/reviews/hero.html>, accessed 12 June 2008.

77. As a film critic, I am not against close reading and analysis of artistic form, as my approach to cinema in this book amply demonstrates; in fact, I believe in its

foundational place in literary and filmic criticism. What I am wary of is New Criticism's dismissal of political modes of reading through their argument that form analysis is in no way ideologically motivated.

78. Providing a rich alternative to my own reductive take on the film (for the immediate purposes of this chapter's argument) is Hwanhee Lee's rather astute reading of the complications of love and the agonizing and contradictory choices one makes in its name. Hwanhee Lee, "*House of Flying Daggers*: A Reappraisal," *Senses of Cinema*, 2005, <http://www.sensesofcinema.com/contents/05/35/house_flying_daggers.html>, accessed 23 May 2007.

79. Again, reviewers from Western media sources rave about the film's lush imagery and spectacular set pieces. See Stephanie Zacharek, "House of Flying Daggers," *Salon.com*, 7 October 2004, <http://dir.salon.com/story/ent/indie/2004/10/07/daggers/index.html>, accessed 22 May 2007; and Stephen Hunter, "'House of Flying Daggers': Symphony in Swords," *Washington Post*, 17 December 2004, <http://www.washingtonpost.com/wp-dyn/articles/A6440-2004Dec16.html?referrer=email>, accessed 22 May 2007. Has an over-familiarity with the genre led to my inability to appreciate these films as spectacular and exquisite instances of movie-making? This question is symptomatic of the challenges for the contemporary makers of the *wuxia pian* in appealing to both new audiences and experienced ones in the global filmic marketplace.

5   Enter the Triads: American Cinema's New Racialized Criminal Other

1. Thomas Leitch, *Crime Films* (Cambridge: Cambridge University Press, 2002). Mark Bould, *Film Noir: From Berlin to Sin City* (London: Wallflower, 2005). See also chapters in Barry Keith Grant, ed., *Film Genre Reader III* (Austin: University of Texas Press, 2003) — chapter 16, Edward Mitchell, "Apes and Essences: Some Sources of Significance in the American Gangster Film"; chapter 17, Paul Schrader, "Notes on Film Noir"; and chapter 18, John G. Cawelti, "*Chinatown* and Generic Transformation in Recent American Films."

2. Read Marchetti's brilliant analysis of racial criminal Otherness in Josef von Sternberg's noir-ish *Shanghai Express*. Gina Marchetti, *Romance and the "Yellow Peril": Race, Sex, and Discursive Strategies in Hollywood Fiction* (Berkeley: University of California Press, 1993), 57–66. Roman Polanski's 1974 crime classic *Chinatown* deploys a racially ghettoized space as "the symbolic locus of darkness, strangeness, and catastrophe." Cawelti, "*Chinatown*," 249. For a wonderful filmic subversion of the roles of racial Otherness in film noir, see Carl Franklin's superb *Devil in a Blue Dress* (1995).

3. David Desser, "Global Noir: Genre Film in the Age of Transnationalism," in *Film Genre Reader III*, ed., Barry Keith Grant (Austin: University of Texas Press, 2003), 516–36.

4. Stanfield offers a list of Chinatown-related films with titles such as *Chinatown*

Villains (1916), *The Tong Man* (1919), *Shadows of Chinatown* (1926), *Chinatown Nights* (1929), *Law of the Tong* (1931), *Chinatown after Dark* (1931), and *The Hatchet Man* (1932). Peter Stanfield, "'American as Chop Suey': Invocations of Gangsters in Chinatown, 1920–1936," in *Mob Culture: Hidden Histories of the American Gangster Film,* eds. Lee Grieveson, Esther Sonnet, and Peter Stanfield (New Brunswick: Rutgers University Press, 2005), 240.

5. Martin Booth, *The Dragon Syndicates: The Global Phenomenon of the Triads* (New York: Carroll & Graf, 1999), 8–9. Booth's book emphasizes the global nature of triad activity, updating his earlier book on the same subject: Martin Booth, *The Triads: The Chinese Criminal Fraternity* (London: Grafton Books, 1990). For more on the beginnings of the triads, see Dian H. Murray, in collaboration with Qin Baoqi, *The Origins of the Tiandihui: The Chinese Triads in Legend and History* (Stanford: Stanford University Press, 1994).

6. Booth, *Dragon Syndicates,* 10.

7. Ibid., 13.

8. Ibid., 14–15.

9. Ibid., 30, 41.

10. Ibid., 46–47, 65, 67.

11. Ibid., 170–261.

12. Ibid., 257.

13. Ibid., 256.

14. Timothy Mo, *Sour Sweet* (London: Paddleless Press, 1999). For more on the triads in North America, check out Peter Houston, *Tongs, Gangs, and Triads: Chinese Crime Groups in North America* (San Jose: Authors Choice Press, 2001).

15. Booth, *Dragon Syndicates,* 298.

16. Ibid., 300–301.

17. Ed Guerrero, *Framing Blackness: The African American Image in Film* (Philadelphia: Temple University Press, 1993), 127–8.

18. Ibid., 129.

19. Louis Althusser, "Marx's Immense Theoretical Revolution," in *Reading Capital,* by Louis Althusser and Étienne Balibar, trans. Ben Brewster (London: Verso, 1997), 188. For more on the concept, see Louis Althusser, *For Marx,* trans. Ben Brewster (London: Verso, 1969), 87–128.

20. One thinks especially of Paul Haggis's intriguing but flawed *Crash,* which won three Academy Awards in 2006, including one for best picture.

21. As this is not the place for me to launch into a detailed critical analysis of this discourse, I wish to point readers to an excellent collection of essays critiquing the politics of the anti-PC agenda: Jeffrey Williams, ed., *PC Wars: Politics and Theory in the Academy* (New York: Routledge, 1995).

22. This is Jet Li's first Hollywood film, which could possibly account for his limited English dialogue.

23. Also, bizarrely in (or out of) character are Mel Gibson's recent allegedly anti-Semitic media spectacles: *The Passion of the Christ* (2004), which he directed; and his 2006 DUI run-in with the law, featuring a drunken tirade against Jews;

both of which serve as rather disturbing extra-textual glosses. See "Gibson: 'I am not an anti-Semite,'" *CNN.com*, 2 August 2006, <http://www.cnn.com/2006/ SHOWBIZ/Movies/08/01/gibson.dui/index.html>, accessed 27 May 2007.

24. Mark A. Reid, "The Black Gangster Film," in *Film Genre Reader III,* ed. Barry Keith Grant (Austin: University of Texas Press, 2003), 486. See also Kenneth Chan, "The Construction of Black Male Identity in Black Action Films of the Nineties," *Cinema Journal* 37, no. 2 (1998): 35–48.

25. According to Booth, *sh'e tau*, or snakehead, is a relatively high-ranking triad member, generally a Red Pole (one of the few leadership positions in the triad hierarchy). The snakehead is the person in charge of the human smuggling operation. Booth, *Dragon Syndicates*, 255.

26. David Harvey, *The Condition of Postmodernity: An Enquiry into the Origins of Cultural Change* (Cambridge: Blackwell, 1990), 121–4.

27. The triads' human smuggling trade is global and international in its reach. Booth, *Dragon Syndicates*, 254–8.

28. Judith Butler, *Precarious Life: The Powers of Mourning and Violence* (London: Verso, 2004), 32.

29. Ibid., 31–2.

30. I borrow the term from Pheng Cheah in his introduction to: Pheng Cheah and Bruce Robbins, eds., *Cosmopolitics: Thinking and Feeling beyond the Nation* (Minneapolis: University of Minnesota Press, 1998).

31. Films like Alejandro González Iñárritu's *Babel* (2006) and Wim Wenders' *Land of Plenty* (2004) grapple with this philosophical question.

32. Producer extraordinaire Terence Chang tells of how Chow Yun-fat was finally convinced to move to Hollywood, a story that weaves the triads, Hong Kong cinema, Hollywood, and Chow Yun-fat into a coincidental relationship: "It took me a long time to convince him. At that time he felt like, you know, I'm a huge star in Asia. Why should I go to Hollywood? Now I would give credit to the gangsters, to the triads, because they started to threaten him. Remember the scene in *The Godfather* where the producer woke up with a horse in his bed. Chow Yun-fat woke up one morning with a cat's head neatly chopped [and] thrown into his garden. And he was so horrified he said, ok, you know, I think I better take your advice. I should try Hollywood." Chang recounts this story in the short documentary video "Chow Yun-fat Goes Hollywood" (2001), directed by Jeffrey Schwarz, available as a special feature in the special edition DVD of Antoine Fuqua's *The Replacement Killers.*

33. Giovanna Borradori, *Philosophy in a Time of Terror: Dialogues with Jürgen Habermas and Jacques Derrida* (Chicago: University of Chicago Press, 2003), 188. See endnote 8, point 2.

34. Booth, *Dragon Syndicates*, 60.

35. Aihwa Ong, *Flexible Citizenship: The Cultural Logics of Transnationality* (Durham: Duke University Press, 1999).

36. See Chapter Two, endnote 49.

37. David Desser, "The Kung Fu Craze: Hong Kong Cinema's First American

Reception," in *The Cinema of Hong Kong: History, Arts, Identity*, eds. Poshek Fu and David Desser (Cambridge: Cambridge University Press, 2000), 19–43. Gina Marchetti, "Jackie Chan and the Black Connection," in *Keyframes: Popular Cinema and Cultural Studies*, eds. Matthew Tinkcom and Amy Villarejo (London: Routledge, 2001), 137–158. Laleen Jayamanne, "Let's Miscegenate: Jackie Chan and His African-American Connection," in *Hong Kong Connections: Transnational Imagination in Action Cinema*, eds. Meaghan Morris, Siu Leung Li, and Stephen Chan Ching-kiu (Durham: Duke University Press, 2005), 151–162.

38. Desser, "The Kung Fu Craze," 38.

39. The image of an Asian asserting his hyper-masculinity through his no-nonsense kung fu moves also subverts the model minority stereotype today, which accounts for the enduring popularity of Bruce Lee among Asian Americans.

40. See Chapter Six of this book, where I explain the significance of "dragon" in both Bruce Lee and Jackie Chan's Chinese names.

41. Marchetti, "Jackie Chan and the Black Connection," 140–3.

42. Ibid., 157. In his reading of *Romeo Must Die*, Lo echoes Marchetti's argument by marking the phenomenon as a form of "racial passing," an ethnic Chinese passing for black as in the case of Jet Li in the film. Kwai-Cheung Lo, *Chinese Face/Off: The Transnational Popular Culture of Hong Kong* (Urbana: University of Illinois, 2005), 154–6.

43. Jayamanne, "Let's Miscegenate," 155.

44. Their screen partnership created such a box-office hit that Ratner released in 2007 *Rush Hour 3*, which again involves, rather unsurprisingly, the triads. *Rush Hour* is Jackie Chan's first slick Hollywood production, with *Rumble in the Bronx* serving as his breakthrough film into the American market. While Chan was involved earlier in his career in a number of failed Hollywood attempts like *The Big Brawl* (1980), *The Cannonball Run* (1981), and *Cannonball Run II* (1984), it is definitely in *Rush Hour* that he has hit upon the right formula for a sustainable Hollywood career.

45. Completely irresistible is the ironic usage of John Lone as Ricky Tan, especially considering the fact that Lone appeared as Song Liling in David Cronenberg's 1993 adaptation of David Henry Hwang's *M. Butterfly*. Consider the scene where Ricky Tan tells Las Vegas partner-in-crime, Steven Reign (Alan King), as he kills him, that he "hate[s] the fortune cookie shit!" For a triad character here to articulate anti-Orientalist critique is to both offer and undermine it at the same time.

46. Jayamanne, "Let's Miscegenate," 159.

47. Lisa Lowe, *Immigrant Acts: On Asian American Cultural Politics* (Durham: Duke University Press, 1996), 91.

48. "*Romeo Must Die* has no significant white character. But whiteness still occupies the privileged place from which to see and make sense of the world." Lo, *Chinese Face/Off*, 157. In his superb discussion of Asian masculinity and its relationship to what he calls the "triangulated racial desire" of "black-white-and-yellow" in the film, James Kim also references the LA riots and how "the contemporary

media had already improvised a triangulation of racial violence, playing black and yellow against each other for the sake of white propertied interests." James Kim, "The Legend of the White-and-Yellow Black Man: Global Containment and Triangulated Racial Desire in *Romeo Must Die*," *Camera Obscura* 55, vol. 19, no. 1 (2004): 165, 168.

49. Walter Benjamin, *Reflections: Essays, Aphorisms, Autobiographical Writings,* ed. Peter Demetz, trans. Edmund Jephcott (New York: Schocken Books, 1978), 286–7.

6 Hollywood's Sino-Chic: Kung Fu Parody, Mimicry, and Play in Cross-Cultural Citationality

1. Unfortunately, the extent of the parody is only in the film's use of animated animal characters. Much of the impressive voice talent is squandered on a weak script that does not sufficiently offer witty banter and clever send-ups of kung fu stereotypes — one hopes for at least some measure of self-irony that films like *The Incredibles* (2004) has offered audiences. To make it worse, the film replicates the narrative arc of *The Forbidden Kingdom* (released at almost the same time) in its believe-in-yourself message that has been remade *ad nauseum* in innumerable animation and children's films. Both *Kung Fu Panda* and *The Forbidden Kingdom*, therefore, demonstrates the way the kung fu genre has been simplistically retooled for rapid Hollywood commodification.

2. I am thinking of the problematic way a television series like BBC's *Little Britain* works through extreme forms of "political incorrectness" for comedic purposes, thus getting away with the crassest and most indecent moments ever seen on television. Because I am still uncertain how to reconcile the pleasure I derive from these moments and the concomitant uneasiness about the notion that it supposedly achieves a critique of racism, sexism, homophobia, and a range of other social offences through parody, a closer study of its mechanics is definitely in order.

3. This cult-to-mainstream phenomenon is significant enough for recent popular/academic monographs to catalog kung fu cinema's development and its essential entries: Leon Hunt, *Kung Fu Cult Masters: From Bruce Lee to Crouching Tiger* (London: Wallflower Press, 2003); Bey Logan, *Hong Kong Action Cinema* (Woodstock: The Overlook Press, 1995); and David West, *Chasing Dragons: An Introduction to the Martial Arts Film* (London: I. B. Tauris, 2006). See also sections of Jeff Yang, *Once Upon a Time in China: A Guide to Hong Kong, Taiwanese, and Mainland Chinese Cinema* (New York: Atria Books, 2003).

4. Siu Leung Li, "The Myth Continues: Cinematic Kung Fu in Modernity," in *Hong Kong Connections: Transnational Imagination in Action Cinema*, eds. Meaghan Morris, Siu Leung Li, and Stephen Chan Ching-kiu (Durham: Duke University Press, 2005), 51, 54. Expanding on this internal citationality is Gary Xu's reading of the Shaw Brothers' filmic influence on Stephen Chow: Gary G. Xu, *Sinascape:*

Contemporary Chinese Cinema (Lanham, MD: Rowman and Littlefield, 2007), 91–3.

5. Peter Hitchcock, "Niche Cinema, or, *Kill Bill* with *Shaolin Soccer*," in *Hong Kong Film, Hollywood and the New Global Cinema: No Film Is an Island*, eds. Gina Marchetti and Tan See Kam (London: Routledge, 2007), 230.

6. This Jackie Chan segment of the chapter constitutes a radically revised version of an essay originally published as "Mimicry as Failure: Jackie Chan in Hollywood, " *Asian Cinema* 15, no. 2 (Fall/Winter 2004): 84–97.

7. Fore examines Chan's work as an instance of "transnational Chinese cinemas." Steve Fore, "Jackie Chan and the Cultural Dynamics of Global Entertainment," in *Transnational Chinese Cinemas: Identity, Nationhood, Gender*, ed. Sheldon Hsiao-peng Lu (Honolulu: University of Hawai'i Press, 1997), 239–62.

8. Scholarly critics have consistently observed and theorized this notion of transformation: see, for instance, Mark Gallagher, "Masculinity in Translation: Jackie Chan's Transcultural Star Text," *The Velvet Light Trap* 39 (Spring 1997): 25–41; and Ramie Tateishi, "Jackie Chan and the Re-invention of Tradition," *Asian Cinema* 10, no. 1 (Fall 1998): 78–84.

9. Read Chan's autobiography *I am Jackie Chan* (co-written with Jeff Yang) for an account of his amazing rags-to-riches story. The narrative ultimately legitimizes stardom and box-office success as the only positive outcome, epitomized by Chan's desire and determination — "Nothing could stop me now" — to join his idols, Sinatra, Chaplin, Keaton, and Lloyd, "in Hollywood's galaxy of stars." Jackie Chan, with Jeff Yang, *I Am Jackie Chan: My Life in Action* (New York: Ballantine, 1999), 253.

10. Kam Louie, *Theorising Chinese Masculinity: Society and Gender in China* (Cambridge: Cambridge University Press, 2002), 152.

11. Rob Wilson and Wimal Dissanayake, eds., *Global/Local: Cultural Production and the Transnational Imaginary* (Durham: Duke University Press, 1996).

12. On the question of Lee's influence, see Teo's account of Chan's career as "The Other Kung Fu Dragon." Stephen Teo, *Hong Kong Cinema: The Extra Dimensions* (London: BFI, 1997), 122. Kam Louie draws similar connections between Lee and Chan in his study of Chinese masculinity. Louie, *Theorising Chinese Masculinity*, 149–50. Chan's autobiography *I am Jackie Chan* also highlights Lee's importance in helping define his sense of identity as an action star.

13. Chan's consciousness of the significance of naming is further featured in a recent documentary about his family: *Traces of a Dragon: Jackie Chan and his Lost Family* (2003). Chan's original family name is Fang, thus tracing his connections to two long lost half-brothers in mainland China, whom Chan oddly did not choose to meet, even at the end of the film's production. One could potentially read in Chan a form of anxiety as star identity comes into collision with familial identity.

14. Lisa Odham Stokes and Michael Hoover, *City on Fire: Hong Kong Cinema* (London: Verso, 1999), 115.

15. Ibid., 116.

16. Teo, *Hong Kong*, 122–3.
17. Gina Marchetti, "Jackie Chan and the Black Connection," in *Keyframes: Popular Cinema and Cultural Studies,* eds. Matthew Tinkcom and Amy Villarejo (London: Routledge, 2001), 138.
18. See my discussion of this issue in Chapter Five.
19. Clearly, these three films are not unproblematic in the way they deal with racial stereotypes and the politics of migrant assimilation and multiculturalism. I am unable to deal with these issues in greater depth here as this is not my chapter's goal. See Marchetti, "Jackie Chan and the Black Connection," for a similar critique of these films.
20. David Bordwell, *Planet Hong Kong: Popular Cinema and the Art of Entertainment* (Cambridge: Harvard University Press, 2000), 58.
21. Homi K. Bhabha, *The Location of Culture* (London: Routledge, 1994), 86.
22. Ibid., 88, 89.
23. Marchetti, "Jackie Chan and the Black Connection," 156.
24. Steve Fore, "Life Imitates Entertainment: Home and Dislocation in the Films of Jackie Chan," in *At Full Speed: Hong Kong Cinema in a Borderless World,* ed. Esther C. M. Yau (Minneapolis: University of Minnesota Press, 2001), 117. Fore borrows the term from Anthony Giddens.
25. Aihwa Ong, *Flexible Citizenship: The Cultural Logics of Transnationality* (Durham: Duke University Press, 1999).
26. Bhabha, *Location of Culture,* 89. Emphasis mine.
27. Ibid., 91.
28. Feng observes that "Asian American [film]makers construct Asian American cinematic identity by locating their subjectivities in relation to dominant cinematic discourses, signifying on cinematic conventions by repeating them ironically or 'splitting' them." Peter X. Feng, *Identities in Motion: Asian American Film and Video* (Durham: Duke University Press, 2002), 2.
29. Li, "The Myth Continues," 60.
30. See Donna Haraway's "A Cyborg Manifesto: Science, Technology, and Socialist-Feminism in the Late Twentieth Century" for a creative use of the cyborg figure as a politically progressive trope. Donna J. Haraway, *Simians, Cyborgs, and Women: The Reinvention of Nature* (New York: Routledge, 1991).
31. "These qualities of self-parody" in the Bond films, observes Toby Miller, "are key aspects to the unstable masculinity on display. The technology of the penis is mockingly troped again and again in details and stories from the series." Toby Miller, "James Bond's Penis," in *Masculinity: Bodies, Movies, Culture,* ed. Peter Lehman (New York: Routledge, 2001), 248.
32. Unbeknownst to many of his US fans, Chan has a moderately successful recording career in Asia. Apart from contributing to various compilation CDs and music soundtracks to his own movies, he has also released, according to the best of my knowledge, two albums: *Diyi qi* (*The First Time*), his first Mandarin CD, and *Long de xin* (*Dragon's Heart*).
33. Chan's leading man appeal is far from that of the traditional sex appeal of Hollywood

male stars. His roles seldom entail a love interest or offer any sexuality on screen. In noting the presence of romance in *Shanghai Noon*, Chan defends his choices: "My fans, especially female ones, are always complaining that I never have romantic scenes in my movies; I always say that people aren't paying to see me kiss, they're paying to see me kick. But maybe this makes up for lost time." Chan, *I Am Jackie Chan,* 347.

34. Chan, *I Am Jackie Chan,* 347.

35. Kwai-Cheung Lo, *Chinese Face/Off: The Transnational Popular Culture of Hong Kong* (Urbana: University of Illinois, 2005), 148. Lo provides an excellent reading of Hung's film as allegorical of the 1997 transitional phase for many Hong Kong film artists who were migrating to Hollywood.

36. Chan, *I Am Jackie Chan,* 347. Fred Zinnemann's 1952 classic *High Noon* actually starred Gary Cooper, not John Wayne.

37. Ella Shohat and Robert Stam, *Unthinking Eurocentrism: Multiculturalism and the Media* (London: Routledge, 1994), 114–5, 118.

38. For close analyses of these series from an Asian American critical perspective, see Darrell Y. Hamamoto, *Monitored Peril: Asian Americans and the Politics of TV Representation* (Minneapolis: University of Minnesota Press, 1994), 32–63. Hamamoto also reminds us that *Kung Fu* (1972–5), starring David Carradine, is really a Western with a Shaolin twist.

39. The significant contribution of Chinese immigrant labor to the American transcontinental railroad project has often been relegated to a historical footnote: "Without Chinese labor and know-how, the railroad would not have been completed. Nonetheless, the Central Pacific Railroad cheated the Chinese railway workers of everything they could. They tried to write the Chinese out of history altogether. The Chinese workers were not only excluded from the ceremonies, but from the famous photograph of white American laborers celebrating as the last spike, the golden spike, was driven into the ground." Iris Chang, *The Chinese in America: A Narrative History* (New York: Penguin, 2003), 64. Asian American history scholars have made a conscious effort to emphasize the important role the Chinese played in this foundational part of United States history. See also Sucheng Chan, *Asian Americans: An Interpretive History* (Boston: Twayne, 1991), 30–32; Ronald Takaki, *Strangers from a Different Shore: A History of Asian Americans* (New York: Penguin, 1989), 84–7.

40. On the other hand, Dyer also cautions that straight audiences can use camp to reclaim John Wayne by questioning the form of masculinity, laughing at it, and then permitting "a certain wistful affection for him to linger on." Richard Dyer, "It's Being So Camp as Keeps Us Going," in *Camp: Queer Aesthetics and the Performing Subject,* ed. Fabio Cleto (Edinburgh: Edinburgh University Press, 1999), 115.

41. David L. Eng, *Racial Castration: Managing Masculinity in Asian America* (Durham: Duke University Press, 2001).

42. For Rathbone to reference in the British Parliament the Sino-British Wars of 1839–42 as the "Opium Wars" is historically inaccurate. Naming the conflicts as

the "Opium Wars" is to relegate blame to the British Empire. It is tempting to see this mistake as another ironic consequence of postmodernist stitching.

43. Chan, *I Am Jackie Chan*, 253.

44. Knopf discusses Chan's indebtedness to Keaton. Robert Knopf, *The Theater and Cinema of Buster Keaton* (Princeton: Princeton University Press, 1999), 152–4.

45. Stokes and Hoover, *City on Fire*, 120.

46. Chan, *I Am Jackie Chan*, 320.

47. "Chan Asks Asians to Shun Hollywood," *CBS News*, 25 November 2005, <http://www.cbsnews.com/stories/2005/11/25/entertainment/main1075637.shtml>, accessed 20 June 2007.

48. Doherty sees "exploitation" not only as a film genre but also as a form of "advertising and promotion that entices an audience into a theater *and* to the way the movie then endears itself to that audience." Thomas Doherty, *Teenagers and Teenpics: The Juvenilization of American Movies in the 1950s* (Boston: Unwin Hyman, 1988), 3. Doherty's point is coincidentally and aptly illustrated by Jami Bernard's opening anecdote in his book on Tarantino, about an incident that occurred during the 1994 New York Film Festival screening of *Pulp Fiction*. Bernard recounts how "at the very moment Travolta plunged the needle [into Uma Thurman], a man in the orchestra keeled over onto the carpet in a dead faint." Rumor has it that this was a publicity stunt, akin to those one finds during the halcyon days of classical exploitation cinema. Jami Bernard, *Quentin Tarantino: The Man and His Movies* (New York: HarperCollins, 1995), 2–3.

49. Eric Schaefer, *"Bold! Daring! Shocking! True!" A History of Exploitation Films, 1919–1959* (Durham: Duke University Press, 1999), 3–4.

50. Ibid., 5.

51. Ibid., 4.

52. Pam Grier graced the screens again as the titular character in Tarantino's *Jackie Brown*, the director's tribute to this genre.

53. For an exposition and analysis of "blaxploitation," see the following: Ed Guerrero, *Framing Blackness: The African American Image in Film* (Philadelphia: Temple University Press, 1993), 69–111; Mark A. Reid, *Redefining Black Film* (Berkeley: University of California Press, 1993), 77–91. Reid rather strategically and less problematically calls these films "black action films."

54. Reid, *Redefining*, 86.

55. David Desser, "The Kung Fu Craze: Hong Kong Cinema's First American Reception," in *The Cinema of Hong Kong: History, Arts, Identity*, eds. Poshek Fu and David Desser (Cambridge: Cambridge University Press, 2000), 25.

56. Jeffrey Sconce, "Trashing the Academy: Taste, Excess and an Emerging Politics of Cinematic Style," *Screen* 36, no. 4 (Winter 1995): 372. Quoted in Paul Watson, "There's No Accounting for Taste: Exploitation Cinema and the Limits of Film Theory," in *Trash Aesthetics: Popular Culture and Its Audience*, eds. Deborah Cartmell, I. Q. Hunter, Heidi Kaye, and Imelda Whelehan (London: Pluto Press, 1997), 67.

57. Watson, "There's No Accounting for Taste," 80.

58. Susan Sontag, "Notes on 'Camp,'" in *Camp: Queer Aesthetics and the Performing Subject*, ed. Fabio Cleto (Edinburgh: Edinburgh University Press, 1999), 61.

59. Judith Butler, *Gender Trouble: Feminism and the Subversion of Identity* (New York: Routledge, 1990).

60. For convenient reference in the rest of this chapter, the title *Kill Bill* will represent both volumes 1 and 2 unless specified for strategic reasons. In any case, one could see the two volumes as constituting a single filmic narrative.

61. In a theoretically dazzling essay on what he calls "visual quotation" in the context of "niche cinema," Peter Hitchcock parses the term's different valences through an intertextual reading of *Kill Bill* and Chow's *Shaolin Soccer*. He argues that "[c]ultural contact enables greater and greater quotation but this accumulation comes with a demand to suffer the consequences of an impossible epistemology, one that actually might embrace knowledge outside the commodity relation (keeping in mind that a quotation is also the offer of a price, hence my preference for it here over intertextuality). This is quotation as acknowledgment and disavowal (of knowledge)." Hitchcock, "Niche Cinema, or, *Kill Bill* with *Shaolin Soccer*," 220.

62. Fred Topel, "Tarantino Talks *Kill Bill Vol. 2*," in *Quentin Tarantino: The Film Geek Files*, ed. Paul A. Woods (London: Plexus, 2005), 183–4.

63. Tomohiro Machiyama, "Quentin Tarantino Reveals Almost Everything That Inspired *Kill Bill*," in *Quentin Tarantino: The Film Geek Files*, ed. Paul A. Woods (London: Plexus, 2005), 173.

64. Topel, "Tarantino Talks," 183.

65. Machiyama, "Quentin Tarantino Reveals," 178.

66. Sontag, "Notes," 56.

67. Terminology I borrow from Rob Wilson and Wimal Dissanayake, "Introduction: Tracking the Global/Local," in *Global/Local: Cultural Production and the Transnational Imaginary*, eds. Rob Wilson and Wimal Dissanayake (Durham: Duke University Press, 1996), 2.

68. Topel, "Tarantino Talks," 183.

69. For more on Shaw's inner workings and production methods, see Stephanie Chung Po-yin, "The Industrial Evolution of a Fraternal Enterprise: The Shaw Brothers and the Shaw Organisation," in *The Shaw Screen: A Preliminary Study*, ed. Wong Ain-ling (Hong Kong: Hong Kong Film Archive, 2003), 1–17.

70. Emphasis mine.

71. Machiyama, "Quentin Tarantino Reveals," 174.

72. Ibid., 177.

73. Desser, "The Kung Fu Craze," 20.

74. Stephen Teo, *Hong Kong Cinema: The Extra Dimensions* (London: BFI, 1997), 114.

75. Machiyama, "Quentin Tarantino Reveals," 174.

76. Desser, "The Kung Fu Craze," 37.

77. Machiyama, "Quentin Tarantino Reveals," 174.

78. Some feminist scholars argue that female screen violence replicates male violence,

but King and McCaughey prefer to see that "visions of sexually attractive women skilled with weaponry, licensed to kill, beating up men might rather take the wind out of the sails of the culture in which sex difference seems unalterable. Such images might challenge smug oppressors." Neal King and Martha McCaughey, "What's a Mean Woman like You Doing in a Movie like This?" in *Reel Knockouts: Violent Women in the Movies*, eds. Martha McCaughey and Neal King (Austin: University of Texas Press, 2001), 6.

79. "Defamiliarization" is a literary critical concept coined by Russian formalist Viktor Šklovskij and later adopted by Bertolt Brecht in his theory of "estrangement effects." M. H. Abrams, *A Glossary of Literary Terms*, 5th ed. (Fort Worth: Holt, Rinehart and Winston, 1988), 44.

80. Topel, "Tarantino Talks," 183.

81. Machiyama, "Quentin Tarantino Reveals," 177.

82. Edward Gallafent, *Quentin Tarantino* (Harlow, England: Pearson, 2006), 113.

83. The status of this production is currently unknown apart from the limited information available on the Internet Movie Database. The production company's webpage <www.burningshaolinproductions.com> is presently unavailable.

7   Chinese Supernaturalism: Mythic Ethnography and the Mystical Other

1. In an excellent essay on the topic, Bliss Cua Lim argues, though, that these new Hollywood remakes are "deracinating acts of cultural appropriation," which I can only partly agree with. Forms of ghostly representation often retain Asiatic traces to register difference as marks of supernatural inexplicability and terror. Bliss Cua Lim, "Generic Ghosts: Remaking the New 'Asian Horror Film,'" in *Hong Kong Film, Hollywood and the New Global Cinema: No Film is an Island*, eds. Gina Marchetti and Tan See Kam (London: Routledge, 2007), 115. Read also a fan-boy account of Asian horror cinemas that delineates East-West differences to explain the shock-value of these films for an American audience: Patrick Galloway, *Asia Shock: Horror and Dark Cinema from Japan, Korea, Hong Kong, and Thailand* (Berkeley: Stone Bridge Press, 2006), 9–14.

2. Robin Wood, "An Introduction to the American Horror Film," in *Movies and Methods: Volume II*, ed., Bill Nichols (Berkeley: University of California Press, 1985), 199–200.

3. Robert G. Lee, *Orientals: Asian Americans in Popular Culture* (Philadelphia: Temple University Press, 1999), 10.

4. Gina Marchetti, *Romance and the "Yellow Peril": Race, Sex, and Discursive Strategies in Hollywood Fiction* (Berkeley: University of California Press, 1993), 2. Emphasis mine.

5. Both Robert Lee and Gina Marchetti offer close analysis of Griffith's film. Lee, *Orientals*, 127–32; Marchetti, *Romance*, 32–45.

6. David Van Biema, "Buddhism in America," *Time,* 13 October 1997, <http://

www.time.com/time/magazine/article/0,9171,987164,00.html>, accessed 6 June 2007.

7. Incidentally, *The Touch* is the first film from Michelle Yeoh's new production company, not so coincidentally called, Mythical Films, which has also two other releases, *Silver Hawk* (2004) and the forthcoming live-action version of *Mulan*.

8. The "*shenguai pian*" are films "dealing with gods and demons, supernatural powers of flight and emission of bodily energy. Fantasy elements from the . . . genre were incorporated into the *wuxia* film early on, and the standard way to refer to the genre from the late 1920s onwards was *shenguai wuxia* which has been translated as 'sword and sorcery' or 'swordplay and magic.'" Stephen Teo, "*Wuxia* Redux: *Crouching Tiger, Hidden Dragon* as a Model of Late Transnational Production," in *Hong Kong Connections: Transnational Imagination in Action Cinema*, eds. Meaghan Morris, Siu Leung Li, and Stephen Chan Ching-kiu (Durham: Duke University Press, 2005), 192.

9. Bhaskar Sarkar, "Hong Kong Hysteria: Martial Arts Tales from a Mutating World, " in *At Full Speed: Hong Kong Cinema in a Borderless World*, ed. Esther C. M. Yau (Minneapolis: University of Minnesota Press, 2001), 171.

10. Kim Soyoung, "Genre as Contact Zone: Hong Kong Action and Korean *Hwalkuk*, " in *Hong Kong Connections: Transnational Imagination in Action Cinema*, eds. Meaghan Morris, Siu Leung Li, and Stephen Chan Ching-kiu (Durham: Duke University Press, 2005), 100. I have applied here to Chinese Supernaturalism Kim's point about "Korean action movies."

11. Ibid., 101. Kim is here channeling Pratt's conception of "transculturation." Mary Louise Pratt, *Imperial Eyes: Travel Writing and Transculturation* (London: Routledge, 1992), 6.

12. Rey Chow, *Primitive Passions: Visuality, Sexuality, Ethnography, and Contemporary Chinese Cinema* (New York: Columbia University Press, 1995), 23.

13. John Woo, foreword to *Bulletproof Monk*, by Michael Yanover and Mark Paniccia (Orange, CA: Flypaper Press, 2002).

14. The film was shot in Toronto and Vancouver.

15. See Chapter One.

16. "Multiculturalism levels the important differences and contradictions within and among racial and ethnic minority groups according to the discourse of pluralism, which asserts that American culture is a democratic terrain to which every variety of constituency has equal access and in which all are represented, while simultaneously masking the existence of exclusions by recuperating dissent, conflict, and otherness through the promise of inclusion." Lisa Lowe, *Immigrant Acts: On Asian American Cultural Politics* (Durham: Duke University Press, 1996), 86.

17. Frantz Fanon, *Black Skin, White Masks*, trans. Charles Lam Markmann (New York: Grove Press, 1967), 47.

18. Emphasis mine.

19. For a discussion of spatiality and special effects in the film, see Ru-shou Robert Chen, "'This Isn't Real!' Spatialized Narration and (In)visible Special Effects in 'Double Vision,'" in *Cinema Taiwan: Politics, Popularity and State of the Arts*,

ed. Darrell William Davis and Ru-shou Robert Chen (London: Routledge, 2007), 108–15.

20. Giorgio Agamben, "The Time That Is Left," *Epoché* 7, no. 1 (Fall 2002): 5. Agamben's analysis of messianic time is too complex to be rendered here in capsule form and, hence, should be read within the context of his essay for a fuller definition.

21. Ibid., 4.

22. Tweedie deliberates on the building as a cultural symptom of global capitalism: "The World Tower (*Shijie Dalou*) that fronts for a Daoist temple becomes the grandest of junkspaces, a spectacle that dazzles because of its incoherent combination of the mythical past and the mythical present, neither imagined as a viable future on a mass scale, neither rooted in a lived history." James Tweedie, "Morning in the New Metropolis: Taipei and the Globalization of the City Film," in *Cinema Taiwan: Politics, Popularity and State of the Arts*, ed. Darrell William Davis and Ru-shou Robert Chen (London: Routledge, 2007), 123.

23. "Jackie Chan Returns to Hong Kong for Artistic Freedom," *Goldsea Asian American Daily*, 15 July 2005, <http://goldsea.com/Asiagate/507/16chan.html>, accessed 17 April 2006.

24. "Aside from unity of the known world, the First Emperor had sought mainly an elixir of immortality for himself. His five royal journeys to sacred mountains had been part of his search." John King Fairbank, *China: A New History* (Cambridge: Belknap Press of Harvard University Press, 1992), 57.

25. Yingjin Zhang, *Chinese National Cinema* (New York: Routledge, 2004), 37.

26. Ibid., 37–41.

27. Discovered in 1974 at the tomb of the First Emperor, these 7500 terracotta warriors are life-sized statues. Fairbank, *China,* 56.

28. See my discussion of Chan's cultural nationalism in *Shanghai Noon* and *Shanghai Knights* in Chapter Six.

29. Emphasis mine. This English translation of the dialogue follows the subtitles in the official Singapore DVD version distributed by Scorpio East Entertainment. I have taken the liberty to adjust them very slightly with my own translations for added clarity.

30. Robert Koehler, "The Promise aka Master of the Crimson Armor," *Variety,* 29 December 2005, <http://www.variety.com/review/VE1117929184.html?categoryid= 1263&cs=1>, accessed 8 June 2007.

31. Christine Chiao, "A Promise Left Unfulfilled," UCLA International Insitute, 13 April 2006, <http://www.international.ucla.edu/article.asp?parentid=42884>, accessed 2 December 2008. My own coincidental use of the Icarus reference marks the contemporaneous negative criticism of Chen's work.

32. Michael Atkinson, "Partial Arts: Former Fifth-Gen Master Proves We Don't Need Another *Hero*," *Village Voice*, 2 May 2006, <http://www.villagevoice.com/film/ 0618,atkinson,73085,20.html>, accessed 9 June 2007.

33. Ty Burr, "Only as a Fairy Tale Does 'Promise' Reach Its Potential," *Boston Globe*, 5 May 2006, <http://www.boston.com/ae/movies/articles/2006/05/05/

only_as_a_fairy_tale_doespromise_reach_its_potential/>, accessed 8 June 2007.

34. Sarkar, "Hong Kong Hysteria," 173.
35. Koehler, "The Promise."
36. This twenty-minute long parody is still available on YouTube at <http://www.youtube.com/watch?v=AQZAcT1xaKk>, accessed 8 June 2007.
37. Dexter Roberts, "A Chinese Blogger's Tale," *Business Week,* 2 March 2006, <http://www.businessweek.com/globalbiz/content/mar2006/gb20060302_026709.htm>, accessed 8 June 2007.
38. Atkinson, "Partial Arts."
39. Spoofs can play a number of functions. The *Austin Powers* movie series provides not only a comic subversion of the James Bond movies, but it also pays an indirect tribute to them.
40. "This intentional rendering of the culture by Chen Kaige and co-writer Zhang Tan refracts negatively as the script neither introduces new approaches nor incorporates any tried and true magical elements that mark great wuxia films. Instead, each supposed nod to Chinese myth becomes a parody of the genre." Chiao, "A Promise Left Unfulfilled."

Coda: Global Cinematic Technologies of Ethnic (Un)Representation

1. The line is from the song "Hollywood's Not America" found in Ferras' album *Aliens and Rainbows* (2008; Capitol Records). The complete lyrics are available on his website at <http://www.ferrasmusic.com/lyrics.aspx>, accessed 18 June 2008.
2. Discussion of future trends in cinema is problematic in that the cinematic references I make of forthcoming films are only "true" during the time of writing and may potentially require correction, which the finality of publication makes utterly impossible.
3. Antonio Gramsci, *Selections from the Prison Notebooks*, ed. and trans. Quintin Hoare and Geoffrey Nowell Smith (New York: International Publishers, 1971). See also Christine Gledhill, "Pleasurable Negotiations," in *Female Spectators: Looking at Film and Television*, ed. E. Deirdre Pribram (London: Verso, 1988), 64–89.
4. Stephen Chow is returning to *Journey to the West* to adapt it for the screen. "Stephen Chow to Remake Classic," *The Straits Times,* 3 December 2007, Life section, 7.
5. Because of *Crouching Tiger, Hidden Dragon*'s box-office success, Columbia Pictures and the Weinstein Company are tussling over the rights to adapt Wang Du Lu's other novels. "Crouching Tiger, Battling Movie Companies," *The Straits Times,* 9 May 2007, Life section, 7.
6. Foong Woei Wan, "Epic Change," *The Straits Times,* 9 April 2008, Life section, 1–3. See also Sonia Kolesnikov-Jessop, "Redefining the Epic," *Newsweek*, 24 December 2007, <http://www.newsweek.com/id/78119>, accessed 18 June 2008.

7. Kwai-Cheung Lo, *Chinese Face/Off: The Transnational Popular Culture of Hong Kong* (Urbana: University of Illinois Press, 2005), 160.

8. Borys Kit, "Disney, Chabon Retelling 'Snow,'" *The Hollywood Reporter*, 29 October 2004, <http://www.hollywoodreporter.com/hr/search/article_display.jsp?vnu_content_id=1000694195>, accessed 18 June 2008. While this article does not mention Chow, internet rumors continue to swirl about his possible presence in the project.

9. "Ten Times More Expensive to Hire Zhang Ziyi Now," *The Straits Times*, 28 April 2006, Life section, 18.

10. Quoted in Tan Dawn Wei, "Sharp and Tough," *The Straits Times*, 29 November 2006, Life section, 2.

11. Chua Beng Huat, "Conceptualizing an East Asian Popular Culture," *Inter-Asia Cultural Studies* 5, no. 2 (2004): 201.

12. Lo, *Chinese Face/Off*, 160.

13. Richard Dyer, *White* (London: Routledge, 1997).

14. Frank H. Wu, *Yellow: Race in America Beyond Black and White* (New York: Basic Books, 2002), 79.

15. "Lee Ang Win Is 'Glory for Chinese,'" *The Straits Times*, 7 March 2006, Life section, 3.

16. Rey Chow, *Sentimental Fabulations, Contemporary Chinese Films: Attachment in the Age of Global Visibility* (New York: Columbia University Press, 2007), 199.

Filmography

The 36th Chamber of Shaolin (Shaolin sanshiliu fang), Liu Chia-liang, Shaw Brothers, 1978.
48 Hours, Walter Hill, Paramount Pictures, 1982.
The 51st State, Ronny Yu, Screen Gems, 2001.
2046 (Erlingsiliu), Wong Kar-wai, Sony Pictures Classics, 2004.
The Accidental Spy (Tewu mi cheng), Teddy Chan, Dimension Films, 2001.
Aladdin, Ron Clements and John Musker, Buena Vista Pictures, 1992.
All about Eve, Joseph L. Mankiewicz, Twentieth Century Fox, 1950.
Another 48 Hours, Walter Hill, Paramount Pictures, 1990.
Anywhere But Here, Wayne Wang, Twentieth Century Fox, 1999.
Armour of God (Long xiong hu di), Jackie Chan, Golden Harvest, 1987.
Armour of God II (Feiying jihua), Jackie Chan, Golden Harvest, 1991.
Around the World in 80 Days, Frank Coraci, Buena Vista Pictures, 2004.
Ashes of Time (Dongxie xidu), Wong Kar-wai, Sony Pictures Classics, 1994.
Autumn in New York, Joan Chen, MGM, 2000.
Babel, Alejandro González Iñárritu, Paramount Vantage, 2006.
Balls of Fury, Robert Ben Garant, Rogue Pictures, 2007.
The Banquet (Ye yan), Feng Xiaogang, Huayi Brothers/Media Asia Films, 2006.
The Beach, Danny Boyle, Twentieth Century Fox, 2000.
Because of Winn-Dixie, Wayne Wang, Twentieth Century Fox, 2005.
Better Luck Tomorrow, Justin Lin, MTV Films/Paramount Pictures, 2002.
A Better Tomorrow (Yingxiong bense), John Woo, Rim, 1986.
Beverly Hills Cop II, Tony Scott, Paramount Pictures, 1987.
Beverly Hills Ninja, Dennis Dugan, Sony Pictures Entertainment, 1997.
The Big Boss (Fists of Fury in the U.S.) (Tangshan daxiong), Lo Wei, Golden Harvest, 1971.
The Big Brawl, Robert Clouse, Warner Bros. Pictures, 1980.
The Big Hit, Kirk Wong, TriStar Pictures, 1998.
Big Trouble in Little China, John Carpenter, Twentieth Century Fox, 1986.
The Birdcage, Mike Nichols, United Artists, 1996.
The Bitter Tea of General Yen, Frank Capra, Columbia Pictures, 1933.
Blood Brothers (Ci ma), Chang Cheh, Shaw Brothers, 1973.
The Blood of Fu Manchu, Jesus Franco, Commonwealth United Entertainment, 1968.
Blue in the Face, Paul Auster and Wayne Wang, Miramax Films, 1995.
Bride of Chucky, Ronny Yu, MCA/Universal Pictures, 1998.

The Bride with White Hair (Baifa monu zhuan), Ronny Yu, Mandarin Films Distribution, 1993.

The Bride Wore Black, François Truffaut, Lopert Pictures Corporation, 1968.

Brokeback Mountain, Ang Lee, Focus Features, 2005.

Broken Arrow, John Woo, Twentieth Century Fox, 1996.

Broken Blossoms, D.W. Griffith, United Artists, 1919.

Buddha's Palm (Rulai shenzhang), Taylor Wong, Shaw Brothers, 1982.

Bulletproof Monk, Paul Hunter, MGM, 2003.

Butch Cassidy and the Sundance Kid, George Roy Hill, Twentieth Century Fox, 1969.

The Cannonball Run, Hal Needham, Twentieth Century Fox, 1981.

Cannonball Run II, Hal Needham, Warner Bros. Pictures, 1984.

The Castle of Fu Manchu, Jesus Franco, International Cinema Corp., 1969.

The Center of the World, Wayne Wang, Artisan Entertainment, 2001.

Chan is Missing, Wayne Wang, New Yorker Films, 1982.

Charlie Chan Carries On, Hamilton MacFadden, Fox Film Corporation, 1931.

Charlie's Angels, McG, Columbia Pictures, 2000.

Chicago, Rob Marshall, Miramax Films, 2002.

China Doll, Frank Borzage, United Artists, 1958.

Chinatown, Roman Polanski, Paramount Pictures, 1974.

Chinatown after Dark, Stuart Paton, States Rights Independent Exchanges, 1931.

Chinatown Nights, William A. Wellman, Paramount Pictures, 1929.

Chinatown Villains, John Francis Dillon, Mutual Film Corporation, 1916.

Chinese Box, Wayne Wang, Lions Gate Films, 1997.

Chinese Rubbernecks, American Mutoscope and Biograph, 1900.

Chungking Express (Chongqing senlin), Wong Kar-wai, Miramax Films, 1994.

City of Sadness (Beiqing chengshi), Hou Hsiao-hsien, 3-H Films/ERA International, 1989.

City on Fire (Long hu feng yun), Ringo Lam, Rim, 1987.

Clan of the White Lotus (Hongwending sanpo bailianjiao) Lo Lieh, Shaw Brothers, 1980.

Cleopatra Jones, Jack Starrett, Warner Bros. Pictures, 1973.

Cleopatra Jones and the Casino of Gold, Charles Bail, Warner Bros. Pictures, 1975.

Clueless, Amy Heckerling, Paramount Pictures, 1995.

Coffy, Jack Hill, American International Pictures, 1973.

Combination Platter, Tony Chan, Arrow, 1993.

Come Drink with Me (Da zui xia), King Hu, Shaw Brothers, 1966.

The Corruptor, James Foley, New Line Cinema, 1999.

Cradle 2 the Grave, Andrzej Bartkowiak, Warner Bros. Pictures, 2003.

Crash, Paul Haggis, Lions Gate Films, 2004.

Crossings (Cuo ai), Evans Chan, Tai Seng Video Marketing, 1994.

Crouching Tiger, Hidden Dragon (Wo hu cang long), Ang Lee, Sony Pictures Classics, 2000.

Curse of the Golden Flower (Man cheng jin dai huangjinjia) Zhang Yimou, Sony Pictures Classics, 2006.

Dancing Chinamen, Marionettes, Edison Manufacturing Company, 1898.

The Darjeeling Limited, Wes Anderson, Fox Searchlight Pictures, 2007.

Dark Matter, Chen Shi-zheng, First Independent Pictures, 2007.

Dark Water, Walter Salles, Buena Vista Pictures, 2005.

Daughter of the Dragon, Lloyd Corrigan, Paramount Pictures, 1931.

Days of Being Wild (*A fei zhengzhuan*), Wong Kar-wai, Rim, 1990.

Dead and Buried, Gary Sherman, AVCO Embassy Pictures, 1981.

Deadly Angels (*Qiao tan nu jiao wa*), Pao Hsueh-li, Shaw Brothers, 1977.

The Deceived Slumming Party, D. W. Griffith, American Mutoscope and Biograph, 1908.

The Departed, Martin Scorsese, Warner Bros. Pictures, 2006.

Devil in a Blue Dress, Carl Franklin, TriStar Pictures, 1995.

Dim Sum: A Little Bit of Heart, Wayne Wang, Orion Classics, 1985.

Double Team, Tsui Hark, Columbia Pictures, 1997.

Double Vision (*Shuang tong*), Chen Kuo-fu, Sony Pictures Entertainment, 2002.

Dr. No, Terence Young, United Artists, 1962.

Dragonball, James Wong, Twentieth Century Fox, 2009.

Drift, Quentin Lee, Margin Films, 2000.

Drunken Master (*Zui quan*), Yuen Wooping, Seasonal Film Corporation, 1978.

Eastern Condors (*Dongfang tuying*), Sammo Hung, Golden Harvest, 1987.

Eat a Bowl of Tea, Wayne Wang, Columbia Pictures, 1989.

Eat Drink Man Woman (*Yin shi nan nu*), Ang Lee, Samuel Goldwyn Company, 1994.

Election (*Heishehui*), Johnnie To, Tartan USA, 2005.

The Emperor and the Assassin (*Jingke ci qinwang*), Chen Kaige, Sony Pictures Classics, 1998.

The Emperor's Shadow, Zhou Xiaowen, Fox Lorber, 1996.

An Empress and the Warriors (*Qin song*), Ching Siu-tung, Golden Network Asia Limited, 2008.

Enter the Dragon, Robert Clouse, Warner Bros. Pictures, 1973.

Enter the Phoenix (*Da lao ai meili*), Stephen Fung, JCE Entertainment, 2004.

Ethan Mao, Quentin Lee, Margin Films, 2004.

The Eye, David Moreau and Xavier Palud, Lionsgate, 2008.

Face/Off, John Woo, Paramount Pictures, 1997.

Fallen Angels (*Duoluo tianshi*), Wong Kar-wai, Kino International Corp., 1995.

Farewell My Concubine (*Bawang bieji*), Chen Kaige, Miramax Films, 1993.

The Fast and the Furious: Tokyo Drift, Justin Lin, Universal Pictures, 2006.

Fearless (*Huo yuan jia*), Ronny Yu, Rogue Pictures, 2006.

Finishing the Game, Justin Lin, IFC Films, 2007.

First Date (*Diyichi yuehui*), Peter Wang, Central Motion Pictures Corporation, 1989.

Fist of Fury (*The Chinese Connection* in the U.S.) (*Jing wu men*), Lo Wei, Golden Harvest, 1972.

Flash Gordon, Mike Hodges, Universal Pictures, 1980.

The Forbidden Kingdom, Rob Minkoff, Lionsgate/The Weinstein Company, 2008.

Foxy Brown, Jack Hill, American International Pictures, 1974.

Freddy vs. Jason, Ronny Yu, New Line Cinema, 2003.
Game of Death, Robert Clouse, Columbia Pictures, 1978.
The God of Cookery (*Shi shen*), Stephen Chow, Star Overseas, 1996.
The Godfather, Francis Ford Coppola, Paramount Pictures, 1972.
The Golden Swallow (*Jin yanzi*), Chang Cheh, Shaw Brothers, 1968.
The Good Earth, Sidney Franklin, MGM, 1937.
A Great Wall, Peter Wang, Orion Classics, 1986.
Grindhouse, Robert Rodriguez and Quentin Tarantino, Dimension Films, 2007.
The Grudge, Takashi Shimizu, Columbia Pictures, 2004.
The Grudge 2, Takashi Shimizu, Columbia Pictures, 2006.
Hannibal Rising, Peter Webber, MGM, 2007.
Hannie Caulder, Burt Kennedy, Paramount Pictures, 1971.
Happy Times (*Xingfu shiguang*), Zhang Yimou, Sony Pictures Classics, 2000.
Happy Together (*Chunguang zhaxie*), Wong Kar-wai, Kino International Corp., 1997.
Hard-Boiled (*Lashou shentan*), John Woo, Rim, 1992.
Hard Target, John Woo, Universal Pictures, 1993.
Harold and Kumar Escape from Guantanamo Bay, Jon Hurwitz and Hayden Schlossberg, Warner Bros. Pictures, 2008.
Harold and Kumar Go to White Castle, Danny Leiner, New Line Cinema, 2004.
The Hatchet Man, William A Wellman, Warner Bros. Pictures, 1932.
Hercules, Ron Clements and John Musker, Buena Vista Pictures, 1997.
Hero (*Yingxiong*), Zhang Yimou, Miramax Films, 2002.
High Noon, Fred Zinnemann, United Artists, 1952.
Horse Thief (*Dao ma zei*), Tian Zhuangzhuang, International Film Circuit, 1986.
The Horsemen, Jonas Åkerlund, Lionsgate, 2008.
House of Flying Daggers (*Shi mian maifu*), Zhang Yimou, Sony Pictures Classics, 2004.
Hulk, Ang Lee, Universal Pictures, 2003.
The Hunchback of Notre Dame, Gary Trousdale and Kirk Wise, Buena Vista Pictures, 1996.
The Ice Storm, Ang Lee, Fox Searchlight Pictures, 1997.
In Hell, Ringo Lam, Millennium Films, 2003.
In the Mood for Love (*Huayang nianhua*), Wong Kar-wai, USA Films, 2000.
In Our Time (*Guangyin de gushi*), Chang Yi, Ko I-chen, Tao De-chen, and Edward Yang, Central Motion Pictures Corporation, 1982.
The Incredibles, Brad Bird, Buena Vista Pictures, 2004.
Indiana Jones and the Temple of Doom, Steven Spielberg, Paramount Pictures, 1984.
Infernal Affairs (*Wu jian dao*), Andrew Lau and Alan Mak, Miramax Films, 2002.
Intimate Confessions of a Chinese Courtesan (*Ai nu*), Chor Yuen, Shaw Brothers, 1972.
Iron and Silk, Shirley Sun, Prestige, 1990.
Jackie Brown, Quentin Tarantino, Miramax Films, 1997.
Jasmine Flower (*Molihuakai*), Yong Hou, 2004.
Joshua Tree, Vic Armstrong, Vision International, 1993.
Journey to Beijing (*Bei zheng*), Evans Chan, Riverside Productions, 1998.

The Joy Luck Club, Wayne Wang, Buena Vista Pictures, 1993.
Judou (Ju dou), Zhang Yimou, Miramax Films, 1990.
Kill Bill: Vol. 1, Quentin Tarantino, Miramax Films, 2003.
Kill Bill: Vol. 2, Quentin Tarantino, Miramax Films, 2004.
The Killer (Diexue shuang xiong) John Woo, Circle Films, 1989.
King Boxer (Five Fingers of Death in the U.S.) *(Tianxia diyi quan)*, Cheng Chang-ho, Shaw Brothers, 1972.
Kiss of Death (Du nu), Ho Meng-hua, Shaw Brothers, 1973.
Knock Off, Tsui Hark, Sony Pictures Entertainment/TriStar Pictures, 1998.
Kundun, Martin Scorsese, Buena Vista Pictures, 1997.
Kung Fu Hustle (Gongfu), Stephen Chow, Sony Pictures Classics, 2004.
Kung Fu Panda, Mark Osborne and John Stevenson, DreamWorks Animation, 2008.
Kung Pow: Enter the Fist, Steve Oedekerk, Twentieth Century Fox, 2002.
Lady Snowblood, Toshiya Fujita, Toho Company, 1973.
Lady Whirlwind (Deep Thrust – the Hand of Death in the U.S.) *(Tiezhang xuanfeng tui)*, Huang Feng, Golden Harvest, 1972.
Lan Yu (Lan yu), Stanley Kwan, Strand Releasing, 2001.
Land of Plenty, Wim Wenders, IFC Films, 2004.
The Laser Man, Peter Wang, Original Cinema, 1988.
The Last Emperor, Bernardo Bertolucci, Columbia Pictures, 1987.
Last Holiday, Wayne Wang, Paramount Pictures, 2006.
The Last Samurai, Edward Zwick, Warner Bros. Pictures, 2003.
Law of the Tong, Lewis D. Collins, Syndicate Film Exchange, 1931.
The Legend of the Seven Golden Vampires, Roy Ward Baker, Dynamite Entertainment, 1974.
Lethal Weapon, Richard Donner, Warner Bros. Pictures, 1987.
Lethal Weapon 2, Richard Donner, Warner Bros. Pictures, 1989.
Lethal Weapon 3, Richard Donner, Warner Bros. Pictures, 1992.
Lethal Weapon 4, Richard Donner, Warner Bros. Pictures, 1998.
Life is Cheap . . . But Toilet Paper Is Expensive, Wayne Wang, Silverlight Pictures, 1989.
Limehouse Blues, Alexander Hall, Paramount Pictures, 1934.
The Lion King, Roger Allers and Rob Minkoff, Buena Vista Pictures, 1994.
Little Buddha, Bernardo Bertolucci, Miramax, 1993.
The Little Mermaid, Ron Clements and John Musker, Buena Vista Pictures, 1989.
Lost Horizon, Frank Capra, Columbia Pictures, 1937.
Lost in Translation, Sophia Coppola, Focus Features, 2003.
Love Is a Many-Splendored Thing, Henry King, Twentieth Century Fox, 1955.
The Love Letter, Peter Chan, DreamWorks Distribution, 1999.
Lust, Caution (Se jie), Ang Lee, Focus Features, 2007.
M. Butterfly, David Cronenberg, Warner Bros. Pictures, 1993.
Maid in Manhattan, Wayne Wang, Columbia Pictures, 2002.
The Man with a Movie Camera, Dziga Vertov, Amkino Corporation, 1929.
The Map of Sex and Love (Qingse detu), Evans Chan, Water Bearer Films, 2001.

The Mask, Chuck Russell, New Line Cinema, 1994.

The Mask of Fu Manchu, Charles Brabin, MGM, 1932.

Master of the Flying Guillotine (*Dubi quanwang dapo xiedizi*), Wang Yu, Shaw Brothers, 1975.

Maximum Risk, Ringo Lam, Columbia Pictures, 1996.

Memoirs of a Geisha, Rob Marshall, Columbia Pictures, 2005.

Men in Black, Barry Sonnenfeld, Columbia Pictures, 1997.

Men in Black II, Barry Sonnenfeld, Columbia Pictures, 2002.

Miami Vice, Michael Mann, Universal Pictures, 2006.

The Mighty Peking Man (*Xingxing wang*), Ho Meng-hua, Shaw Brothers, 1977.

Mission Impossible II, John Woo, Paramount Pictures, 2000.

Mommie Dearest, Frank Perry, Paramount Pictures, 1981.

Monkey Goes West (Xiyou ji), Ho Menghua, Shaw Brothers, 1966.

Mr. Magoo, Stanley Tong, Buena Vista Pictures, 1997.

Mulan, Tony Bancroft and Barry Cook, Buena Vista Pictures, 1998.

The Mummy: Tomb of the Dragon Emperor, Rob Cohen, Universal Pictures, 2008.

My American Vacation, V. V. Dachin Hsu, Santa Monica Pictures, 1999.

My Blueberry Nights, Wong Kar-wai, Studio Canal, 2007.

The Myth (*Shenhua*), Stanley Tong, China Film Group/JCE Entertainment, 2005.

Na Cha the Great (*Nazha*), Chang Cheh, Shaw Brothers, 1974.

Once Upon a Time in China and America (*Huangfeihong: Zhi xi yu xiong shi*), Sammo Hung, China Star Entertainment, 1997.

One-Armed Swordsman (*Dubi dao*), Chang Cheh, Shaw Brothers, 1967.

The Opium War (*Yapian zhanzheng*), Xie Jin, United International Pictures, 1997.

Pale Blood, V. V. Dachin Hsu, Nobel Entertainment, 1990.

The Passion of the Christ, Mel Gibson, Newmarket Films, 2004.

Paycheck, John Woo, Paramount Pictures, 2003.

Pirates of the Caribbean: At World's End, Gore Verbinski, Buena Vista Pictures, 2007.

Pocahontas, Mike Gabriel and Eric Goldberg, Buena Vista Pictures, 1995.

Police Story (*Jingcha gushi*), Jackie Chan, Cinema Group, 1985.

The Princess of Nebraska, Wayne Wang, Center for Asian American Media, 2007.

Project A (*'A' jihua*), Jackie Chan, Golden Harvest, 1983.

The Promise (*Wu ji*), Chen Kaige, Warner Independent Pictures, 2005.

Proud and Confidence (*Aoqi xiongying*), Lee King Chu, 1989.

Psycho, Gus Van Sant, MCA/Universal Pictures, 1998.

Pulp Fiction, Quentin Tarantino, Miramax Films, 1994.

Pushing Hands (*Tui shou*), Ang Lee, Cinépix Film Properties/Good Machine, 1992.

Quantum of Solace, Marc Forster, Columbia Pictures, 2008.

Raise the Red Lantern (*Da hong denglong gaogao gua*), Zhang Yimou, Orion Classics, 1991.

Red Cliff (*Chi bi*), John Woo, Avex Entertainment, 2008.

Red Corner, Jon Avnet, MGM, 1997.

The Replacement Killers, Antoine Fuqua, Columbia Pictures, 1998.

Replicant, Ringo Lam, Millennium Films, 2001.

Reservoir Dogs, Quentin Tarantino, Miramax Films, 1992.

Return to the 36th Chamber (Shaolin dapeng dashi), Liu Chia-liang, Shaw Brothers, 1980.

Ride with the Devil, Ang Lee, USA Films, 1999.

The Ring, Gore Verbinski, DreamWorks Distribution, 2002.

The Ring 2, Hideo Nakata, DreamWorks Distribution, 2005.

Ringu, Hideo Nakata, Kadokawa Shoten Publishing Co., 1998.

The Road Home (Wo de fuqin muqin), Zhang Yimou, Sony Pictures Classics, 1999.

The Road to Guantanamo, Mat Whitecross and Michael Winterbottom, Roadside Attractions, 2006.

Romance of the Songsters, Joe Chiu, Grandview, 1933.

Romeo + Juliet, Baz Luhrmann, Twentieth Century Fox, 1996.

Romeo Must Die, Andrzej Bartkowiak, Warner Bros. Pictures, 2000.

Rumble in the Bronx (Hong fan qu), Stanley Tong, New Line Cinema, 1995.

Rush Hour, Brett Ratner, New Line Cinema, 1998.

Rush Hour 2, Brett Ratner, New Line Cinema, 2001.

Rush Hour 3, Brett Ratner, New Line Cinema, 2007.

Safety Last!, Fred C. Newmeyer and Sam Taylor, Pathé Exchange, 1923.

The Sandwich Man (Erzi de da wanou), Hou Hsiao-hsien, Wan Jen, and Zeng Zhuang-xiang, Central Motion Pictures Corporation, 1983.

Saving Face, Alice Wu, Sony Pictures Classics, 2004.

Sayonara, Joshua Logan, Warner Bros. Pictures, 1957.

Se7en, David Fincher, New Line Cinema, 1995.

Sense and Sensibility, Ang Lee, Columbia Pictures, 1995.

Seven Years in Tibet, Jean-Jacques Annaud, TriStar Pictures,1997.

Shadows of Chinatown, Paul Hurst, States Rights Independent Exchanges, 1926.

Shanghai Express, Josef von Sternberg, Paramount Pictures, 1932.

Shanghai Knights, David Dobkin, Buena Vista Pictures, 2003.

Shanghai Noon, Tom Dey, Buena Vista Pictures, 2000.

Shaolin Girl, Katsuyuki Motohiro, Toho Company, 2008.

Shaolin Soccer (Shaolin zuqiu), Stephen Chow, Miramax Films, 2001.

Shatter, Michael Carreras, AVCO Embassy Pictures, 1974.

The Silence of the Lambs, Jonathan Demme, Orion Pictures Corporation, 1991.

The Silent Flute (or Circle of Iron), Richard Moore, AVCO Embassy Pictures, 1978.

Silver Hawk (Fei ying), Jingle Ma, Media Asia Distribution, 2004.

Silver Streak, Arthur Hiller, Twentieth Century Fox, 1976.

Singin' in the Rain, Stanley Donen and Gene Kelly, MGM, 1952.

Slam Dance, Wayne Wang, Island Pictures, 1987.

The Slanted Screen, Jeff Adachi, Center for Asian American Media, 2006.

Smoke, Wayne Wang, Miramax Films, 1995.

Snake in the Eagle's Shadow (Shexing diaoshou), Yuen Woo-ping, Seasonal Film Corpration, 1978.

So Close (Xiyang tianshi), Corey Yuen, Columbia Pictures, 2002.

Spirit of the Raped (Suo ming), Kuei Chih-hung, Shaw Brother, 1976.

Star Wars, George Lucas, Twentieth Century Fox, 1977.
Star Wars: Episode I – The Phantom Menace, George Lucas, Twentieth Century Fox, 1999.
The Stepford Wives, Bryan Forbes, Columbia Pictures, 1975.
The Stepford Wives, Frank Oz, Paramount Pictures, 2004.
Stir Crazy, Sidney Poitier, Columbia Pictures, 1980.
Supercop (*Jingcha gushi san: chaoji jingcha*), Stanley Tong, Golden Harvest, 1992.
Sweet Sweetback's Baadasssss Song, Melvin Van Peebles, Cinemation Industries, 1971.
Switchblade Sisters, Jack Hill, Surrogate, 1975.
Taiga, Ulrike Ottinger, New Yorker Films, 1993.
Temptress Moon (*Feng yue*), Chen Kaige, Miramax Films, 1996.
Thelma and Louise, Ridley Scott, MGM, 1991.
A Thousand Years of Good Prayers, Wayne Wang, Magnolia Pictures, 2007.
Three Kingdoms: Resurrection of the Dragon (*Sanguo zhi jian long xie jia*), Daniel Lee, Visualizer Film Productions, 2008.
Time and Tide (*Shun liu ni liu*), Tsui Hark, TriStar Pictures, 2000.
To Liv(e) (*Fushi lianqu*), Evans Chan, 1992.
Tomorrow Never Dies, Roger Spottiswoode, United Artists, 1997.
The Tong Man, William Worthington, Exhibitors Mutual Distributing Company, 1919.
Top Gun, Tony Scott, Paramount Pictures, 1986.
The Touch, Peter Pau, Miramax Films, 2002.
Touch of Zen (*Xianu*), King Hu, International Film Company, 1969.
Traces of a Dragon: Jackie Chan and his Lost Family, Mabel Cheung, Fortissimo Films, 2003.
Trading Places, John Landis, Paramount Pictures, 1983.
Triad Election (*Heishehui er: yiheweigui*), Johnnie To, Tartan USA, 2006.
Triumph of the Will, Leni Riefenstahl, Contemporary Films, 1935.
The Tuxedo, Kevin Donovan, DreamWorks Distribution, 2002.
The Vengeance of Fu Manchu, Jeremy Summers, Warner Brothers/Seven Arts, 1967.
War, Philip G. Atwell, Lions Gate Films, 2007.
The Warlords (*Tou ming zhuang*), Peter Chan, Media Asia Distribution/ARM Distribution, 2007.
Warriors of Heaven and Earth (*Tiandi yingxiong*), He Ping, Sony Pictures Classics, 2003.
The Way of the Dragon (*Menglong guojiang*), Bruce Lee, Concord/Golden Harvest, 1972.
The Web of Death (*Wudu tianluo*), Chor Yuen, Shaw Brothers, 1976.
The Wedding Banquet (*Xiyan*), Ang Lee, Good Machine/Samuel Goldwyn Company, 1993.
Welcome Danger, Clyde Bruckman and Malcolm St. Clair, Paramount Pictures, 1929.
White Men Can't Jump, Ron Shelton, Twentieth Century Fox, 1992.
Who Am I? (*Wo shi shei*), Benny Chan and Jackie Chan, Golden Harvest, 1998.
Who Framed Roger Rabbit, Robert Zemeckis, Buena Vista Pictures, 1988.
Windtalkers, John Woo, MGM, 2002.

The Wisdom of Crocodiles, Leong Po-chih, Miramax Films, 1998.
The Wizard of Oz, Victor Fleming, MGM, 1939.
The World of Suzie Wong, Richard Quine, Paramount Pictures, 1960.
Xiu Xiu: the Sent-Down Girl (*Tian yu*), Joan Chen, Stratosphere Entertainment, 1998.
Yellow Earth (*Huang tude*), Chen Kaige, International Film Circuit, 1984.
Zhuangzi Tests His Wife (*Zhuangzi shi qi*), Li Minwei, Huamei, 1913.

Bibliography

Abbas, Ackbar. *Hong Kong: Culture and the Politics of Disappearance.* Minneapolis: University of Minnesota Press, 1997.

Abrams, M. H. *A Glossary of Literary Terms.* 5th ed. Fort Worth: Holt, Rinehart and Winston, 1988.

Abramson, Marc. "Mountains, Monks, and Mandalas: *Kundun* and *Seven Years in Tibet.*" *Cineaste* 23, no. 3 (April 1998): 8–12.

Achebe, Chinua. *Hopes and Impediments: Selected Essays 1965–1987.* London: Heinemann, 1988.

Agamben, Giorgio. *Homo Sacer: Sovereign Power and Bare Life.* Translated by Daniel Heller-Roazen. Stanford: Stanford University Press, 1998.

—. "The Time That Is Left," *Epoché* 7, no. 1 (Fall 2002): 1–14.

Althusser, Louis. *For Marx.* Translated by Ben Brewster. London: Verso, 1969.

Althusser, Louis, and Étienne Balibar. *Reading Capital.* Translated by Ben Brewster. London: Verso, 1997.

Ang, Ien. *On Not Speaking Chinese: Living between Asia and the West.* London: Routledge, 2001.

"Apology: Stone and Dior Differ." *The Straits Times*, 2 June 2008, Life section, 12.

Atkinson, Michael. "Partial Arts: Former Fifth-Gen Master Proves We Don't Need Another *Hero.*" *Village Voice*, 2 May 2006, <http://www.villagevoice.com/film/0618,atkinson, 73085,20.html>, accessed 9 June 2007.

Aufderheide, Patricia. "Made in Hong Kong: Translation and Transmutation." In *Play It Again, Sam: Retakes on Remakes,* edited by Andrew Horton and Stuart Y. McDougal. Berkeley: University of California Press, 1998.

Avedon, John F. *In Exile from the Land of Snows: The Definitive Account of the Dalai Lama and Tibet Since the Chinese Conquest.* New York: HarperCollins, 1997.

Barshay, Robert. "Ethnic Stereotypes in Flash Gordon." *Journal of Popular Film* 3, no. 1 (Winter 1974): 15–30.

Benjamin, Walter. *Illuminations.* Edited by Hannah Arendt. Translated by Harry Zohn. New York: Schocken Books, 1968.

—. *Reflections: Essays, Aphorisms, Autobiographical Writings.* Edited by Peter Demetz. Translated by Edmund Jephcott. New York: Schocken Books, 1978.

Bernard, Jami. *Quentin Tarantino: The Man and His Movies.* London: HarperCollins, 1995.

Berry, Chris. "Market Forces: China's 'Fifth Generation' Faces the Bottom Line." In *Perspectives on Chinese Cinema,* edited by Chris Berry. London: BFI, 1991.

Berry, Chris, and Mary Farquhar. *China on Screen: Cinema and Nation.* Hong Kong: Hong Kong University Press, 2006.

Berry, Chris, and Feii Lu, eds. *Island on the Edge: Taiwan New Cinema and After.* Hong Kong: Hong Kong University Press, 2005.

Bhabha, Homi K. *The Location of Culture.* London: Routledge, 1994.

Booth, Martin. *The Dragon Syndicates: The Global Phenomenon of the Triads.* New York: Carroll & Graf, 1999.

—. *The Triads: The Chinese Criminal Fraternity.* London: Grafton Books, 1990.

Bordwell, David. *Planet Hong Kong: Popular Cinema and the Art of Entertainment.* Cambridge: Harvard University Press, 2000.

Borradori, Giovanna. *Philosophy in a Time of Terror: Dialogues with Jürgen Habermas and Jacques Derrida.* Chicago: University Of Chicago Press, 2003.

Bould, Mark. *Film Noir: From Berlin to Sin City.* London: Wallflower, 2005.

Bourdieu, Pierre. *The Logic of Practice.* Translated by Richard Nice. Stanford: Stanford University Press, 1990.

Brunette, Peter. *Wong Kar-wai.* Urbana: University of Illinois Press, 2005.

Burr, Ty. "Only as a Fairy Tale Does 'Promise' Reach Its Potential." *Boston Globe,* 5 May 2006, <http://www.boston.com/ae/movies/articles/2006/05/05/only_as_a_fairy_tale_doespromise_reach_its_potential/>, accessed 8 June 2007.

Butler, Judith. *Bodies That Matter: On the Discursive Limits of "Sex."* New York: Routledge, 1993.

—. *Gender Trouble: Feminism and the Subversion of Identity.* New York: Routledge, 1990.

—. *Precarious Life: The Powers of Mourning and Violence.* London: Verso, 2004.

Cawelti, John G. "*Chinatown* and Generic Transformation in Recent American Films. " In *Film Genre Reader III,* edited by Barry Keith Grant. Austin: University of Texas Press, 2003.

"Celebrities Mark Tibetan Uprising." *BBC News,* 10 March 1999, <http://news.bbc.co.uk/2/hi/entertainment/294210.stm>, accessed 5 June 2008.

Certeau, Michel de. *The Practice of Everyday Life.* Translated by Steven Rendall. Berkley: University of California Press, 1984.

"Chan Asks Asians to Shun Hollywood," *CBS News,* 25 November 2005, <http://www.cbsnews.com/stories/2005/11/25/entertainment/main1075637.shtml>, accessed 20 June 2007.

Chan, Evans. "Postmodernism and Hong Kong Cinema." In *Postmodernism and China,* edited by Arif Dirlik and Xudong Zhang. Durham: Duke University Press, 2000.

—. "Zhang Yimou's *Hero*: The Temptations of Fascism." *Film International* 2, no. 8 (March 2004): 14–23.

Chan, Felicia. "*Crouching Tiger, Hidden Dragon*: Cultural Migrancy and Translatability." In *Chinese Films in Focus: 25 New Takes,* edited by Chris Berry. London: BFI, 2003.

Chan, Jachinson. *Chinese American Masculinities: From Fu Manchu to Bruce Lee.* New York: Routledge, 2001.

Chan, Jackie, with Jeff Yang. *I Am Jackie Chan: My Life in Action.* New York: Ballantine, 1999.

Chan, Kenneth. "The Construction of Black Male Identity in Black Action Films of the Nineties." *Cinema Journal* 37, no. 2 (1998): 35–48.

—. "The Global Return of the *Wu Xia Pian* (Chinese Sword-Fighting Movie): Ang Lee's *Crouching Tiger, Hidden Dragon.*" *Cinema Journal* 43, no. 4 (Summer 2004): 3–17.

—. "Mimicry as Failure: Jackie Chan in Hollywood." *Asian Cinema* 15, no. 2 (Fall/Winter 2004): 84–97.

Chan, Sucheng. *Asian Americans: An Interpretive History.* Boston: Twayne, 1991.

Chang Cheh. *Chang Cheh: A Memoir.* Translated by Teri Chan and Agnes Lam. Hong Kong: Hong Kong Film Archive, 2004.

Chang, Hsiao-hung. "The Unbearable Lightness of Globalization: On the Transnational Flight of *Wuxia* Film." In *Cinema Taiwan: Politics, Popularity and State of the Arts*, edited by Darrell William Davis and Ru-shou Robert Chen. London: Routledge, 2007.

Chang, Iris. *The Chinese in America: A Narrative History.* New York: Penguin, 2003.

Chang, Yahlin. "Can You Go Home Again?" *Newsweek*, 10 November 1997, 78.

Cheah, Pheng, and Bruce Robbins, eds. *Cosmopolitics: Thinking and Feeling beyond the Nation.* Minneapolis: University of Minnesota Press, 1998.

Chen, Ru-shou Robert. "'This Isn't Real!' Spatialized Narration and (In)visible Special Effects in 'Double Vision.'" In *Cinema Taiwan: Politics, Popularity and State of the Arts*, edited by Darrell William Davis and Ru-shou Robert Chen. London: Routledge, 2007.

Cheng, Ien. "Hero's Success Sweeps the US." *Financial Times*, 13 September 2004, Arts and Style section, 12.

Cheng, Scarlet. "The Homecoming." *Far Eastern Economic Review*, 15 May 1997, 66–68.

Chiang, Mark. "Coming Out into the Global System: Postmodern Patriarchies and Transnational Sexualities in *The Wedding Banquet.*" In *Screening Asian Americans*, edited by Peter X. Feng. New Brunswick: Rutgers University Press, 2002.

Chiao, Christine. "A Promise Left Unfulfilled." UCLA International Insitute, 13 April 2006, <http://www.international.ucla.edu/article.asp?parentid=42884>, accessed 2 December 2008.

Chin, Frank, and Jeffrey Paul Chan. "Racist Love." In *Seeing Through Shuck,* edited by Richard Kostelanetz. New York: Ballantine, 1972.

"China Blocks YouTube over Tibet Protests." *MSNBC.Com*, 16 March 2008, <http://www.msnbc.msn.com/id/23657906/>, accessed 7 June 2008.

"China Censors 'Cut' Pirates Film." *BBC News*, 12 June 2007, <http://news.bbc.co.uk/2/hi/entertainment/6744245.stm>, accessed 15 June 2007.

"Chinese Student in US Dubbed 'Traitor,' Threatened with Violence." *The Straits Times*, 23 April 2008, 8.

Chopin, Kate. *The Awakening.* New York: Norton, 1994.

Chow, Rey. "King Kong in Hong Kong: Watching the 'Handover' from the U.S.A." *Social Text* 55, vol. 16, no. 2 (Summer 1998): 93–108.

—. "Nostalgia of the New Wave: Structure in Wong Kar-wai's *Happy Together.*" In

Keyframes: Popular Cinema and Cultural Studies, edited by Matthew Tinkcom and Amy Villarejo. London: Routledge, 2001.

—. *Primitive Passions: Visuality, Sexuality, Ethnography, and Contemporary Chinese Cinema.* New York: Columbia University Press, 1995.

—. *Sentimental Fabulations, Contemporary Chinese Films: Attachment in the Age of Global Visibility.* New York: Columbia University Press, 2007.

—. *Woman and Chinese Modernity: The Politics of Reading between West and East.* Minneapolis: University of Minnesota Press, 1991.

Chua Beng Huat. "Conceptualizing an East Asian Popular Culture." *Inter-Asia Cultural Studies* 5, no. 2 (2004): 200–21.

Chung Po-yin, Stephanie. "The Industrial Evolution of a Fraternal Enterprise: The Shaw Brothers and the Shaw Organisation." In *The Shaw Screen: A Preliminary Study,* edited by Wong Ain-ling. Hong Kong: Hong Kong Film Archive, 2003.

Clark, Mike. "Bai Ling Adds Dimension to 'Red Corner' Thrills." *USA Today*, 31 October 1997, Life section, 1D.

—. "'Hero': Easy on the Eyes But a Little Too Plodding." *USA Today*, 26 August 2004, <http://www.usatoday.com/life/movies/reviews/2004-08-26-hero_x.htm>, accessed 12 June 2008.

Clark, Paul. *Reinventing China: A Generation and its Films.* Hong Kong: The Chinese University Press, 2005.

Coonan, Clifford. "'Memoirs of a Geisha' Banned by Beijing in Row over Chinese Stars." *The Independent*, 2 February 2006, <http://www.independent.co.uk/arts/film/news/article342661.ece>, accessed 15 June 2007.

Corliss, Richard. "Asian Invasion." *Time*, 14 August 1995, <http://www.time.com/time/magazine/article/0,9171,983301-1,00.html>, accessed 27 May 2008.

—. "Hollywood's Asian Romance." *Time*, 14 November 2005, <http://www.time.com/time/asia/covers/501051121/story.html>, accessed 15 June 2007.

—. "In the Mood for Swordplay," *Time*, 15 December 2002, <http://www.time.com/time/magazine/article/0,9171,501021223-400044,00.html>, accessed 17 May 2007.

"Crouching Tiger, Battling Movie Companies." *The Straits Times,* 9 May 2007, Life section, 7.

Dariotis, Wei Ming, and Eileen Fung. "Breaking the Soy Sauce Jar: Diaspora and Displacement in the Films of Ang Lee." In *Transnational Chinese Cinemas: Identity, Nationhood, Gender*, edited by Sheldon Hsiao-peng Lu. Honolulu: University of Hawai'i Press, 1997.

Davis, Darrell William, and Ru-shou Robert Chen, eds. *Cinema Taiwan: Politics, Popularity and State of the Arts.* London: Routledge, 2007.

Deleuze, Gilles. *Cinema 1: The Movement-Image.* Translated by Hugh Tomlinson and Barbara Habberjam. Minneapolis: University of Minnesota Press, 1986.

Derrida, Jacques. *Margins of Philosophy.* Translated by Alan Bass. Chicago: University of Chicago Press, 1982.

—. *Writing and Difference.* Translated by Alan Bass. London: Routledge, 1978.

Desser, David. "Global Noir: Genre Film in the Age of Transnationalism." In *Film Genre Reader III,* edited by Barry Keith Grant. Austin: University of Texas Press, 2003.

—. "The Kung Fu Craze: Hong Kong Cinema's First American Reception." In *The Cinema of Hong Kong: History, Arts, Identity,* edited by Poshek Fu and David Desser. Cambridge: Cambridge University Press, 2000.

Dinmore, Guy. "Hollywood Filmstar Urges Congress to Act Over Tibet." *Financial Times,* 14 March 2007, Asia edition, 3.

Dissanayake, Wimal. *Ashes of Time.* Hong Kong: Hong Kong University Press, 2003.

Doherty, Thomas. *Teenagers and Teenpics: The Juvenilization of American Movies in the 1950s.* Boston: Unwin Hyman, 1988.

Dyer, Richard. "It's Being So Camp as Keeps Us Going." In *Camp: Queer Aesthetics and the Performing Subject,* edited by Fabio Cleto. Edinburgh: Edinburgh University Press, 1999.

—. *White.* London: Routledge, 1997.

Ebert, Roger. "Hero." *rogerebert.com,* 27 August 2004, <http://rogerebert.suntimes.com/apps/pbcs.dll/article?AID=/20040826/REVIEWS/408260304/1023>, accessed 12 June 2008.

Eng, David L. *Racial Castration: Managing Masculinity in Asian America.* Durham: Duke University Press, 2001.

Eng, Robert Y. "Is Hero a Paean to Authoritarianism?" *AsiaMedia,* 7 September 2004, <http://www.asiamedia.ucla.edu/article.asp?parentid=14371>, accessed 22 May 2007.

Fairbank, John King. *China: A New History.* Cambridge: The Belknap Press of Harvard University Press, 1992.

Faison, Seth. "Hong Kong Plays the Role of a Drama-Filled City." *New York Times,* 1 July 1997, C9, C12.

Fanon, Frantz. *Black Skin, White Masks.* Translated by Charles Lam Markmann. New York: Grove Press, 1967.

Farquhar, Mary. "Zhang Yimou." *Senses of Cinema,* May 2002, <http://www.sensesofcinema.com/contents/directors/02/zhang.html>, accessed 17 May 2007.

Feng, Peter X. *Identities in Motion: Asian American Film and Video.* Durham: Duke University Press, 2002.

—. "Recuperating Suzie Wong: A Fan's Nancy Kwan-dary." In *Countervisions: Asian American Film Criticism,* edited by Darrell Y. Hamamoto and Sandra Liu. Philadelphia: Temple University Press, 2000.

—, ed. *Screening Asian Americans.* New Brunswick: Rutgers University Press, 2002.

Fonoroff, Paul. *Silver Light: A Pictorial History of Hong Kong Cinema, 1920–1970.* Hong Kong: Joint Publishing, 1997.

Foong Woei Wan. "Epic Change." *The Straits Times,* 9 April 2008, Life section, 1–3.

"Forbidden Kingdom is No. 1 in US" *The Straits Times,* 22 April 2008, Life section, 18.

Fore, Steve. "Jackie Chan and the Cultural Dynamics of Global Entertainment." In *Transnational Chinese Cinemas: Identity, Nationhood, Gender,* edited by Sheldon Hsiao-peng Lu. Honolulu: University of Hawai'i Press, 1997.

—. "Life Imitates Entertainment: Home and Dislocation in the Films of Jackie Chan." In *At Full Speed: Hong Kong Cinema in a Borderless World,* edited by Esther C. M. Yau. Minneapolis: University of Minnesota Press, 2001.

Foucault, Michel. *Discipline and Punish: The Birth of the Prison.* Translated by Alan Sheridan. New York: Vintage Books, 1977.

Friedman, Lester D., ed. *Unspeakable Images: Ethnicity and the American Cinema.* Urbana: University of Illinois Press, 1991.

Fu, Poshek, and David Desser, eds. *The Cinema of Hong Kong: History, Arts, Identity.* Cambridge: Cambridge University Press, 2000.

Gallafent, Edward. *Quentin Tarantino.* Harlow, England: Pearson, 2006.

Gallagher, Mark. "Masculinity in Translation: Jackie Chan's Transcultural Star Text." *The Velvet Light Trap* 39 (Spring 1997): 25–41.

Galloway, Patrick. *Asia Shock: Horror and Dark Cinema from Japan, Korea, Hong Kong, and Thailand.* Berkeley: Stone Bridge Press, 2006.

Garcia, Roger. *Out of the Shadows: Asians in American Cinema.* Milano: Olivares, 2001.

Gateward, Frances, ed. *Zhang Yimou: Interviews.* Jackson: University Press of Mississippi, 2001.

"Geisha Film Reveals 'Hidden Culture.'" *BBC News*, 1 January 2006, <http://news.bbc.co.uk/1/hi/entertainment/4503454.stm>, accessed 15 June 2007.

"Gibson: 'I Am Not an Anti-Semite,'" CNN.com, 2 August 2006, <http://www.cnn.com/2006/SHOWBIZ/Movies/08/01/gibson.dui/index.html>, accessed 27 May 2007.

Gilroy, Paul. *The Black Atlantic: Modernity and Double Consciousness.* Cambridge: Harvard University Press, 1993.

Gledhill, Christine. "Pleasurable Negotiations." In *Female Spectators: Looking at Film and Television*, edited by E. Deirdre Pribram. London: Verso, 1988.

Goh Sui Noi. "Slap in the Face for Chinese." *The Straits Times*, 24 April 2008, 22.

Goldstein, Melvyn C. *The Snow Lion and the Dragon: China, Tibet, and the Dalai Lama.* Berkeley: University of California Press, 1997.

Gramsci, Antonio. *Selections from the Prison Notebooks.* Edited and translated by Quintin Hoare and Geoffrey Nowell Smith. New York: International Publishers, 1971.

Grant, Barry Keith, ed. *Film Genre Reader III.* Austin: University of Texas Press, 2003.

"The Guardian/NFT Interview: Ang Lee and James Schamus," *Guardian Unlimited*, 7 November 2000, < http://film.guardian.co.uk/interview/interviewpages/0,6737,394676,00.html#early>, accessed 23 May 2007.

Guerrero, Ed. *Framing Blackness: The African American Image in Film.* Philadelphia: Temple University Press, 1993.

Haenni, Sabine. "Filming 'Chinatown': Fake Visions, Bodily Transformations." In *Screening Asian Americans,* edited by Peter X. Feng. New Brunswick: Rutgers University Press, 2002.

Hajari, Nisid. "Erasing the Boundaries." *Newsweek*, special ed., Issues Asia, July-September 2001, 79.

Hamamoto, Darrell Y. *Monitored Peril: Asian Americans and the Politics of TV Representation.* Minneapolis: University of Minnesota Press, 1994.

Hamamoto, Darrell Y., and Sandra Liu, eds. *Countervisions: Asian American Film Criticism.* Philadelphia: Temple University Press, 2000.

Haraway, Donna J. *Simians, Cyborgs, and Women: The Reinvention of Nature.* New York: Routledge, 1991.

Harrer, Heinrich. *Seven Years in Tibet.* New York: Tarcher/Putnam, 1981.

Harvey, David. *The Condition of Postmodernity: An Enquiry into the Origins of Cultural Change.* Cambridge: Blackwell, 1990.

Hills, Matt. "*Star Wars* in Fandom, Film Theory, and the Museum: The Cultural Status of the Cult Blockbuster." In *Movie Blockbusters,* edited by Julian Stringer. London: Routledge, 2003.

Hilton, James. *Lost Horizon: A Novel.* New York: HarperCollins, 1960.

Hitchcock, Peter. "Niche Cinema, or, *Kill Bill* with *Shaolin Soccer.*" In *Hong Kong Film, Hollywood and the New Global Cinema: No Film Is an Island,* edited by Gina Marchetti and Tan See Kam. London: Routledge, 2007.

Hoberman, J. "Man with No Name Tells a Story of Heroics, Color Coordination: Hero." *Village Voice,* 17 August 2004, <http://www.villagevoice.com/film/0434,hoberman2,56140,20.html>, accessed 21 May 2007.

Hohenadel, Kristin. "A Human Face for Hong Kong's Identity Crisis." *New York Times,* 19 April 1998, 29, 38.

Holden, Stephen. "A Meditation on the Meaning of Hong Kong." *New York Times,* 17 April 1998, B18.

"Hong Kong Set for Chinese Influx." *BBC News,* 28 April 1999, <news.bbc.co.uk/1/hi/world/asia-pacific/330923.stm>, accessed 16 June 2007.

Hong Xiaoyong. "China Did Well by Tibet." *The Straits Times,* 23 April 2008, 20.

hooks, bell. *Reel to Real: Race, Sex, and Class at the Movies.* New York: Routledge, 1996.

Horton, Andrew, and Stuart Y. McDougal, eds. *Play It Again, Sam: Retakes on Remakes.* Berkeley: University of California Press, 1998.

Hunt, Leon. *Kung Fu Cult Masters: From Bruce Lee to Crouching Tiger.* London: Wallflower Press, 2003.

Hunter, Stephen. "'House of Flying Daggers': Symphony in Swords." *Washington Post,* 17 December 2004, <http://www.washingtonpost.com/wp-dyn/articles/A6440-2004Dec16.html?referrer=email>, accessed 22 May 2007.

Huston, Peter. *Tongs, Gangs, and Triads: Chinese Crime Groups in North America.* San Jose: Authors Choice Press, 2001.

"Jackie and Jet: Friends, Not Foes." *The Straits Times,* 19 April 2008, Life section, 12.

"Jackie and Jet's Movie 'Isn't Great.'" *The Straits Times,* 20 September 2007, Life section, 12.

"Jackie Chan Returns to Hong Kong for Artistic Freedom." *Goldsea Asian American Daily,* 15 July 2005, <http://goldsea.com/Asiagate/507/16chan.html>, accessed 17 April 2006.

Jakes, Susan. "Playing Safe." *Time,* 15 December 2002, <http://www.time.com/time/magazine/article/0,9171,501021223-400042,00.html>, accessed 17 May 2007.

Jameson, Fredric. *The Political Unconscious: Narrative as a Socially Symbolic Act.* Ithaca: Cornell University Press, 1981.

—. *Postmodernism, or, the Cultural Logic of Late Capitalism.* Durham: Duke University Press, 1991.

—. "Third-World Literature in the Era of Multinational Capitalism." *Social Text* 15 (Autumn 1986): 65–88.

Jayamanne, Laleen. "Let's Miscegenate: Jackie Chan and His African-American Connection." In *Hong Kong Connections: Transnational Imagination in Action Cinema,* edited by Meaghan Morris, Siu Leung Li, and Stephen Chan Ching-kiu. Durham: Duke University Press, 2005.

Jones, Dorothy B. *The Portrayal of China and India on the American Screen, 1896–1955.* Cambridge: Center for International Studies, Massachusetts Institute of Technology, 1955.

Kim, James. "The Legend of the White-and-Yellow Black Man: Global Containment and Triangulated Racial Desire in *Romeo Must Die." Camera Obscura* 55, vol. 19, no. 1 (2004): 151–79.

Kim Soyoung. "Genre as Contact Zone: Hong Kong Action and Korean *Hwalkuk."* In *Hong Kong Connections: Transnational Imagination in Action Cinema,* edited by Meaghan Morris, Siu Leung Li, and Stephen Chan Ching-kiu. Durham: Duke University Press, 2005.

King, Neal, and Martha McCaughey. "What's a Mean Woman Like You Doing in a Movie like This?" In *Reel Knockouts: Violent Women in the Movies,* edited by Martha McCaughey and Neal King. Austin: University of Texas Press, 2001.

Kingston, Maxine Hong. *The Woman Warrior: Memoirs of a Girlhood Among Ghosts.* New York: Vintage International, 1976.

Kit, Borys. "Disney, Chabon Retelling 'Snow.'" *The Hollywood Reporter,* 29 October 2004, <http://www.hollywoodreporter.com/hr/search/article_display.jsp?vnu_content_id=1000694195>, accessed 18 June 2008.

Klein, Christina. *Cold War Orientalism: Asia in the Middlebrow Imagination, 1945–1961.* Berkeley: University of California Press, 2003.

—. "*Crouching Tiger, Hidden Dragon*: A Diasporic Reading." *Cinema Journal* 43, no. 4 (Summer 2004): 18–42.

Knopf, Robert. *The Theater and Cinema of Buster Keaton.* Princeton: Princeton University Press, 1999.

Koehler, Robert. "The Promise aka Master of the Crimson Armor." *Variety,* 29 December 2005, <http://www.variety.com/review/VE1117929184.html?categoryid=1263&cs=1>, accessed 8 June 2007.

Koh, Bernard, and Douglas Tseng. "Who Packs a Bigger Punch?" *The Sunday Times,* 27 April 2008, Lifestyle section, 2.

Kolesnikov-Jessop, Sonia. "Redefining the Epic." *Newsweek,* 24 December 2007, <http://www.newsweek.com/id/78119>, accessed 18 June 2008.

Kraicer, Shelley. "Absence as Spectacle: Zhang Yimou's *Hero.*" <http://www.chinesecinemas.org/hero.html>, accessed 22 May 2007.

Kwok Ching-ling and Grace Ng, eds. *Director Chor Yuen.* Hong Kong: Hong Kong Film Archive, 2006.

LaCapra, Dominick. *History in Transit: Experience, Identity, Critical Theory*. Ithaca: Cornell University Press, 2004.

Lalanne, Jean-Marc, et al., eds. *Wong Kar-wai*. Paris: Dis Voir, 1997.

Lam, Michael. "The Mysterious Gayness in Chang Cheh's Unhappy World." Translated by Sam Ho. In *The Shaw Screen: A Preliminary Study*, edited by Wong Ain-ling. Hong Kong: Hong Kong Film Archive, 2003.

Landreth, Jonathan. "China's Huayi Bros. Thinking Big." *The Hollywood Reporter*, 24 May 2005, <http://www.hollywoodreporter.com/hr/search/article_display.jsp?vnu_content_id=1000930260>, accessed 18 May 2008.

Lau, Jenny Kwok Wah. "*Farewell My Concubine*: History, Melodrama, and Ideology in Contemporary Pan-Chinese Cinema." *Film Quarterly* 49, no. 1 (Fall 1995): 16–27.

—. "*Hero*: China's Response to Hollywood Globalization." *Jump Cut: A Review of Contemporary Media*, no. 49 (Spring 2007), <http://www.ejumpcut.org/trialsite/Lau-Hero/text.html>, accessed 22 May 2007.

—, ed. *Multiple Modernities: Cinemas and Popular Media in Transcultural East Asia*. Philadelphia: Temple University Press, 2003.

Law Kar. "The American Connection in Early Hong Kong Cinema." In *The Cinema of Hong Kong: History, Arts, Identity*, edited by Poshek Fu and David Desser. Cambridge: Cambridge University Press, 2000.

—. "An Overview of Hong Kong's New Wave Cinema." In *At Full Speed: Hong Kong Cinema in a Borderless World*, edited by Esther C. M. Yau. Minneapolis: University of Minnesota Press, 2001.

"Lee Ang Win Is 'Glory for Chinese.'" *The Straits Times*, 7 March 2006, Life section, 3.

Lee, Hwanhee. "*House of Flying Daggers*: A Reappraisal." *Senses of Cinema*, 2005, <http://www.sensesofcinema.com/contents/05/35/house_flying_daggers.html>, accessed 23 May 2007.

Lee, Ken-fang. "Far Away, So Close: Cultural Translation in Ang Lee's *Crouching Tiger, Hidden Dragon*." *Inter-Asia Cultural Studies* 4, no. 2 (2003): 281–95.

Lee, Min. "Kung Fu Film 'The Forbidden Kingdom' a Hit in China." *Yahoo! News*, 8 May 2008, <http://news.yahoo.com/s/ap/20080508/ap_en_mo/film_forbidden_kingdom>, accessed 15 May 2008.

Lee, Robert G. *Orientals: Asian Americans in Popular Culture*. Philadelphia: Temple University Press, 1999.

Lee Sze Yong. "Enter the New Dragon." *The Straits Times*, 31 May 2007, Life section, 20.

Leitch, Thomas. *Crime Films*. Cambridge: Cambridge University Press, 2002.

Li, Siu Leung. "The Myth Continues: Cinematic Kung Fu in Modernity." In *Hong Kong Connections: Transnational Imagination in Action Cinema*, edited by Meaghan Morris, Siu Leung Li, and Stephen Chan Ching-kiu. Durham: Duke University Press, 2005.

Lim, Bliss Cua. "Generic Ghosts: Remaking the New 'Asian Horror Film.'" In *Hong Kong Film, Hollywood and the New Global Cinema: No Film Is an Island*, edited by Gina Marchetti and Tan See Kam. London: Routledge, 2007.

Lim, Song Hwee. *Celluloid Comrades: Representations of Male Homosexuality in Contemporary Chinese Cinemas.* Honolulu: University of Hawai'i Press, 2006.

Liu, Cynthia W. "When Dragon Ladies Die, Do They Come Back as Butterflies?: Re-Imagining Anna May Wong." In *Countervisions: Asian American Film Criticism,* edited by Darrell Y. Hamamoto and Sandra Liu. Philadelphia: Temple University Press, 2000.

Liu, Sandra. "Negotiating the Meaning of Access: Wayne Wang's Contingent Film Practice." In *Countervisions: Asian American Film Criticism,* edited by Darrell Y. Hamamoto and Sandra Liu. Philadelphia: Temple University Press, 2000.

Lo, Kwai-Cheung. *Chinese Face/Off: The Transnational Popular Culture of Hong Kong.* Urbana: University of Illinois Press, 2005.

—. "Copies of Copies in Hollywood and Hong Kong Cinemas: Rethinking the Woman-Warrior Figures." In *Hong Kong Film, Hollywood and the New Global Cinema: No Film Is an Island,* edited by Gina Marchetti and Tan See Kam. London: Routledge, 2007.

Logan, Bey. *Hong Kong Action Cinema.* Woodstock, NY: The Overlook Press, 1995.

Lorenz, Andreas. "China's 'Geisha' Complex." *Spiegel Online,* 7 February 2006, <http://www.spiegel.de/international/0,1518,399593,00.html>, accessed 15 June 2007.

Louie, Kam. *Theorising Chinese Masculinity: Society and Gender in China.* Cambridge: Cambridge University Press, 2002.

Lowe, Lisa. *Immigrant Acts: On Asian American Cultural Politics.* Durham: Duke University Press, 1996.

Lowenstein, Stephen, ed. *My First Movie: Twenty Celebrated Directors Talk about Their First Film.* New York: Pantheon, 2000.

Lu, Sheldon H. "Crouching Tiger, Hidden Dragon, Bouncing Angels: Hollywood, Taiwan, Hong Kong, and Transnational Cinema." In *Chinese-Language Film: Historiography, Poetics, Politics,* edited by Sheldon H. Lu and Emilie Yueh-yu Yeh. Honolulu: University of Hawai'i Press, 2005.

Lu, Sheldon H., and Emilie Yueh-yu Yeh, eds. *Chinese-Language Film: Historiography, Poetics, Politics.* Honolulu: University of Hawai'i Press, 2005.

Lu, Sheldon Hsiao-peng, ed. *Transnational Chinese Cinemas: Identity, Nationhood, Gender.* Honolulu: University of Hawai'i Press, 1997.

Lu, Tonglin. *Confronting Modernity in the Cinemas of Taiwan and Mainland China.* Cambridge: Cambridge University Press, 2002.

Ma, Sheng-mei. *Immigrant Subjectivities in Asian American and Asian Diaspora Literatures.* Albany: State University of New York Press, 1998.

—. "Kung Fu Films in Diaspora: Death of the Bamboo Hero." In *Masculinities and Hong Kong Cinema,* edited by Laikwan Pang and Day Wong. Hong Kong: Hong Kong University Press, 2005.

Machiyama, Tomohiro. "Quentin Tarantino Reveals Almost Everything That Inspired *Kill Bill.*" In *Quentin Tarantino: The Film Geek Files,* edited by Paul A. Woods. London: Plexus, 2005.

Mackey, Robert. "Cracking the Color Code of 'Hero.'" *New York Times,* 15 August 2004, <http://www.nytimes.com/2004/08/15/movies/15MACK.html?ex=

1250308800&en=314c0d1ef8845f23&ei=5088&partner=rssnyt>, accessed 17 May 2007.

Marchetti, Gina. *From Tian'anmen to Times Square: Transnational China and the Chinese Diaspora on Global Screens, 1989–1997.* Philadelphia: Temple University Press, 2006.

—. "Jackie Chan and the Black Connection." In *Keyframes: Popular Cinema and Cultural Studies,* edited by Matthew Tinkcom and Amy Villarejo. London: Routledge, 2001.

—. *Romance and the "Yellow Peril": Race, Sex, and Discursive Strategies in Hollywood Fiction.* Berkeley: University of California Press, 1993.

Marchetti, Gina, and Tan See Kam, eds. *Hong Kong Film, Hollywood and the New Global Cinema: No Film Is an Island.* London: Routledge, 2007.

Martin, Fran. "The China Simulacrum: Genre, Feminism, and Pan-Chinese Cultural Politics in *Crouching Tiger, Hidden Dragon*." In *Island on the Edge: Taiwan New Cinema and After,* edited by Chris Berry and Feii Lu. Hong Kong: Hong Kong University Press, 2005.

Marx, Karl, and Frederick Engels. *The German Ideology.* Edited by C. J. Arthur. New York: International Publishers, 1947.

Metz, Christian. "The Imaginary Signifier." In *Narrative, Apparatus, Ideology: A Film Theory Reader*, edited by Philip Rosen. New York: Columbia University Press, 1986.

Michelson, Annette. Introduction to *Kino-Eye: The Writings of Dziga Vertov*, by Dziga Vertov, translated by Kevin O'Brien. Berkeley: University of California Press, 1984.

Miller, Toby. "James Bond's Penis." In *Masculinity: Bodies, Movies, Culture*, edited by Peter Lehman. New York: Routledge, 2001.

Mitchell, Edward. "Apes and Essences: Some Sources of Significance in the American Gangster Film." In *Film Genre Reader III*, edited by Barry Keith Grant. Austin: University of Texas Press, 2003.

Mo, Timothy. *Sour Sweet.* London: Paddleless Press, 1999.

Morris, Meaghan. "Learning from Bruce Lee: Pedagogy and Political Correctness in Martial Arts Cinema." In *Keyframes: Popular Cinema and Cultural Studies,* edited by Matthew Tinkcom and Amy Villarejo. London: Routledge, 2001.

Morris, Meaghan, Siu Leung Li, and Stephen Chan Ching-kiu, eds. *Hong Kong Connections: Transnational Imagination in Action Cinema.* Durham: Duke University Press, 2005.

Mulvey, Laura. "Visual Pleasure and Narrative Cinema." In *Feminism and Film,* edited by E. Ann Kaplan. Oxford: Oxford University Press, 2000.

Murray, Dian H., in collaboration with Qin Baoqi. *The Origins of the Tiandihui: The Chinese Triads in Legend and History.* Stanford: Stanford University Press, 1994.

Ngai, Jimmy and Wong Kar-wai. "A Dialogue with Wong Kar-wai." In *Wong Kar-wai,* edited by Jean-Marc Lalanne, et al. Paris: Dis Voir, 1997.

"The One That Got Away." *The Straits Times,* 8 March 2006, Life section, 6.

Ong, Aihwa. *Flexible Citizenship: The Cultural Logics of Transnationality.* Durham: Duke University Press, 1999.

Overstreet, Jeffrey. "Hero." *Christianity Today*, 20 August 2004, < http://www.christianitytoday.com/movies/reviews/hero.html>, accessed 12 June 2008.

Pang, Laikwan, and Day Wong, eds. *Masculinities and Hong Kong Cinema.* Hong Kong: Hong Kong University Press, 2005.

Pham, Minh-Ha T. "The Asian Invasion (of Multiculturalism) in Hollywood." *Journal of Popular Film and Television* 32, no. 3 (Fall 2004): 121–131.

Plate, Tom. "When Hollywood Hijacks the Plot." *The Straits Times*, 14 April 2008, 20.

"Politically Minded Stars Split on Skipping Beijing Olympics." *CNN.com*, 8 May 2008, <http://edition.cnn.com/2008/US/05/07/olympic.boycott/index.html?eref= edition>, accessed 5 June 2008.

Poon, Wena. Review of *Chinese Box* by Wayne Wang. *Film Quarterly* 52, no. 1 (1998): 31–4.

Prasso, Sheridan. *The Asian Mystique: Dragon Ladies, Geisha Girls, and Our Fantasies of the Exotic Orient.* New York: Public Affairs, 2005.

Pratt, Mary Louise. *Imperial Eyes: Travel Writing and Transculturation.* London: Routledge, 1992.

Pribram, E. Deirdre, ed. *Female Spectators: Looking at Film and Television.* London: Verso, 1988.

Rayns, Tony. "Breakthroughs and Setbacks: The Origins of the New Chinese Cinema. " In *Perspectives on Chinese Cinema,* edited by Chris Berry. London: BFI, 1991.

—. "Bruce Lee: Narcissism and Nationalism." In *A Study of the Hong Kong Martial Arts Film.* Hong Kong: The Urban Council, 1980.

Reid, Mark A. "The Black Gangster Film." In *Film Genre Reader III,* edited by Barry Keith Grant. Austin: University of Texas Press, 2003.

—. *Redefining Black Film.* Berkeley: University of California Press, 1993.

Roberts, Dexter. "A Chinese Blogger's Tale." *Business Week,* 2 March 2006, <http://www.businessweek.com/globalbiz/content/mar2006/gb20060302_026709.htm>, accessed 8 June 2007.

Rodriguez, Hector. "The Emergence of the Hong Kong New Wave." In *At Full Speed: Hong Kong Cinema in a Borderless World,* edited by Esther C. M. Yau. Minneapolis: University of Minnesota Press, 2001.

—. "The Fragmented Commonplace: Alternative Arts and Cosmopolitanism in Hong Kong." In *Multiple Modernities: Cinemas and Popular Media in Transcultural East Asia.* Edited by Jenny Kwok Wah Lau. Philadelphia: Temple University Press, 2003.

Rushdie, Salman. *Imaginary Homelands: Essays and Criticism 1981–1991.* London: Granta Books, 1991.

Said, Edward W. *Orientalism.* New York: Vintage, 1978.

Sarkar, Bhaskar. "Hong Kong Hysteria: Martial Arts Tales from a Mutating World." In *At Full Speed: Hong Kong Cinema in a Borderless World,* edited by Esther C. M. Yau. Minneapolis: University of Minnesota Press, 2001.

Schaefer, Eric. *"Bold! Daring! Shocking! True!": A History of Exploitation Films, 1919–1959.* Durham: Duke University Press, 1999.

Schamus, James. "Aesthetic Identities: A Response to Kenneth Chan and Christina Klein." *Cinema Journal* 43, no. 4 (Summer 2004): 43–52.

Schatz, Thomas. "The New Hollywood." In *Movie Blockbusters,* edited by Julian Stringer. London: Routledge, 2003.

Schell, Orville. "Virtual Tibet." Harper's Magazine, April 1998, 39–50.

Schoof, Renee. "Zhang Yimou: Only Possible Work Environment Is China." In *Zhang Yimou Interviews,* edited by Frances Gateward. Jackson: University Press of Mississippi, 2001.

Schrader, Paul. "Notes on Film Noir." In *Film Genre Reader III,* edited by Barry Keith Grant. Austin: University of Texas Press, 2003.

Sconce, Jeffrey. "Trashing the Academy: Taste, Excess and an Emerging Politics of Cinematic Style." *Screen* 36, no. 4 (Winter 1995): 371–93.

Sedgwick, Eve Kosofsky. *Between Men: English Literature and Male Homosocial Desire.* New York: Columbia University Press, 1985.

Shakya, Tsering. *The Dragon in the Land of Snows: A History of Modern Tibet Since 1947.* New York: Columbia University Press, 1999.

Shohat, Ella, and Robert Stam. *Unthinking Eurocentrism: Multiculturalism and the Media.* London: Routledge, 1994.

Short, Stephen, and Susan Jakes. "Making of a Hero," *TIMEasia.com,* <http://www.time.com/time/asia/features/hero/story2.html>, accessed 17 May 2007.

—. "This Film Was My Boyhood Dream." *TIMEasia.com,* <http://www.time.com/time/asia/features/hero/int_zhang_yimou.html>, accessed 17 May 2007.

—. "Violence Doesn't Solve Anything." *TIMEasia.com,* <http://www.time.com/time/asia/features/hero/int_jet_li.html>, accessed 17 May 2007.

Showalter, Elaine. "Sex Goddess." *The American Prospect,* 21 May 2001, 38.

Smith, Craig S. "'Hero' Soars, and Its Director Thanks 'Crouching Tiger.'" *New York Times,* 2 September 2004, E1.

Sontag, Susan. "Notes on 'Camp.'" In *Camp: Queer Aesthetics and the Performing Subject,* edited by Fabio Cleto. Edinburgh: Edinburgh University Press, 1999.

Spivak, Gayatri Chakravorty. *Outside in the Teaching Machine.* New York: Routledge, 1993.

Stanfield, Peter. "'American as Chop Suey': Invocations of Gangsters in Chinatown, 1920–1936." In *Mob Culture: Hidden Histories of the American Gangster Film,* edited by Lee Grieveson, Esther Sonnet, and Peter Stanfield. New Brunswick: Rutgers University Press, 2005.

"Stephen Chow to Remake Classic." *The Straits Times,* 3 December 2007, Life section, 7.

Sterngold, James. "Wang's World in a Love Story." *New York Times,* 9 January 1998, B7.

Stokes, Lisa Odham, and Michael Hoover. *City on Fire: Hong Kong Cinema.* London: Verso, 1999.

"Stone Says Quake Was 'Karma,'" *The Straits Times,* 27 May 2008, Life section, 14.

"Stone Sorry for 'Karma' Comment," *The Straits Times*, 30 May 2008, Life section, 10.

Sunshine, Linda, ed. *Crouching Tiger, Hidden Dragon: A Portrait of the Ang Lee Film.* New York: Newmarket Press, 2000.

Tajima, Renee. "Moving the Image: Asian American Independent Filmmaking 1970–1990." In *Moving the Image: Independent Asian Pacific American Media Arts,* edited by Russell Leong. Los Angeles: UCLA Asian American Studies Center, and Visual Communications, Southern California Asian American Studies Central, 1991.

Takaki, Ronald. *Strangers from a Different Shore: A History of Asian Americans.* New York: Penguin, 1989.

Tam, Kwok-Kan. "Cinema and Zhang Yimou." In *Zhang Yimou Interviews,* edited by Frances Gateward. Jackson: University Press of Mississippi, 2001.

Tambling, Jeremy. "The History Man: The Last Governor of Hong Kong." *Public Culture* 9 (1997): 355–75.

—. *Wong Kar-wai's* Happy Together. Hong Kong: Hong Kong University Press, 2003.

Tan Dawn Wei. "Sharp and Tough." *The Straits Times,* 29 November 2006, Life section, 2.

Tan See Kam. "From *South Pacific* to *Shanghai Blues*: No Film Is an Island." In *Hong Kong Film, Hollywood and New Global Cinema: No Film Is an Island,* edited by Gina Marchetti and Tan See Kam. London: Routledge, 2007.

Tasker, Yvonne. *Spectacular Bodies: Gender, Genre and the Action Cinema.* London: Routledge, 1993.

Tateishi, Ramie. "Jackie Chan and the Re-invention of Tradition." *Asian Cinema* 10, no. 1 (Fall 1998): 78–84.

Taylor, Charles. "Hero." *Salon.com*, 27 August 2004, <http://dir.salon.com/story/ent/movies/review/2004/08/27/hero/index_np.html>, accessed 17 May 2007.

"Ten Times More Expensive to Hire Zhang Ziyi Now." *The Straits Times,* 28 April 2006, Life section, 18.

Teo, Stephen. *Hong Kong Cinema: The Extra Dimensions.* London: BFI, 1997.

—. "'We Kicked Jackie Chan's Ass!': An Interview with James Schamus." *Senses of Cinema*, March-April 2001, <http://www.sensesofcinema.com/contents/01/13/schamus.html>, accessed 11 June 2008.

—. *Wong Kar-wai: Auteur of Time.* London: BFI, 2005.

—. "*Wuxia* Redux: *Crouching Tiger, Hidden Dragon* as a Model of Late Transnational Production." In *Hong Kong Connections: Transnational Imagination in Action Cinema,* edited by Meaghan Morris, Siu Leung Li, and Stephen Chan Ching-kiu. Durham: Duke University Press, 2005.

Topel, Fred. "Tarantino Talks *Kill Bill Vol. 2*." In *Quentin Tarantino: The Film Geek Files,* edited by Paul A. Woods. London: Plexus, 2005.

Trumpbour, John. *Selling Hollywood to the World: U.S. and European Struggles for Mastery of the Global Film Industry, 1920–1950.* Cambridge: Cambridge University Press, 2002.

Tsang, Steve. *A Modern History of Hong Kong.* Hong Kong: Hong Kong University Press, 2004.

Turan, Kenneth. *Sundance to Sarajevo: Film Festivals and the World They Made.* Berkeley: University of California Press, 2002.

Tweedie, James. "Morning in the New Metropolis: Taipei and the Globalization of the City Film." In *Cinema Taiwan: Politics, Popularity and State of the Arts,* edited by Darrell William Davis and Ru-shou Robert Chen. London: Routledge, 2007.

Van Biema, David. "Buddhism in America." *Time,* 13 October 1997, <http://www.time.com/time/magazine/article/0,9171,987164,00.html>, accessed 6 June 2007.

Vertov, Dziga. *Kino-Eye: The Writings of Dziga Vertov.* Translated by Kevin O'Brien. Berkeley: University of California Press, 1984.

Wang, Yiman. "The Art of Screen Passing: Anna May Wong's Yellow Yellowface Performance in the Art Deco Era." *Camera Obscura* 60, vol. 20, no. 3 (2005): 159–91.

Watson, Paul. "There's No Accounting for Taste: Exploitation Cinema and the Limits of Film Theory." In *Trash Aesthetics: Popular Culture and Its Audience,* edited by Deborah Cartmell, I. Q. Hunter, Heidi Kaye, and Imelda Whelehan. London: Pluto Press, 1997.

Wei, William. *The Asian American Movement.* Philadelphia: Temple University Press, 1993.

West, David. *Chasing Dragons: An Introduction to the Martial Arts Film.* London: I. B. Tauris, 2006.

"'Wheelchair Angel' Feted for Fending Off Protesters." *The Straits Times*, 12 April 2008, 8.

White, Hayden. *Metahistory: The Historical Imagination in Nineteenth Century Europe.* Baltimore, MD: Johns Hopkins University Press, 1975.

Williams, Jeffrey, ed. *PC Wars: Politics and Theory in the Academy.* New York: Routledge, 1995.

Wills, David. "The French Remark: *Breathless* and Cinematic Citationality." In *Play It Again, Sam: Retakes on Remakes,* edited by Andrew Horton and Stuart Y. McDougal. Berkeley: University of California Press, 1998.

Wilson, Rob, and Arif Dirlik, eds. *Asia/Pacific as Space of Cultural Production.* Durham: Duke University Press, 1995.

Wilson, Rob, and Wimal Dissanayake, eds. *Global/Local: Cultural Production and the Transnational Imaginary.* Durham: Duke University Press, 1996.

Wollen, Peter. *Readings and Writings: Semiotic Counter-Strategies.* London: Verso, 1982.

Wong Ain-ling, ed. *The Shaw Screen: A Preliminary Study.* Hong Kong: Hong Kong Film Archive, 2003.

Wong, Eugene Franklin. "The Early Years: Asians in the American Films Prior to World War II." In *Screening Asian Americans,* edited by Peter X. Feng. New Brunswick: Rutgers University Press, 2002.

—. *On Visual Media Racism: Asians in the American Motion Pictures.* New York: Arno Press, 1978.

Woo, John. Foreword to *Bulletproof Monk*, by Michael Yanover and Mark Paniccia. Orange, CA: Flypaper Press, 2002.

Wood, Robin. "An Introduction to the American Horror Film." In *Movies and Methods: Volume II,* edited by Bill Nichols. Berkeley: University of California Press, 1985.

Wu, Frank H. *Yellow: Race in America Beyond Black and White.* New York: Basic Books, 2002.

Xiao, Zhiwei. "Anti-Imperialism and Film Censorship During the Nanjing Decade, 1927–1937." In *Transnational Chinese Cinemas: Identity, Nationhood, Gender,* edited by Sheldon Hsiao-peng Lu. Honolulu: University of Hawai'i Press, 1997.

Xing, Jun. *Asian America through the Lens: History, Representations, and Identity.* Walnut Creek, CA: AltaMira Press, 1998.

Xu, Gary G. *Sinascape: Contemporary Chinese Cinema.* Lanham, MD: Rowman and Littlefield, 2007.

Yang, Jeff. *Once Upon a Time in China: A Guide to Hong Kong, Taiwanese, and Mainland Chinese Cinema.* New York: Atria Books, 2003.

Yang, Mayfair Mei-Hui. "Of Gender, State, Censorship, and Overseas Capital: An Interview with Chinese Director Zhang Yimou." In *Zhang Yimou Interviews,* edited by Frances Gateward. Jackson: University Press of Mississippi, 2001.

Yau, Esther C. M., ed. *At Full Speed: Hong Kong Cinema in a Borderless World.* Minneapolis: University of Minnesota Press, 2001.

Yeh, Emilie Yueh-yu, and Darrell William Davis. *Taiwan Film Directors: A Treasure Island.* New York: Columbia University Press, 2005.

"You Are Either With Us or Against Us," *CNN.com*, 6 November 2001, <http://archives.cnn.com/2001/US/11/06/gen.attack.on.terror/>, accessed 31 May 2008.

Zacharek, Stephanie. "House of Flying Daggers." *Salon.com*, 7 October 2004, <http://dir.salon.com/story/ent/indie/2004/10/07/daggers/index.html>, accessed 22 May 2007

Zhang, Yingjin. *Chinese National Cinema.* New York: Routledge, 2004.

Žižek, Slavoj. *The Sublime Object of Ideology.* London: Verso, 1989.

Index